THE DUPLICITY OF PHILOSOPHY'S SHADOW

The Duplicity of Philosophy's Shadow

HEIDEGGER, NAZISM, AND THE JEWISH OTHER

Elliot R. Wolfson

Columbia University Press
New York

Columbia University Press
Publishers Since 1893
New York   Chichester, West Sussex
cup.columbia.edu
Copyright © 2018 Columbia University Press
All rights reserved

Library of Congress Cataloging-in-Publication Data

Names: Wolfson, Elliot R., author.
Title: The duplicity of philosophy's shadow: Heidegger, Nazism, and the Jewish other / Elliot R. Wolfson.
Description: New York: Columbia University Press, 2018. | Includes bibliographical references and index.
Identifiers: LCCN 2017049988 | ISBN 9780231185622 (cloth) | ISBN 9780231185639 (pbk.) | ISBN 9780231546249 (e-book)
Subjects: LCSH: Heidegger, Martin, 1889-1976. | National socialism.
Classification: LCC B3279.H49 W627 2018 | DDC 193—dc23
LC record available at https://lccn.loc.gov/2017049988

Cover design: Noah Arlow

To Aaron
For abiding when many others absconded

As every past generation has had to disenthrall itself from an inheritance of truisms and stereotypes, so in our time we must move on from the reassuring repetition of stale phrases to a new, difficult, but essential confrontation with reality. For the great enemy of the truth is very often not the lie—deliberate, contrived and dishonest—but the myth—persistent, persuasive and unrealistic. Too often we hold fast to the clichés of our forebears. We subject all facts to a prefabricated set of interpretations. We enjoy the comfort of opinion without the discomfort of thought.

—JOHN F. KENNEDY, "COMMENCEMENT ADDRESS AT YALE UNIVERSITY,"
JUNE 11, 1962

The matter of thinking is always confounding—all the more in proportion as we keep clear of prejudice. To keep clear of prejudice, we must be ready and willing to listen.

—MARTIN HEIDEGGER, *WHAT IS CALLED THINKING?*

CONTENTS

PREFACE: CALCULATING HEIDEGGER'S MISCALCULATION   xi

Chapter One
Barbaric Enchantment: From Existential Ontology to Abyssal Meontology   1

Chapter Two
Nomadism, Homelessness, and the Obfuscation of Being   33

Chapter Three
Jewish Time and the Historiographical Eclipse of Historical Destiny   87

Chapter Four
Being's Tragedy: Heidegger's Silence and the Ring of Solitude   109

Chapter Five
Political Disavowal: Truth and Concealing the Unconcealment   131

Chapter Six
Heidegger, Balaam, and the Duplicity of Philosophy's Shadow   154

Afterword   169

NOTES   173

BIBLIOGRAPHY   267

INDEX   301

PREFACE

Calculating Heidegger's Miscalculation

> into the book
> —whose name did it take in
> before mine?—
> the line written into
> this book about
> a hope, today,
> for a thinker's
> (un-
> delayed coming)
> word
> in the heart
>
> —CELAN, "TODTNAUBERG"

Martin Heidegger (1889–1976) powerfully transformed the twentieth-century philosophical landscape and exercised an inordinate influence on a wide variety of other disciplines. His personal shortcomings and lapses in ethical judgment, attested in his explicit complicity with National Socialism, are well known and cannot be easily justified or dismissed as miscalculations based on inadequate knowledge or lack of savvy.[1] In this book I will focus on Heidegger's embrace of Nazism—the so-called *affaire Heidegger*—and its connection to some crucial aspects of his philosophical enterprise. Needless to say, the bibliography on this sensitive, and what has become sensational, topic, largely due to the publication of the *Schwarze Hefte*, the personal notebooks covering the years 1931–1948, is considerable in size and scope. There is no pretense to treat the subject comprehensively or exhaustively. My contribution will, hopefully, consist of shedding new light on the vexing labyrinth of issues by approaching it not as a member of the Heideggerian guild, as it were, or as an intellectual historian of National Socialism, anti-Semitism, or even twentieth-century philosophy, but as a scholar of Jewish mysticism, albeit one whose work has been deeply informed by the disciplines of hermeneutics and phenomenology and especially by Heidegger.

PREFACE: CALCULATING HEIDEGGER'S MISCALCULATION

In the infamous *Der Spiegel* interview, "Nur ein Gott kann uns noch retten," conducted in September 1966, Heidegger demonstrated that he was cognizant of what his fate would be: "Probably the polemics will flare up again and again, whenever the occasion presents itself."[2] As a framework for my investigation of what Heidegger rightly identified as a matter that is polemical to its core, I will adopt the eminently sensible sentiment expressed by Jacques Derrida on the first day of the Heidelberg conference on Heidegger's philosophy and politics, which took place on February 5–6, 1988:

Often, when I see so many people in France suddenly interested in Heidegger's Nazism, shouting loudly and accusing philosophers of having said nothing to them, and setting out to condemn not only Heidegger but also the living, I would like to ask them a very simple question: okay, let's talk; have you read *Sein und Zeit*? . . . to take only that example. Those of us who began to read this book, to confront it in a close explication, in a questioning and nonorthodox way, know well that, among others, it is still waiting to be read; that there are still, in this text of Heidegger, immense resources. Consequently, one has a right to ask those who wish to draw very rapid conclusions linking the philosophical text and a political comportment that they begin at least to try to read.[3]

I trust the readers of this book will agree unconditionally to the condition laid down by Derrida: no thinker is above criticism, certainly not one as controversial as Heidegger, but even he, nay especially he, deserves to be read before he is castigated as an outcast and his lifework deemed irredeemable. As Derrida added, philosophers particularly are obliged to read Heidegger's entire oeuvre rigorously and scrupulously so that they do not relinquish their individual political responsibility.[4] In his comments at the colloquium "Reading Heidegger" held at the University of Essex in May 1986, Derrida makes clear that what is at stake is not only the fairly banal and eminently sensible plea to read Heidegger if one wants to understand his thought, but the far more provocative and unexpected assertion that to understand Nazism philosophically one must go through the questions proffered directly and indirectly by Heidegger.

Are we sure today that we can understand what Nazism was, without asking all the questions, the historical questions, Heidegger asks? I am not sure. I am not sure that we have today really understood what Nazism was. And if we have to think and think about that, I believe we will have to *go through*, not to stop, at Heidegger's questions, *go through* Heidegger's trajectory and his project. We cannot understand what Europe is and has been during this century, what Nazism has been ... without integrating what made Heidegger's discourse possible. And then you will have to *read* Heidegger to see what has occurred.[5]

The burden marked by Derrida—to wrestle with Heidegger as a way to think through to the depth of what we condemn[6]—is, I am afraid to say, one that can be borne only by those willing to invest an inordinate amount of time and energy in reading through this vastly arduous corpus.

This, it will be recalled, is also the crux of Derrida's caustic reprimand of Victor Farías's *Heidegger et le nazisme*, in the interview with Didier Eribon published in *Le Nouvel Observateur*, November 6–12, 1987: "Beyond certain aspects of the documentation and some factual questions, which call for caution, discussion will focus especially ... on the interpretation, let us say, that relates these 'facts' to Heidegger's 'text,' to his 'thinking.' The reading proposed, if there is one, remains insufficient or questionable, at times so shoddy that one wonders if the investigator began to read Heidegger more than an hour ago."[7] Some have defended Farías,[8] but it seems to me that on the essential point of contention Derrida is correct. The real scandal is to scandalize Heidegger with such platitudes as that he was a fascist from start to finish or that anti-Semitism was at the heart of his philosophy without scrutinizing his writings to determine meticulously the contours of his dystopian misadventure, as Miguel de Beistegui has argued.[9] Before one presumes an indissoluble link between Heidegger's politics and his thought, one is obligated to submit oneself—in the sacrificial spirit of the piety of thinking—to the subtleties and complexities of his writings and, most of all, to be faithful to the centrality of questioning by questioning the questions so that new questions emerge to elucidate what was left unquestioned.[10] And only if one is committed to that effort is it possible to embark upon the mission that Derrida boldly articulates:

Is not the task, the duty, and in truth the only new or interesting thing to try to recognize the analogies and the possibilities of rupture between, on the one hand, what is called Nazism—that enormous, plural, differentiated continent whose roots are still obscure—and, on the other hand, a Heideggerian thinking that is also multiple and that, for a long time to come, will remain provocative, enigmatic, still to be read? Not because it would hold in reserve, still encrypted, a good and reassuring politics, a "Heideggerianism of the left," but because it opposed to actual Nazism, to its dominant strain, only a more "revolutionary" and purer Nazism! . . . But from the moment one is having it out with [*s'explique avec*] Heidegger in a critical or deconstructive fashion, must one not continue to recognize a certain necessity of his thinking, its character, which is inaugural in so many respects, and especially what remains to come for us in its deciphering? This is a task of thinking, a historical task and a political task. A discourse on Nazism that dispenses with this task remains the conformist opinion of "good conscience."[11]

Walking this fine line by resisting those who disqualify Heidegger as a Nazi ideologue, on the one hand, but recognizing that the greatness and relevance of his work is linked precisely to the fact that he affords us the opportunity to think conceptually about some of the basic tenets of National Socialism, on the other hand, is what Derrida tried to execute in his own writing, especially *De l'esprit, Heidegger et la question* (1987). As he writes near the conclusion of that monograph, "Nazism was not born in the desert. We all know this, but it has to be constantly recalled. And even if, far from any desert, it had grown like a mushroom in the silence of a European forest, it would have done so in the shadow of big trees, in the shelter of their silence or their indifference but in the same soil."[12] It is noteworthy that in the Heidelberg conference Hans-Georg Gadamer offered a related rationale for the need to continue to ponder Heidegger's thought earnestly. Noting that he and other students were troubled and surprised by Heidegger's engagement with the National Socialist movement from the moment they began working with him, Gadamer suggests that the sense of astonishment they felt can serve as an impetus "to pose the crucial and absolutely inevitable problem, which is, through Heidegger, the problem of German Nazism." Although the question is not easy to answer, Gadamer does not hesitate to proclaim, "it is clear that one cannot dissociate Heidegger's philosophy from the fact of the extermination that took place in the history of our century."[13] In a note from 2014, which has now been reprinted as the foreword to the published proceedings of the conference, Jean-Luc Nancy similarly wrote, "However much time has passed, one thing remains certain and continues to be confirmed: there is no sense in judging Heidegger except on the condition of judging, along with him,

PREFACE: CALCULATING HEIDEGGER'S MISCALCULATION

ourselves and our history."[14] In *The Banality of Heidegger* Nancy extends his argument:

> To condemn is one thing, to analyze is another, which in any case cannot damage the condemnation, any more than it can favor it. The obligation that we face today belongs above all to analysis, not because we ought to forget moral judgment (or political or philosophical judgment), but because up to now we still have not gone far enough in *thinking the deep reasons for our condemnations*.... What is at stake in the reading of Heidegger, and specifically of the texts most exposed to condemnation or anathema, is that they place us once again, but with a very particular force, before the exigency of interrogating that which, with "the modern world," happened to the world—and to the world as such—that is, as a presumed configuration of one or several possibilities of making, of receiving, and of dividing up and sharing sense (whatever one may understand with this word). Now it was Heidegger who operated the first metamorphosis of the philosophical question of sense (or meaning: *Sinn*) by designating it as the question of "the meaning of being."... There is something a little ridiculous in having to make such a reminder, but it does seem necessary, given the widespread opinion that Heidegger could without further ado be struck from the ranks of the philosophers on the grounds of his Nazism. This amounts to piling one serious error on top of another: first, that the event of Nazism... would not pose any philosophical problems... and then that Heidegger was simply a Nazi... whereas in fact the *Black Notebooks* demonstrate exactly the inverse.[15]

The space we must inhabit, as uncomfortable as it might be, is one in which we acknowledge that Heidegger was both a Nazi given to anti-Semitic jargon and an incisive philosopher whose thinking not only was responding to the urgencies of his epoch but also contains the potential to unravel the thorny knot of politics and philosophy relevant for the present as much as for the past. As Alexander Duff put it, "Dismissing Heidegger by reducing his thought to his political biography lets us off the hook for rethinking the premises of our own political arrangements and the extent to which they may be implicated by his broadly critical assessment of the nihilism of Western civilization and philosophy."[16] Heidegger is thus neither defensible nor disposable; his thinking—and this includes, above all, his philosophical scapegoating of Jews under the rubric of *das*

Judentum—demands reflective analysis and critical questioning. This injunction is not fulfilled by refutation. As Heidegger himself noted,

> The first and thus all-inclusive and constantly self-intensifying insight of contemplative thinking [*denkerischen Denkens*] must be: every thinker who has established a basic position in the history of Western thought is irrefutable. In other words, the mania to refute is the first fall from authentic thinking. By that measure, all philosophical bustle [*Philosophiebetrieb*], especially the "National Socialistic" one, remains outside the domain of essential knowledge [*wesentlichen Wissens*]. This does not prevent such bustling about from attempting to make itself publicly respectable by means of boundless, noisy, and—thievish "literature," one which corresponds down to a hair with the pen pushing that, as "Catholic philosophy," has created an entry for itself among the "intelligentsia" of all "confessions" and "stations." How long can this bustling about still endure? Or is its time only now arriving with the consummation of modernity?[17]

No one who reads this passage from the notebooks honestly and dispassionately can deny Heidegger's disdain for National Socialism. To highlight the irrefutability of authentic thinkers, Heidegger mentions Nazism explicitly as an example of philosophical bustle that is not worthy of refutation because it falls outside the domain of essential knowledge and, in the end, signifies the consummation of modernity. To apply this measure to Heidegger himself, as Nancy has done, the objective should not be to refute, and certainly not to ignore him, because only "by designating clearly the way in which he let himself be carried away and stupefied in the worst of heinous banalities, to the point of the intolerable, one can shed more light on what he himself should have seen and what in any case he allows us to discern."[18] Particularly with respect to the notebooks, as I will argue at several points in this study, it is vital to stress that they equally prove Heidegger's avowal and denunciation of certain elemental principles of National Socialism. To cite Nancy again, the *Schwarze Hefte* "show that Heidegger wanted to consider all of Germany as a 'concentration camp,' because it handed its fate over to the sorry 'world view' of the Nazis, whose racism and technical calculating machination remained deeply foreign to the meaning of *beyng* and of its other beginning."[19] Grotesquely, and unforgivably, the logic of Heidegger's cultural appraisal of metaphysics and the decline of the West leads to his positing that the agent of destruction must destroy itself and the people that personify exclusivity must be excluded.

The typical problem posed by Heidegger that has dominated the scholarly and more popular discussions is stated succinctly by Mireille Calle-Gruber in the opening remarks of the conference in Heidelberg: "how was it possible for a thinker who is considered to be the greatest philosopher of our time to have engaged in the National-Socialist movement? And still more grave: how could one be silent on his postwar silence, and how could one accept that he never publicly retracted what he had said, thus failing to think the greatest horror that has ever been—the industrial extermination of the Jews?"[20] These questions are unquestionably legitimate and to avoid them is to forsake the moral imperative of critical thinking. However, philosophical audacity requires as well that one illumine the shadows of Heidegger's brilliance by attending even more carefully to his silence than to what was overtly spoken. This is neither evasion nor vindication; on the contrary, failure to be attuned to the unspoken is to circumvent the circumvention and thereby skirt one of the most important lessons that Heidegger's all-too-human fragility has to teach us about the accountability of a thinker to the exigencies of history, especially when the debacle is one to which, paraphrasing Hannah Arendt, we can never finally reconcile ourselves.[21]

Parenthetically, I note that it is apposite to heed Heidegger's distinction between talking about philosophy (*Reden über die Philosophie*) and actual philosophizing (*Philosophieren*).[22] The latter cannot be experienced

by reading or reviewing philosophical literature, but only by making the effort to philosophize. This must bring us to the point where we can understand a philosopher better than he understood himself. . . . If someone does not summon up the inner freedom as a philosopher to be such a person to whose essence it necessarily belongs to be better understood than he understands himself—then philosophy has passed that person by, in spite of all philosophical erudition. Philosophy is only there to be overcome. Yet it can only be overcome if it stands in the first place, and can be overcome all the more essentially the more profound the resistance is that it summons up through its being there.[23]

It is surely reasonable to assume that Heidegger would have wished his legacy to be engaged philosophically in these very terms, that his greatness would be measured by the extent to which others might understand him better than he understood himself, that the overcoming of his thought would be commensurate to the resistance it provokes. To paraphrase Habermas, to think against Heidegger we must think with Heidegger.

Following the lead of Derrida, Calle-Gruber observes in a second passage that we are faced with the dilemma that only through the thought of Heidegger can we attempt to evaluate philosophically the crime of the Nazis in its specificity.[24] For his part, Phillipe Lacoue-Labarthe articulated a similar stance: "I know that this may sound like a pure paradox, but, for me at least, it is the reading of Heidegger that, I believe . . . can give access to a certain reality of Nazism. An access that the univocal moral and political accusation . . . has continued to mask."[25] Lacoue-Labarthe even went so far as to declare that the "secret of Nazism" is buried in Heidegger, and that the way to retrieve it is to read his texts against the author's idiosyncratic reading.[26] Echoing this perspective, Calle-Gruber affirms in the introduction written for the published record of the aforementioned conference that the task of critique "is to pose questions precisely where Heidegger's questioning failed—that is, to take up questions at the place where Heidegger's thought remained incomplete, in the hiatus in which his ethical failure is inscribed, his unforgivable silence regarding Auschwitz."[27]

In a note to *De l'esprit*, Derrida delineates what it means to read Heidegger *après la lettre*:

Heidegger's journey crosses, constitutes, or leaves certain strata up until now scarcely visible, less massive, sometimes almost imperceptible—for Martin Heidegger as much as for anyone. In their rarity, precariousness, or very discretion, these strata appear prominent after the event, to the extent that they restructure a space. But they do this only by assigning so many new tasks to thought, and to reading. . . . Beyond an always necessary exegesis, this re-reading sketches out another topology for new takes, for what remains to be situated of the relationships between Heidegger's thought and other places of thought.[28]

What Derrida articulates more generally can surely be applied to the specific case of engaging the relevance of Heidegger's thought to comprehending the historical destiny of National Socialism. The mandate, as Lacoue-Labarthe also emphasized,[29] is to probe Heidegger's writings to expose what remains unthought (*Ungedachte*) in the phenomenon of Nazism, an undertaking that Heidegger himself considered essential to the inquiry into the nature of thinking: "What a thinker has thought can be mastered only if we refer everything in his thought that is still unthought back to its originary truth [*anfängliche Wahrheit*]."[30] We are prevented from "hearing" the language of thinkers as long as the "self-deception about history" prevails and we construe tradition as something that "lies behind us" rather than as something that "comes toward us because we are its captives and destined to it."[31] The reversal of time—the recollection of the future dissimulating as the anticipation of the past—is related to the hermeneutic of attunement to a thinker's language, which, in turn, requires that we acknowledge and respect that language, but this can come about only if one is attentive to what is unique and inexhaustible in each thinker through "being shaken to the depths by what is unthought in his thought. What is unthought in a thinker's thought is not a lack inherent in his thought. What is *un*-thought is there in each case only as the un-*thought* [*Das Un-Gedachte ist je nur als das Un-gedachte*]. The unthought is the greatest gift that thinking can bestow."[32] The unthought is not something that can be thought once and for all or something that can never be thought, but the unspoken that pervades all thought, the potential of the text to yield new meaning unremittingly in the curvature of time, the gift of the most thought-provoking that delivers us constantly to what is to be thought (*das Zu-denkende*),[33] the "true endowment that keeps itself concealed in our essential nature."[34] The more original the thinking—the deeper it wells forth from the origin that stays hidden with every disclosure—the more fecund will be the attempts to articulate what remains unthought.

Derrida summarizes his method programmatically in the Eribon interview: "For a long time I have been trying to displace the old alternative between an 'external' history or sociology, which in general is powerless to take the measure of the philosophemes that it claims to explain, and on the other hand, the 'competence' of an 'internal' reading, which for its part is blind to historico-political inscription and first of all to the pragmatics of discourse. In the case of Heidegger, the difficulty of articulating the two is particularly serious. There is the seriousness of what it at stake: Nazism from the day before yesterday to tomorrow."[35] My own path similarly seeks to maintain a balance between the external and the internal, the historical and the philosophical, by interrogating not only the said but, more important, the unsaid in Heidegger's thinking and action as they pertain to what Derrida appropriately called the "abysmal monstrosity."[36] Instead of marginalizing Heidegger, and ostracizing all those who would continue to mine his writings, what is necessary is to engage him critically, to deconstruct his deconstructive hermeneutic, to emulate his propensity for questioning everything but the need to question, to pave the way to what persists as unthought in his thinking or, echoing Heidegger's mystifying cadence, to heed the stillness of the passing by of the last god.[37] Here it is pertinent to cite the sagacious words of Gadamer that ring even truer in the present environment than when he wrote them, "Whoever believes that today one need no longer be concerned with Martin Heidegger has not taken the measure of how difficult it will always be for us to debate with him, instead of making oneself ridiculous by looking down on him with an air of superiority."[38]

The position I take resonates as well with the stance espoused by Marc Froment-Meurice in his attempt to speculate on the *past that will not pass away*, that is, the question of Heidegger and Nazism—the philosophical notion of annihilation and the political-militaristic goal of extermination—as it relates to his thinking about metaphysics and ontology.[39] To quote one passage that encapsulates the author's view:

If Heidegger was blind, it was not for want of judgment; nor was it on account of some stupidity ... but rather, on account of being caught by want: by the want of sight, of knowledge, of thought—even, by want of everything. Being "itself" is nothing; it cannot be identified with anything whatsoever: neither with the Idea nor absolute knowledge nor the will to power nor planetary technology. And yet, it makes possible all identification and therefore all annihilation. The retreat shall be seen precisely in the calling into question of both the identity of Being and the identity of identity. Also, it is a calling into question of the identity of thought: from the first beginnings of philosophy—from Parmenides to Plato—to the last—from Nietzsche to Heidegger. In the end, Being returns to nothing more—than itself. It disappears within the tautology. For perhaps there is no other way for it "to be" (nothing but a tautology saying nothing: Being as the Same—*logos*). And perhaps there is no other way to disappear: to a-void or/and to give out itself.[40]

I will side with those who have challenged the tendency to bifurcate the relationship of the political and the philosophical in Heidegger's thought, but I will argue that Heidegger's partisan activism and his rejection thereof are two sides of the selfsame coin,[41] originating in the philosophical impulse to become the dwelling within which being is disclosed as nothing, the clearing within which givenness pours forth in its withholding and truth is revealed in its concealment.

For Heidegger, this unconcealment of the concealment may have involved his silence about the Jewish victims of Nazi persecution as well as his deliberate avoidance in analyzing Jewish thinkers in any serious or sustained manner—and this despite the fact that he had a number of Jewish students.[42] By attending to these silences, we may be able to fill in the blank spaces of his thinking.[43] It is germane to call to mind the words of Jean-François Lyotard, "The Forgotten is not to be remembered for what it has been and what it is, because it has not been anything and is nothing, but must be remembered as something that never ceases to be forgotten."[44] What never ceases to be forgotten—the jews—is the semiotic marker of the unrepresentable otherness that does not thwart representation but rather is the non-representable that all representation must strive to represent, the unthinkable alterity that all thought must seek to think in its unthinkability. To cite Lyotard again, "Here lies the paradox and even the scandal: how could this thought (Heidegger's), a thought so devoted to remembering that a forgetting (of Being) take place in all thought, in all art, in all 'representation' of the world, how could it possibly have ignored the thought of 'the jews,' which, in a certain sense, thinks, tries to think, nothing but that very fact? How could this thought forget and ignore 'the jews' to the point of suppressing and foreclosing to the very end the horrifying (and inane) attempt at exterminating, at making us forget forever what, in Europe, reminds us, even since the beginning, that 'there is' the Forgotten?"[45] Only if the forgotten continue to be forgotten—as they surely are in Heidegger—will the forgotten be remembered as the ones who were forgotten. Both the Jews and Heidegger's Nazism belong to the economy of the *Unheimliche*, the uncanny that is simultaneously familiar and strange—indeed, familiar as that which is strange. "For the one and the other repeat, in their essence and in their effect on our thinking, a foreclosure that is constitutive of Western thought as philosophy and as politics. An unforgettable continues to forget itself, reiterates its forgetting, in Heidegger's 'politics' as in our politics regarding that 'politics.'"[46]

Tenaciously, Heidegger avoided personalizing his descent into the void—now rendered even more transparent by the black night of the *Black Notebooks*, to borrow the redolent expression of Babette Babich[47]—whence he glimpsed the tautological truth of the identity of nonidentity that undergirds his meontological notion of the nihilating abyss (*Abgrund*) that is the primordial ground (*Urgrund*) of the nonground (*Ungrund*). The entanglement with National Socialism and what transpired under the auspices of the Third Reich cast a cold and stark light on the watchword of the nihilistic foundation of Heidegger's *Seinsgeschichte*: being is the nothing that is nothing but being.[48] Luce Irigaray astutely noted that the goal of Heidegger's thinking is to get beyond "the circularity of discourse, of the nothing that is in and of being. When the copula no longer veils the abyssal burial of the other in a gift of language which is neuter only in that it forgets the difference from which it draws strength and energy."[49] To overcome the oblivion of that difference, one must go through Heidegger's path, and this includes the twists and turns suffused in the discordant tropes of Nazi ideology.

The issue, then, as Dominique Janicaud argued, is not choosing between the false dichotomy of condemning and ignoring Heidegger, on one hand, or admiring and maintaining an uncritical allegiance to him, on the other hand, but rather "to propose a reading of Heidegger from the perspective of the political question, which would bring the lancet onto the most sensitive points—those where truth and error, errancy and perhaps a certain greatness are at play."[50] To disregard Heidegger because of his Nazi patronage, therefore, runs the risk of denying us the opportunity to think the unthinkable that must be thought as part of our communal human lot as being historical. In contrast to the thoughtlessness (*Gedankenlosigkeit*) grounded in a flight from thinking (*auf der Flucht vor dem Denken*), the unthinkable is the catalyst that stimulates our capacity to think.[51] At the same time, we must remember, as Heidegger remarked in the 1955 memorial address he gave in honor of Conradin Kreutzer, "the master's presence *in the work* is the only true presence. The greater the master, the more completely his person vanishes behind his work."[52] In my estimation, these words can be applied to Heidegger: the work he produced is what best preserves his presence, but in that very work the personal gravitas of that presence dissipates in the dark luminosity of his—sometimes paradoxical and virtually impenetrable—cogitations on the essence of being, truth, time, and language. Our hermeneutical obligation, to invoke

Calle-Gruber again, is "to strive to read Heidegger as he did not read himself—that is, rather than limiting ourselves to condemning him, to make it such that his silence on Auschwitz carries us toward the difficult courage of thinking."⁵³ The deliberations in the following pages are a modest attempt to comply with this directive.

Chapter One

BARBARIC ENCHANTMENT

From Existential Ontology to Abyssal Meontology

He who thinks greatly must err greatly.
—HEIDEGGER, *POETRY, LANGUAGE, THOUGHT*

The closer we come to the danger, the more brightly do the ways into the saving power begin to shine and the more questioning we become. For questioning is the piety of thought.
—HEIDEGGER, "THE QUESTION CONCERNING TECHNOLOGY"

Let me begin this chapter with the following methodological caveat: moral condemnation does not necessarily interfere with the stated objective of this study, to consider Nazism philosophically in the shadow of Heidegger's thinking. On the contrary, to suspend all judgment would compromise the ability to provide the historical context wherein the piety of Heidegger's thought will illumine and be illumined by the impiety of National Socialism. By casting aspersions on some of the dicta and actions of Heidegger, I am not reducing the intricacy and originality of his thought to the brutality exemplified by the Nazi movement. Furthermore, the rebuke of Heidegger does not interfere with the ability to hear the thinker in an unbiased way. In particular, the Heideggerian presumption that questioning is the means to reveal the matter of thought is not forfeited by adopting a critical stance regarding the monstrosity of Nazism nor is there justification to argue that objectivity can be achieved only by abandoning oneself to a thinking that would preclude the ability to discriminate between right and wrong. After all, Heidegger did not relinquish the sanction of good and evil, even if he thought their valence was determined by historical destiny and the world-play of the shining forth and withdrawing of being rather than by some metaphysical ground of transcendence.[1]

I do not deny that on occasion Heidegger does explicitly speak as if the truth of beyng is beyond the duality of good and evil. Consider, for example, the following description of the plight (*die Not*) of the human being in the *Beiträge zur Philosophie (Vom Ereignis)*, composed between 1936–1938 but not published until 1989: "That which compels, and is retained without being grasped, essentially surpasses all 'progress.' For that which compels is itself what is genuinely to come and thus resides completely outside of the distinction between good and evil and withdraws itself from all calculation."[2] Unlike progress, the plight of what is to come in the future cannot be calibrated and hence cannot be defined as either good or evil. This is not to say, however, that historical instantiations of the event of beyng—or what Heidegger called the essential occurrences—are not subject retroactively to an evaluation of those instantiations within a larger enframing of sociocultural mores. Such an appraisal is an inherent component of the plight of the thinker to transform the question of being by relentless interpretive questioning out of the ground of Dasein.[3] This, I submit, is the intent of Heidegger's comment in the *Schwarze Hefte*, "The whither is not the concerning-what! Instead, the concerning-what belongs to the questioning itself, which as a whole—as this whole of the question concerning being—has its whither."[4] This interrogation is no doubt part of the "all-embracing disclosive questioning," whose purpose is "to impart to beings their full empowerment and to lead humanity to a more originary *poetry*—i.e., to one by which humanity can become great and can experience the bliss of high spirits."[5]

To sharpen my perspective, it is pertinent to recall the divergent observation of Hans Jonas regarding the inherently amoral, if not immoral, nature of Heidegger's thought: "But as to Heidegger's *being*, it is an occurrence of unveiling, a fate-laden happening upon thought: so was the Führer and the call of German destiny under him: an unveiling of something indeed, a call of being all right, fate-laden in every sense: neither then nor now did Heidegger's thought provide a norm by which to decide how to answer such calls—linguistically or otherwise: no norm except depth, resolution, and the sheer force of being that issues the call."[6] The "adequate response to the call of being" is identified as thinking about being, which is inseparable from speaking about being, but not as "action, brotherly love, resistance to evil, promotion of the good."[7] The ostensibly irredeemable corollary of Heidegger's primal thinking centered on the eventfulness of being is thus condemned by Jonas:

But the terrible anonymity of Heidegger's "being," illicitly decked out with personal characters, blocks out the personal call. Not by the being of another person am I grasped, but just by "being"! And my responsive thought is being's own event. But called as person by person—fellow beings or God—my response will not primarily be thinking but action (though this involves thinking), and the action may be one of love, responsibility, pity; also of wrath, indignation, hate, even fight to the death: it is him or me. . . . In this sense indeed also Hitler was a call. *Such calls are drowned in the voice of being to which one cannot say No*; as is also, we are told, the separation of subject from object. This is the final claim of pride, and the betrayal of man's task growing from the acceptance of his lot.[8]

There is no doubt that Heidegger challenged the conventional measure of moral agency connected to the sovereignty of a willful and self-legislating subject, but perhaps in its place, as François Raffoul argued,[9] he maintained an alternate notion of responsibility as exposure to the inappropriable. The latter, however, is not the opposite of what is appropriable, but rather the play of expropriation that delimits the very limits of the aporia in which ethics is grounded as the inappropriation of the event of the appropriable. That there is no appropriation without expropriation means, as Reiner Schürmann deduced, there is no centripetal aggregation without a centrifugal disaggregation, no universalization without singularization, no legislation without transgression. Hence the henological difference between being and beings "makes the law by binding us both to the dissolution of the phenomena of the world and to their consolidation that is under way. . . . This double bind is embedded in our condition as mortals. We can call it the *henological differend*."[10] Thinking incessantly demands of one to ascertain if the historical destiny wherein one is situated—or into which one is thrown—is the means by which that differend is manifest in the concealment of being that is concealed and therefore revealed or if the concealment of concealment is concealed such that the nothingness is enveloped by the abyss of nihilism rather than nihilism being enveloped by the abyss of nothingness. I concur, therefore, with the assessment of Alexander Duff, "The politics that issue from Heidegger's thought—his teaching on community, as well as the impetus his thinking gives beyond or in spite of this teaching—derive from his formulation of the problem of Being and its presentation to us as a perplexing, anxiety-inducing, disintegrating question. Given that our finite understanding has us apprehend Being as distinct from the beings when we can see its 'sameness' with the nothing, then a time when we are surrounded by the phenomena of nihilism may be a uniquely disclosive moment in the history of Being."[11]

Tragedy, wrote Karl Jaspers, obliquely responding to Heidegger, "depicts a man in his greatness beyond good and evil."[12] This does not mean that the categories of good and evil are no longer relevant to substantiating the contours of greatness. The beyond encompasses what is trespassed; overcoming (*Überwindung*) is always a transition (*Übergang*) that signals an undergoing (*Untergang*).[13] Alternatively expressed, the ungrounding of the ground is an upholding of the ground, an eradication that is taking hold of the root. Any attempt to elicit a radical politics from Heidegger should be tempered by the astute formulation of Pierre Bourdieu that Heidegger's ontologization of history and the understanding of alienation in the *völkisch* sense of uprooting foster a "radical overcoming of all possible radicalism, which provides conformism with its most water-tight justification. To identify ontological alienation as the foundation of all alienation is, in a manner of speaking, to banalize and yet simultaneously dematerialize both economic alienation and any discussion of this alienation, by a radical but imaginary overcoming of any revolutionary overcoming."[14] As Heidegger explicitly noted in the late 1930s, "*Our own hour is the era of downgoing* [das Zeitalter des Untergangs]. The down-going, in the essential sense, is the path to the reticent preparation for what is to come, i.e., for the moment in which and the site in which the advent and the remaining absent of the gods will be decided. This downgoing is the utterly first beginning." The first beginning is of the past, but it belongs to the future, and thus those who go down are designated the "futural ones" (*die Zukünftigen*). The knowledge attained by these individuals is not subject to calculation (*errechnen*) or compulsion (*erzwingen*); from the scientific-technological standpoint, it is useless (*nutzlos*) and without value (*Wert*) and, consequently, it "cannot be taken as an immediate condition for a currently ongoing business." As historical cognition (*geschichtliche Erkenntnis*), this knowledge "never consists in determining and delineating current incidents in their circumstances and orientations and in their cherished goals and claims," but it is decidedly concerned "with knowledge of the domain out of which future history is decided and with (questioning) steadfastness in that domain."[15] To suggest that the unrest (*Un-ruhe*) integral to this questioning of what is

BARBARIC ENCHANTMENT

most steadfast, literally, the standing-in (*Innestehen*), the questioning into the essence of truth and into the essential occurrence of being, excludes or bans moral evaluation is unjustified and imprudent.

I concur with William Franke's comparison of Heidegger's piety of thinking to the phenomenon of apophaticism inasmuch as both summon one methodologically to "an ardent questioning for the sake of opening all beliefs to their furthest reach of possibility. Among such beliefs, traditional religious teachings often prove to be the richest and the most laden with symbolic meaning and implication for ethics and for life in general."[16] The questioning Heidegger demands subjects these beliefs to their potential undoing, but in the undoing they are preserved as what is undone. Moreover, the presumption that adherence to truth pursued through radical questioning can only be achieved by breaking the circle of self-validation fails to take seriously Heidegger's embrace of circularity to explain the hermeneutical structure of human understanding and the attendant comportment of temporality.[17] Insofar as the circular movement (*Kreisbewegung*) requires that one always leap to the ground upon which one is already standing, to return to where one has never been,[18] every act of thinking involves a "resolute openness toward the mystery" (*die Ent-schlossenheit zum Geheimnis*) whereby "the question of the essence of truth gets asked more originally" and "the ground of the intertwining [*Verflechtung*] of the essence of truth with the truth of essence reveals itself."[19]

For Heidegger, to be enlightened philosophically consists of unmasking the shadow as shadow, that is, discerning the shadow as a form of luminescence and not as the privation of light. I will explore this insight in more detail in the fourth chapter, but suffice it here to emphasize that the moral denunciation of Heidegger's supporting Hitler and espousing some of his disconcerting ideas about Judaism does not represent an a priori commitment to an ethical worldview that prohibits the ability to think the unthought in Heidegger's thinking. I am cognizant of the fact that some might construe this outcry as antagonistic to Heidegger's own suspension of an axiological valuation, attested, for instance, in the following statement in *Einführung in die Metaphysik*, published in 1953, based on a lecture course offered at the University of Freiburg in the summer semester of 1935: "The essence of Being-human, as thus experienced and placed back poetically into its ground, remains closed off to understanding in its character as a mystery if understanding hastily takes refuge in some moral appraisal [*Abschätzungen*]."²⁰ I would argue, nonetheless, that reproof is precisely the means to open the way of questioning so that we can attend to Heidegger's surpassing of ethics buoyed by his insight that the untruth (*Un-wahrheit*) as errancy (*Irre*) is "the essential counteressence [*Gegenwesen*] to the originary essence of truth. Errancy opens itself up as the open region for every counterplay [*Widerspiel*] to essential truth. . . . The disclosure of beings as such is simultaneously and intrinsically the concealing of beings as a whole. In the simultaneity [*Zugleich*] of disclosure and concealing, errancy holds sway. Errancy and the concealing of what is concealed belong to the originary essence of truth."²¹

Errancy—in the double sense of the Latin *errare* as "to wander" and "to err"²²—is not set against the truth, nor does it disappear with the appearance of truth. Rather, errancy is the clearing (*Lichtung*) or openness (*Offenheit*) of being, and thus it "is the appearing of the truth itself in its own sway [*das Erscheinen der Wahrheit selbst in ihrem eigenen Wesen*]. Errancy is that within which a particular interpretation of be-ing must err, which erring alone traverses the clearing of refusal [*die Lichtung der Verweigerung*]—traverses in accord with the clearing of what is lighted up." The consequence of this notion of errancy as the sway of the truth of being is that "any being that enters into and stays within the openness and can possibly preserve this openness, simultaneously resides in 'un-truth' in the double sense of sheltering-concealing [*Verborgenheit*] and dissembling [*Verstellung*]."²³ Embedded in the essence of truth, therefore, is the counteressence of the errancy of untruth, which is related by Heidegger to his signature idea of the contemporaneity (*Gleichzeitigkeit*)—or what he would more typically call the belonging-together (*Zusammengehörigkeit*)-of disclosure and concealment: every being disclosed in the opening of unconcealment is at the same time concealed, and hence every truth is at the same time untruth. Heidegger draws the logical conclusion: "But because the full essence of truth contains the nonessence [*Unwesen*] and above all holds sway as concealing, philosophy as a questioning into this truth is intrinsically discordant [*zwiespältig*]."²⁴ To be faithful to the conflictual and ambivalent mode of questioning for which Heidegger advocated, we must be able to question the questioning so that we gain access to the intermediate zone between the truth of untruth and the untruth of truth where the transparency of the shadow—the nonessence of the essence—is exposed in a thinking forward (*Vordenken*) that frees us from thinking back (*Nachdenken*).

However, the thinking forward, the turning to what must still be thought, even if unthinkable, can only come about by turning thoughtfully toward what has already been thought.[25]

How, then, do we think Nazism in the shadow of Heidegger rather than fixate on how Nazism cast a shadow on Heidegger? It is appropriate to start by summarily dismissing those who have unwaveringly adopted a defensive posture impervious to doubt or to investigation. Typical of this approach is Hermann Heidegger's contention that his father "never denied his entanglements in the movement" and he owned up to the mistakes he made as rector, but "he was neither an uncritical fellow traveler, nor an active party member. From the very beginning he kept a clear distance from the party leadership."[26] Along parallel lines, Heinrich Petzet offered the following meager vindication of Heidegger: "He had a clear conscience and saw no reason to go on a humiliating penitential pilgrimage that would be a retrospective apology for his activities, especially for his thinking, and therefore an acknowledgment that they were wrong. . . . In his opinion he had made it clear that he had never been a National Socialist through his resignation of the rectorate in February 1934."[27]

Such an artless whitewashing of the facts hardly calls for a rejoinder. Nor can we acquiesce to Jean Baudrillard's argument that efforts to ponder Heidegger's "intellectual treachery," centered about his relationship to Nazism, are futile, since this concern is naught but a "perverse fascination with a return to the wellsprings of violence, a collective attempt to hallucinate the historical truth of evil. . . . What is happening, then, is a desperate attempt to snatch a posthumous truth from history, a posthumous exculpation—and this at a moment when there is precisely not enough truth around to allow us to arrive at any sort of verification, nor enough philosophy to ground any relation whatever between theory and practice, nor enough history to produce any kind of historical proof of what happened."[28] Baudrillard himself considers revisionist denials of the Holocaust to be abominable,[29] but he does have qualms about the legitimacy of rendering the cataclysm historically intelligible. His criticism of the quarrel over Heidegger's Nazi affiliation, accordingly, is one example of a larger cultural trend he bemoans. As much as I am sympathetic to the notion of an open past constantly reshaped by the narrative retellings of our historical sensibility, I cannot accept his argument regarding the events of the Second World War in general or with respect to Heidegger in particular.

The mandate to honor the memory of the victims obligates us to take a stand, to repudiate this sense of "necrocultural pathos" and the tactless comparison of the "endless lamentations, commemorations and mummifications" of the Holocaust to walking aimlessly on the "same old treadmill."[30] As Edith Wyschogrod reminded us, the scholarly task is to resuscitate through historical remembrance the spirits still lurking in the smoldering ashes of the death event.[31]

Recent publications, including especially the *Schwarze Hefte*, have provided new and incontrovertible evidence of Heidegger's susceptibility to crass anti-Semitic tropes that prevailed in Germany in the time of Hitler's reign of terror. However, contra to the view expressed by Richard Wolin that the *Black Notebooks* of the 1930s and early 1940s give the reader "access to Heidegger's *innermost philosophical thoughts*: the elaboration of an extensive 'hidden doctrine' that the philosopher developed in the solitude of his Black Forest ski hut,"[32] I agree with the view of David Krell that these notebooks should not be regarded as *Denktagebücher*, that is, philosophical diaries that preserve and do justice to the core of Heidegger's thinking; rather, they "represent a tragic collapse" when compared to the books and essays that Heidegger wrote "with greater care, rigor, and insight" and in which the thinking is "not merely *provoking* but *thought* provoking."[33] It is apposite to keep in mind Heidegger's prefatory remark, "*The entries in the black notebooks* are at their core attempts at simple designation [*einfachen Nennens*]—not statements [*Aussagen*] or even sketches [*Notizen*] for a planned system [*geplantes System*]."[34] And yet, even though these notebooks are not a systematic exposition of an esoteric doctrine,[35] and there is certainly much in them that "one wishes Heidegger had never written," as Krell put it,[36] he did in fact write them, and, alas, they include passages that one ignores only at one's own peril. These comments, as repulsive as they may seem, must now be used to gauge other statements made by Heidegger or his supporters regarding his political activities and beliefs.

It is worth beginning our analysis with Heidegger's portrayal of his involvement with Nazism in a letter he wrote to the rector of the University of Freiburg on November 4, 1945:

After my resignation from the rectorship it became clear that by continuing to teach, my opposition to the principles of the National Socialist world-view would only grow. There was little need for me to resort to specific attacks; it sufficed for me to express my fundamental philosophical positions against the dogmatism and primitivism of Rosenberg's biologism.... Since National Socialist ideology became increasingly inflexible and increasingly less disposed to a purely philosophical interpretation, the fact that I was active as a philosopher was itself a sufficient expression of opposition. During the first semester that followed my resignation I conducted a course on logic and under the title, the doctrine of *logos*, treated the essence of language. I sought to show that language was not the biological-racial essence of man, but conversely, that the essence of man was based in language as a basic reality of *spirit*.[37]

In 1933, based on what he understood to be Hitler's message, Heidegger presumed that his own "spiritual position" and "conception of the task of the university" had the potential to "be reconciled with the political will of those in power."[38] As George Steiner put it, Heidegger's dream was to act as "the *Führer's Führer*, as Plato had striven to do in Sicily."[39] This self-exculpation is corroborated in "Erläuterungen und Grundsätzliches," a letter written on December 15, 1945, to Constantin von Dietze.[40] Heidegger admits that his belief in 1933 that, after Hitler "assumed responsibility for the whole nation," he "would rise above the party and its doctrine and everything would come together" proved to be a mistake (*ein Irrtum*), as he discerned from the events that began on June 30, 1934, the so-called *Nacht der langen Messer*. The discrepancy between his original expectations and the facts on the ground brought him to an intermediary position (*Zwischenstellung*) whereby he could affirm the social and national (*Soziale und Nationale*) but not the nationalistic (*nationalistische*) aspects of the movement. The nationalism, which he rejected, entailed a "spiritual and metaphysical grounding based on the biologism of the Party doctrine" (*die geistige und metaphysische Grundlegung durch den Biologismus der Parteidoktrin*). By contrast, the social and the national were "not necessarily linked to the biological-racist worldview" (*nicht wesensmäßig an die biologisch-rassische Weltanschauungslehre geknüpft war*).[41] As the following passage in the notebooks indicates, Heidegger's rejection of the biological racism has to be cast in a wider epistemological framework: Contemplative thinking, "the asking of the question of beyng" (*Fragen der Seynsfrage*), a meditation that is not teleologically oriented and that is unaffected by what is public, is contrasted with "all biological-characterological analysis" (*biologisch-charakterologische Zergliedern*), which entails a "shirking of the decisions" and the "last flight into an extreme anthropomorphizing of everything."[42] Understanding anti-Semitism metaphysically, as opposed to biologically, is a direct result of this distinction between contemplative and inauthentic modes of thinking. But we cannot forget Derrida's rumination about this "equivocal strategy" of Heidegger elicited from the latter's lectures on Friedrich Nietzsche: "the thought of race [*Rassengedanke*] is interpreted in metaphysical and not biological terms. . . . By thus inverting the direction of determination, is Heidegger alleviating or aggravating this 'thought of race'? Is a metaphysics of race more or less serious than a naturalism or a biologism of race?"[43] Derrida does not answer his own questions, but I trust levelheaded people would agree his silence speaks loudly.

In the continuation of the aforementioned letter to the rector, Heidegger offers other examples, especially the courses and lectures on Nietzsche from 1936–1945, to demonstrate that his teaching was often a clandestine declaration of "spiritual resistance" to the totalitarian and nihilist tendencies of National Socialism.[44] In this regard, it is also of interest to note Heidegger's attempt in *Einführung in die Metaphysik* to protect Nietzsche's philosophy against "all the clumsy and trifling importunities of the horde of scribblers that is becoming ever more numerous around him today. It seems that his work hardly has the worst of this misuse behind it. In speaking of Nietzsche here, we want nothing to do with all this—nor with a blind hero worship."[45] Around the same time that this text was written, Heidegger began his lecture course on Nietzsche by stating that it was necessary to contextualize him as a thinker who asked the grounding question of philosophy concerning the essence of being and therefore he is "not at all so modern as the hubbub that has surrounded him makes it seem. . . . He and we have not yet been sufficiently separated in history; we lack the distance necessary for a sound appreciation of the thinker's strength."[46] I surmise that in both of these passages Heidegger sought to distance himself from the Nazi's partisan use of Nietzsche, especially his doctrines of the superman (*Übermensch*) and the will to power (*Wille zur Macht*).[47] It is instructive that he felt it necessary to add this stipulation lest someone erroneously attribute to him a comparable misreading of Nietzsche.

I take Heidegger at his word when he said in the *Die Spiegel* interview that anyone with ears would hear in the Nietzsche lectures "a confrontation with National Socialism."[48] A comparable defense was offered years before by Heidegger in a letter from January 20, 1948, responding to Herbert Marcuse's request that he explain his commitment to the Nazi regime and his reasons for not publicly denouncing its actions or ideologies. In his reply, Heidegger emphasized that in 1933 "he expected from National Socialism a spiritual renewal of life in its entirety, a reconciliation of social antagonisms and deliverance of Western Dasein from the dangers of communism," but by 1934 he recognized his "political error" and resigned from the rectorate "in protest against the state and party." Heidegger stressed as well that in his lectures and courses from 1933–1944 he took a stand against Nazism.[49] Some may object that Heidegger's reply is inadequate, but there is a degree of consistency in his self-justification, even if it is refuted by other evidence, such as the testimony of Karl Löwith that, when he met Heidegger in 1936, his former teacher still maintained trust in Hitler and wore the Nazi insignia in his lapel. But even Löwith reported that Heidegger alleged to have distanced himself from those who promulgated a biological-racist ideology, which he considered akin to pornography.[50] Human beings, even those who envision themselves to be morally upright and unshakably convinced of an ethical rectitude, are plagued by comporting inconsistent and even contradictory perspectives. I can thus accept that Heidegger was speaking candidly when he mentions the difficulties he endured as a result of his unwillingness to obey certain ultimatums imposed by the very party to which he swore allegiance.[51]

In his *Das Rektorat 1933/34: Tatsachen und Gedanken*, the reflections on his experience as rector written shortly after the collapse of the Nazi regime in 1945 but not published until 1983, Heidegger wrote that he saw in National Socialism a movement that had "the possibility of an inner recollection and renewal of the people and a path that would allow it to discover its historical vocation in the Western world." He also believed that the university could "contribute to this inner self-collection of the people, providing it with a measure."[52] Entries to the notebooks prior to his assuming the rectorate indicate Heidegger's disenchantment with the German university for becoming a "professional school" (*Fachschule*) and his hope for the possibility of reformation based on an authentic desire for knowledge.[53] As in the rectoral address, delivered on May 27, 1933,[54] he maintains that the goal of the university is not "scientific progress in itself" or "professional training and technical preparation," but rather "teaching as *education* [Erziehung]," which involves guiding students toward "*knowingness*" (Wissendsein) or mastery in "genuine questioning." Only then can the university be said to fulfill its mission of "*knowledge cultivation*" (Wissenserziehung) in response to the need and basic character of the German people.[55] In no uncertain terms, he insists that "National Socialism can never be the principle of a philosophy but must always be placed under philosophy as the principle." Heidegger believed, in an almost Platonic way,[56] that this political ideology could "coeffectuate a new basic posture toward beyng," but he did stipulate unreservedly that this could only come about "under the presupposition that National Socialism knows itself in its limits—i.e., realizes that it is true only if it is able—only if it is in condition—to prepare and set free an original truth."[57] Yet, as Heidegger writes in the notebooks, "One regrets the absence of '*spirit*' in National Socialism and fears and laments the destruction [*Zerstörung*] of spirit. Indeed; but what is understood here by 'spirit'? Some sort of unclear vocation [*Berufung*] to something hitherto—which had validity in its time." Heidegger goes on to say that some were frivolous with respect to what was happening, and with regard to what should have been obligatory, but "in such frivolity one always easily finds support and nourishment in order to participate continually in such activity. . . . One adheres obstinately to something one *has not created oneself* but has only taken over; such a one is not at all in the condition of those who are striving to create that which is coming. Frivolity [*Leicht-fertigkeit*] goes together with *recklessness* [Leicht-mütigkeit]."[58]

In another diary entry, Heidegger bemoaned the fact that the movement might be disparaged as a gimmick (*Dreh*) that introduces rigidity under the semblance of spiritual vitality. What is necessary to offset this possibility is an attunement to the fact that "a quite new and unprecedented spiritual mission" is required.[59] Elsewhere he asserts that the "essential character" and the "possible greatness" of National Socialism is that it is a *barbaric principle*. He goes on to explain: "The danger is not National Socialism itself—but, rather, its trivialization into a sermon on the true, the good, and the beautiful (as in an indoctrination session). And the danger is also that those who want to form its philosophy are able to base the latter on nothing other than the traditional 'logic' of common thinking and of the exact sciences, instead of realizing that precisely now 'logic' is newly coming into urgency and necessity and must spring forth as new."[60] The import of the term *barbaric* must be gleaned from its Greek root *barbaros*, the foreign, and thus what Heidegger was affirming here is not brute savagery or belligerence,⁶¹ but rather the hermeneutical violence⁶² that ensues from the altercation (*Streit*) or the confrontation (*Auseinandersetzung*)—which Heidegger contrasts with opposition (*Gegnerschaft*) understood as either rejection (*Ablehnung*) or sublation (*Aufhebung*)⁶³—with the unfamiliar, the uncanny (*Unheimlich*) or unhomely (*Unheimische*). The encounter with the unordinary (*Ungeheure*) facilitates the return home (*Heimat*). Only in this way—the disposition proper to the poeticizing of the poet—can one recover the historical event (*geschichtlich ereignishaft*) that is the question of origin (*Ursprungsfrage*),⁶⁴ the "original strife" (*ursprüngliche Streit*) that arises from "the intimacy of the '*not*' in beyng [*der Innigkeit des* Nicht im Seyn]," that is, the struggle of the oscillation (*Gegenschwung*) between being (*Seyn*) and nonbeing (*Nichtseyn*) in the essence of being.⁶⁵ In *Besinnung*, written in 1938–1939, Heidegger differentiates war (*Krieg*) identified as "the uncontrolled machination of beings" (*die unbeherrschte Machenschaft des Seienden*)—conversely, peace (*Frieden*) is "the seeming suspension of that uncontrolledness"—and struggle (*Kampf*) depicted as the distress that arises from the countering (*Entgegnung*) of god and man crossing with the strife of the earth and the world, a crisscrossing (*Durchkreuzung*) that is "the en-owning [*Er-eignis*] wherein beings are 'owned over' [*übereignet*] again to the belongingness to be-ing [*Zugehörigkeit zum Seyn*]." The struggle, which is thought "out of the stillness of the swaying [*der Stille der Wesung*]," is "the mirroring of the gifting of the sway from out of the mildness of the pride of refusal [*Verweigerung*]."⁶⁶ In contrast to the aggression of war, the confrontation of struggle is peaceful resistance akin to the refusal that is essential to the bestowal of being.

Heidegger came to realize that National Socialism failed miserably to meet these conditions.⁶⁷ Indeed, in a revealing comment in the fifth of the *Black Notebooks*, he decisively expressed his disappointment at any effort to blend the political and the philosophical: "Therefore, philosophy—assuming it actually is such—can also never be appraised 'politically,' neither in an affirmative or negative direction. A 'National Socialist' philosophy is neither a 'philosophy' nor a service to 'National Socialism'—but instead simply runs behind it as burdensome | pedantry—an attitude which is already sufficient to demonstrate its incapacity for actual philosophy. To say a philosophy is 'National Socialist,' or is not so, means the same as to say a triangle is courageous or not so—and therefore is cowardly."⁶⁸ In diametric opposition to the hopes expressed during the rectoral period,

Heidegger here states unequivocally that classifying Nazism as philosophy is a categorical mistake akin to attributing or denying the property of courage to a geometric figure.

There is no question, however, despite his awareness of potential pitfalls from a much earlier period, that Heidegger proclaimed his optimism in the notebooks and in political lectures and writings from 1933, for example, in a speech he gave on June 30 of that year, organized by the Heidelberg Student Association and subsequently published in the *Heidelberger Neuste Nachrichten*, July 1, 1933: "We have the new Reich and the university that is to receive its tasks from the Reich's will to existence.... The possibility could exist that the university will suffer death through oblivion and forfeit the last vestige of its educational power. It must, however, be *integrated again into the Volksgemeinschaft* and *be joined together with the State*. The university must again become an educational force that draws on knowledge to educate the State's leaders to knowledge."[69] Heidegger's commitment to Hitler and encouraging students to engage the escalating battle (*Kampf*) were justified by his belief that true research could only emerge from "rootedness in the Volk and its bond to the State."[70] In a speech delivered in August 1933 on the occasion of the fiftieth anniversary of the *Instituts für Pathologische Anatomie* at the University of Freiburg, Heidegger remarked, "The German people is now in the process of again finding its own essence and of making itself worthy for its great destiny. Adolf Hitler, our great leader and chancellor, has produced a new state through the National Socialist revolution, by means of which the people should again secure a persistence and steadiness of its history.... The German people itself will rediscover genuine self-responsibility [*Selbstverantwortung*]."[71]

Hitting a concordant note many years later in the *Der Spiegel* interview,[72] Heidegger professed that his attraction to National Socialism was sparked by the need "to find a national, and above all a social, point of view."[73] Additionally, responding to the charge that the expression "self-assertion" (*Selbstbehauptung*) in the rectoral address was ill-conceived, Heidegger argued that it actually went "against the so-called 'political science' which was demanded at that time in the Party and by the National Socialist Students. At that time the title had a completely different meaning: it did not mean the science of politics . . . rather it meant: science as such in the meaning and worth, is devalued in favor of the practical needs of the people. The counterposition to such politicizing of science is rightly expressed in the rectoral address."⁷⁴ The main objective of assuming the rectorate was the desire to combat the "technical organization" of the university and the "politicization of science," which Heidegger considered the dubious corollaries of the Nazi agenda, in the hopes of retrieving the true intellectual mission of Western European thought.⁷⁵ In the same interview, Heidegger insisted that his resignation was due to his unwillingness to comply with the request that he replace certain deans he had appointed as part of the university reform because they were not acceptable to the party.⁷⁶

Before one dismisses these statements as examples of Heidegger's dissimulation,⁷⁷ it is imperative to recall that he began the lecture course *Der Wille zur Macht als Kunst*, taught in the winter semester of 1936–1937, with the following aphorism from Nietzsche's notebooks, "I do not wish to persuade anyone to philosophy; it is inevitable, it is perhaps also desirable, that the philosopher should be a *rare* plant. . . . Philosophy has little to do with virtue. . . . What I desire is that the genuine concept of the philosopher should not utterly perish in Germany."⁷⁸ This passage encapsulates two elements well entrenched in Heidegger's path: philosophy has little to do with virtue and the desire to establish the conditions that would make it possible for the philosopher to flourish in Germany, and here I would add uniquely so, that is, philosophy, he thought, belongs in an essential way to the German. Given the events of the Second World War, both of these proved to be problematic, but to some extent they validate his postfactum rationalizations that early on he felt National Socialism offered the possibility of a "new dawn" for the German people.⁷⁹ However, even if we accept this to be the case, we cannot assent to the one-sided and self-serving recounting of Heidegger's adherence to Nazism, epitomized by Walter Biemel, who argued that his teacher's "political error of 1933 was of short duration" and therefore should not be invoked to discredit him as a philosopher. Somewhat pigheadedly, Biemel reasons, "Had the error been a result of his philosophical thought, this thinking would have come to an end with the correction of the error. What actually happened was just the opposite, for it was after 1934 that his thinking really began to unfold."⁸⁰ Heidegger may not have proposed a political philosophy in the wake of resigning from the rectorate, but this does not mean that the topics that engaged his thinking were any less political in nature.⁸¹ As Bourdieu felicitously put it, "Whether they are opponents who reject his philosophy in the name of its affiliation to Nazism or apologists who separate the philosophy from its author's sympathy for Nazism, all the critics contrive to ignore the fact that Heidegger's philosophy might be only a sublimated philosophical version, imposed by the forms of censorship specific to the field of philosophical production, of the political or ethical principles which determined the philosopher's support for Nazism."[82] When we properly fathom the field of philosophical production in which Heidegger's thought was engendered, then it becomes clear that the two domains of the social-political and the academic-theoretical intersect in such a way that it is inappropriate to reduce one to the other. An "adequate analysis" of Heidegger, consequently, "must accommodate a dual refusal, rejecting not only any claim of the philosophical text to absolute autonomy, with its concomitant rejection of all external reference, but also any direct reduction of the text to the most general conditions of its production.... Thus we must abandon the opposition between a political reading and a philosophical reading and undertake a simultaneously political and philosophical *dual reading* of writings which are defined by their fundamental *ambiguity*, that is, by their reference to two social spaces, which correspond to two mental spaces."[83]

One would also be hard-pressed to accede to Hannah Arendt's apologetic assessment in her essay "What Is Existenz Philosophy?" (1946) that Heidegger's behavior is a vestige of the Romanticism that fostered a "genuinely abysmal state of political thought in German universities" rather than the result of "a purely personal failure of character." Arendt goes so far as to say that Heidegger's "complete lack of responsibility is attributable to a spiritual playfulness that stems in part from delusions of genius and in part from despair," which she assumes are features of a shared Romantic spirit rather than a consequence of his individual shortcomings.[84] In a review of *The Black Book: The Nazi Crime Against the Jewish People*, also published in 1946, Arendt described Heidegger as being amongst the "scholars first put to one side by the Nazis as of relatively little use to them," and she notes, perhaps with a touch of defensiveness, that his "enthusiasm for the Third Reich was matched only by his glaring ignorance of what he was talking about."[85] Interestingly, Jaspers offered a similar analysis in a letter, written to Heidegger on March 19, 1950: "You will excuse me when I say what I sometimes thought: that you seemed to behave toward the manifestations of National Socialism like a boy who dreams, who doesn't know how blindly and forgetfully he gets mixed up in an undertaking that looks to him like something completely different than what it is in reality, and then stands before a pile of rubble and allows himself to be driven further."[86] Heidegger responded on April 8, 1950: "You are completely accurate with your image of the dreaming boy." After offering a detail account of the circumstances leading up to his decision to assume the rectorate, Heidegger reiterated the point, "I dreamed and thought fundamentally only about *the* university that I had a vague notion of, but I immediately fell into the machinery of the office: the influences, the power struggles, and the factions, I was lost and fell, if only for a few months, into what my wife describes as an 'intoxication of power.'"[87]

Heidegger offers an explanation, and not an excuse, that he was misled by the realpolitik of the situation and the ideals he harbored inevitably were shown to be imprudent. I am prepared to grant some veracity to this defense, but more troubling is Arendt's assertion in her tribute to Heidegger on his eightieth birthday (September 26, 1969)[88] that he "once succumbed to the temptation to change his 'residence' and to get involved in the world of human affairs. . . . He was still young enough to learn from the shock of the collision, which after ten short hectic months thirty-seven years ago drove him back to his residence, and to settle in his thinking what he experienced. . . . For the wind that blows through Heidegger's thinking—like that which still sweeps toward us after thousands of years from the works of Plato—does not spring from the century he happens to live in."[89] In an accompanying note, added to what was originally delivered as an oral address, Arendt refers to the "episode" of Heidegger's flirtation with National Socialism as an "error" and a "misunderstanding of what it was all about"—indeed, she assumes that he was ignorant of the fundamental tenets of Nazism and probably did not even read Hitler's *Mein Kampf*.[90] To buttress her suggestion, Arendt cites Heidegger's parenthetical statement in *Einführung in die Metaphysik*,[91] that the "inner truth and greatness" of the movement[92] consisted in "the encounter between global technology and modern humanity" (*der Begegnung der planetarisch bestimmten Technik und des neuzeitlichen Menschen*).[93] Despite Heidegger's statement concerning these words in the *Die Spiegel* interview, it is probable that the parenthetical remark was interpolated into the text when it was prepared for publication,[94] but even if it was part of the original, it would not alter the fact that the gloss hardly bolsters Arendt's dismissal of the seriousness of Heidegger's understanding of the dogma of the Third Reich, nor does it lend support to her view that her teacher's reflections on history reinforced an old hostility between the philosopher and the realm of the political.[95]

Heidegger's former student, although faithful to her master and onetime lover, was capable of criticizing him and even expressed distrust in his ability to be honest,[96] but this defense rings hollow.[97] One may contend, as we find in the case of Richard Rorty,[98] that the cogency of a philosophy is not compromised by the moral depravation of the philosopher, but it is not satisfactory to say a thinker's thoughts do not, at least in part, both spring from and have an impact on the era in which he or she lives.[99] Jaspers put it bluntly, "Philosophy is not without political consequences."[100] To portray Heidegger's participation with the Nazis as a temporary aberration from the presumed apolitical nature of his thinking, which allegedly has no relation to his own historical time and is merely circumstantial, as Alain Badiou has argued,[101] is indefensible both empirically and conceptually. One might challenge those who argue for an indisputable relation between Heidegger's thought and his politics, but the insufficiency of Arendt's position regarding his naïveté is so obvious that it does not merit a lengthy rebuttal. Closer to the mark is another statement where Arendt notes that a crucial part of the turn of Heidegger's path in the 1930s had to do with his rejection of the Nietzschean will-to-power in favor of his emphasis on the will-not-to-will.[102] Focusing on the two volumes on Nietzsche, which contain the lecture courses from the years 1936–1940, Arendt noted that "what the reversal originally turns against is primarily the will-to-power. In Heidegger's understanding, the will to rule and to dominate is a kind of original sin, of which he found himself guilty when he tried to come to terms with his brief past in the Nazi movement."[103]

A more careful examination of Heidegger's words does not support the transition proposed by Arendt. On the contrary, Heidegger's adopting the quietistic ideal of self-sacrifice—expressed dialectically as the willing of nonwilling (*Wollen des Nicht-Wollens*) and the nonwilling of willing (*Nicht-Wollen des Wollens*)[104]—was a continuation of the political hyperactivism pursuant to his acceptance of the Nazi demand for submission of the individual's volition to the collective will determined by the Führer. I concur with the conclusion reached by Peter S. Dillard:

Initially, Heidegger's later view of *Ereignis* as *Da-sein*'s passively withstanding the wrathful storm of being by becoming gradually and variously appropriated into a radically non-metaphysical mode of dwelling seems clearly superior to Heidegger's 1933 view of *Ereignis* as *Führer* and *Volk* proving themselves worthy to possess and exercise power through issuing and skillfully completing feasible arguments. For even if the 1933 view avoids the philosophical confusions of crude "blood-and-soil" Nazism, it tacitly assumes a metaphysical conception of being as objectively subordinate to collective willing (planning, designing, deciding, and executing).[105]

An allusion to this is thinly veiled in the rectoral address of 1933, "The will to the essence of the German university is the will to science [*Wissenschaft*] as the will to the historical spiritual mission [*geschichtlichen geistigen Auftrag*] of the German Volk as a Volk that knows itself in its state."[106] The model is the Greeks for whom "science is not a 'cultural treasure,' but the innermost determining center of their entire existence as a Volk and a state."[107] To reactivate the Greek ideal, Heidegger implored the students "to stand firm [*standzuhalten*] in the face of the extreme distress of German fate," for out of this resolve (*Entschlossenheit*) there would come the "will to the essence of the university. This will is a true will, provided that the German students . . . place themselves under the law of their essence and thereby delimit this essence for the very first time. To give law to oneself is the highest freedom [*Sich selbst das Gesetz geben, ist höchste Freiheit*]. . . . Out of this freedom will develop for German students certain bonds and forms of service."[108] The will is realized most veritably when it is delimited in accord with the law of one's essence. The ultimate freedom, however, is to give law to oneself, which is to say, to surrender the individual caprice and to be bound by the service of labor (*Arbeitsdienst*) to the national community (*Volksgemeninschaft*).

In the *Beiträge*, Heidegger translated this idea by noting that the task to ground the domain of decision making (*Entscheidungsbereich*) regarding the truth of being—a domain identified as *Da-sein*, the between (*Zwischen*) that sets human and divine apart and thus appropriates each to the other—requires a "surrendering" (*Entäußerung*) that is the opposite of "self-renunciation" (*Selbstaufgabe*). This grounding (*Gründung*) "can be carried out only by courageously facing the abyss [*Ab-grund*]."[109] Heidegger's understanding of the will can be clarified from his essay on Friedrich Hölderlin's

"Andenken," written in 1942, whence he elicits the following from the poet's words "Yet here comes that which I will" (*Doch kommt das, was ich will*): "Here 'will' does not at all mean the egotistically driven compulsion of a selfishly calculated desire. Will is the knowing readiness for belonging to one's destiny. This will wills only what is coming, for what is coming has already addressed this will, summoning it to know and to stand in the wind of the promise."[110] In 1945 Heidegger continued this line of thought by developing the notion of the will to not will, the higher activity that is not an activity, identified as "releasement" (*Gelassenheit*). Explicitly distinguishing his usage of this term from Meister Eckhart, Heidegger writes that for the medieval Dominican monk the will-not-to-will was still considered an expression of willfulness, whereas for him releasement does not belong to the domain of the will and is thus "outside the distinction between activity and passivity."[111] This may be what Heidegger intended by the aforementioned distinction between relinquishing and repudiating the self. To face the abyss requires a divestiture of self that is realized through beckoning and abiding "in the open realm [*Offenen*] of the 'there,' which is precisely the clearing-concealing fulcrum of this turning [*der lichtend-verbergende Wendungspunkt in dieser Kehre*]."[112] What is required of the human, in kenotic emulation of the withdrawal of the ground of the truth of being that marks the delay in the transition from what Heidegger called the first beginning and the other beginning, is "to withstand a self-refusal of being [*Versagung des Seins*] all the way up to the abandonment by being [*Seinsverlassenheit*]."[113] Only by negating oneself by keeping silent can one be attuned to and interrogate the self-revealing concealing of being.[114]

The example of Heidegger's quietism gives us reason to reject the unconditional proposition that Heidegger's "turning to Nazism cannot be explained through his thought and remains inexplicable."[115] However, it also seems to me excessively reductive to evaluate a thinker's thought merely in light of historical circumstances and the existential decisions they elicit, as we find, for example, in Emmanuel Levinas's unyielding assertion that Heidegger's philosophy rests on a "peasant enrootedness" that glorifies the "pagan" existence and "earth-maternity" emblematic of Nazism,[116] the "eternal seductiveness of paganism" that instigates the *sacred filtering into the world* and the superstitious "attachment to *Place*,"[117] the antithesis of the "abstract universalism" of Judaism expressed in its preference for densely populated urban centers over the countryside, a proclivity that it shared with the Socratic origins of the philosophic disposition: "Socrates preferred the town, in which one meets people, to the countryside and trees. Judaism is the brother of the Socratic message.... Judaism has not sublimated idols—on the contrary, it has demanded that they be destroyed. Like technology, it has demystified the universe. It has freed Nature from a spell. Because of its abstract universalism, it runs up against imaginations and passions. But it has discovered man in the nudity of his face."[118] Alternatively, Levinas expresses his conviction that the "bloody barbarism of National Socialism . . . stems from the essential possibility of *elemental Evil* . . . inscribed within the ontology of a being concerned with being [*de l'être soucieux d'être*], a being, to use the Heideggerian expression,[119] 'dem es in seinem Sein um dieses Sein selbst geht.'"[120] Simply put, Levinas's inability to find a way to absolve Heidegger suggests that in some sense he placed him beyond the pale of being human, since the ability to forgive is commensurate to the infinite ethical responsibility he imparts to every individual vis-à-vis the transcendence of the Other. In language that seems to be an implicit assault on Heidegger's Nazism, Levinas writes that this transcendence "is not to be described negatively, but is manifested positively in the moral resistance of the face to the violence of murder. The force of the Other is already and henceforth moral."[121]

There is a notable aside in one of Levinas's talmudic readings offered at a colloquium held in October 1963 dedicated to the topic of forgiveness, specifically as it pertains to the problems confronting French Jews in their relations with Germans. On this occasion, Levinas chose to concentrate on a passage from the Babylonian Talmud, Yoma 87a–b, which illumines the matter of forgiveness with several anecdotes, including one that deals with Rav and Ḥanina bar Ḥama. According to the talmudic narrative, Rav was commenting on a text before Judah the Prince, and each time a different rabbi entered the room he would start the reading from the beginning. However, when Ḥanina entered, Rav complained about being interrupted and did not start anew, thereby wounding Ḥanina's pride. For thirteen years on Yom Kippur eve, Rav went to seek forgiveness from Ḥanina but the latter refused to be appeased. The master's refusal to accept the disciple's request to be pardoned is explained in terms of a dream in which Ḥanina became aware of Rav's secret ambitions to succeed him as head of the academy. By not exonerating Rav, Ḥanina thwarted his plans and coerced him instead to leave Palestine and to establish a school in

Babylonia in the town of Sura. Levinas adds that it was difficult for Ḥanina to forgive Rav, since it was prophetically revealed to him that he "was fully aware and destined for a great fate." Remarkably, this affords Levinas the opportunity to assert the following: "One can forgive many Germans, but there are some Germans it is difficult to forgive. It is difficult to forgive Heidegger. If Hanina could not forgive the just and humane Rab because he was also the brilliant Rab, it is even less possible to forgive Heidegger. Here I am brought back to the present, to the new attempts to clear Heidegger, to take away his responsibility—unceasing attempts which, it must be admitted, are at the origin of this colloquium."[122] Levinas sharply contrasts Heidegger and Rav—if Ḥanina could not forgive Rav, how much more inconceivable is it to imagine that Heidegger could be forgiven. And yet the pairing of these two figures is jarring and leads us to ask if anything else may be adduced from the juxtaposition. We expect better from the philosopher, especially one as great as Heidegger, just as we expect better from the rabbinic sage to whom is assigned a laudable destiny. Precisely because of those expectations, however, Heidegger is the one German whose guilt cannot be assuaged.

The publication of the diaries has only enhanced those who wish to follow Levinas's intransigent unwillingness to forgive Heidegger, even to the point of some scholars identifying the intellectual turn in the 1930s as a break with National Socialism,[123] thus understanding the philosophical underpinning of the political decision as the shift from beginning with an analysis of Dasein and delimiting the meaning of being based thereon to beginning with *Ereignis*, the appropriating event of being, and understanding Dasein as the possibility that is required if that event is to take place, or, as Krell expressed it, the "turn away from forgottenness of Being to its revealing/concealing clearing."[124] Part of the turning doubtlessly coincided with Heidegger's grappling with Nazism. Years before the diaries were published, Jürgen Habermas already explained Heidegger's change from the phenomenological ontology of *Sein und Zeit* to the pursuit of a new understanding of being (*Seinsverständis*) as a result of the involvement with the Nazis. "I suspect," he writes, "that Heidegger could find his way to the temporalized *Ursprungsphilosophie* of the later period only by way of his temporary identification with the National Socialist movement—to whose inner truth and greatness he still attested in 1935."[125]

Notwithstanding the cogency of Habermas's approach, it is reductionist to think, as some have more recently argued,[126] that the whole of the turn should be comprehended as the break with the aberrant Nazi ideology. A more balanced view is offered by Marcuse, another of Heidegger's Jewish students, who pointedly wrote to him in a letter dated August 28, 1947, "The philosopher of 1933–34 cannot be completely different than the one prior to 1933; all the less so, insofar as you expressed and grounded your enthusiastic justification of the Nazi state in philosophical terms."[127] Elaborating on the nexus of the philosophical and the political in a 1977 interview with Frederik Olafson, Marcuse responded to the query whether Heidegger's Nazism was discernible in his thinking prior to 1933. Marcuse states without equivocation that when he studied with Heidegger there was no hint of any sympathies for Nazism in his lectures, seminars, or private communications. On the contrary, as Marcuse reminisces, between 1928 and 1932, "there were relatively few reservations and relatively few criticisms on my part. I would rather say on *our* part, because Heidegger at that time was not a personal problem, not even philosophically.... We saw in Heidegger what we had first seen in Husserl, a new beginning, the first radical attempt to put philosophy on really concrete foundations—philosophy concerned with human existence, the human condition, and not with merely abstract ideas and principles."[128] No politics were discussed in this period and Heidegger continued to speak highly of the two Jews to whom he dedicated his books, Edmund Husserl and Max Scheler. However, once Heidegger became the rector and openly declared his support for Hitler, Marcuse recounts—in a manner similar to Gadamer, noted in the preface—that he and other students began to wonder if the Nazi outlook was indicated or presaged in earlier work. "And we made one interesting observation, ex-post... If you look at his view of human existence, of being-in-the-world, you will find a highly repressive, highly oppressive interpretation."[129] The essential characteristics of Dasein delineated by Heidegger in *Sein und Zeit*, therefore, present a "picture which plays well on the fears and frustrations of men and women in a repressive society—a joyless existence: overshadowed by death and anxiety; human material for the authoritarian personality.... I see now in this philosophy, ex-post, a very powerful devaluation of life, a derogation of joy, of sensuousness, fulfillment. And we may have had the feeling of it at that time, but it became clear only after Heidegger's association to Nazism became known."[130]

In "An Introduction to Heideggerian Existentialism," Leo Strauss similarly remarked that Heidegger's becoming a Nazi "was not due to a mere error of judgment on the part of a man who lived on great heights high above the low land of politics. Everyone who read his first great book and did not overlook the wood for the trees could see the kinship in temper and direction between Heidegger's thought and the Nazis. What was the practical, that is to say, serious meaning of the contempt for reasonableness and the praise of resoluteness except to encourage that extremist movement?"[131] In a second passage, Strauss gives voice to a different sentiment, one that succinctly frames the dilemma we face in trying to square Heidegger's intellectual prowess and his moral cowardice: "Only a great thinker could help us in our intellectual plight. But here is the great trouble: the only great thinker in our time is Heidegger. The only question of importance, of course, is the question whether Heidegger's teaching is true or not. But the very question is deceptive because it is silent about the question of competence—of who is competent to judge. Perhaps only great thinkers are really competent to judge the thought of great thinkers."[132] There is, of course, no logical way out of the impasse laid out by Strauss. If the only question that matters is whether a teaching of a great thinker is true, but the only one competent to make that judgment is a great thinker, and the only great thinker in our time is Heidegger, then no one but Heidegger would be equipped to render a decision about the significance of his own thinking. Despite this caution, Strauss affirmed that the philosophy of the most important thinker of the twentieth century is marred by its conceptual affinity to Nazism.

In a consonant vein, Amos Funkenstein argued that, even though Heidegger maintained that the distinction he made in *Sein und Zeit* between authentic and inauthentic modes of human existence implied no moral judgment,[133] it was, in fact, "an intrinsic assault on the *dignitas hominis*, the integrity and worthiness of each concrete individual life, however lived. The latter attitude, with its difficulties and paradoxes, must constitute the absolute center of humanistic ethical theories, even at the cost of subscribing to a one-dimensional, flat philosophical anthropology. At best, Heidegger's distinction diverts from this focus; at the worst, it undermines it."[134] As Thomas Sheehan put it more recently, "despite the magnitude of Heidegger's intellectual achievement, major elements of his philosophy are deeply flawed by his notions of politics and history—and that this is so quite apart from the fact that he joined the Nazi party and, for whatever period of time, ardently supported Hitler. Heidegger's engagement with

Nazism was a public enactment of some of his deepest, and most questionable, philosophical convictions."[135]

Even if we grant that the worldview expressed in Heidegger's early philosophical treatises could partially explain the subsequent allure that Hitler and Nazism had upon him—as Löwith explicitly recounted, in their meeting in Rome in 1936 Heidegger acknowledged that "National Socialism lay in the essence of his philosophy" and that his concept of historicity (*Geschichtlichkeit*) in particular was the "basis of his political engagement"[136]—it would be unwarranted to say unqualifiedly that his thinking from the beginning was tainted by this ideological stance and thus a question mark must be placed after his philosophy,[137] an opinion that has been endorsed by a number of scholars, including Victor Farías,[138] Richard Wolin,[139] Hugo Ott,[140] Hans Sluga,[141] Tom Rockmore,[142] Johannes Fritsche,[143] Emmanuel Faye,[144] but also criticized by others, such as Dominique Janicaud,[145] Fred Dallmayr,[146] Julian Young,[147] and Peter Trawny,[148] just to mention a few of the better-known examples. The most extreme expression of the former sentiment is Faye's incendiary proposal to move Heidegger's *Gesamtausgabe* from the "philosophy section of libraries" to the "historical archives of Nazism and Hitlerism."[149] It is more judicious to assume that the affinities between Heidegger's thinking and Nazism led him to the belief that the latter was an effective political way to implement what he believed to be the true philosophical essence of German culture and language. The political repercussions of Heidegger's thought are not coextensive with his Nazism even if the latter is clearly an essential component of the former.

Many of the major ideas in *Sein und Zeit* were consistent with Heidegger's devotion to National Socialism, but as Löwith pointed out in an essay written in 1939, particularly relevant to understand Heidegger's political involvement with Nazism was the theory of historical existence outlined in *Sein und Zeit*, understood from the standpoint of an *Existenzphilosophie* that celebrates the naked facticity[150] of individual mineness (*Jemeinigkeit*) as the measure of authentic community (*Gemeinschaft*); that is, the essential constitution (*Grundverfassung*) of Dasein's historicity, its being-in-the world (*In-der-Welt-sein*), specific to the possibilities of existence, is determined by the anticipatory resoluteness (*vorlaufenden Entschlossenheit*) of its ownmost thrownness (*Geworfenheit*) without recourse to any transcendental ontology or axiology.[151] In Löwith's words:

"*Being and Time* also represents—and in a far from inessential manner—a theory of historical existence; whereas, on the other hand, the practical application of this project to an actual historical situation is only possible insofar as *Being and Time* already contains a relation to contemporary reality. It is this practical-political application in terms of an actual commitment to a determinate decision that in truth justifies or condemns the philosophical theory that serves as the basis of this commitment."[152] Rejecting the choice between defense of Heidegger's philosophy or condemnation of his political attitudes, Löwith insists that "the historical importance of Heideggerianism rests to a large extent on the fact that he took on political responsibilities and involvements in a manner consistent with the fundamental thesis of *Being and Time*."[153] The rhetoric of the lectures connected to Heidegger's assuming the rectorate not only conformed entirely with the National Socialist idiom but also represented a "popularized version" of his philosophy.[154] Löwith thus concludes: "Given the significant attachment of the philosopher to the climate and intellectual habitus of National Socialism, it would be inappropriate to criticize or exonerate his political decision in isolation from *the very principles* of Heideggerian philosophy itself. It is not Heidegger, who, in opting for Hitler, 'misunderstood himself'; instead, those who cannot understand why he acted this way have failed to understand him."[155]

In a later essay, Löwith reiterated his perspective on the political horizons of Heidegger's existential ontology:

For the "spirit" of National Socialism has to do not so much with the national and the social as with the kind of radical resoluteness and dynamic which rejects all discussion and genuine communication because it relies exclusively on itself—on the (German) capacity-for-Being which is always one's own. Without exception, it is expressions of power and resoluteness which characterize the vocabulary of National Socialist politics and Heidegger's philosophy. . . . In light of Heidegger's substantial adherence to the National Socialist attunement and manner of thinking, it was inappropriate to criticize, as well as to offer excuses for, his political decision in isolation, rather than explaining it on the basis of the *principle* of his philosophy. Heidegger did not "misunderstand himself" when he supported Hitler; on the contrary, anyone who did not comprehend how he could do this, did not understand him.[156]

An analogous rationale can be elicited from Gianni Vattimo's more recent observation that Heidegger "really believed that the nonmetaphysical civilization of pre-classical Greece could be reborn through the antimodernity and anticapitalism of the Nazis."[157] Without condoning Heidegger's "tragic error," Vattimo argues that his taking sides with Hitler should be seen as a "matter of deciding upon a historical commitment" that he regarded as "philosophically determining" but not as "responding to a metaphysically universal value." That is, in Löwith's formulation, Heidegger understood his mission as translating the existential belief of one's ownmost individual Dasein into the more specifically cultural German Dasein,[158] a destiny that is "no less particular by virtue of its generality,"[159] indeed, its generality bespeaks an even more acute particularism as Dasein is delimited in its most pristine and superior sense as German. According to Vattimo, the destiny allocated to the Germans by Heidegger was seen as the "call of Being, but exactly of a Being that announces itself only as a particular historical sending, within the limits of a situation (the prevailing power of capitalistic America and Stalinist Russia) that is also unreadable—in its perspective—in terms of universal values and essence."[160]

I accept Theodor Adorno's argument that Heidegger's anti-Judaism is stoked by the implementation of the jargon of existential authenticity and cultural destiny,[161] but, as Karl Löwith, Giorgio Agamben, and others have argued, Heidegger's support of Nazism did not embroil him in positing any pretense of metaphysical access to first principles or absolute truths. On the contrary, the political engagement with National Socialism stems from his categorical rejection of categorical absolutes, the debunking of the universal dictates of reason in favor of an uncompromising acceptance of human finitude or what Wolin, indebted to Löwith, labels a counter-enlightenment.[162] However, this does not imply that his philosophical legacy is contaminated by fascism; it bespeaks rather that critical aspects of his philosophical anthropology intersected with the political goals laid out by the National Socialist agenda. That intersection led Heidegger to believe that the party would serve as a good practical platform to propagate his thought, and, consequently, he would rescue the German people at a critical juncture and help them retrieve their destiny as the ethnos that would bring about the new beginning marked by meditative thinking (*Besinnung*)—to gather oneself into reflection (*sich sammeln ins Nachdenken*)[163]—as opposed to the calculative thinking that shaped Western metaphysics. As farfetched as it seems to us in retrospect, Heidegger viewed National Socialism as a movement that had the potential to advance his notion of a contemplative openness to the essential occurrence of truth wherein what is true has its ground,[164] the opening in which beings are manifest in the concealment of their being.

It is germane to note Marcuse's deduction that Heidegger's assertion in November 1933 that "only the *Führer* himself is German reality and its law" was "the betrayal of philosophy as such," inasmuch as the exhortation to idolize Hitler entails abdication and surrender, two responses that are antithetical to the spirit of philosophical inquiry.[165] The irrefutable fact is that Heidegger not only did not discard the rudimentary dogma of National Socialism, he offered as an ideational validation for such base prejudices the widespread notion of the rootless and nomadic quality of the Jewish people and the politically subversive potential of the conspiracy of world Jewry (*Weltjudentum*), an expression appropriated by Heidegger[166] either from the *Protocols of the Elders of Zion*[167] or from the Nazi rhetoric based thereon as is attested in various iterations in Hitler's *Mein Kampf* and in many of his political speeches.[168] In the aforementioned letter to the rector of the University of Freiburg, Heidegger admitted, albeit self-defensively, that he committed an error and misjudged Hitler and Nazism: "But I was equally convinced, especially following Hitler's May 1933 speech asking for peace, that my basic spiritual position and my conception of the task of the university could be reconciled with the political will of those in power.... During the few days of Christmas vacation I realized that it was a mistake to believe that, from the basic spiritual position that was the result of my long years of philosophical work, I could immediately influence the transformation of the bases—spiritual or non-spiritual—of the National Socialist movement."[169]

Heidegger's attempt to vindicate his actions is feeble, but the evidence is persuasive that he consistently saw his role as imputing spiritual meaning to the historical process underfoot. Consider his comment in a letter written to Carl Schmitt on August 22, 1933, the year they both joined the Nazi party, thanking him for sending a copy of *Der Begriff des Politischen*, referred to as his "written work" (*Schrift*): "Your quote from [Fragment 53 of] Heraclitus particularly pleased me in that you did not forget the *basileus*, which gives the fragment its full meaning, if one interprets it completely. I have had such an interpretation with respect to the concept of truth set down for years.... But now I myself stand in the midst of the polemos [that is, in his role as rector] and all literary projects must give way."[170] In the continuation of the letter, Heidegger notes that the current situation in which he finds himself is "very bleak" (*sehr trostlos*), and that what is most urgent is to gather the "spiritual forces" (*geistigen Kräfte*), "which will be necessary to usher in what is to come" (*die das Kommende heraufführen sollen*).[171]

Heidegger allowed his critique of Western metaphysics to become entangled with some of the crudest expressions of anti-Semitism, or perhaps anti-Judaism would be the more appropriate locution,[172] creating what Trawny has labeled a "being-historical anti-Semitism" (*seinsgeschichtlichen Antisemitismus*).[173] Especially pernicious was his eventual embrace of the idea of *Volksgemeinschaft*, that is, a racially unified community of people with a privileged role to play in claiming their authentic destiny within the history of being (*Seinsgeschichte*).[174] The measured evaluation of Roberto Esposito is worthy of citation: "This and nothing else was Heidegger's Nazism: the attempt to address directly the proper, to separate it from what is improper, and to make the improper speak affirmatively the primigenial voice; to confer upon it a subject, a soil, and a history, as well as a genealogy and a teleology. A teleology through *its* genealogy."[175]

The seeds to destabilize this unfortunate turn can be drawn from Heidegger himself. In an aphorism in the *Beiträge*, Heidegger writes that the essence of a people (*Volk*) can only be grasped on the basis of Dasein, "which means at the same time to know that a people can never be a goal and a purpose." He goes on to say that the essence of a people is its voice (*Stimme*), but that voice "does precisely *not* speak in the so-called immediate outpourings of the common, natural, unspoiled, and unrefined 'man.' . . . The *voice* of a people seldom speaks and speaks only in a few individuals."[176] Setting aside the elitism implied in this statement, what is relevant to our discussion is Heidegger's explicit rejection of an instrumentalism—a people can never be objectified as a goal or as a purpose—and his pronouncement that the sense of peoplehood cannot be expressed through the common and unrefined person. In the same spirit, Heidegger warned in the *Schwarze Hefte*, "This 'folkish' animalization and mechanization [*völkische Vertierung und Mechanisierung*] of the people cannot see that a people 'is' only on the ground of Da-sein, in whose truth for the first time nature and history—in general, a world—come into the open and liberate the earth to its closedness."[177] We can safely assume that these qualifications would have excluded the Nazis. Heidegger's sine qua non for the makeup of the *Volk* is in accord with his disapproval of both teleology and genealogy because neither arche nor telos can be fixed ontologically. Utilizing Nietzsche's *Wille zur Macht* to eschew the systematic and to extol the fragmentary, Heidegger writes in the notebooks, "the essential end cannot be something finished, as little as can the beginning. Instead, it must remain ungraspable and thus inexhaustible."[178] The hope of inaugurating a new future by retrieving an authentic way to the past—what Heidegger designates as the second beginning that would reclaim the origin of thinking (*Andenken*) that reigned before the advent of metaphysics, the ground in virtue of which the history of being first reveals its essence—led the philosopher to fall prey to the cultural psychosis that gripped many German intellectuals during this dark time. Surely, the statement that in the other beginning "all beings are sacrificed up to beyng, and only from there do beings as such receive their truth" takes on an ominous tone when thought in conjunction with Nazi ideology,[179] even if this sacrifice was never meant to be ascribed literally to one ethnic group. To add insult to injury, as many have noted, Heidegger never publicly acknowledged his culpability for statements such as this, not to mention others that are more overtly toxic, nor did he avow that what he did or said was merely a temporary aberration, leaving one to infer that he did not regret his actions and words even if privately he confessed that they were foolhardy and ill-advised.[180] The recent publication of the diaries only adds fuel to the flame.

Particularly damning is the fact that these notebooks yield ample proof that, contrary to his self-portrait,[181] Heidegger's caricature of the Jews long outlived his resignation from the rectorate in April 1934 and his removal from having an official role in the Nazi organization.[182] The newly divulged material confirms that Heidegger's indiscretion was more deeply rooted in the ground of his thinking than he was willing to concede, but the same notebooks also yield evidence that Heidegger found serious and seemingly irreparable fault with National Socialism. Let me cite one illustration from the autumn of 1932:

Why National Socialism in its current configuration [Gestalt] *is still hardly a "worldview"* [»Weltanschauung«] *and, as long as it insists on this "configuration," can never become one*—because it misunderstands the basic condition of all "viewing" [»*Anschauung*«]—all intuiting [*Schauens*] and seeing [*Sehens*]—and is untroubled by such misunderstanding; indeed it thwarts all striving for such understanding— out of fear for its own bravery. It misunderstands that everything near and actual is seen, viewed, only on the basis of what is remote. And that the greatest remoteness of Da-sein is necessary and constitutes Da-sein's own proper grounding. Can come back to what is near only on the basis of this remoteness. What is *seen* is first visible on the basis of the remote, only so—in *such* seeing—does the *world* come to be.[183]

In this relatively early entry, long before Heidegger accepted the rectorate, he already expressed philosophical misgivings about National Socialism's inability to comprehend the principle that Dasein's grounding is dependent on the remote that makes possible the seeing of what is proximate. Passages such as these give us ample reason to reject the claim that the *Black Notebooks* reveal anti-Semitism at the core of Heidegger's philosophy as sensationalistic and inaccurate.[184]

I am of the opinion that Heidegger was sincere when he spoke privately of his political loyalty to the Nazis as the "greatest act of stupidity" (*die grösste Dummheit*).[185] Personal correspondence demonstrates that he was humiliated and dishonored.[186] One of the more moving articulations of Heidegger's disgrace is found in his letter to Jaspers from March 7, 1950: "Since 1933, I no longer came to your house, not because a Jewish woman lived there, but *because I simply felt ashamed*."[187] In response to this letter, dated March 19, 1950, to which I have already briefly referred, Jaspers wrote, "That you felt ashamed means a lot to me. With that, you enter into the community of all of us who have lived and live in a condition for which *shame* is also an appropriate word."[188] And in response to Jaspers, in a letter written on April 8, 1950, Heidegger goes into greater detail about his decision to accept and then to reject the rectorate, and at one point he professes, "What I have reported can excuse nothing; it can only explain to what extent and how from year to year, as more viciousness came out, the sense of shame also grew over having here and there, directly and indirectly, contributed to it."[189] To my ear, these words convey heartfelt remorse and guilt.

I concur, moreover, with Marcel Conche that some credence is to be given to Heidegger's postwar protestation that he sought to purify the vulgar and prosaic elements of National Socialism—including the racism and anti-Semitism—by advocating for a more exalted image of the movement based on the belief that the Germans were the paradigmatic philosophical nation.[190] The chauvinism of this stance is surely reprehensible, but it does suggest, when viewed in historical context, that Heidegger's strategy was to reform the party's platform. It is important to recall as well that Emil Fackenheim, an escapee from Nazi Germany, who roundly criticized Heidegger for endorsing Hitler's program *with the weight of his philosophy* and not impelled by either personal considerations or capitulation to the hysteria of the time,[191] nevertheless documented the ways in which he offered criticism of Nazi ideology both during the war and after its cessation.[192] Heidegger fell short of outwardly and forthrightly rejecting the movement or admitting that his own decision was a symptom of a philosophical catastrophe and not merely a political blunder, but this moral failing provides the opening through which the concealed of the unconcealed of his thinking may be revealed as the entanglement of truth and untruth, an entanglement that sheds light on the shadow so that the substance of the shadow is unveiled as the shadow of the substance.

Chapter Two

NOMADISM, HOMELESSNESS, AND THE OBFUSCATION OF BEING

> The poet is now no longer far away from home; he is near the source.... He is only beginning to learn the free use of what is his own. That is why the foreign must remain near. That is why, for the future poets, the journey preserves what is unavoidable according to the law whereby they must become-at-home. That is why he who is alone and ponders what is his own at the same time commemorates his companions.
>
> —HEIDEGGER, *ELUCIDATIONS OF HÖLDERLIN'S POETRY*

As troublesome as are the conclusions reached in the previous chapter, the position I take must be differentiated from the view that Heidegger was articulating Nazi principles intentionally in the guise of his hermeneutic phenomenology. Not only is there no compelling evidence that Heidegger subscribed to the vulgar biological racism of blood and soil infamously promulgated by the Nazi ideologues,[1] but there is ample proof that he was critical of these excesses, as we find in his explicit rejection of the doctrinaire primitivism of Alfred Rosenberg.[2] One passage from the *Schwarze Hefte* is particularly significant in this regard. Heidegger admits that the longer he carries out his work in his "adopted homeland" (*Wahlheimat*), the more clearly has he seen that he does "*not* belong, and *cannot* belong, to Alemannia as it is behaving convulsively and barrenly here on the upper Rhine.... But—over and above all distribution into belonging to a line of descent and a class—what alone is decisive is *how* one does belong, i.e., whether one merely gives 'expression' to the common and familiar qualities of the line of descent or rather, through one's course of life and achievements, sets forth undeveloped tasks and new possibilities. All of this makes otiose the talk—even rational talk—about belonging to a line of descent."[3] Heidegger is patently disputing two of the pillars of the Nazi creed, the privileging of Germany as the fatherland (*Vaterland*) based solely on the criterion of blood and soil and the supremacy accorded the

Aryan race. The valorization of both is not automatically linked to ethnocultural descent or to socioeconomic class; inheritance depends on the actions and decisions that determine the manner in which one belongs to country and race.[4]

Lest there be misunderstanding, let me be clear that none of this puts into relief the evidence that Heidegger continued to entertain derogatory and perilous views about Jews. One of the most unnerving passages is from the seminar *Vom Wesen der Wahrheit*, offered in the winter semester of 1933–1934. In his explication of the Heraclitean saying that struggle (*polemos*) is the essence or inner necessity of being,[5] Heidegger notes that the nemesis that "poses an essential threat to the Dasein of the people and its individual members" is not the external enemy but rather the more insidious enemy, who may not even appear on the surface to be an enemy, but who has nonetheless "attached itself to the innermost roots of the Dasein of a people." Heidegger admonished his students that it is a "fundamental requirement to find the enemy, to expose the enemy to the light, or even first to make the enemy, so that this standing against the enemy may happen and so that Dasein may not lose its edge. . . . The struggle is all the fiercer and harder and tougher, for the least of it consists in coming to blows with one another; it is often far more difficult and wearisome to catch sight of the enemy as such, to bring the enemy into the open, to harbor no illusions about the enemy, to keep oneself ready for the attack, to cultivate and intensify a constant readiness and to prepare the attack looking far ahead with the goal of total annihilation."[6] There is little doubt, as Faye duly noted,[7] that this solicitation of others to join the struggle against the internal enemy, who threatens the existence and innermost essence of the German people, that will lead to complete annihilation (*Vernichtung*), is a terrifying anticipation of Hitler's own forecast in a speech on January 30, 1939, that the outcome of the world war would be "the extermination of the Jewish race in Europe."[8] That Heidegger's language approximates the malevolent oratory of Hitler's final solution is a chilling damnation of his philosophical imprudence and moral decadence at that time.

The recklessness of Heidegger's political interventions in the 1930s is highlighted by the soberer reflection on war and peace found in the course he offered at the University of Freiburg during the winter and summer semesters of 1951–1952, the first lectures he was permitted to give since 1944 and the last before his formal retirement:

NOMADISM, HOMELESSNESS, AND THE OBFUSCATION OF BEING

With a wink the nations are informed that peace is the elimination of war, but that meanwhile this peace which eliminates war can be secured only by war. Against this war-peace, in turn, we launch a peace offensive whose attacks can hardly be called peaceful. War—the securing of peace; and peace—the elimination of war. How is peace to be secured by what it eliminates? Something is fundamentally out of joint here, or perhaps it has never yet been in joint.[9]

Sadly, it took the carnage of the Second World War for Heidegger to realize the ineffectiveness of military power and the absurdity of the ubiquitous assumption of nation-states that peace can be gained only through war. In this spirit, we should understand the comment in the "Supplements" to the *Feldweg-Gespräche*:

> The War at an end, nothing changed, nothing new, on the contrary. What has long subsisted must now noticeably come out.
> The *devastation*—that it goes onward.
> Onward? So much as possible.
> What initially comes, only the emerging, less and less hiding.
> *The terrible non-essence* of beyng [Unwesen *des Seyns*]—evil—the will.[10]

These words stand in striking contrast to Heidegger's truculent rhetoric directed against the Jews and his appeal to German students to join the struggle in preparation for the total annihilation of the enemy. Presumably, at this vital moment in his own biography and in the drama of world history, he had not yet gained the wisdom to comprehend the futility of the bluster of confrontation and the dire ramifications of the unfettered manifestation of the nonessence of being, the evil that proceeds from the unmitigated expression of the will, culminating in unforgiveable acts of genocide. As Derrida rightly surmised, Heidegger's devotion to Nazism was fueled by a desire to save "a purity internal to spirit, even though he recognizes that evil (*das Böse*) is spiritual (*geistlich*)."[11]

To add insult to injury, in a passage from the diaries that has recently come to light, written sometime in 1942, Heidegger further dehumanized the Jewish victims of Nazi atrocities by utilizing the language of self-destruction to mark the "Jewish" struggle against the Jews understood philosophically as part of the purification of being in the culminating stages of overcoming metaphysics: "When what is essentially 'Jewish'

[»Jüdische«] in the metaphysical sense struggles against the Jewish [*das Jüdische*], the highpoint of self-destruction [*Höhepunkt der Selbstvernichtung*] in history is reached—assuming that the 'Jewish' everywhere has completely arrogated to itself domination [*Herrschaft*], so that even the struggle [*Bekämpfung*] against what is 'Jewish' [»*des Jüdischen*«], and that first and foremost, is the dominance [*Botmäßigkeit*] handed to him."[12] In what can only be considered a convoluted mode of reasoning bordering on madness—an illustration of the demon complaining about being demonized[13]—Heidegger identifies the violence of National Socialism against the Jews as a form of Jewish machination, linked to the long-standing trope of the Jews as the Antichrist, which he relates more specifically to the principle of destruction (*Prinzip der Zerstörung*) connected to metaphysics in the Christian West.[14] The pinnacle of self-destruction instantiated in history by the Nazis, therefore, is referred to bizarrely as a Jewish form of battling the menacing impact of the Jews.[15] The latter play a disproportionate part in Heidegger's mind, functioning as the prime representatives of the orientation that interprets being from the standpoint of a thinking dominated by calculation (*Rechnung*) and machination (*Machenschaft*), a mode of philosophizing that has contributed immeasurably to the obfuscation of being (*Seinsvergessenheit*).[16]

That Heidegger was aware of the absurdity of identifying all calculative thinking as Jewish is evident in the following passage from the *Beiträge*, which, as Trawny has pointed out,[17] implicitly criticizes the Nazi distinction between Aryan and Jewish science: "*Because* modern 'science' (physics) is mathematical (not empirical), it is necessarily experimental in the sense of the measuring experiment. *Sheer idiocy* to say that experimental research is Nordic-Germanic and the rational research, on the contrary, is of *foreign extraction* [fremdartig]! We would then have to resolve to number Newton and Leibniz among the 'Jews.'"[18] While not all those who uphold the modern scientific mode of mathematical experimentation should be identified as Jewish, it is still the case that Heidegger viewed Jewish thinking as inherently calculative. Insofar as the Jews ethnically embody the "empty rationality and calculability" (*leeren Rationalität und Rechenfähigkeit*), which gains a foothold in spirit (*Geist*) but without being able to grasp the "hidden realms of decision" (*die verborgenen Entscheidungsbezirke*),[19] their self-destruction would herald the nihilism of nihilism achieved as the "highest level of technology" (*die höchste Stufe der Technik*), that is, the

NOMADISM, HOMELESSNESS, AND THE OBFUSCATION OF BEING

self-annihilation (*Selbstvernichtung*) implemented when technology, as consumption, has nothing more to consume than itself (*wenn sie als Verzehr nichts mehr zu verzehren hat—als sich selbst*).[20]

Building on the much older negative stereotypes of the Jew as itinerant, scheming, and impetuous, Heidegger gives expression to a topological anti-Semitism[21] in passages such as the one where he writes that the "worldlessness of Jewry" (*Weltlosigkeit des Judentums*) is grounded in "the tenacious facility in calculating, manipulating, and interfering" (*die zähe Geschicklichkeit des Rechnens und Schiebens und Durcheinandermischens*).[22] Inasmuch as the basic comportment of being human, according to Heidegger's existential analytic of Dasein, is being-in-the-world (*in-der-Welt-sein*), his translation of the leitmotif of the wandering Jew as an inherent worldlessness can be seen as a form of philosophic dehumanization in both spatial and temporal terms. Concerning the former, an indissoluble link is forged between the physical location of space and the ontological locality of place.[23] This dislocation is to be distinguished from the feeling of the uncanny (*unheimlich*) that Heidegger analyzed in *Sein und Zeit* in conjunction with the basic attunement (*Grundbefindlichkeit*) to the mood of anxiety that leaves one disoriented as the tranquility and self-assurance of "being-at-home" (*Zuhause-sein*) in the everyday world slip away and one enters the existential state of "uncanniness" (*Unheimlichkeit*), the sense of "not-being-at-home" (*Nicht-zuhause-sein*),[24] an ontological condition in which the familiar becomes strange.[25] The nomadism of the Jew is indicative of a more persistent ontic condition of homelessness, of not having a world altogether and not merely the anxiety about being-in-the-world as such and the consequent flight of Dasein from itself. As Heidegger writes in one passage from the *Black Notebooks*, utilizing the term coined by Hans Grimm as the title of his novel published in 1926 and later exploited in Nazi propaganda, a *people without space* (Volk ohne Raum) are a people "without an essential world [*wesentliche Welt*] and without essentially occurring truth [*wesende Wahrheit*]—in which the people can surmount themselves [*sich überhöhen*]—in order for the first time—to be themselves [*es selbst zu sein*]."[26] The placeless Jews suffer alienation from a sense of worldhood that would afford them the opportunity to surmount and thereby become themselves. Significantly, even though Heidegger's thought pivoted from examining the nature of being through an analysis of Dasein to understanding the latter as the vehicle that facilitates the appropriating event of being, a turn on the path that results in a reorientation in the correlationality of humanity and the world, there is a thread that ties together the two phases of Heidegger's thought with respect to this essential mode of belonging together as a hermeneutical plight. As Sheehan astutely noted, Heidegger's thought in toto can be viewed as a "phenomenological reduction of being to meaning," and the two critical terms, *facticity* in the earlier period and *Ereignis* in the later period, both portend "the a priori appropriation of man to the meaning process."[27]

That process, I would contend, is conditioned by a cultural sense of geolinguistic emplacement and thus Heidegger was not able to get out from under an overbearing *echontology*,[28] a neologism that communicates through the amalgamation of being (*ontos*) and having (*ekhōn*) the revered state of "*belongingness in being* [Zugehörigkeit in das Seyn], *in the event as deliverance* [in das Ereignis als Austrag]. . . . *Silencing of the deliverance*—(event) *original clearing* [ursprüngliche Lichtung]."[29] From both the earlier and the latter Heideggerian perspectives, the Jew is marginalized and excluded from the very language—the act of naming—that grounds the world and preserves the clearing of being-there. Caputo succinctly summarized Heidegger's perspective, "The Jews, the Judeo-Christian tradition generally, indeed virtually *everybody* except a short list of Greco-Germans, figure not at all in this rival sacred history, this narrative of the history of being, except as distortions of the early Greek dawn. The Jews do not speak words of being, and being does not speak Hebrew. The two are separated by an abyss."[30] With regard to this matter, Heidegger revitalized an older anti-Semitic stereotype, exploited by the Nazis, that Jews were incapable of an authentic German expression and hence their linguistic skills were predictably inferior and derivative, sometimes even depicted—as it relates to Yiddish—as a meager translation from Hebrew.[31] Heidegger adopted this bias and interpreted it as a consequence of the Jews wanting a sense of the world and their being denied a meaningful claim to historical destiny, as he despicably argued in *Logik als die Frage nach dem Wesen der Sprache* (1934) regarding "human groups" like the "Negros" to whom he also refers as "Kaffirs," a pejorative term for black Africans: "If we now take up the question concerning the essence of history, one could think that we have arbitrarily decided what history is, namely, that history is that which is distinctive for the being of the human being. One could object, on the one hand, that there are human beings and human groups (Negros like, for example, Kaffirs) [*Neger wie z. B. Kaffern*] who have no history, of which we say that they are without history. On the other hand, however, animal and plant life has a thousand year long and eventful history."[32]

In an undeniable racist tone, Heidegger suggests that perhaps we can attribute to African blacks the sense of history (*Geschichte*) in the manner that animals and plants have a history but not a proper human history. Alas, even this suggestion is rejected since it remains questionable if the concept of history at all should be associated with the former:

But, how do we come to say that Kaffirs are without history? They have history just as well as the apes and the birds. Or do earth, plants, and animals possibly have after all no history? Admittedly, it seems indisputable that that which goes by, immediately belongs to the past; however, not everything that passes and belongs to the past needs to enter into history. . . . We have confined history to the being of the human being. . . . We determine, with this restriction, *history as being of the human being* [Geschichte als Sein des Menschen], and reject "animal history" and "earth history" as vacuous. History is a distinctive character of human being.[33]

The restricting of history as a viable phenomenon to humanity, and excluding thereby vegetal and animalistic life, parallels Heidegger's argument in the "Brief über den 'Humanismus'" (1946): "Because plants and animals are lodged in their respective environments [*Umgebung*] but are never placed freely into the clearing of being [*die Lichtung des Seins*] which alone is 'world' [»*Welt*«], they lack language."[34] Heidegger goes on to say that lacking language does not mean that plants and animals are "suspended worldlessly [*weltlos*] in their environment."[35] However, the distinction he has made between world and environment is such that the lack of language does, in fact, mean that these species are worldless. Moreover, insofar as language is defined by Heidegger as "the clearing-concealing advent of being itself" [*lichtend-verbergende Ankunft des Seins selbst*],[36] it follows that plants and animals have no access to being. The Jews would be placed in the same category; at best, they live within an environment that sustains their ontic-biological existence, but they have no world ontologically and therefore no language and no being.

In the essay "Die Überwindung der Metaphysik" (1938–1939),[37] Heidegger writes that the meaning of the history of being (*seynsgeschichtlichen Sinne*) yields a conception of the "world" that is indexical of the "nonobjective presencing [*ungegenständliche Wesung*] of the truth of Being for man in that man is essentially delivered over to Being." However, as a consequence of the "abandonment of beings by Being's truth" (*Verlassenheit des Seienden von einer Wahrheit des Seins*), the "world" has become an unworld (*Unwelt*) in which there is still the presence of being but without the sense of its reigning.³⁸ Expanding this theme in *Besinnung*, also written in 1938–1939, Heidegger distinguishes *Geschichte* and *Historie*, the former is an "objectification [*Vergegenständlichung*] of the past into what is situational [*Zuständliche*] in the present," whereas the latter is the "domain of man insofar as this domain . . . on the ground of its hidden allotment [*Zugewiesenheit*] to be-ing 'comports' itself towards 'beings in the whole' and towards itself. *The ground of the historicality* [Geschichtlichkeit] *of the domain of man is its allotment unto the truth of be-ing*, which as the domination of *ratio* and thus as the domination of 'irrational' 'lived-experience' can prevail on the foreground for a long time."³⁹ History and the lack of history, therefore, are determined from the perspective of this comportment (*Verhalten*) to beings. Insofar as "the historicality of the domain of man is grounded in the enowning-character of *be-ing* [*Ereignis-Charakter des Seyns*]," a person can be historical or unhistorical, but if one is entirely "without history," then the human becomes an animal.⁴⁰

Here is it well to mention the passing comment in *Sein und Zeit* in which Heidegger already wondered if we could phenomenologically attribute time to animals in light of the link he established between temporality (*Zeitlichkeit*), understanding (*Verstehens*), and attunement (*Befindlichkeit*):

Only beings that in accordance with the meaning of their being [*Seinssinne*] are attuned—that is, beings which, as existing, have in each instance already been and exist in a constant mode of having-been—can be affected. Ontologically, affection presupposes making present [*Gegenwärtigen*] in such a way that in it Dasein can be brought back to itself as having-been. How the *stimulation* [Reiz] and *touching* [Rührung] of the senses in beings that are simply alive [*Nur-Lebenden*] are to be ontologically defined, for example, how and where in general the being of animals [*das Sein der Tiere*] is constituted by a "time" [*eine »Zeit«*], remains a problem for itself.⁴¹

Heidegger's denying the Jews a sense of *Geschichtlichkeit* robs them of the fundamental sense of the temporally conceived understanding and

NOMADISM, HOMELESSNESS, AND THE OBFUSCATION OF BEING

attunement basic to being human and thus condemns them to the fate of being animalistic,[42] a theme that accords with a well-known stratagem in Nazi propaganda.[43] The name "world history" (*Weltgeschichte*), as Heidegger noted in *Was Heißt Denken?*, "means the *fatum* [*das Geschick*] that there *is* world and that man *is* as its inhabitant. The world-historical question, 'What is it that calls on us to think?' asks: That which really is—in what way does it come to touch the man of our era"[44] This comment sheds light on what was intended in his earlier depiction of the Jews as having no world: not only do they lack a secure place geopolitically but they are *geschichtslos*, that is, they have no legitimate claim to being-historically and thus they cannot espouse a genuine sense of living in time.[45] To divest the Jew of both spatial and temporal coordinates is an act of supreme degradation by which the world invariably becomes an unworld, a place of utter discord with no possibility of reconciliation.

In a captivating note in *De l'espirit*, Derrida beckons the reader:

Pause for a moment: to dream of what the Heideggerian corpus would look like the day when, with all the application and consistency required, the operations prescribed by him at one moment or another would indeed have been carried out: "avoid" the word "spirit," at the very least place it in quotation marks, then cross through all the names referring to the world whenever one is speaking of something which, like the animal, has no *Dasein*, and therefore no or only a little world, then place the word "Being" everywhere under a cross, and finally cross through without a cross all the question marks when it's a question of language, i.e., indirectly, of everything, etc. One can imagine the surface of a text given over to the gnawing, ruminant, and silent voracity of such an animal-machine and its implacable "logic." This would not only be simply "without spirit," but a figure of evil. The perverse reading of Heidegger. End of pause.[46]

The immediate issue that occasioned Derrida's remark is Heidegger's call for the necessity "of crossing through again the question marks (*die Fragezeichen wieder streichen*)."[47] Reflecting on this note in a later publication, Derrida highlights that he was concerned with the so-called animal-machine, which he further glosses as an "animal of reading and rewriting." Moreover, this peculiar monstrosity, which is neither animal nor nonanimal, neither organic nor inorganic, neither living nor dead, is compared to a computer virus. Insofar as this being is invasive in nature, it is described as a "malign and hence perverse beast," and Derrida even suggests that there is an affinity between it and the demonic.[48] What I would extrapolate from this parenthetical annotation—admittedly a conclusion not drawn by Derrida—is that the portrait of the Jew that emerges from Heidegger is not conceptually far from this quasi-animal that is incapable of relating to being and, as a consequence, is extrinsic to the horizon of language.

It is worth recalling Levinas's description of his own incarceration with fellow Jewish prisoners of war, "We were subhuman, a gang of apes. A small inner murmur, the strength and wretchedness of persecuted people, reminded us of our essence as thinking creatures, but we were no longer part of the world. . . . We were beings entrapped in their species; despite all their vocabulary, beings without language."[49] The loss of language poignantly delineates the forfeiture of being human. From his particular experience, Levinas proffered the following generalization, which well captures the repercussions of the perspective promoted by Heidegger: "Racism is not a biological concept; anti-Semitism is the archetype of all internment. Social aggression, itself, merely imitates this model. It shuts people away in a class, deprives them of expression and condemns them to being 'signifiers without a signified' and from there to violence and fighting." Ironically, the "cherished dog" named Bobby, the very animal associated with Nazi ruthlessness, was the one being that still recognized—through his jumping up and down and his barking in delight—that the Jewish captives were men, and thus Levinas sardonically brands the canine "the last Kantian in Nazi Germany, without the brain needed to universalize maxims and drives."[50] Levinas transposes one of the greatest symbols of the Jewish dread of Nazi sovereignty into the ideal of what was once most noble in German culture. The crucial point is that Heidegger conceptually performed what Levinas described by depriving Jews of the endowment of language and hence leaving them in a state of desertion and dispossession.

In the protocols to his seminar on nature, history, and the state, which took place in 1933–1934, Heidegger offers the following disparaging portrayal of the disenfranchised status of the Jews:

History teaches us that nomads have not only been made nomadic by the desolation of wastelands and steppes, but they have also often left wastelands behind them where they found fruitful and cultivated land—and that human beings who are

NOMADISM, HOMELESSNESS, AND THE OBFUSCATION OF BEING

rooted in the soil have known how to make a home for themselves even in the wilderness. Relatedness to space, that is, the mastering of space and becoming marked by space, belong together with the essence and the kind of Being of a people.... From the specific knowledge of a people about the nature of its space, we first experience how nature is revealed in this people. For a Slavic people, the nature of our German space would definitely be revealed differently from the way it is revealed to us; to Semitic nomads, it will perhaps never be revealed at all.[51]

Heidegger's comment about the Semitic nomads—apparently the worst kind of nomadism, since the nature of German space cannot be disclosed to them at all—has to be weighed against his overall thinking regarding the themes of enrootedness, dwelling, homelessness, and homecoming,[52] as they relate to the destiny of the human being in the world,[53] or, to be more precise, the triangulation of the concepts of groundedness (*Bodenstädigkeit*), homeland (*Heimat*), and peoplehood (*Volkstum*) as markers of German identity.[54] In *Sein und Zeit* Heidegger wrote, "Dasein itself has its own 'being-in-space' [*ein eigenes »Im-Raum-sein«*], which in its turn is possible only *on the basis of being-in-the-world in general* [auf dem Grunde des In-der-Welt-seins überhaupt].... The understanding of being-in-the-world as an essential structure of Dasein first makes possible the insight into its *existential spatiality* [existenziale Räumlichkeit]."[55] The ontic characteristic of being-in-space is dependent on the ontological condition of being-in-the-world, and the latter is not a quality of corporeal extension but rather the spiritual constitution of care (*Sorge*): "Dasein can be spatial [*räumlich*] only as care, in the sense of factically entangled existing [*des faktisch verfallenden Existierens*].... Rather, because Dasein is 'spiritual' [*»geistig«*], *and only because it is spiritual*, can it be spatial in a way that essentially remains impossible for an extended corporeal thing."[56] Expressing the same motif concerning the connection between the spiritual and the spatial, albeit as it pertained specifically to the compatibility of his philosophical contemplation and the manual labor of the peasants in the mountains, Heidegger wrote in "Warum bleiben wir in der Provinz?" (1934): "The inner relationship of my own work to the Black Forest and its people comes from a centuries-long and irreplaceable rootedness in the Alemannian-Swabian soil."[57] To deny the Jews the possibility of this rootedness in the soil is to deny them the possibility of being in the world in a spatial sense, and this is to deny them something essential about the spiritual dimension of being human. By contrast, the space demarcated as German is most properly bequeathed to the German people because of their unique way of being in the world, which is intricately connected to their linguistic legacy. Thus, Heidegger writes in the *Schwarze Hefte*, "The Germans will not grasp—let alone fulfill—their Western destiny, unless they are equipped for it by the originality of their language [*die Ursprünglichkeit ihrer Sprache*], which must ever again find its way back to the simple, uncoined word, where the closeness to beyng bears and refreshes the imprintability of discourse [*die Prägsamkeit des Sagens*]."[58] This is the principle by and through which the Germans "struggle over their most proper *essence*" embodied in their history as the "people of poets and thinkers" (»*Volk der Dichter und Denker*«).[59]

Heidegger's take on Jewish nomadism can be further elucidated by comparing it to the following comment in Carl G. Jung's lecture "Zur gegenwärtigen Lage der Psychotherapie" (1934)[60]: "The Jew, who is something of a nomad, has never yet created a cultural form of his own and as far as we can see never will, since all his instincts and talents require a more or less civilized nation to act as host for their development."[61] On the one hand, Jung links the nomadic quality of the Jews to the assumption that they lack a cultural form of their own and thus, like women, who are "physically weaker," they parasitically thrive off their host nations and are better protected and less vulnerable; on the other hand, he contrasts what he identifies as the ancient civilization of the Jews and the cultural makeup of the younger Aryans. Because the Jew is "a member of a race with a three-thousand-year-old-civilization," he is more adept at dealing with the shadow side of the unconscious than the Germanic peoples.[62] If ever there was a left-handed compliment, Jung's impudent attempt to distinguish between Jew and Aryan certainly qualifies. To cite his words verbatim: "The Jewish race as a whole—at least this is my experience—possesses an unconscious which can be compared with the 'Aryan' only with reserve. Creative individuals apart, the average Jew is far too conscious and differentiated to go about pregnant with the tensions of unborn futures. The 'Aryan' unconscious has a higher potential than the Jewish; that is both the advantage and the disadvantage of a youthfulness not yet fully weaned from barbarism."[63]

Jung goes on to criticize Freud for applying "Jewish categories... indiscriminately to Germanic and Slavic Christendom." As a consequence

NOMADISM, HOMELESSNESS, AND THE OBFUSCATION OF BEING

of this "grave error in medical psychology," the "most precious secret of the Germanic peoples—their creative and intuitive depth of soul—has been explained as a morass of banal infantilism." If that were not bad enough, Jung whines that his own "warning voice" has been suspected of anti-Semitism, a suspicion he traces to Freud, based on the latter's inability to understand the "Germanic psyche." The same can be said of his "Germanic followers," a surreptitious reference to the German-Jewish disciples of Freudian psychoanalysis. With callous disdain, Jung writes, "Has the formidable phenomenon of National Socialism, on which the whole world gazes with astonished eyes, taught them better? Where was that unparalleled tension and energy while as yet no National Socialism existed? Deep in the Germanic psyche, in a pit that is anything but a garbage-bin of unrealizable infantile wishes and unresolved family resentments. A movement that grips a whole nation must have matured in every individual as well. That is why I say that the Germanic unconscious contains tensions and potentialities which medical psychology must consider in its evaluation of the unconscious."[64] A full analysis of Jung's thinking about National Socialism and the Germanic unconscious is beyond my immediate concerns. Without absolving the Nazis, Jung emphasizes that this movement unleashed the dark energies of the German people, forces that are sinister but creative. These forces of the unconscious comprise future possibilities and therefore cannot be explained by the Freudian emphasis on past repression.[65] By contrast, Heidegger finds no redeeming quality in the Semitic nomadism vis-à-vis German culture. The Jew has no home, no language, no world, no historical destiny.

The confluence of the ethnolinguistic and the geopolitical in Heidegger's thought is already attested in the rectoral address of 1933,[66] where he spoke of the essence of the German university related to the "the inexorability of that spiritual mission which impresses onto the fate of the German Volk the stamp of their history."[67] The essential character of the university is self-governance (*Selbstverwaltung*), but the latter, Heidegger told the professors and students in attendance, involves determining through self-examination (*Selbstbesinnung*) the way to realize the task of becoming what one ought to be.[68] Crucial to this task is the act of "self-limitation" (*Selbstbegrenzung*) by which the German people will that essence and, in so willing, assert their own essential being. A nexus is thus drawn between self-governance, self-examination, self-limitation, and self-assertion (*Selbstbehauptung*). The reclaiming of science—the word *Wissenschaft* denotes authentic knowing, in which the question of being occupies a central place, as opposed to more contemporary forms of positivism or empiricism—bespeaks the historical spiritual mission of the German university, which, in turn, embodies the essence of the German people fully incorporated in the state.[69] This knowledge, Heidegger told his audience on that fateful day, could be attained only "when we submit to the power of the *beginning* of our spiritual-historical existence. This beginning [*Anfang*] is the commencement [*Aufbruch*] of Greek philosophy.... All science remains bound to that beginning of philosophy and draws from it the strength of its essence, assuming that it still remains at all equal to this beginning."[70]

Several years later, in *Einführung in die Metaphysik*, Heidegger articulated the dilemma of modernity as follows:

This Europe, in its unholy blindness always on the point of cutting its own throat, lies today in the great pincers between Russia on the one side and America on the other. Russia and America, seen metaphysically are both the same: the same hopeless frenzy of unchained technology and of the rootless organization of the average man. When the farthest corner of the globe has been conquered technologically and can be exploited economically; when any incident you like, in any place you like, at any time you like, becomes accessible as fast as you like; when you can simultaneously "experience" an assassination attempt against a king in France and a symphony concert in Tokyo; when time is nothing but speed, instantaneity, and simultaneity, and time as history has vanished from all Dasein of all peoples; when a boxer counts as the great man of a people; when the tallies of millions at mass meetings are a triumph; then, yes then, there still looms like a specter over all this uproar the question: what for?—where to?—and what then? The spiritual decline of the earth has progressed so far that peoples are in danger of losing their last spiritual strength, the strength that makes it possible even to see the decline [which is meant in relation to the fate of "Being"] and to appraise it as such.[71]

As is well known, the critique of the technological and materialistic predilection of modernity is a central theme in Heidegger's writings. In this context, what I wish to emphasize is that the spiritual decline is also expressed as ethnicities losing their sense of history, which is tied to their individual cultural-linguistic foundations. The favoring of the German *Volk*, therefore, is intrinsically related to the German language, which cannot be separated from the physical land of Germany. Heidegger did not practically, and could not theoretically, embrace Adorno's rhetoric, a "language without earth, without subjection to the spell of historical existence, a utopia that lives on unawarely in the childlike use of language."[72] For Heidegger, the notion of language without soil is preposterous; language is rooted in soil and hence in the absence of the latter we cannot speak about the former. Heidegger could not envision the possibility of Arendt's identification of her homeland as the German language separated from the land and the consequent decoupling of language and people,[73] or what Agamben has more recently called, influenced by Scholem's account of the linguistic theory of the kabbalah,[74] language without name, which similarly entails the severing of language from the people who speak it as part of their national identity and, by extension, from the land where it is spoken.[75] Elias Canetti and Paul Celan are mentioned by Agamben as individuals who wrote in German without any relation to the German people, and thus they sought to save the language from its people.[76] Moreover, they serve as a model for a future anonymous, anarchic, and antinomian intertwining of politics and poetry. For Heidegger, despite his efforts to extend beyond the more constricted nationalism of Nazi ideology, the political dimension of poetry was still tied to the intricate connection between land, language, and peoplehood, and, in that respect, the figure of poetry effaces plurality.[77]

German identity, therefore, is grounded in homeland, and homeland in language, which is to be interpreted in a particularistic as opposed to a universalistic register, since German, above all, is the matrix language, the *Muttersprache*, the mother tongue.[78] As Peter Blickle reminds us, "In German philosophy the word *Grund*, no matter how abstract its application, never seems to come away entirely from its concrete and literal root in 'ground' or 'earth.'"[79] This philological insight can surely be applied to Heidegger. In the introduction to his 1934–1935 lecture course on Hölderlin's "Germanien," Heidegger wrote, "The fatherland, our fatherland Germania—most forbidden, withdrawn from the haste of the everyday and the bustle of activity. The highest and therefore most difficult, that which comes last, because fundamentally first—the origin withheld in silence [*verschwiegene Ursprung*]."[80] The confrontation with the "primordial power" of that origin encompasses "a questioning that is truly necessitated, one that has the task of once again first bringing about a historically spiritual space. This can occur only if such questioning is necessitated from out of the ownmost need of our historical Dasein.... It is the need of needlessness, the need of the complete inability to experience the innermost question-worthiness of Dasein."[81] The topological connotation of the *Vaterland* cannot be denied, but geographic place is important only insofar as the physical space facilitates "the innermost and most far-reaching historical vocation [*geschichtlichen Bestimmung*] of the people."[82] For Hölderlin, the fatherland "does not mean some dubious greatness of an even more dubious patriotism full of noise." The fatherland, the land of the fathers, relates to the Germans as the "people of this Earth as a historical people, in its historical being. Such beyng, however, is founded poetically, articulated and placed into knowing in thinking; it is rooted in the actions of those of the Earth who are responsible for the establishing of the state, and in historical space."[83]

The fatherland thus primarily signifies the historical being of the German people, a being established poetically but expressed politically. Still, the historical being of the people—the fatherland—is sealed essentially and forever in the mystery (*Geheimnis*) of the poetic saying (*dichterische Sagen*).[84] I shall elaborate on the nature of this mystery in chapter 4, but suffice it here to note that Heidegger alludes to it when he writes that the fatherland is "*beyng itself* [das Seyn selbst], which from the ground up bears and configures the history of a people [*die Geschichte eines Volkes*] as an existing [*daseienden*] people: the historicity of its history [*die Geschichtlichkeit seiner Geschichte*]. The fatherland is not some abstract, supratemporal idea in itself; rather, the poet sees the fatherland as historical in an original sense."[85] The way to dwell poetically within the *Vaterland* is through the *Muttersprache*; the saying/showing of the concealed can transpire solely through the poet's native language. As Heidegger expressed it in "Hebel—der Hausfreund" (1957): "Man speaks from within that language to which his essence is commended. We call this language 'the mother tongue.' With regard to the language that has grown historically—that it is the mother tongue—we may say: *It is language, not man, which genuinely speaks. Man speaks only to the extent that he in each case co-responds to language.*"[86] Heidegger never swerved from his commitment to the proposition that language confers the abode in which human beings may dwell,[87] but the language most apposite to that conferral and the awakening of poetry that ensues therefrom is

German. The linguistic character of poeticizing as the configuring ground (*Grundgefüge*) of historical Dasein should apply to all people without partiality, since language is presumed to constitute the originary essence of the historical being of human beings,[88] and yet it is identified exemplarily as German. Indeed, in one context, Heidegger pridefully avers that the German song entails the greatest facility to bring one into nearness to the mystery of beyng because it is the most joyful.[89]

The argument made here about space corresponds to Heidegger's conjecture about time based on his reading of the eleventh chapter of Augustine's *Confessions* in the 1930 Beuron lecture: the aporetic questionability of time—the not-knowing (*Nichtwissen*) that one inevitably encounters in posing the question of the nature of time[90]—strikes a deeper chord than the cognizant seeking proper to the ontological examination of entities. By contrast, the ignorance about the eventfulness of time occasions an incessant interrogation that is itself the enactment of true temporality as the distention of life and its stretching out to eternity.[91] Analogously, albeit with a focus on extensionality, in the lecture "... dichterisch wohnet der Mensch..." given on October 6, 1951, Heidegger elicits from Hölderlin that humankind's dwelling rests most aptly in the poetic, "the taking of the measure by which the measure-taking [*Maß-Nahme*] of human being is accomplished,"[92] and consequently only the poetic word—epitomized in German—can awaken humankind to the obligation of constructing a spiritual space, that is, a space calibrated to the physical site wherein the spiritual can materialize on earth and not in some otherworldly domain. "Poetry does not fly above and surmount the earth in order to escape it and hover over it. Poetry is what first brings man onto the earth, making him belong to it, and thus brings him into dwelling."[93]

From the time Heidegger abandoned the rectorate in 1934, he shifted from a purely geopolitical denotation of "the homeland" (*die Heimat*) and of "the German" (*das Deutsche*) to a theological-political sense, which is bound up with the theological-poetical, in Philippe Lacoue-Labarthe's terminology.[94] Somewhat more sanguinely, Jennifer Anna Gosetti-Ferencei argues, "Poetic dwelling in the later works is characterized by the nonviolence of *Gelassenheit*, a letting-be that escapes representational thinking and refuses the technological objectification of things in favor of a more essential, poetic revealing; this is the 'turning around' that also motivates and arises from factical life. Dwelling here reflects Hölderlin's notion of peaceful dwelling."⁹⁵ Richard Polt, in a similar vein, notes that, already in the years that he served as rector, "Heidegger's collaboration with the regime fit poorly with his insistence on silence, poetry, and philosophy. The later political, and ultimately apolitical, evolution of his thought consists in a growing disenchantment with the reality of the 'movement,' as opposed to its ever more distant and nebulous 'inner truth and greatness.'"⁹⁶

I am sympathetic to this approach, but I would question the suitability of using the terms *nonviolence* and *apolitical* to describe Heidegger's turn. Regarding the issue of the nonviolent, I will mention this arresting passage from *Einführung in die Metaphysik* that describes the breaking forth (*Ausbrechen*) or breaking up (*Umbrechen*) by which the powers of language, understanding, mood, and building are all surmounted:

The violence-doing [*Gewalttätigkeit*] of poetic saying, of thoughtful projection, of constructive building, of state-creating action, is not an application of faculties that the human being has, but is a disciplining and disposing of the violent forces by virtue of which beings disclose themselves as such, insofar as the human being enters into them. This disclosedness of beings is the violence [*Gewalt*] that humanity has to surmount [*bewältigen*] in order to be itself first of all—that is, to be historical in doing violence in the midst of beings.... Only when we grasp that the need to use violence in language, in understanding, in constructing, in building, co-creates [and this always means: brings forth] the violent act of laying out the paths into the beings that envelop humanity in their sway—only then do we understand the uncanniness of all that does violence.⁹⁷

The poetic calls for an overcoming of violence, but this can come about only through the doing of violence that is essential to the uncanniness of the inception—the beginning that is an irruption—that makes possible the formation and revelation of language as poetry and the consequent endowment of historical destiny on the particular Dasein that shapes and is shaped by that language. As Heidegger elaborated in another passage from this treatise:

The character of mystery belongs to the essence of the origin of language. But this implies that language can have begun only from the overwhelming [*Überwältigenden*] and the uncanny [*Unheimlichen*], in the breakaway [*Aufbruch*] of humanity into Being. In this breakaway, language, the happening in which Being becomes word, was poetry [*In diesem Aufbruch war die Sprache als Wortwerden des Seins: Dichtung*]. Language is the primal poetry [*Urdichtung*] in which a people [*ein Volk*] poetizes Being. In turn, the great poetry by which a people steps into history begins the formation [*Gestaltung*] of its language. The Greeks created and experienced this poetry through Homer. Language was revealed [*offenbar*] to their Dasein as a breakaway into Being, as the formation that opens being up.[98]

With respect to the matter of the apolitical, I would counter that the prominence accorded the poetic summons a different sense of the political and not its dismissal. Appealing to Lacoue-Labarthe again,[99] we must attend to the *politics of poetry* enunciated by Heidegger, beginning already in 1934, a recalibration of the nationalist spirit of Nazism by turning to the ontomythologizing potential of poetry—especially Hölderlin, identified by Heidegger as "the poet of poets and of poetizing" (*der Dichter des Dichters und der Dichtung*) and "the poet of the Germans" (*der Dichter der Deutschen*)[100]—to substantiate the Germanic claim to the threefold distinctiveness of peoplehood, homeland, and language. I note parenthetically that Heidegger's path converges with the esoteric tradition of the kabbalah on this matter of divergence, a topic that I will address elsewhere.[101] Returning to the main point concerning the resounding "aesthetic-political echo" of Heidegger's postrectorate thought,[102] this can be bolstered by a plethora of texts. I will concentrate on Heidegger's explanation that he chose the poetry of Hölderlin for two reasons: first, to bring his readers "into the domain in which an actual poetizing [*wirklichen Dichtung*] unfolds its power," and second, to advocate that this poet, in particular, become a force in the history of the German people.[103] "In this process," writes Heidegger, "we must keep in mind 'politics' in the highest and authentic sense [›*Politik‹ im höchsten und eigentlichen Sinne*], so much so that whoever accomplishes something here has no need to talk about the 'political' [*das ›Politische‹*]."[104] The politics of the poetic—the most authentic German politics elicited through proper attunement to Hölderlin—is a politics that dispenses with pedestrian chatter[105] and reclaims the originary silence that is "the fundamental orientation of the poetic telling" (*die Grundstellung des dichterischen Sagens*).[106] The political is aestheticized to the extent that it is identified with poiēsis as the bringing forth of being in the appearance of the nonappearance. As Andrew Cooper has recently written, "Heidegger no longer considers his vocation in terms of political confrontation as he did in his Rector's Address.... Heidegger's goal is no longer to organize the self-assertion of a nation against a configuration of political meaning. Rather, it is to transform the 'problem of politics' into a task of unveiling the origin of the political as such: a philosophical task of *techne*, of transgressive knowing."[107]

In the essay "Der Ursprung des Kunstwerkes" (1935–1936), Heidegger lucidly expressed the interweaving of the political and the poetic centered around the depiction of the latter as the saying of the unsayable that accommodates the disclosure of beings and the grounding of the historicity of the Dasein of a particular ethnic community:

Poetry is the saying of the unconcealment of beings [*die Sage der Unverborgenheit des Seienden*]. The prevailing language is the happening of that saying in which its world rises up historically for a people and the earth is preserved as that which remains closed. Projective saying [*entwerfende Sagen*] is that in which the preparation of the sayable [*Sagbaren*] at the same time brings the unsayable [*Unsagbare*] as such to the world. In such saying, the concepts of its essence—its belonging to world-history [*Welt-Geschichte*], in other words—are formed, in advance, for a historical people [*geschichtlichen Volk*].[108]

Utilizing Heidegger's own distinction, discussed in the previous chapter, we can propose that he professed a national as opposed to nationalistic ideology; that is, he affirmed a worldview that sponsored the cultural-linguistic superiority of the German people without allocating to them the biological-racial supremacy that would justify vilification of the other.[109] In a passage from the *Schwarze Hefte*, Heidegger tacitly criticized the nationalistic sense of ethnicity (*Volkstum*) promulgated by the Nazis: "Which of us will then presume, in a 'time' that is so confused, to settle for 'all eternity' what is German and what is a people and do so at a time which is perhaps itself only the consequence of an essential misunderstanding of what is German, a misunderstanding due to nationalism? And even if one could say something about the German essence, how can one pretend to have grasped the entire essence? Whence this raving blindness which now sets about spoiling the most concealed German possessions?"[110]

In the "Brief über den 'Humanismus,'" Heidegger noted that in his lecture on Hölderlin's elegy "Heimkunft/An die Verwandten" (1943), the nearness to being (*die Nähe zum Sein*), which is the clearing of the "there" (*da*) of being-there (Dasein), "is perceived as spoken from the minstrel's poem; from the experience of the oblivion of being it is called the 'homeland.' The word is thought here in an essential sense, not patriotically [*patriotisch*] or nationalistically [*nationalistisch*], but in terms of the history of being [*seinsgeschichtlich*]. The essence of the homeland, however, is also mentioned with the intention of thinking the homelessness of contemporary human beings from the essence of being's history."[111] In an obvious polemical poke at Nazi ideology, Heidegger goes on to write that the poem of Hölderlin on the theme of homecoming was meant to help his "countrymen" (»*Landesleute*«) find their essence but not by seeking that essence in "an egoism [*Egoismus*] of his people. He sees it rather in the context of a belongingness to the destiny of the West. But even the West is not thought regionally as the Occident in contrast to the Orient, nor merely as Europe, but rather world-historically out of nearness to the source."[112] Even with respect to the matter of language, Heidegger insists that the poet does not speak German "to the world so that the world might be reformed through the German essence [*deutschen Wesen*]; rather, it is spoken to the Germans so that from a destinal belongingness [*geschickhaften Zugehörigkeit*] to other peoples they might become world-historical [*weltgeschichtlich*] with them."[113] Heidegger's words present an unmistakable rebuke of the Nazi standpoint. From this reading of Hölderlin we can elicit that Heidegger sought to locate the universal calling of becoming world-historical in the individuated destiny of the German people and its language. There is no transition, therefore, from a Dasein that is always particular to a Dasein that is always universal, insofar as the notion of the German Dasein universalizes the particularity and particularizes the universality.[114]

Further proof may be culled from the following exposition in 1942 of these lines from Hölderlin's hymn "Der Ister," "A sign is needed, / Nothing else, plain and simple" (*Ein Zeichen braucht es, / Nichts anderes, schlecht und recht*): "This alone is the singular need of journeying into the locality of what for the Germans is their ownmost [*der Wanderschaft in die Ortschaft des Eigensten der Deutschen*]: 'A sign' (a poet), 'Nothing else, plain and simple'—there is need of this unconditional founding of what remains."[115] In an accompanying note, Heidegger admonishes his potential readers: "There is no need for the affected extravagance, the loud gestures and bewildering din, or the immense monuments characteristic of the un-German monumental of the Romans and Americans. And such things are not needed if the sign remains plain, that is, oriented directly toward that which is to be said, and it has nothing to do with all those other things that are adverse and detrimental to one's own."[116] There is surely justification to argue that Heidegger espoused a different relation to the topographical, eventually advocating for a thinking poetics that celebrated the sense of the unhomely (*das Unheimische*) as essential for the possibility of the human being—τὸ δεινότατον, the uncanniest of the uncanny[117]—feeling at home (*einheimisch*) in the world.[118] The historicality of humankind "resides in being homely," but "being homely is a becoming homely in being unhomely" (*das Heimschwerden im Unheimischsein ist*).[119] One is reminded of Celan's directive to the heart, "Cry out the shibboleth / into your homeland strangeness" (*Ruf's, das Schibboleth, hinaus / in die Fremde der Heimat*).[120] The idiomatic marker, *shibboleth*, whose variation in pronunciation based on a narrative in Hebrew scripture (Judges 12:6) determines to which speech community one belongs, is translated subversively by Celan into an emblem of *homeland strangeness*, an oxymoron that effaces the demarcation of boundaries such that for the human being to be at home cannot be experienced except as the unhomely; it is the very sense of unhomeliness that enables one to feel at home.

Similarly, Heidegger deduced from the fact that the human being is the most uncanny of all beings that "humankind emerges from uncanniness and remains within it. . . . The uncanny itself is what looms forth in the essence of human beings and is that which stirs in all stirring and arousal: that which presences and at the same time absences [*das Anwesende und zugleich Abwesende*]."[121] *That which presences and at the same time absences*—not successively but synchronously; the presencing comes to pass by means of the absencing and the absencing by means of the presencing. The prefix of *Unheimische*, therefore, does not signify the negation of *Heimische*, the lack of a home, but rather the interplay of presence and absence such that the absence of being at home is the way of being present at home. "The unhomely one is deprived of the homely; deprivation is the way in which the unhomely one possesses the homely, or to put it more precisely, the way in which whatever is homely possesses the unhomely one. What becomes manifest in these relations is the essence of uncanniness itself, namely, presencing in the manner of an absencing [*die Anwesung in der Art einer Abwesung*], and in such a way that whatever presences and absences here is itself simultaneously the open realm of all presencing and absencing."¹²² The uncanny exhibits a counterturning (*Gegenwendigkeit*),¹²³ a turning to self that is a turning away from self.¹²⁴ Already in the essay "Vom Wesen der Wahrheit" (1930), Heidegger argued that the ek-sistence of Dasein is such that the human being is subject to both the rule of mystery and the oppression of errancy. "The full essence of truth," he concluded, "including its most proper nonessence [*Unwesen*], keeps Dasein in need by this perpetual turning to and fro."¹²⁵ The challenge, therefore, is to remain "within the grounds of that which is counterturning" without "taking flight into one or the other side,"¹²⁶ to stay in the open of the between where opposites belong together in the sameness of their difference. In the clearing, pervaded by the constant concealment of refusal and obstructing, the ordinary (*das Geheure*) is not ordinary but extra-ordinary (*un-geheuer*), and the essence of truth as unconcealment is ruled by denial (*Verweigerung*).¹²⁷ "The great doom is nearing," he warned in his notebooks, "if searching is suffocated and the need for searching is blocked. The concealed errancy in the semblance of the homeland!"¹²⁸

Perhaps Heidegger was expressing something similar to Lacan's remark concerning Freud, "the *Unheimliche* is defined as *Heimliche* [*c'est que la définition de* l'unheimlich, *c'est d'être* heimlich]. The *Unheim* is poised in the *Heim* [*C'est ce qui est au point du* Heim *qui est* Unheim]."¹²⁹ What does it mean to say that the definition of *Unheimliche* is to be *Heimliche*, that the point of the *Heim* is the *Unheim*? Lacan elaborates, "Man finds his home at a point located in the Other that lies beyond the image from which we are fashioned. This place represents the absence where we stand."¹³⁰ One locates one's home at the domicile of the unhomely, marked symbolically by Lacan as *minus-phi* ($-\varphi$), which signifies the imaginary castration, the lack for which there is no image—not even the image of lack—because there is nothing visible, tangible, or presentifiable.¹³¹ The presence of being at home is thus experienced most acutely in the absence of not being at home, in the place of the Other that is always the other place, the *virtual image of the real image*, the absolute appearance wherein nothing appears.¹³² Bracketing the psychoanalytic slant of Lacan's interpretation, there is conceptual affinity between his posture and Heidegger with respect to the crucial entwining of *Heimliche* and *Unheimliche*; indeed, I would go so far as to hypothesize that Lacan endorsed a Heideggerian interpretation of Freud's idea of the uncanny.¹³³

Support for my contention can be gleaned from the section on "becoming homely" (*das Heimischwerden*) in the exposition of "Der Ister." Heidegger notes that, for Germans, to come into one's own is to belong to the fatherland, but whatever is of the fatherland is at home only in relation to mother earth. To be at home, therefore, depends on an encounter between these two axes:

> This *coming to be* at home in one's own in itself entails that human beings are initially, and for a long time, and sometimes forever, not at home. And this in turn entails that human beings fail to recognize, that they deny, and perhaps even have to deny and flee what belongs to the home. Coming to be at home is thus a passage through the foreign. And if the becoming homely of a particular humankind sustains the historicality of its history, then the law of the encounter [*Auseinandersetzung*] between the foreign and one's own is the fundamental truth of history, a truth from out of which the essence of history must unveil itself.[134]

In a later section from the same work, Heidegger further elucidates the juxtaposition of the themes of homeliness and unhomeliness. To appreciate his insights regarding this matter, we must bear in mind his reading of the internal guidance reported by Antigone in response to Ismene: "Yet leave this to me, and to that within me that counsels the dangerous and difficult: / to take up into my own essence the uncanny that here and now appears. / For everywhere shall I experience nothing of the fact / that not to being my dying must belong." Heidegger focuses especially on the crucial phrase "to take up into my own essence the uncanny," which reads in the Greek of Sophocles παθεῖν τὸ δεινὸν τοῦτο, and in the German translation *ins eigne Wesen aufzunehmen das Unheimliche*.[135]

For Heidegger, the charge to suffer the uncanny (τὸ δεινὸν, *das Unheimliche*) is the decisive word that points to the choral ode of the poem (lines 332–375),[136] which begins "Manifold is the uncanny, yet nothing / more uncanny looms or stirs beyond the human being" (*Vielfältig das Unheimliche, nichts doch / über den Menschen hinaus Unheimlicheres ragend sich regt*), and ends "Such shall not be entrusted to my hearth, / nor share their delusion with my knowing, / who put such a thing to work" (*Nicht werde dem Herde ein Trauter mir der, / nicht auch teile mit mir sein Wähnen mein Wissen, / der dieses führet ins Werk*).[137] Heidegger deduces from these words that Antigone "is utterly unhomely. τὸ δεινὸν τοῦτο—this uncanny that Antigone takes upon herself is by no means the fearful and inhabitual experience of an early death, which she herself faces with certainty. For her dying is, if it is anything at all, that which constitutes καλῶς, a belonging to being [die Zugehörigkeit zum Sein]. Her dying is her becoming homely, but a becoming homely within and from out of such being unhomely."[138] This, too, is the figurative import of the symbol of the hearth that appears near the conclusion of the choral ode, the "site of being homely." It is through the fire, whose essence prevails in radiating light as the force that illumines, warms, nourishes, purifies, refines, and glows, that "the hearth is the enduring ground and determinative middle—the site of all sites, as it were, the homestead pure and simple, toward which everything presences alongside and together with everything else and thus first is." The homely ones, who belong to the radiance and warmth of the hearth, are human beings, the most uncanny of all beings. The knowledge that issues from the homestead, therefore, "must be closer to the unhomely, indeed closer to the homely, and from such nearness have some intimation of the law of being unhomely."[139]

Heidegger educes from Hölderlin, "the first to experience poetically, that is, to say poetically, the German need of being unhomely,"[140] that the law of destiny that sends forth the poet into the foundation of the history of the fatherland is the love of not being at home for the sake of becoming at home in what is one's own.[141]

The law of being homely as a becoming homely consists in the fact that historical human beings, at the beginning of their history, are not intimate with what is homely, and indeed must even become unhomely with respect to the latter in order to learn the proper appropriation of what is their own in venturing to the foreign, and to first become homely in the return from the foreign. The historical spirit of the history of a humankind must first let what is foreign come toward that humankind in its being unhomely so as to find, in an encounter with the foreign, whatever is fitting for the return to the hearth. For history is nothing other than such return to the hearth.[142]

The benchmark by which to assess the historical spirit of history is the poetic journey to the homeland, the return to the hearth, but the homecoming to what is proper to oneself can be attained only by undergoing the passage away from home to the foreign land, bearing the homelessness that stimulates the venturing toward and confrontation with the unknown. The hearth, as Heidegger states explicitly in his exposition of Hölderlin's poem "Wie wenn am Feiertage . . . ," is the place of light that "has already come to presence in everything that emerges and goes away within the open."[143] The lighting of the clearing—the opening into which beings are manifest in their concealment—orients the poet in the homeward excursion in nature (*phusis*).[144] From wandering in the uncanny, which Heidegger also labels "the district of the extraordinary" (*die Ortschaft des Ungeheuren*)[145] and "the field of withdrawing concealment" (*das Feld der entziehenden Verbergung*), the place of *lēthe*, the oblivion of the demonic (*dämonisch*) objectified as the "nothing in itself" (»*Nichts an sich*«) and experienced as the "empty nothingness" (*leeren Nichtigkeit*) where everything disappears, the poet finds the way back to *alētheia*, the realm of finitude where what shows itself appears in the nonshowing of the appearing and thus there holds sway "a concealment and a withdrawal of beings, so that a being only is insofar as at the same time and in opposition to this concealment and this withdrawal there also prevails an unconcealedness in which the unconcealed is conserved."[146]

The emphasis on language[147] as the poetic dwelling that provides the means of respite by which Dasein is settled in being and overcomes the feeling of homelessness (*Unheimlichkeit*)—and the potential of violence contained therein[148]—replaces the ethnic-biological foundations of Nazi nationalism as well as its emphasis on the polis.[149] Thus, in the conclusion of "Bauen Wohnen Denken," a lecture given on August 5, 1951, Heidegger shuns the technological, political, and militaristic explanations of the idea of dwelling by emphasizing that the "real plight of dwelling is indeed older than the world wars with their destruction, older also than the increase of the earth's population and the condition of the industrial workers."[150] In its place, Heidegger offers a concept of home based on thinking: "The real dwelling plight lies in this, that mortals ever search anew for the nature of dwelling, that they *must ever learn to dwell*. What if man's homelessness consisted in this, that man still does not even think of the *real* plight of dwelling as *the* plight? Yet as soon as man *gives thought* [bedenkt] to his homelessness, it is a misery no longer. Rightly considered and kept well in mind, it is the sole summons that *calls* mortals into their dwelling."[151] The sense of *Heimat* is cast here in seemingly less provincial terms—just as homelessness consists of the inability to think about homelessness, so the plight of real dwelling is linked to learning how to dwell. Thinking is that which beckons the human being on the way to the homecoming. The more universal undertone notwithstanding, one must not lose sight of the fact that Heidegger never let go of a inseparable bond of language and the homeland, and indeed in that very lecture Heidegger emphasized that thinking implicates one in listening to what language has to say, since language "tells us about the nature of a thing, provided that we respect language's own nature."[152]

The codependency of dwelling and speaking is epitomized best in the 1960 lecture "Sprache und Heimat,"[153] which concludes with the observation that, on account of its poetic essence (*dichtenden Wesens*), language is "concealed [*verborgenste*] and therefore the most extensive [*weitesten auslangende*], the intensely granting inculcation of the homeland [*das inständig schenkende Hervorbringen der Heimat*]." Hence we should no longer speak of "language and homeland" (*Sprache und Heimat*) but rather of "language as homeland" (*Sprache als Heimat*).[154] This veneration of language as home can only be applied to German because this is the dialect most suited to the poeticizing that discloses the concealment of the event of being in its unconcealment and thereby provides the conditions for Dasein's historical dwelling on earth. Heidegger's politicized interpretation of Hölderlin, and of poiēsis more broadly, engenders its own form of xenophobia that carries the potential to render the other as an intrusive organism feeding off the host or as a vagrant resident trespassing the boundaries of the homeland.[155] Indeed, on occasion the more restricted nationalistic understanding of the homeland surfaces in Heidegger's words, as we find, for example, in the following passage near the conclusion of the study of Hölderlin's poem "Heimkunft/An die Verwandten":

Assuming then that those who are merely residents on the soil of the native land are those who have not yet come home to the homeland's very own; and assuming, too, that it belongs to the *poetic* essence of homecoming, over and above the merely casual possession of domestic things and one's personal life, to be open to the origin of the joyful; assuming *both* of these things, then are not the sons of the homeland, who though far distant from its soil, still gaze into the gaiety of the homeland shining toward them, and devote and sacrifice their life for the still reserved find, are not these sons of the homeland the poet's closest kin? Their sacrifice shelters in itself the poetic call to the dearest in the homeland, so that the reserved find may remain reserved.... Then there will be a homecoming. But this homecoming is the future of the historical being of the German people. They are the people of poetry *and* of thought.[156]

Needless to say, Heidegger is not the first thinker who esteemed the German language as most suitable to the path of thinking. We are reminded, for instance, of Hegel's remark in the preface to the second edition of *Wissenschaft der Logik*, written in 1831, concerning the relationship of language and thought: "In this respect, the German language has many advantages over other modern languages, for many of its words also have the further peculiarity of carrying, not just different meanings, but opposite ones, and in this one cannot fail to recognize the language's speculative spirit [*ein speculativer Geist der Sprache*]. It can delight thought to come across such words, and to discover in naïve form, already in the lexicon as one word of opposite meanings, that union of opposites which is the result of speculation but to the understanding is nonsensical."[157] Influenced by previous thinkers, especially Herder, Hegel championed the view that a particular language effectively expresses the representations, thoughts, and concepts of spirit/consciousness to the degree that the nationalistic and universalistic elements are interwoven. As he put in the *Philosophie des Geistes*, the third part of *Das System der spekulativen Philosophie* (1803–1804), "*speech only is as the speech of a people*, and *understanding and Reason* likewise. Only as the work of a people is *speech* the ideal *existence of the spirit*, in which it expresses what it is in its essence and its being; speech is a universal [mode of expression], recognized in itself, and resounding in the same way in the consciousness of all; every speaking consciousness comes immediately to be another consciousness in it. In respect of *its content too*, speech comes to be true speech for the first time in a people, for now it expresses what each one means.... Only in a people is it already posited as *superseded*, *present* as *ideal*, universal *consciousness*."[158] Reiterating this perspective in the *Wissenschaft der Logik*, the first part of the *Enzyklopädie der philosophischen Wissenschaften* (1830), Hegel wrote, "Given that *language* is the product of thought, nothing that is not universal can be expressed in it either. What I only *mean* [*meyne*], is *mine* [*mein*], belonging to me as this particular individual. If, however, language expresses only what is universal, then I cannot say what I *mean* only.... When I say 'the *individual*,' '*this* individual,' 'here,' 'now,' then these are all universalities.... This I is the universal in and for itself, and the commonality is also a universal, albeit only an outer form of universality."[159]

Heidegger was heir to this attitude and thus believed that German was superior as the language most suitable to the enterprise of thinking, the language whose particularity was most universal. Indeed, the reader is misled if he or she is not cognizant of the fact that Heidegger's many reflections on the nature of *Sprache* are not about language in general but more specifically about German or, to be even more precise, about German and its special relationship to Greek, as Derrida argued, in "Interpretations at War: Kant, the Jew, the German," concerning

a German tradition which survives as far as Heidegger: the German holds an absolutely privileged relation to the Greek—descent, *mimesis*, and rivalry with all the consequent paradoxes.... No other European people is supposed to share this competitive affinity with Greece. If the Greek tradition is safeguarded in a privileged manner within German culture and more specifically within German philosophy, then the syllogism implies the German spirit. Cohen emphasizes this already at the end of the first paragraph: "Now, as Christianity is unthinkable without the logos, Hellenism is one of its sources. *But thus, and with equal impact, Hellenism appears as one of the fundamental sources* (Grundquelle) *of Germanity*."[160]

The affiliation of Greek and German was upheld by other thinkers, including Hermann Cohen, who argued that both cultural formations displayed the same exemplarity (*Eigentümlichkeit*), based on the paradoxical conjunction of universality and particularity, that is, the particular national specificity is in each case expressive of the universal ideal.[161] Heidegger's espousal of what has been called the chiasmic structure of the Dionysian-Greek/Apollonian-German, which has shaped the historical fate of the West,[162] likely tends toward a racial component as his Germanism, and we can assume his sense of Greekism as well, is not inclusive of other ethnicities indelicately condemned as barbarian. The point is made explicitly by Heidegger in *Vom Wesen der menschlichen Freiheit: Einleitung in die Philosophie*, a text based on the lecture course delivered at the University of Freiburg in the summer semester of 1930. From the observation that the word οὐσία is not an artificial philosophical expression but a term that belonged to the everyday language of the Greeks, Heidegger draws the following conclusion:

The history of the basic word of Greek philosophy is an exemplary demonstration of the fact that the *Greek language is philosophical*, i.e. not that Greek is loaded with philosophical terminology, but that it philosophizes in its basic structure and formation. The same applies to every genuine language, in different degrees to be sure. The extent to which this is so depends on the depth and power of the people who speak the language and exist within it. Only our German language has a deep and creative philosophical character to compare with the Greek.¹⁶³

Along similar lines, Heidegger brazenly proclaimed in one of the notebook entries from October 1931, "Only someone who is German can in an originarily new way poetize being and say being—he alone will conquer anew the essence of θεωρία . . . and finally create *logic*."¹⁶⁴

An attenuation of the Hellenic-Teutonic ethnocentrism, however, may be extracted from Hölderlin's letter to Casimir Ulrich Böhlendorff in December 1801 prior to his departure from Germany to southern France. I cite the relevant passage as it appears in Heidegger's study of Hölderlin's "Andenken" (1942):

We shall learn nothing more difficult than to freely use our national character. And as I believe, it is precisely the clarity of presentation which is as natural to us as the fire of heaven was to the Greeks. But what is proper to us [*Eigene*] must be learned as well as what is foreign [*Fremde*]. That is why the Greeks are indispensable to us. Only we will not match them precisely in what is proper to us, our national character, because, as I said, the *free* use of *what is proper to one* [*der freie Gebrauch des Eigenen*] is the most difficult.¹⁶⁵

What are we to make of the concluding statement, why is the free use of one's own the most difficult? Presumably because the ability to be self-collected (*Sichfassenkönnen*)—to come into one's own and to appropriate one's destiny—is effectuated through learning what is foreign.¹⁶⁶ As Heidegger put it in his exegesis of "Der Ister," "What is properly one's own, and appropriating it, is what is most difficult. Yet learning what is foreign, as standing in the service of such appropriation, is easier for precisely this reason. That which is easier lets one more readily excel."¹⁶⁷

From the poet Heidegger thus adduced that "the Greek world is what is foreign with respect to the historical humankind of the Germans. . . . The Greek world is not identical to, or even the same as, the 'German world.' The relationship to the Greek world, therefore, cannot at all be one of identification or assimilation, not even in the sense of taking the Greek world as the measure or model for the perfection of humankind."[168] Instead of integrating or obliterating what is alien, the modus operandi is to acknowledge the foreign in its "essential oppositional character" (*wesenhaften Gegensätzlichkeit*), for only by doing so is there "the possibility of a genuine relationship [*die Möglichkeit der echten Beziehung*], that is, of a uniting [*der Einigung*] that is not a confused mixing [*wirre Vermischung*] but a conjoining in distinction [*fügende Unterscheidung*]. By contrast, where it remains only a matter of refuting, or even of annihilating the foreign, what necessarily gets lost is the possibility of a passage through the foreign [*die Möglichkeit des Durchgangs durch das Fremde*], and thereby the possibility of a return home into one's own [*der Heimkehr ins Eigene*], and thereby that which is one's own itself."[169]

In the continuation, Heidegger speaks of the resolve of the spirit of Americanism, which has dominated the Anglo-Saxon world, to vanquish the homeland of Europe.[170] It is beyond my concerns to assess the credibility of that hypothesis, but I would suggest that the principle of the homecoming he articulates, which presumes that the essence of one's own "unfolds its ownmost essential wealth only from out of a supremely thoughtful acknowledgement of the foreign,"[171] stands as a counter to the Nazi condemnation and subjugation of the non-Aryan. And this is nowhere more strikingly articulated by Heidegger than in his comments on translation and interpretation:

Every translation is interpretation. And all interpreting is translating, To the extent that we have the need to interpret works of poetry and of thought in our own language, it is clear that each historical language is in and of itself in need of translation, and not merely in relation to foreign languages. . . . If becoming homely belongs essentially to historicality, then a historical people can never come to satisfy the essence of its own accord or directly within its own language. A historical people *is* only from the dialogue between its language and foreign languages. . . ."Translating" [»*Übersetzen*«] is not so much a "*trans*-lating" [»*Übersetzen*«] and passing over into a foreign language with the help of one's own. Rather, translation is more an awakening, clarification, and unfolding of one's own language with the help of an encounter with the foreign language.[172]

Translation is a mode of interpretation, and interpretation a mode of translation, but what the two share in common is that they are hermeneutical processes that arise from the belonging together of the familiar and the strange.¹⁷³ To be sure, there is still a privileging of German as the essential language, the "concealed shrine that, in belonging to being, preserves within it the essence of human beings."¹⁷⁴ Specifically, with respect to the Greek language, the exhortation to enter into the singularity of its linguistic spirit is ultimately so that Germans gain a deeper access to their own language. "We learn the Greek language so that the concealed essence of our own historical commencement can find its way into the clarity of our word.... We may learn the Greek language only when we must learn it out of an essential historical necessity for the sake of our own German language."¹⁷⁵

The lingering ethnocentrism is modified to the extent that the encounter with the foreign language through translation is necessary for the sake of appropriating one's own language.¹⁷⁶ At its extreme, the practice of translation as confrontation with the foreign sheds light on the fact that every verbal utterance is an act of translation of the language into itself. As Heidegger expressed it in his lectures on Parmenides:

It is said that "translating" is the transposing of one language into another, of the foreign language into the mother tongue or vice versa. What we fail to recognize, however, is that we are also already constantly translating our own language, our native tongue, into its genuine word. To speak and to say is in itself a translation, the essence of which can by no means be divided without remainder into those situations where the translating and translated words belong to different languages. In every dialogue and in every soliloquy an original translating holds sway.¹⁷⁷

The shift from considering every translation an interpretation, and every interpretation a translation, to viewing every utterance as a translation of the language within itself undercuts the rigid line separating self and other. Translation of a foreign word into one's own language entails at the same time the more difficult translation of one's own language into its genuine and ownmost word; the former is the making of that which is foreign familiar, the latter the familiar foreign. In either case the translation and paraphrase "are always subsequent and follow upon the transporting of our whole being into the realm of a transformed truth. Only if are already appropriated by this transporting are we in the care of the word."¹⁷⁸ To translate is be transported into a realm of transformed truth—a conceptual point underscored philologically by the fact that the same word *Übersetzen* is used to name both activities. The nature of that transformation is the discernment that not only is the foreign not disposable, but its very alterity compels a deeper appreciation of the intimacy of the space of the between where the division of the same and the different prevails in the concord of their discord.

Peter Warnek well expressed the import of Heidegger's uncanny perspective on the uncanny implicit in his view on translation as a movement into what is most strange in order to encounter what is properly one's own being:

What is *most difficult* is precisely this decisive reversal in which the proper as such finds itself displaced, expropriated *into itself* as strange. This, however, should not be mistaken for the utter abandonment of the proper, should not be confused with the simple privileging of the strange, whereby, through mere inversion, the strange would now be given a priority over the proper. Instead, through this decisive reversal, the proper as such appears itself as the most strange, as if, therefore, it lacked propriety.[179]

I would add that the estranging movement, the expropriation of the *Muttersprache* by its appropriation of the *Fremdsprache*, is a tacit criticism of the Nazi construal of homeliness. The reproach is discernible as well in the contrast between the Greek and the German that Heidegger adopts from Hölderlin: what is proper to the former is the fire of heaven (*Feuer vom Himmel*) and to the latter the clarity of presentation (*Klarheit der Darstellung*) that is oriented more to the earth.[180] What is natural to the Germans and what captivates them, accordingly, is the "ability to grasp, the designing of projects, the erection of frameworks and enclosures, the construction of boundaries and divisions, dividing and classifying." The native trait, however, "does not become authentically their own as long as this ability to grasp is not tested by the need to grasp the ungraspable. . . . What the Germans must encounter as foreign to them, and what they must become experienced with in the foreign land, is the *fire of heaven*. Through the shock of being struck by this fire, they will be compelled to appropriate and to need and use their own proper character."[181]

Heidegger continued to speak of the homecoming (*Heimkunft*) as the "return to the nearness to the origin" (*die Rückkehr in die Nähe zum*

Ursprung), but this is qualified by an emphasis on the expedition, the roaming that secures that nearness to the origin is a mystery predicated on keeping at a distance that which is proximate: "Only he can return home who previously, and perhaps for a long time, has wandered as a traveler and borne upon himself the burden of the journey upon his shoulders, and has crossed over into the origin, so that there he might experience what that is which was to be sought, in order then, as the seeker, to come back more experienced.... The nearness that now prevails lets what is near be near, and yet at the same time lets it remain what is sought, and thus not near."[182] By eliciting from Hölderlin the poetic gnosis that there is no being at home that is not concomitantly a striving to return home, no nearness to origin that is not concurrently remoteness from origin, Heidegger dissociates from the cruder understanding of homeland and fatherland propagated by the Nazis. Minimally, one would be hardpressed to deny that his attitude toward the nomadic underwent a drastic revision after the so-called turn or reversal (*Kehre*) in the mid-1930s, when he came to affirm that the homecoming necessarily entails a journey that brings one nearer to the origin from which one remains distant.

This viewpoint is accentuated in the address Heidegger delivered on July 22, 1961, "Ansprache zum Heimatabend," published as "700 Jahre Meßkirch."[183] On this occasion Heidegger reiterated his concern that in the age of augmented technology, with its characteristic homogeneity of form, humans have lost a sense of home (*Heimat*), living predominantly in a state of homelessness (*Heimatlosigkeit*) or the uncanny (*das Unheimische*), that is, a state of uprootedness from the earth and alienation from the homeland.[184] Already in the 1955 memorial address in honor of Kreutzer, also delivered in Meßkirch, Heidegger remarked that in the wake of the war many Germans were driven from their native soil, others were forced out of rural areas and resettled in large industrial cities, still others stayed in their homeland but are even more homeless as they are overpowered by radio and television,[185] technological media that leave human beings with the sense that they no longer are at home in the place in which they dwell, since they are pulled into what we would today call realms of virtual reality.[186] Estrangement—the movement from home into the alien (*aus dem Heimischen ins Unheimische*)[187]—is thus not only a matter of dislodgment from one's indigenous place.[188] Indeed, the deepest homelessness is felt when the feeling of homesickness (*Heimweh*) has died out because one finds oneself at home everywhere and nowhere (*weil er überall zu Hause ist und nirgends*),[189] a curious modification of Novalis's claim that philosophy is homesickness because it expresses the *urge to be at home everywhere* (*Die Philosophie ist eigentlich Heimweh, ein Trieb überall zu Hause zu sein*).[190] Commenting on this fragment in *Die Grundbegriffe der Metaphysik*, the lecture course given at the University of Freiburg in the winter semester of 1929–1930, Heidegger wrote:

> A strange definition, romantic of course. Homesickness—does such a thing still exist today at all? Has it not become an incomprehensible word, even in everyday life? Has not contemporary city man [*städtische Mensch*], the ape of civilization [*Affe der Zivilisation*], long since eradicated homesickness?... What is all this talk about philosophy as homesickness? Novalis himself elucidates: "an urge to be everywhere at home." Philosophy can only be such an urge if we who philosophize are *not* at home everywhere [*wenn wir, die philosophieren, überall* nicht *zu Hause sind*].... To be at home everywhere—what does that mean? Not merely here or there, nor even simply in every place, in all places taken together one after the other. Rather, to be at home everywhere means to be at once and at all times within the whole [*im Ganzen sein*]. We name this *"within the whole"* [›im Ganzen‹] and its character of wholeness the *world*. We are, and to the extent that we are, we are always waiting for something. We are always called upon by something as whole. This "as a whole" is the world.[191]

From Novalis Heidegger found confirmation of the idea that the philosophical condition—indeed, the more general human condition—is one of inherent restlessness (*Getriebenheit*). The philosopher is perpetually adrift; hence the urge to be at home everywhere results from the fact that one is at home nowhere. Heidegger adds that to be at home everywhere would mean to be within the whole, which is to say, the world. However, since to be human is to be in a constant state of waiting, the longing to be as a whole is experienced as the nostalgia to return home.

We have somehow always already departed toward this whole, or better, we are always already on the way [*unterwegs*] to it. But we are driven on, i.e., we are somehow simultaneously torn back by something, resting in a gravity that draws us downward. We are underway to this "as a whole." We ourselves are this underway [*Unterwegs*], this transition [*Übergang*], this "neither the one nor the other." What is this oscillating to and fro between this neither/nor? Not the one and likewise not the other, this "indeed, and yet not, and yet indeed". What is the unrest of this "not" [*Unruhe des Nicht*]? We name it *finitude* [Endlichkeit].¹⁹²

Finitude is surely our fundamental way of being, we are in a permanent condition of being underway, vacillating and fluctuating, but the restlessness and homelessness have been exacerbated by the modern technological environment and the detachment from the soil to the point that urbanity runs the risk of eradicating homesickness from such a deep alienation, the alienation from being alienated. As Heidegger's put it elsewhere, "The loss of rootedness [*Bodenständigkeit*] is caused not merely by circumstance and fortune, nor does it stem only from the negligence and the superficiality of man's way of life. The loss of autochthony springs from the spirit of the age into which all of us were born."¹⁹³ Therefore the great threat of the shift in the industrial age from feeling at home in the world to feeling dispossessed is that the very notion of homeland as critical to our life experience will disintegrate,¹⁹⁴ and in its place we will frantically chase the "constantly self-surpassing machinations" (*überbietenden Machenshaften*).¹⁹⁵

Heidegger suggests, however, that perhaps a new relation to the homeland is being prepared precisely in the midst of the pressing force of the alien, for the homeland is more hauntingly present in the homesickness than in anywhere else.¹⁹⁶ More specifically, Heidegger notes that the deep boredom (*tiefe Langeweile*), which has penetrated our existence to the core in the form of the passion for killing time, "is the hidden, unavowed pull of the homeland, pushed aside but still inescapable: the hidden homesickness [*das verborgene Heimweh*].... Probably these belong together: the alienation of the technological world and the deep boredom that is the hidden pull of a sought-for homeland [*Vermutlich gehören das Unheimische der technischen Welt und die tiefe Langeweile als der verborgene Zug zu einer gesuchten Heimat zusammen*]."¹⁹⁷

To grasp the import of this statement, we must recall that the expression "belonging together" (*zusammengehören*) in Heidegger denotes the juxtaposition of the same as opposed to the identical. In contrast to the ideal of the *coincidentia oppositorum*, wherein the incongruence between opposites is collapsed, or even the Hegelian dialectic, wherein the difference between identity and difference is sublated, Heidegger's *Zusammengehörigkeit* implies the concurrence of what is kept apart,[198] which in this case relates more specifically to the homelessness of technological alienation and the desire for an originary homeland. The two ostensibly conflictual sentiments—corresponding to the two primary modes of thinking, the calculative and the meditative—are juxtaposed as the same that persist in their difference. "The deep boredom, the long time, homesickness: they attest unceasingly and quietly to the pull of the homeland, our indestructible affiliation [*Zugehörigkeit*] with it."[199] Only through the unhomely can one experience the power of the home, albeit veiled, and hence rootlessness itself serves the positive role as the impetus to be rooted in the ground. Just as the recollective thinking or the thoughtful recollection (*Andenken*) affirmed by Heidegger must retrieve all modes of thought, including the representational, so the homecoming comprises a return to the familiar that requires remaining in and with the strange.[200]

The ideal of sheltering—as opposed to eradicating—the foreign notwithstanding, Heidegger continued to display an ethnocultural chauvinism by insisting that Greek and German are the philosophical languages par excellence: "For along with the German language, Greek (in regard to the possibilities of thinking) is at once the most powerful and the most spiritual of languages."[201] Heidegger never wavered from the conviction that the retrieval of thinking—the second beginning that is the return to origin—must be realized by the German people through their indigenous language and preferably, I surmise, in their native land. Nor did he abandon the belief that German derives its ultimate worth as the most suitable means to reclaim Greek.[202] In the Le Thor seminar from 1969, Heidegger offered the following romanticized version of Hellenic thought: "The Greeks are those human beings who lived immediately in the openness of phenomena [*Offenbarkeit der Phänomene*]—through the expressly ek-static capacity of letting the phenomena speak to them (modern man, Cartesian man, *se solum alloquendo*, only talks to himself). No one has ever again reached the heights of the Greek experience of a being as phenomenon."[203] To attain those heights is precisely the undertaking Heidegger set for himself.

There is much more to say about this topic, but what I have written is sufficient to demonstrate that a deeper understanding of Heidegger's fondness for the simplicity of rural life in southwest Germany, the aversion to the metropolitan centers, and his denying the Jews a sense of being in the world, expose the inadequacy and flimsiness of the explanation proffered by Heinrich Petzet, "If Heidegger lacked a certain 'urbanity' and was estranged from everything pertaining to city life, this was particularly so in the case of the urbane spirit of the Jewish circles in the large cities of the West. But this attitude should not be misconstrued as anti-Semitism, although Heidegger's attitude has often been interpreted in that way."[204] The urbane spirit of the Jews is a sanitized way of expressing the fallenness that is the consequence of being submerged in the dark shadows of technological hegemony. For Heidegger, this submersion is indicative of a more foreboding alienation from possessing a homeland, which he describes as "the appropriation of the earth [*Er-eignung der Erde*] to become the place [*Ortschaft*] for the preparation of dwelling [*Bereitung des Wohnens*], which safeguards the arrival of Beyng from whose truth [*Wahr-heit*] gods and humans first conceived the region of their response. Homeland is this appropriation of the destiny of Beyng [*Ereignung das Geschick des Seyns*]. Homeland is the historical site of the truth of Beyng [*geschichtliche Ortschaft der Wahrheit des Seyns*], called and received by the earth, rooted in it and sheltered in it."[205]

The peripatetic nature of Jewish existence precludes the possibility of the Jewish people having a land of origin,[206] and by consequence they have no stake in the destiny of being and no historical site for the disclosure of the truth of being, which is the true nature of time.[207] Deploying Heidegger's categorization in *Die Grundbegriffe der Metaphysik*, we would say that to deny the Jews a sense of having a world strips them of their humanity and animality, demoting them to the level of inanimate stone, which is described as "worldless" (*weltlos*), as opposed to both the human, who is "world-forming" (*weltbildend*), and the animal, who is "poor in the world" (*weltarm*).[208] The decidedly more anthropocentric language used five years later in *Einführung in die Metaphysik* reflects greater negative implications for the societal status of the Jews: "World is always *spiritual* world [geistige Welt]. The animal has no world, nor any environment [*Umwelt*]. The darkening of the world [*Weltverdüsterung*] contains within itself a *disempowering of the spirit* [Entmachtung des Geistes], its dissolution [*Auflösung*], diminution [*Auszehrung*], suppression [*Verdrängung*], and misinterpretation [*Mißdeutung*]."[209] The darkening includes the flight of the gods, the destruction of the earth, the reduction of human beings to a mass, and the preeminence of the mediocre. Heidegger summons the notion of the world to highlight the destitution and spiritual decline of European society. If worldhood (*Weltlichkeit*) is a spiritual phenomenon, and spiritual is distinctively human, it follows that animals lack a sense of world. By this criterion the worldless Jews are reduced to the level of the beasts.

Even more precarious is the fact that removing from the Jews the sanctuary of topographic emplacement transforms their nomadism into a parasitism. In contrast to Herder, who extricated from the resilience and tenacity of the Jews as the consummate pariahs a key to explain the universal meaning of *Volksgeist*,[210] Heidegger highlights the provincial and egocentric implication of the Jews' claim to separatism: "World Judaism, spurred by the emigrants let out of Germany, is everywhere elusive. In all the unfurling of its power, it need nowhere engage in military actions, whereas it remains for us to sacrifice the best blood of our own people."[211] Leaving aside the altogether impertinent and inappropriate way of referring to Jews who were forcefully deported from Germany as emigrants,[212] and the patently absurd anti-Semitic allegation concerning the Jewish ambition for world domination at exactly the time when Germans themselves were guilty of this aspiration,[213] one cannot but be struck by Heidegger's utilization of a central theme in Hitler's diatribe against the alleged parasitic nature of the Jews[214] and their instinct for self-preservation and racial solidarity that prevents them from being willing to sacrifice for others.[215]

Despite the inexcusable bigotry of Heidegger, it is of interest, nonetheless, to compare his stance about the worldlessness of the Jews with the view expressed by Franz Rosenzweig concerning Judaism's essentially diasporic nature. What Heidegger considered a blight on the body politic of the Jewish people, Rosenzweig considered a badge of cultural distinction and honor. In contrast to other nations, the sense of peoplehood for the Jews is based on the ancestral blood community (*Blutsgemeninschaft*), which is construed neither as the ethnic attachment to land secured by territorial occupation, as Zionism advocates, nor the racial purity decreed by the Nazis,[216] but rather as the ontological-temporal self-sufficiency that preserves Jewish identity through participation in liturgy, ritual, and textual study.[217]

The peoples of the world cannot be satisfied with a community made up of the same blood; they put forth their roots into the night of the earth, itself dead yet life-bestowing, and appropriate from its permanence a guarantee of their own permanence. Their will to eternity clings to the soil and to the soil's dominion, the territory.... We alone have put our trust in the blood and have parted with the land; in this way we saved the precious life fluid that offered us a guarantee of our own eternity and alone among all peoples of the earth we have awakened out of every community our living with the dead.[218]

Turning the vile rhetoric about Jewish parasitism and cowardice on its head, Rosenzweig praises the withdrawal of Jews from messianic politics as a means to secure their eternity.[219] The eternality of the Jewish nation is such that its temporality is not a matter of teleology, or, in Rosenzweig's language, there is no growing (*Wachsen*), which would be a disavowal of eternity, but only waiting (*Warten*) or wandering (*Wandern*).[220] Indeed, the waiting is the wandering, and the wandering the initiation and terminus of the journey. "Waiting and wandering are affairs of the soul; only growing falls on the side of the world. And the eternal people forgo precisely this growing. Its peoplehood is already at that place to which the peoples of the world only aspire. Its world is at the goal."[221]

Having already reached the objective toward which other people are striving, the Jews are beyond history and thus they have grown numb to the mundane struggles and maneuverings indispensable to worldly affairs.[222] The ontological condition of the temporality of the Jewish people exemplifies, in Peter Gordon's felicitous locution, a "rooted unrootedness," that is, a temporality grounded in the sense of self determined by allegiance to the blood community rather than in adherence to the dictates of spatial territoriality.[223] The unrootedness—the inherently uncanny nature of blood[224]—is an inevitable consequence of the revelatory experience by which the community was formed, the incursion of an Archimedean point of orientation that disorients one from the quotidian sense of space and time. As Rosenzweig expressed it, "But after entering the world of Revelation [*die Welt der Offenbarung*], this same homely image [*heimelige Bild*] of the ancient world, where one felt well before, this Platonic and Aristotelian cosmos suddenly became an unhomely and disquieting world [*eine unheimelige, unheimliche Welt*]."[225] Insofar as the eternal people are shaped historically and phenomenologically by revelation, it follows that they must continually endure disenchantment in nature. The yearning for a homeland, accordingly, cannot be determined by the metrics of

NOMADISM, HOMELESSNESS, AND THE OBFUSCATION OF BEING

rootedness in a particular land, even the land that is promised to them as part of the scripturally mandated covenant with God. It is incumbent on the Jew to remember "the lack of constraints on a traveler" and to emulate the "knight truer to his land when he lingers in his travels and adventures and longs for the homeland."[226] The Jew is most fully at home as the stranger seeking a fixed residence, a destiny well captured in the biblical idiom *ivri*, the Hebrew, that is, the one identified as the immigrant whose forebears dwelt beyond the river, *be-ever ha-nahar* (Joshua 24:2), the refugee blemished as one who persistently originates from another place.

In support of his interpretation, Rosenzweig appeals to the unique role of exile in the Jewish tradition. Indeed, as he perceptively notes, the incipient episode of Israelite history—"the tribal legend of the eternal people"—begins with God's commandment to Abram to leave his native land and to go to the land he will be shown (Genesis 12:1). But since the "full proprietorship" of that homeland is disputed—an allusion to the biblical admonition that "the Canaanites were then in the land" (Genesis 12:6)—the Jewish people "is itself only a stranger and tenant in its land."[227] Rosenzweig intuits a profound irony in the positing of exile at the outset of Jewish history, an irony that has informed the religious sensibility of Jews through the ages. On the one hand, the destiny of the Jewish people is tied intrinsically to a homeland that provides the geographical and metaphysical boundaries of the nation. But, on the other hand, the physical space of that territory belonged to another, and hence the bond between the Jews and the country obtains its validity from the fact that God commanded Abraham to leave his place of origin to enter the land of promise. Tragically, the displacement of Abraham occasions the displacement of the other, leading inescapably to a political-military dispute over which nation should occupy the land rightfully. In the end, however, more momentous is the matter of spiritual ownership, and this results not from an intrinsic connection between the people and the land but from the fact that God decrees that the land belongs to him and thus even the Israelites themselves can reside therein only as foreigners and strangers (Leviticus 25:23). The Jew belongs to this home, we might say, by not belonging. As Rosenzweig perspicaciously remarked, this is precisely the import of the holiness attached to the land of Israel: "The land is in the deepest sense its own only as land of longing, as—holy land. . . . The holiness of the land removes the land from its natural hold as long as it could take hold of it; the holiness infinitely increases its longing for the lost land and henceforward no longer lets it feel entirely at home in any other land [*in keinem andern Land mehr ganz heimisch werden*]."[228]

Just as the holiness of the land precludes the possibility of the Jews feeling at home in their homeland, so too Hebrew denies them the sense of linguistic custody: "The holiness of its own language has the same effect as the holiness of its own land: it deflects the ultimate of feeling from the everyday; it prevents the eternal people from ever living entirely at one with the times."[229] The enduring state of disjointedness resonates with what Rosenzweig marks as the distinctive sense of alienation that the Jewish poet feels in the world, experienced especially as an exile from language that is perpetuated by being surrounded by the scriptural word.[230] This accords with Rosenzweig's more general characterization of poetry as "at home neither in time nor in space, but where time and space have their inner origin, in imagistic thinking [*vorstellenden Denken*]."[231] Aligned with the view latter expressed by both Maurice Blanchot—partially in response to Heidegger—for whom the poem is innately a state of exile and hence the poet is a wanderer expelled interminably from a true abode,[232] and Celan, who wrote that authentic poetry is antibiographical, since the home of the poet is in the poem, which changes from one poem to another,[233] Rosenzweig likewise maintained that the poet, constitutionally, is in a state of *Unheimlichkeit*,[234] a condition that is especially fitting for the Jews, the eternal people, since they do not feel at home even in their homeland. As the metahistorical reference point in history, the Jewish nation is fundamentally at odds with the vagaries of the sociopolitical world.[235]

It is edifying to compare Rosenzweig's portrayal of Abraham with the following depiction of Levinas:

A work conceived radically is a movement of the same unto the other which never returns to the same. To the myth of Ulysses returning to Ithaca, we wish to oppose the story of Abraham who leaves his fatherland forever for a yet unknown land, and forbids his servant to even bring back his son to the point of departure. A work conceived in its ultimate nature requires a radical generosity of the same who in the work goes unto the other. It then requires an *ingratitude* of the other. Gratitude would in fact be the *return* of the movement to its origin.[236]

One can hear the echo of Rosenzweig as well in the following words of Levinas: "Judaism has always been free with regard to place. It remained faithful in this way to the highest value. The Bible knows only a Holy Land, a fabulous land that spews forth the unjust, a land in which one does not put down roots without certain conditions."[237] I cannot enter here into the complexity of the Jewish perspective on place according to Levinas, but let me note briefly that he is not consistent. On the one hand, he distinguishes Judaism from paganism—which is a cipher for Heidegger—on the grounds that the former affirms a universalism that is disentangled from place, but, on the other hand, he does acknowledge the special allegiance that Jews have for the land of Israel. No doubt, in Levinas's mind, the holiness of Israel is precisely what precludes loyalty to that land devolving into the pagan and idolatrous attachment to physical space. The designation of Israel as the holy land secures the ethical universalism of the Jewish people, their mission to promote a universalism aimed at nurturing the potential unique to each particular ethnocultural entity, a universalism embodied in the particularism of a given nationalist identity.[238] Thus, as he puts it in another passage:

It is not because the Holy Land takes the form of a State that it brings the Reign of the Messiah any closer, but because the men who inhabit it try to resist the temptations of politics; because this State, proclaimed in the aftermath of Auschwitz, embraces the teaching of the prophets; because it produces abnegation and self-sacrifice. And certainly, this identity, geographically localizable through all Sacred History and nearly all Western history, holds great power over failings and wills. But it lends this power to all the messianic institutions of Israel, all those that tear us out of our conformism and material comforts, dispersion and alienation, and reawaken in us a demand for the Absolute.[239]

Levinas positions the identity of nonplace in Judaism as an alternative to the Heideggerian notion of homeland based on enrootedness in the soil. In a spirit closer to Rosenzweig, Levinas disentangles the promise of the promised land from territorial occupation, but he privileges the ethical demand that the land imposes on its inhabitants:

Nothing is more strange or foreign than the other man, and it is in the light of utopia that man shows himself. Outside all enrootedness and all dwelling: statelessness as authenticity!. . . It is as if in going toward the other I met myself and implanted myself in a land, henceforth native, and I were stripped of all the weight of my identity. A native land owing nothing to enrootedness, nothing to first occupation; a native land owing nothing to birth. A native, or a promised, land? Does it vomit out its inhabitants when they forget the circular journey that made that land familiar to them, and their wanderings, which were not for a change of scenery, but for de-paganization? But habitation justified by movement toward the other is essentially Jewish.[240]

Turning Heidegger's perspective on its head, Levinas maintained that, for the Jew, *expulsion from the worldliness of the world* is the truest sense of being at home and returning to the autochthonous land of their covenantal pledge; to be entrenched in the world is a form of imprisonment applicable to the pagan. "The world conceived as *Heimat* [homeland] is to be brought together with the notion of the *promised land*, expelling [*vomissant*] unjust societies, but which is neither a living space nor a native land above all."[241]

Whereas Levinas's notion of the foreign or the nonspatial outside is dependent on the strangeness of the stranger, and not the strangeness of art and the openness of beings on being,[242] there is a greater congruity between Rosenzweig's sense of Jewish existence as an exilic state of spatiotemporal ungroundedness and Heidegger's emphasis on the unhomeliness of the human condition in the face of the nothingness of being[243]—an affinity that becomes even more pronounced in Heidegger's later thought, due primarily to the influence of Hölderlin,[244] as we saw earlier, wherein the poet is idealized as the most suitable guide to the thinker trying to find the language that allows one to be at home in a thinking always underway. Curiously, the metahistorical status Rosenzweig assigned to the Jews has some affinity to the superlative politics Heidegger ascribes to the poetic dwelling that withdraws one from the haste of the everyday. The poet plunges into the meandering of homelessness through which the homecoming to where one has never been is enacted. As Reiner Schürmann summarized Heidegger's view on the poiēsis of the traveler steadied in the waywardness of the road, "This errant one dwells in joy. Through his wanderings the origin beckons."[245]

The kinship of which I speak was deliberately denied or more likely unknown to Heidegger. In his contorted thinking, worldlessness is connected to three other purported Jewish qualities, social tenacity, calculative reasoning, and a penchant to combine things in a disorderly fashion.

The diasporic rootlessness advances the "*Jewish* comportment" (jüdisches *Gebahren*) in the domain of culture politics (*Kulturpolitik*), which consists of arrogating "culture" as a means of power (*Machtmittel*) to assert oneself as superior.[246] In another diary entry, Heidegger remarked that Jewry's "temporary increase in power" (*zeitweilige Machtsteigerung*) is because Western metaphysics, especially in its modern unfolding, is beholden to "empty rationality" (*leeren Rationalität*) and "computational ability" (*Rechenfähigkeit*), the very characteristics that he attributes to the Jews. As a consequence, the more originary (*ursprünglicher*) and primordial (*anfänglicher*) the nature of future decisions and questions, the more they remain inaccessible to those who belong to this "race" (*Rasse*). Heidegger even included Husserl in this ludicrous platitude about the Jewish people's inability to philosophize.[247] Despite acknowledging the significance of Husserl's disapproval of psychological and historical reductionism in his phenomenology—qualities, incidentally, that Heidegger commandeered in his own thinking—he remained bound to "the historical tradition of philosophy" and hence was not able to approach the domain of "essential decisions" (*wesentlicher Entscheidungen*). Heidegger maintained that his "attack" (*Angriff*) against Husserl was not directed to him exclusively but was aimed at all those who enhance the "neglect of the question of being" (*Versäumnis der Seinsfrage*), that is, "the essence of metaphysics as such, on the ground of which the machination of beings can determine history." The denigration of Husserl, who is indicative of the Jewish modality of thought more generally, "grounds a historical moment of the highest adjudication [*Entscheidung*] between the primacy of beings and the grounding of the truth of beyng."[248] Heidegger's essentializing the Jews as those who forsake the *Seinsfrage* is eerily evocative of what Hitler ignobly called the *Judenfrage*.[249]

The distinctively anti-Jewish sentiment expressed by Heidegger cannot be exonerated, but it behooves me to say that the dominance of the technological control of events is a phenomenon that he cataloged as a more general condition of modern Western culture and not limited to the Jews, a point eclipsed in much of the scholarly literature. Indeed, at times in his writings, Heidegger utilizes this rubric to signify the transformation and adulteration of inceptual—i.e., Greek—philosophy, the originary questioning of the meaning or truth of being, traceable to Rome, Judaism, and

Christianity.²⁵⁰ It is especially the latter that is the object of Heidegger's critique, even if in some passages the brunt of his ire is turned against the Jews.²⁵¹ Thus, in one passage, Heidegger commented on "the Christian obliviousness to all truth of beyng" (*die christliche Verkennung aller Wahrheit des Seyns*),²⁵² and in another he remarked, "Through metaphysics, i.e., through Christianity, we are misled and accustomed to seeing in 'unsettlement' [»*Entsetzen*«] . . . only the wild and the ghastly instead of experiencing it as disposing toward the truth of beyng and, on the basis of that disposition, coming to a steadfast knowledge of the essential occurrence of beyng."²⁵³ In a section from the notebooks that deals with what is required for a people to become a "people" (*Volk*), Heidegger ponders, "What if that which, *prior* to the excessive demand of an intimation and word, must be drawn out of beyng and inserted into its essence, namely, the people of the Germans—makes itself into a 'myth' in what is first to be attained through the truth of beyng and thereby transformed—without the facile and 'refined' escape into Christianity?"²⁵⁴ And, what is perhaps the most unsettling, in another entry from the notebooks, Heidegger says of Catholic philosophy that it is not much different than Nazi science (»*Katholische Philosophie*«—*das ist nicht viel anders als* »*nationalsozialistische Wissenschaft*«), comparing them both to a square circle (*ein viereckiger Kreis*) or to a wooden iron (*ein hölzernes Eisen*) that instead of being hardened in the fire is pulverized to ashes.²⁵⁵ Both images are meant to convey the inherent absurdity of the category. The comparison of Catholic philosophy to Nazi science is jarring, but it does offer another example of Heidegger's blatant dissatisfaction with Hitler's official party line.

I do not mean to placate Heidegger's anti-Judaism, nor do I dispute the fact that he never retracted the unseemly bigotries that were an incontestable feature of his thinking, but academic integrity obliges me to state that proper contextualization requires one to acknowledge that the criticism he makes of the Jews is allotted to others as well. The animus toward Jews is pitched more in socioeconomic than theological terms, whereas the degrading of Christianity reflects, in all probability, Heidegger's existential struggle with and yet philosophical indebtedness to his Catholic upbringing.²⁵⁶ Following the path paved by Nietzsche, which marks the "end of Western metaphysics" and the beginning of an "entirely different question of the truth of Being,"²⁵⁷ Heidegger views Christianity as the embodiment of the ontotheological obscuration of being. Thus, commenting on

Nietzsche's remark that the "feast is paganism *par excellence*,"²⁵⁸ Heidegger writes that "the feast of thinking never takes place in Christianity. That is to say, there is no Christian philosophy. There is no true philosophy that could be determined anywhere else than from within itself. For the same reason there is no pagan philosophy, inasmuch as anything 'pagan' is always still something Christian—the counter Christian."²⁵⁹ In *Schelling: Vom Wesen der menschlichen Freiheit*, Heidegger noted that the term *theology* first evolves within philosophy and not "in the framework and service of an ecclesiastical system of faith." From that standpoint every philosophy as metaphysics "is theology in the primordial and essential sense that comprehension (*logos*) of beings as a whole asks about the ground of Being, and this ground is called *theos*, God." Even Nietzsche's philosophy, which contains the statement that "God is dead," is to be considered theological. Rather than viewing modern philosophy as a "secularization of Christian theology," it is more accurate to characterize modern philosophy as the "Christianization of an extra-Christian philosophy." All theology is possible only on the basis of philosophy, even if the latter is identified as the work of the devil. Heidegger concludes, therefore, that the questioning of philosophy "is always and in itself both onto-logical and theological in the very broad sense. Philosophy is *Ontotheology*. The more originally it is both in one, the more truly it is philosophy."²⁶⁰

Here it is apposite to recall as well Heidegger's explication in the lecture "Die Zeit des Weltbildes," delivered on June 9, 1938, of the loss of gods (*Entgötterung*) as the fifth phenomenon of modernity. The expression is not to be understood as the "mere elimination of the gods, crude atheism." On the contrary, the loss of the gods is a twofold process intimately related to Christianity: "On the one hand, the world picture Christianizes itself [*sich verchristlicht*] inasmuch as the ground of the world is posited as infinite and unconditioned, as the absolute. On the other hand, Christendom reinterprets its Christianity as a world view (the Christian world view) and thus makes itself modern and up to date." Contrary to what one might assume, the loss of the gods does not imply an atheistic abolition of the gods. In a far more complicated way, the loss of the gods is related to the Christianization of the world picture (*Weltbild*) by positing the ground of the world (*Weltgrund*) as the infinite and unconditioned absolute. The shift in orientation results in Christianity becoming a worldview (*Weltanschauung*), which reflects the "condition of indecision [*Entscheidungslosigkeit*] about

God and the gods." Heidegger is quick to point out, however, that the loss of the gods does not exclude religiosity (*Religiosität*). Rather, the relation to the gods, which ensues from the loss of the gods, "is transformed into religious experience [*Erleben*]. When this happens, the gods have fled [*entflohen*]. The resulting void is filled by the historical and psychological investigation of myth."[261]

Heidegger offers a shrewd analysis of the modern predicament and the role played by Christianity in fostering the religious experience centered on the flight of the gods that results from a worldview positing God as the absolute that supplants the theistic image. The void created by this displacement is filled by turning one's attention to myth. Here it is germane to remember that Heidegger argued in *Einführung in die Metaphysik* that it is mythology, in lieu of natural science (*Naturwissenschaft*), that makes possible the knowing of primal history (*Ur-geschichte*) and the understanding of its inception (*Anfang*)—depicted as both uncanny (*Unheimlichste*) and most powerful (*Gewaltigste*)—as a mystery related to the "poetic projection of the human being."[262] In some sense this is a continuation of Heidegger's argument in *Sein und Zeit* regarding the existential origin of historiography (*Historie*) from the historicity (*Geschichtlichkeit*) of Dasein; that is, the assertion that the sciences originate ontologically from the constitution of Dasein's being, which is rooted in the temporality that temporalizes itself in the ecstatic-horizonal unity of past, present, and future. Heidegger thus boldly concludes that "the *historiographical disclosure of history is in itself rooted in the historicity of Dasein in accordance with its ontological structure*, whether it is carried out or not."[263] After Heidegger's turn, that constitution is identified more specifically with art whose essence is poetry, which is defined as the founding of truth (*die Stiftung der Wahrheit*). It follows that only through dwelling poetically can the human—and in the most exacting sense this means the German—be transported out of the habitual and into what is opened by the poetic saying so that one's essence can take a stand within the truth of beings.[264] Poesy, therefore, is the way of being in the world that bestows upon Dasein its historical destiny.

The appropriate response to the dominance of the technoscientific phenomenon of modernity is to recover through "meditative thought" (*Besinnung*) and "genuine questioning" (*echten Fragen*) the wisdom of the Greek poets and thinkers that is neither Christian nor pagan,[265] a possibility of

NOMADISM, HOMELESSNESS, AND THE OBFUSCATION OF BEING

forging a course of thinking beyond the binary, a strategy that to my ear augurs Derrida's attempt to demarcate the space of discourse between and therefore neither Jewish nor Greek, a space that some have argued should be identified as Egyptian.[266] The crucial difference, however, is that Heidegger's thought remains resolutely parochial as it revolves about what Derrida named the "Greek-German axis,"[267] and particularly the idolizing of these two languages as the most spiritual (*geistigste*) and hence the most conducive to thinking about the question of being.[268] Be that as it may, a point that has often been downplayed in the clamor about Heidegger's sporadic remarks about Judaism is that he offers an equally reproachful perspective on Christianity. Indeed, it appears that his "ontological" or "metaphysical" anti-Semitism is notionally on a par with the problem posed by Christianity,[269] which Heidegger attacks with much more vitriol and fervor.[270] The deficiency of world Jewry is not primarily racial in a physical but rather in a metaphysical sense, related especially to the Jews assuming—exacerbated in the mediocrity of both Anglo-American capitalism and Bolshevism[271]— the type of humanity (*Menschentümlichkeit*)[272] that can take on unreservedly the world-historical task (*weltgeschichtliche »Aufgabe«*) of uprooting all beings from being (*die Entwurzelung alles Seienden aus dem Sein*).[273] As Nancy put it, "But in these notebooks ... the Jewish people—this people considered at least as a remarkable exception at the heart of all the forces of destruction that it accompanies and of which it seems to provide the type. The Jewish people is the identifiable agent, properly identifiable (or *more properly*, a bizarre notion that must no doubt be recognized), of what at the same time is a broad composition of masses and identities, American or Americanism, communism and technics, French, English, Europeans, Germans even, and '*Abendland*,' evening, decline, collapse."[274] The problem with Judaism is a quandary related to the nature of being or, more specifically, to the cloaking of the ontological difference between being (*Sein*) and beings (*Seienden*), the very duality (*Zwiefalt*) that "gives food for thought," the self-concealing revealing of the "presence of what is present," the given that is "the gift of what is most worthy of question [*die Gabe des Fragwürdigsten*]."[275] Inasmuch as the essential nature of being human cannot be severed from the question of being and its distinction from beings,[276] the suggestion that Jews uproot all beings from being means that, philosophically, they are less than fully human.

NOMADISM, HOMELESSNESS, AND THE OBFUSCATION OF BEING

The allegation that the Jewish question is a matter of metaphysics and not just race is an even more deleterious prejudice, as it denies the Jews the possibility of being circumscribed in the hermeneutic circularity of the historical self-understanding of Dasein. "History is a distinctive character of human being. But, it is this human being that we shall understand precisely first from the concept of the essence of history! Thus, once again, we are going in a circle: We determine history from the human being and the human being from history [*Die Geschichte bestimmen wir aus dem Menschen und den Menschen aus der Geschichte*]. We are going in a circle and are, therefore, on the right way."[277] As a consequence of having no claim to history, the Jews have no access to the essence of their humanness or to the essence of philosophy, and hence they can have nothing but an antagonistic role in the history of being. It should not be forgotten that Heidegger also speaks of the Jews in racial terms, and on occasion he even draws a connection between the metaphysical and the biological. Thus, in the passage to which I already referred, which depicts the pinnacle of self-annihilation metaphysically as the Jewish struggle against the Jews,[278] after stating that the Antichrist must come from the same essential ground (*Wesensgrund*) as Christ—based on the assumption that antinomies originate from one essence—and the Christian stems from Jewry (*aus der Judenschaft*),[279] Heidegger further speculates that the Jews are "the principle of destruction" (*das Prinzip der Zerstörung*) in the "time-space [*Zeitraum*] of the Christian West," also identified as the time-space of metaphysics. But what does it mean to identify Jewry with the principle of destruction? Heidegger explains: "The destructive aspect of the inversion [*Umkehrung*] of the completion of metaphysics—i.e., in Hegel's metaphysics through Marx. Spirit [*Geist*] and culture [*Kultur*] are the superstructure [*Überbau*] of 'life'—i.e., of the economy, i.e., of the organization—i.e., of the biological—i.e., of the people [*des »Volkes«*]."[280] Apparently reversing a position articulated by Heidegger at an earlier date in a passage from the *Beiträge* wherein the "final form" of Marxism is said to have "essentially nothing to do with Jewishness [*Judentum*]," even though Bolshevism is labeled as Jewish (*jüdisch*) and Christianity is labeled as Bolshevist (*bolschewistisch*) due to its Jewish origin (*jüdischen Ursprungs*),[281] Marx is here identified as the representative of the Jews whose status as Antichrist is positioned as the adversary to the time-space of Christianity, which understood philosophically, implies the antipathy to the completion of metaphysics expressed as the reversal of the Hegelian dialectic such that spirit and culture become the superstructure or epiphenomenon of life related respectively to the economy, organization, biology, and peoplehood. It is difficult to exempt Heidegger from the charge of biological racism even though it appears, astonishingly, that he is suggesting that the *völkische* ideology of the Third Reich is a direct consequence of Jewish ethnocentrism refracted through the prism of Marx's spurious revision of Hegel.[282]

In another exceptionally confused passage, Heidegger notes that because of their "calculative talent" (*rechnerischen Begabung*) the Jews live longer than anyone else according to the "principle of race" (*Rasseprinzip*), but this is the reason "why they defend themselves and most violently against the full application" of this very principle. To the Jews is ascribed an "overpowering of life through machination" (*Übermächtigung des Lebens durch die Machenschaft*) that has led to the "establishment of racial breeding" (*Einrichtung des rassischen Aufzucht*). The eugenics, which does not originate in the life force itself but in the cunning character of modern technology, particularly as it is exemplified by the Jews,[283] has as its aim the "complete de-racialization" (*vollständige Entrassung*) of all peoples by clamping (*Einspannung*) them in a uniformly constructed constitution (*Einrichtung*) of all beings.[284] The calculating propensity of the Jewish race is responsible for this uprooting or deracination (*Entrassung*) and self-alienation of peoples (*Selbstentfremdung der Völker*), which is expressive of the loss of history (*Verlust der Geschichte*) as it pertains to the decisive regions of being (*Entscheidungsbezirke zum Seyn*).[285] Nancy well expressed the point when he noted that "the anti-Semitic motif is inscribed very clearly at the heart of this configuration: the Jewish people belongs in an essential way to the process of the devastation of the world. It is the most identifiable agent of this devastation in that it presents a figure, a form, or a type, a Gestalt—the figure of the aptitude for calculation, of traffic, and of shrewdness.... The figure of the Jew configures the very type of a devastating necessity: the gigantic, calculation, and a rationality that is busy de-differentiating the world and properly dislodging it: withdrawing from it every kind of ground and soil."[286]

The Jew, then, is the figure that configures the disfiguration of being, the groundlessness (*Bodenlosigkeit*)—the lack of place, destiny, historical time, decision, and peoplehood—that precludes the opening to the self-concealed revealing of being. This exclusivity can be overcome only when it excludes itself, that is, when the principle of destruction is destroyed.[287] Is there a reverberation here of the long-standing Christian attitude, codified by Augustine,[288] that the Jews, as a consequence of being in error, stand as witnesses to the truth to be revealed in the future through their conversion, that Jewish blindness harbors the possibility of eschatological vision? Transmuted into Heideggerian terms, the unconcealment of being at the first beginning contained within itself its own forgetting, but the forgetting of this self-betrayal can be forgotten only in the final disbanding when the forgetfulness is remembered—the exclusion thereby excluded—and the advent of the other beginning begins and being will no longer be occluded by beings. To cite Nancy again, "The West will not have ceased betraying itself, essentially, and this betrayal is at the same time the condition for another beginning. Such is the complexity of the 'forgetting of being' insofar as this forgetting is inherent to the first destining of being, and moreover without anything allowing us to specify either the reason for this inherence or the reason for its disappearance in the event of a new destining."[289]

But what is clear is that world Jewry assumed a lopsidedly ominous role in the forgetting of this forgetting. Indeed, the higher truth of anti-Semitism is that *Judentum*, the being that is associated singularly with the Jews, embodies the

> devouring banalization of the world—the loss of the spirit of peoples in the universal-vulgar.... For Heidegger, anti-Semitism is not only ambient, for this ambience also bears within itself an entire vein of thought that in certain respects is already traditional... Heidegger ties together the deconstruction (*Abbau*) of metaphysical ontology—a grand philosophical gesture that extends and pushes further the premises of Nietzsche, Kierkegaard, and Husserl—and the destruction (*Zerstörung*) of that which and of those who seem to him precisely to be destroying the world and history.[290]

The denunciation of an agent defined by destruction is part of the long legacy of salvation history that has united and separated Jews and Christians through the centuries.[291] The knot that emerged from Heidegger's conjoining the mandate to deconstruct the devastation of metaphysics and to

NOMADISM, HOMELESSNESS, AND THE OBFUSCATION OF BEING

destroy the leading agent of that devastation turned out to be a costly misjudgment as the fires of Nazi hatred raged and the Jews—icons of self-hatred hewn from an internalized anti-Semitism—were forced to confront a mode of exclusion by being included in the renunciation of the self-destruction that sought to destroy their status as the ones excluded in the inclusion manifest as the repudiation of their identity as the other, the contemptible exception that sustains what is presumed to be the norm, the limb that is both attached to and detached from the main body. Heidegger seemed inattentive to the fact that, by advocating the liquidation of the ethnos that embodied alterity, he was complicit in the technological and calculative machination attributed to Judaism and the other political ideologies against which the notebooks took aim. Heidegger's portrayal of Judaism confirms the thesis of Dana Villa that despite his tireless disparagement of metaphysics and the reification of presence, and the attempt to recover finitude through the temporalization of being without recourse to a standard of truth distinguishable from the semblance of untruth, the nonpolitical essence of the political that he embraced in his aestheticism did not allow him to escape entirely from the "productionist paradigm" and the "teleocratic concept of action,"[292] and thus he remained "curiously blind to plurality and intersubjectivity."[293] Regrettably, Heidegger forgot the counsel he offered in his comments on Jaspers's *Psychologie der Weltanschauungen* (1920–1921):

One thereby fails to appreciate the peculiar character of any intuition, namely, that it is always actualized in a particular orientation [*Orientierung*] and by way of a *preconception* [*Vorgriff*] that anticipates its region of experience [*regionvorwegnehmenden*]. An intuiting that is concerned with immediacy only in its simplistic "objective" sense, and is thereby diligent in avoiding all constructivistic viewpoints [*Konstruktionsgesichtspunkte*] foreign to its subject matter, can easily become oblivious of its own ultimately unoriginal motivational basis. The *sense of originality* [*Ursprünglichkeit*] is not an extra-historical or supra-historical idea; it can attain its sense of *freedom from presuppositions* [*Voraussetzungslosigkeit*] only in a *factically and historically oriented self-critique* [*faktisch historisch orientierter Eigenkritik*]. . . . It may well be that even the routes of access to the matters of philosophy lie hidden and require a *radical deconstruction and reconstruction* [*radikalen Ab- und Rückbauens*] to be carried out along philosophical lines.[294]

When it came to the inane and at times pugnacious views about the Jews that he mindlessly ratified in his metaphysical anti-Semitism, Heidegger failed to achieve this measure of originality, the presuppositionlessness that is actualized only in the radical deconstruction and reconstruction of ideas based on factical and historical self-criticism.

Chapter Three

JEWISH TIME AND THE HISTORIOGRAPHICAL ECLIPSE OF HISTORICAL DESTINY

> Does a *truth* arise from the coupling of two errors? No. Then a third error? No. Instead, something much more dangerous, because more pertinacious, namely, the *semblance* of a truth and indeed mostly a semblance which cannot be surpassed with respect to all self-evidence.
>
> —HEIDEGGER, *ÜBERLEGUNGEN VI*, § 88

In the previous chapter I noted that a consequence of Heidegger's denying the Jews a sense of *Geschichtlichkeit* was to rob them of the temporal comportment that is basic to Dasein's being-in-the-world. A more careful scrutiny of Heidegger's remarks indicates that he prejudicially linked the Jews to a mathematical and historicist conception of time as opposed to what he considered the authentic mode of time that endows one with historical destiny. This negative valorization of Jewish time has its roots in Heidegger's youthful theological training and his acceptance of the contrast between Jewish messianism and Christian soteriology as we find, most explicitly, in a section from the 1920–1921 lecture course, *Einleitung in die Phänomenologie der Religion*.[1] Expounding the fifth chapter of 1 Thessalonians, Heidegger argues that, for Paul, the anticipation of the reappearance of the Messiah is not a matter of waiting for a future event. On the contrary, the structure of Christian hope, which is the relational sense of the parousia, is radically different from all expectation. The "when" of the second coming is not a moment of time but the "enactment of life" (*Vollzug des Lebens*), which gives rise to a knowledge of self lived in a temporal interval that cannot be measured or calibrated objectively. Heidegger distinguishes Jesus's announcement of the coming of the kingdom of God in the synoptic gospels and Paul's notion of enactment, which in turn is based on the "factical life experience" (*faktische Lebenserfahrung*) whose object is Jesus, the savior that has already come.² To understand Heidegger's scriptural exegesis, it is necessary to bear in mind that *Vollzugssinn* denotes that *experience at its fullest takes place in its properly factic context of actualization in the historically existing self*.³ Sheehan details the crucial transition in Heidegger's phenomenological nomenclature from *Bezugssinn*, the relational meaning of sense, to *Vollzugssinn*, the enactment sense:

Now that Husserl had broken the stranglehold of the apophantic assertion in ontology, now that he has rescued beingness from the copula and had rendered it present for itself as an immediately intuitable phenomenon, Heidegger could ask how *it* is given. If beingness is the givenness of beings, and if this givenness-of . . . is itself given, then it too can be treated as a phenomenon and questioned as to the "how" of its becoming present. To use language that Heidegger developed in his earliest courses after World War I, Husserl had uncovered the *Bezugssinn* operative in ontology, the sense of relation between man and beingness; but the *Vollzugssinn* remained to be settled, the sense of the "how" in which the *Bezugssinn* is carried out. For Heidegger that *Vollzugssinn* essentially has to do with man's temporality: his presence-by-absence, his having of himself and his world by being out beyond himself in self-absence. That dimension of *absence* into which man is *appropriated* lets happen the *presence* or beingness of all that is.⁴

Heidegger's reading of Paul is an application of his phenomenology of *Vollzugssinn*. The life experience of the enactment demands the ability to relive the moment—the Christ-event of the crucifixion—which from its inception heralds a past that can always become future in the present. This is the import of Heidegger's claim that "Christian factical life experience is historically determined [*historisch bestimmt*] by its emergence with the proclamation [*Verkündigung*] that hits the people in a moment, and then is unceasingly also alive in the enactment of life. . . . For all its originality, primordial Christian facticity gains no exceptionality. . . . In all its absoluteness of reorganizing the enactment, everything remains the same in respect to the worldly facticity."⁵

The eschaton for the committed Christian is a future enacted in the present as a form of gnostic self-revelation rather than a future anticipated as a historical event that is to come in the homogeneous sequence of quantitatively calculable and qualitatively interchangeable now points, an event that changes the course of what Heidegger calls "worldly facticity" (*weltlichen Faktizität*). To deny that the future is an event that can be expected to occur in historical time is not to deny the historicity of Christian facticity, which, as we have seen, is embedded in the original statement. Indeed, Heidegger's analysis of the primordial Christian religiosity turns on two axes: first, that this religiosity is to be sought in a factical life experience and, second, that this experience is historical.[6] But what is the nature of the historical? "The task," writes Heidegger, "is to gain a real and original relationship to history, which is to be explicated from out of our own historical situation and facticity. At issue is what the sense of history can signify for us, so that the 'objectivity' of the historical 'in itself' disappears. History exists only from out of a present. Only thus can the possibility of a philosophy of religion be begun."[7]

Contrary to what one might assume, Heidegger argues that the gaining of an original relationship to history is dependent on the meaning of the historical that we elicit from our own factical state, and this expedites the disappearance of the objectivity of the historical in itself. Heidegger is here gesturing to a critical distinction he will make in *Sein und Zeit* between the authentic temporality (*eigentlichen Zeitlichkeit*) of the "existential and ontological constitution of historicity [*Geschichtlichkeit*]" and the inauthentic time of everydayness (*Alltäglichkeit*) related to the "vulgar interpretation of the history [*Geschichte*] of Dasein."[8] According to the latter, which is also referred to as the "astronomical and calendrical *time-reckoning*" (*astronomische und kalendarische* Zeitrechnung),[9] the computable now of the present is the metrics by which we chronoscopically measure past and future: the past is the irretrievable no-longer-present (*Nicht-mehr-Gegenwart*), and the future the indeterminate not-yet-present (*Noch-nicht-Gegenwart*).[10] The everyday standpoint presumes, therefore, both the irreversibility (*Nicht-Umkehrbarkeit*) of time and its assimilation into space expressed as the homogenization into now-points (*Homogenisierung auf Jetztpunkte*),[11] a perspective informed by the Aristotelian conception of time as the measure of bodies in motion and the consequent characterization of duration as a sequential progression.[12] Authentic time, alternatively, is lived from the futural retrieval of the past in the present, an act that constitutes the nature of Dasein as historicity, namely, the enigma of history that unravels in our being historical, which is to be distinguished from the historian's concern with analyzing and classifying "world-historical occurrences" (*weltgeschichtliches Geschehen*). The historiographical (*historisch*) explanation is thus differentiated from historical (*geschichtlich*) thinking; the latter cannot be subsumed under scientific or systematic reflection.¹³ Elsewhere Heidegger depicts the discrepancy by noting that the historiographical refers to the past as an object that can be explored and presented from the perspective of the present, whereas the historical is not a manner of grasping or exploring but relates to "the very happening itself" (*das Geschehen selbst*). Consequently, the historical is not focused on the past or even the present, but on the eventfulness of the future, which is commended to the will, to expectation, and to care. The passing of the past (*das Vergehen*) is the "gathering of what endures" (*die Versammlung des Währenden*) and not simply "what has been" (*das Gewesen*).¹⁴ From that perspective the future can be identified as the "origin of history" (*Ursprung der Geschichte*), but what is most futural (*Zukünftigste*) is the "great beginning [*große Anfang*], that which—withdrawing itself constantly [*sich ständig entziehend*]—reaches back the farthest and at the same time reaches forward the farthest."¹⁵

In *Sein und Zeit*, Heidegger described the equiprimordiality (*Gleichursprünglichkeit*) of the three ecstasies of temporality (*Ekstasen der Zeitlichkeit*)—the future (*Zukunft*), the having-been (*Gewesenheit*), and the present (*Gegenwart*)¹⁶—in the unity of the structure of care along similar lines:

The wholeness of the being [*Seinsganzheit*] of Dasein as care means: ahead-of-itself-already-being-in [*Sich-vorweg-schon-sein-in*] (a world) as being-together-with [*Sein-bei*] (beings encountered within the world).... Being-ahead-of-oneself [*Sich-vorweg*] is grounded in the future. Already-being-in... makes known having-been. Being-together-with... is made possible in making present.... The "ahead" does not mean the "before" in the sense of a "not-yet-now, but later." Nor does the "already" mean a "no-longer-now, but earlier."... The "before" and the "ahead of" indicate the future that first makes possible in general the fact that Dasein can be in such a way that it is concerned *about* its potentiality-of-being [*Seinkönnen*]. The self-project [*Sichentwerfen*] grounded in the "for the sake of itself" in the future is an essential quality of *existentiality* [Existenzialität]. *Its primary meaning is the future.*¹⁷

The primordial temporality (*ursprünglichen Zeitlichkeit*) is thus experienced in the ecstatic compresence of past, present, and future, as opposed to the vulgar understanding (*vulgären Verständnis*) of time as the ceaseless succession of nows (*Jetzt-folge*).[18] "This simultaneous totality of perspective in which Dasein constantly moves—even if one perspective is obscured or clouded, even if another is one-sidedly favoured—the simultaneity of these three perspectives proceeds to distribute itself into *present, having-been*, and *future*. These three perspectives are not lined up alongside one another, but originarily simply united in the horizon of time as such. Originarily, there is the *single* and *unitary universal horizon of time*."[19] The concurrence of the heterogeneity of the homogeneous and the homogeneity of the heterogeneous within that temporal horizon undergirds Heidegger's contention that the historicity of Dasein is not determined from the human being existing in history; on the contrary, the human being exists historically because in the very ground of its being Dasein is temporal.[20] Put differently, Heidegger did not consider history as "equivalent to what is past; for this is precisely what is no longer happening. But much less is history what is merely contemporary, which also never happens, but always just 'passes,' makes its entrance and goes by. History as happening is determined from the future, takes over what has been, and acts and endures its way through the *present*."[21] The linearity of the temporal grid is upended by the portrayal of the future as the past ceaselessly withdrawing so that distending mentally to the end is concurrently distending mentally to the beginning, albeit a beginning whose mystery is not revealed until the unconcealment of the end when the concealment is concealed.

As a passage from the *Beiträge* indicates, Heidegger recognized that history (*Geschichte*) is always determined by historiology (*Historie*), but the predicament of modernity is that the latter has dominated. To reclaim the historical, so that the essence of history can be known, "the essence of the human being must become questionable [*fraglich*] above all and being must become question-worthy [*fragwürdig*]. . . . History can be grounded only in the essence of beyng itself, i.e., only in the relation of beyng to the human being who is equal to that relation."[22] In the continuation, Heidegger opines, "Today, at the start of the decisive phase of modernity, this dominance already extends so far that historiology determines the understanding of history in such a way this history is thrust aside into what lacks history, and its essence is sought therein. Blood and race become the bearers of history."[23] In fairness to Heidegger, we must note that this passage lends credibility to his dogged insistence that he was critical of National Socialism and its brutal tactics. He is implying here, it seems, that the modernist dominance of the historiological is behind the privileging of genetic racism at the hands of the Nazis. Historiology, however, at its base, "is the explanation which establishes facts about the past out of the horizon of a calculative bustling about [*berechnenden Betreibungen*] with the present. Beings are thereby preconceived as the orderable, the producible, and the establishable (ἰδέα)." The historicist mentality, accordingly, obscures time by eternalizing the present "as that which is objectively present." History, by contrast, "*is beyng as appropriating event and must receive the determination of its essence on that basis, i.e., independently of any notion of becoming or development, independently of historiological considerations and explanations.*"²⁴ In the final analysis, historiology, which is based on the subject-object relation, "ends in an anthropological-psychological biographism" because the subject itself is objectified and hence there is no real opposition between subjective and objective.²⁵

The historical is a mode of reinscribing the past to lay the bridge to the future. For Heidegger, this is the first principle of all hermeneutics: "*The possibility of access to history* [Zugangsmöglichkeit zur Geschichte] *is grounded in the possibility according to which any specific present understands how to be futural* [zukünftig]."²⁶ In *Sein und Zeit*, Heidegger similarly argued that the "being of Dasein finds its meaning in temporality," which is defined more specifically as "the condition of the possibility of historicity [*Möglichkeit von Geschichtlichkeit*] as a temporal mode of being [*zeitlichen Seinsart*] of Dasein itself." As the determination of the constitution of the being of Dasein, historicity is prior to the world-historical occurrences (*weltgeschichtliches Geschehen*), the delineation and classification of which constitute the contours of what we call history. On the face of it, the historical propensity of the human being, which eludes the historicist perspective, is dependent on the fact that in its factical being (*faktischen Sein*) Dasein always is how and what it already was, that is, it possesses the past as a property that is still objectively present. However, the appropriation and narration of the past is possible only because Dasein is "its past in the manner of *its* being which, roughly expressed, on each occasion 'occurs' out of its future. In its manner of existing at any given time, and thus also with the understanding of being that belongs to it, Dasein grows into a customary interpretation of itself and grows up on that interpretation. . . . Its own past . . . does not *follow after* Dasein but rather always already goes ahead of it."²⁷ This articulation portends the anti-Hegelian emphasis in Heidegger's later thought on the historical destiny of the unthought of being as the "it gives" (*es gibt*), which comes into language in the words of essential thinkers, that is, thinkers who think one thought essentially, albeit always from different vantage points and in a decidedly unsystematic manner befitting the gesture of poetizing.²⁸

Therefore the thinking that thinks into the truth of being is, as thinking, historical [*geschichtlich*]. There is not a "systematic" thinking and next to it an illustrative history of past opinions.²⁹ ... Thought in a more primordial way, there is the history of being [*Geschichte des Seins*] to which thinking belongs as recollection [*Andenken*] of this history, propriated [*ereignet*] by it. Such recollective thought differs essentially from the subsequent presentation of history in the sense of an evanescent past. History does not take place primarily as a happening [*Geschehen*]. And its happening is not evanescence [*Vergehen*]. The happening of history occurs essentially as the destiny of the truth of being and from it [*Das Geschehen der Geschichte west als das Geschick der Wahrheit des Seins aus diesem*]. ... Being comes to its destiny in that It, being, gives itself. But thought in terms of such destiny this says: It gives itself and refuses itself simultaneously [*Es gibt sich und versagt sich zumal*].³⁰

I agree with those who detect in Heidegger's discussion of the parousia a foreshadowing of his more mature reflections on ecstatic temporality, and especially the principle of individuation, which entails privileging the moment as that which projects to the future and thereby affords one the possibility of reclaiming the past in the present.³¹ Within the hermeneutical circle of the word coming to language, and being bringing itself to the word (*Das Wort kommt zur Sprache, das Seyn bringt sich zum Wort*), the alignment of time is such that destining toward the end is a return to the beginning that is yet to be. The performativity of language as saying thus preserves the event in the past and in what is coming (*Die Sprache als Sage wahrt das Ereignis ... sie wahrt das Gewesene und das Kommende*).³² In the uncertainty of the future, one is always becoming what one has already not been. Suffice it here to cite one illustration: "In being futural in running ahead, the Dasein that on average is becomes itself; in running ahead it becomes visible as this one singular uniqueness of its singular fate in the possibility of its singular past."³³ In his earlier phenomenology of religion, Heidegger relatedly argued that the parousia is not a matter of anticipating the literal return of Christ but an "obstinate waiting" (*Erharren*) that "does not wait for the significances of a future event, but for God. The meaning of temporality determines itself out of the fundamental relationship [*Grundverhältnis*] to God—however, in such a way that only those who live temporality in the manner of enactment [*vollzugsmäßig*] understand eternity."[34] The "eschatological problem," which the young Heidegger identified as "the center of Christian life" (*das Zentrum des christlichen Lebens*),[35] is tied to a waiting that is not a waiting for some event in spacetime that will repeat what happened in the past, but rather an expectation of the future that will bring about the "transformation before God,"[36] the enactment of the moment, being-present in the presence of God. The messianic annunciation is not simply a "thankful memory" (*dankbare Erinnerung*) of an historical past, but the "having-become" (*Gewordensein*) that engenders the possibility of a "new becoming" that "always remains co-present as alive [*immer mitlebendig dableibt*]."[37] Heidegger alludes to this mode of realization in the statement, "Christian experience lives time itself [*Die christliche Erfahrung lebt die Zeit selbst*],"[38] and in the parallel formulation, "Christian religiosity lives temporality [*daß christliche Religiosität die Zeitlichkeit lebt*]."[39] Commenting on Paul's observation that the appointed time (*kairos*) has grown short (1 Corinthians 7:29), Heidegger writes that the "primordial Christian religiosity" demands that one live incessantly in the distress of the only-yet (*Nur-Noch*), a "compressed temporality" (*zusammengedrängte Zeitlichkeit*) in the moment of vision (*Augenblick*), in which there is no time for postponement. The true believer ascertains that since there is nothing to be attained, nothing for which to wait, there is nothing to be postponed. The time of salvation is thereby endowed with a special character, a mode of temporality that cannot be encountered "in some sort of objective time." The "when" of the factical life experience, which converts the temporal into the eternal, is thus not "objectively graspable."[40]

Even at this early stage, Heidegger—in consonance with Augustine[41] and strikingly similar to Rosenzweig[42]—does not sanction a metaphysical conception of eternity that is the ontological negation of time, but rather eternity is to be construed as the moment that instantiates the limiting idea that determines the horizon of and intensifies our experience of time. "A remarkable error dominates human thinking, to the effect that eternity could be explained by timelessness [*Zeitlosigkeit*], whereas the essence of eternity can be nothing other than the deepest oscillation *of time* [*die tiefste Duchschwingung der Zeit*] in its refusing and bestowing, preserving and losing."[43] In *Die Grundbegriffe der Metaphysik*, Heidegger expresses this idea as the spell of time broken by the moment of vision rooted in the essence of temporality: "The temporal entrancement [*Zeitbann*] can be ruptured only through time itself, through that which is of the proper essence of time and which, following Kierkegaard, we call the moment of vision [*Augenblick*]. The moment of vision ruptures the entrancement of time, and is able to rupture it, insofar as it is a specific possibility of time itself."[44] Elaborating on this theme in *Schelling: Vom Wesen der menschlichen Freiheit*, in an effort to account for the temporal becoming of the eternal God—a process that embraces the paradox, similar to what is articulated in kabbalistic theosophy, that the being of God is a becoming to himself out of himself (*Das Seyn Gottes ist ein Zuschselbstwerden aus sich selbst*)[45]—Heidegger remarked that

original simul-taneity [*Gleich-Zeitigkeit*] consists in the fact that being past and being present assert themselves and mingle with each other together with being present as the essential fullness of time itself. And this mingling of *true temporality* [*eigentlichen Zeitlichkeit*], this Moment [*Augenblick*], "is" the essence of eternity [*das Wesen der Ewigkeit*], but not the present which has merely stopped and remains that way, the *nunc stans*. Eternity can only be thought truly, that is, poetically, if we understand it as the most primordial temporality, but never in the manner of common sense which says to itself: Eternity, that is the opposite of temporality. Thus, in order to understand eternity, all time must be abstracted in thought.[46]

In light of this discussion, it is of interest to consider the marginal note that Heidegger added to his copy of *Sein und Zeit*, "Transcendence as the ecstatic—timeliness—temporality, but 'horizon'! Being covered up as being. Transcendence, however, of the truth of Being: the Event of appropriation" (*Transzendenz als das Ekstatische—Zeitlichkeit—Temporalität; aber "Horizont"! Seyn hat Seyendes "überdacht." Transzendenz aber von Wahrheit des Seyns her: das Ereignis*).[47] The annotation is especially noteworthy as it attests to Heidegger's attempt to link the discussion in *Sein und Zeit* on the temporality of being-in-the-world and the problem of the transcendence of the world to terminology that is reflective of the turn in his thinking. Transcendence is not something with metaphysical approbation (*metaphysischen Anklangs*) that would diminish the sense of the temporal in the face of that which is timeless, but rather the horizon of ecstatic temporality, the timeliness that is the truth of being, the event through which being is covered up as a being.

The intensification of the time of the moment as eternity is the phenomenological content of the enactment of life identified by Heidegger at an earlier stage as the essence of what it is to be Christian. In *Der Begriff der Zeit*, a lecture delivered a few years after the seminar on the phenomenology of religion, Heidegger defines Christian faith (*Glaube*) as that which "is in itself supposed to stand in relation to something that happened in time—at a time, we are told, of which it is said: It was the time 'when time was fulfilled.'"[48] Heidegger distinguishes between the theologian's concern to understand time in relation to eternity (*Ewigkeit*), which is a matter of faith, and the philosopher's quest to understand time through time (*die Zeit aus der Zeit*) or in terms of that which exists everlastingly (*aei*), which appears to be eternal but is actually a derivative of being temporal.[49] The dichotomy seems definitive: the theologian comprehends time from the standpoint of eternity, and the philosopher eternity from the standpoint of time. And yet Heidegger is clear that faith dictates that the believer experiences eternity in relation to what has occurred at a given moment in time, an eternity that should be understood neither as *sempiternitas*, "the ongoing continuation of time" (*das fortgesetzte Weitergehen der Zeit*), nor as *aeternitas*, the "ever-enduring presence" (*immerwährende Gegenwart*) of the "standing now" (*nunc stans*), the two explanations of eternity offered by Heidegger in the lecture course on Hölderlin's hymn "Germanien," delivered in the winter semester 1934–1935 at the University of Freiburg.[50]

Correspondingly, Heidegger's reading of Pauline eschatology and his construal of Christianity based thereon rest upon a third possibility that postulates the eternalization of the temporal without appeal to the two conceptions of eternity (*Ewigkeitsbegriffe*)—the incessant flow of time, a "never-ending sequence of 'nows,'" and the motionless and everlasting present, "an encompassing 'now' that remains standing ahead of time"— that spring from the experience of time as a *"pure sequential passing of 'nows'"* (reinen Vergehens des Jetzt im Nacheinander). Insofar as this notion of time "does not grasp the essence of time"—the view already championed in *Sein und Zeit*—it follows that the concepts of eternity dependent upon it also will not "reach the essence of eternity."⁵¹ In addition to these perspectives, Heidegger proposes a third notion of eternity that is tagged as "the time that is essentially long" (*die wesenhaft lange Zeit*). Utilizing the following lines from the second version of Hölderlin's poem "Mnemosyne" as a springboard, "Long is / The time, yet what is true / Comes to pass" (*Lang ist / Die Zeit, es ereignet sich aber / Das Wahre*), Heidegger distinguishes the ascription of the quality of length to "everyday time" (*alltägliche Zeit*) and to "time of the peaks" (*die Zeit der Gipfel*), an expression derived from the poem "Patmos." In the case of the former, the feeling that time is long is a sign of boredom, whereas in the case of the latter it signifies that at the height of sublimity there "reigns a persistent waiting for and awaiting the event [*Ereignis*]. . . . There is no passing or even killing of time there, but a struggle for the duration and fullness of time that is preserved in awaiting."⁵² In this context Heidegger has unquestionably departed from the theistic mind-set operative in his reading of Paul. However, there is a thread that ties together that discussion and his analysis of Hölderlin. Both instances demonstrate that Heidegger did not think of eternity as atemporal or supratemporal, but rather as the elongation of time experienced in the obdurate waiting for the event that is "the becoming manifest of beyng" (*das Offenbarwerden des Seyns*),⁵³ the repeatedly renewed conferral of the origin that remains permanently still to come. As Heidegger expressed the matter in the *Beiträge*, "The eternal is not the incessant [*das Fort-währende*]; it is instead that which can withdraw [*entziehen*] in a moment so as to recur [*wiederzukehren*] later. What can recur: not as the *identical* [*das* Gleiche] but as the newly transforming [*Verwandelnde*], the one and unique [*Eine-Einzige*], i.e., beyng, such that it is not immediately recognized, in this manifestness, as the same [*das Selbe*]!"⁵⁴ The end exemplifies the eternal recurrence of the same that is uniquely different. The anticipation of the end, accordingly, reveals a delicate interplay between foresight and reminiscence, between the experience of absence and the nonexperience of presence, between the nongivenness of an event and the givenness of the nonevent, between the disappearance that has appeared and the appearance that will disappear.⁵⁵

Not surprisingly, Heidegger distinguishes Christian and Jewish eschatological perspectives. In one passage, he grants that the "basic direction" of this eschatology is "already late Judaic" (*spätjüdisch*), but he immediately adds that the "Christian consciousness" (*christliche Bewuβtsein*) is a "peculiar transformation thereof."[56] The degree to which Heidegger viewed this transformation as a radical break is underscored in a second passage: "In late-Judaism [*Spätjudentum*], the anticipation [*Erwartung*] of the Messiah refers primarily to such a futural event [*zukünftiges Ereignis*], to the appearance [*Erscheinung*] of the Messiah at which other people will be present." In a manner intriguingly reminiscent of Scholem's celebrated distinction between the historical-political nature of Jewish messianism and the internal-spiritual nature of Christian messianism,[57] Heidegger argued that the hope for redemption in the two faiths must be diametrically differentiated: in Judaism it is tied to the "event complex" (*Ereigniszusammenhang*), which is expected to occur at a future point in time, whereas in Christianity it is connected to the "complex of enactment with God" (*Vollzugszuammenhang mit Gott*), which is realized fully in the present in light of the fact that the Messiah has already come historically.[58] The distinction that Heidegger makes is rooted in the age-old contrast between Jewish literalism and Christian spiritualism, not to mention the altogether problematic and prevalent taxonomy *Spätjudentum*. For Heidegger, Jewish messianism—a remnant of which is still to be found in the synoptic gospels—is expressive of chronological time, and Christian eschatology of kairetic time; that is, the fullness of time is realized not as the climax of a linear process but in the potentiality of each moment disrupting the temporal sequence. The Jew, according to this calibration, lacks the midpoint that conjoins and disjoins the beginning and the end to which the Christian can lay claim.

Heidegger's assumption that Jewish messianism necessarily and in every case implies the directive to wait for an incident in history that has not yet occurred—the temporal analogue to spatial dislocation and the diasporic desire to return to the homeland—can surely be challenged. Needless to say, the distinction that he draws is too simplistic. One can discover in Jewish sources the chiastic paradox that Heidegger associates with the structure of hope and the temporality of the enactment of life ritualized sacramentally by the Christian parousia: the future is already present as the present that is always future. This form of hope is not expressed by waiting for something to come to pass in the ordinary procession of time but as an expectation of the unexpected, the unforeseeable intrusion that occasions the renewal of what has previously transpired as what is yet to transpire, the disjuncture within time through which we grasp the conjuncture of tenses that are constellated in the configuration of time. On this score, as Rosenzweig well understood, the messianic doctrine of Judaism—congruent to, even though not identical with, Christian faith—betokens a tension between the absent presence of the past and the present absence of the future. That is to say, redemption is always of the future, but a future that retrieves the past and ruptures the present, thereby bending the time line such that not-yet is already-there insofar as already-there is not-yet.[59] Redemption is not the consequence of historical development, the effect of a causal chain that links the retention of the past and the protection of the future, but rather the corollary of an expectation that is realized as the expectation of what cannot be realized,[60] or, as Levinas put it, to wait for the Messiah requires the patience that is indicative of the duration of time, referred to as diachrony,[61] "an awaiting without anything being awaited, without the intention of awaiting."[62] The allure of the future, accordingly, is not to be assessed from the standpoint of an achievable objective but from the standpoint of the activity that the waiting for that objective incites. Belief in a savior always in the process of coming and not in one that has already come transposes the temporal order by inverting the causal succession—what determines the present is not the past but the future.[63]

Heidegger was obviously oblivious to this facet of Jewish messianic speculation and thus rigidly distinguished it from Christianity. Even more crucial is the fact that in the 1930s the kairological dimension of time was transferred from primordial Christian temporality to the authentic time of German destiny from which the Jews are excluded. Heidegger's intent is clarified by another passage from the notebooks where he writes that the present condition is marked by "the *ending* of the history of the great beginning of Western humanity" (*das Ende der Geschichte des großen Anfangs des abendländischen Menschen*), the beginning in which humanity "was called to the stewardship of beyng" (*zur Wächterschaft des Seyns berufen wurde*), a vocation (*Berufung*) that "was immediately transformed into the claim of representing beings" (*Vor-stellung des Seienden*) in their "machinational unessence" (*machenschaftlichen Unwesen*). The current state of the lack of history (*Geschichtslosen*) is one in which there is the "unity of a complete commixture" (*Einheit der völligen Vermischung*), that is, the abysmal (*Bodenlose*) state wherein the "apparent buildup and renewal" (*scheinbare Aufbauen und Erneuern*) and the "complete destruction" (*völlige Zerstörung*) are the same, the state of "those addicted to mere beings and those alienated from beyng" (*dem nur Seienden Verfallene und dem Seyn Entfremdete*). This state is described further as one in which historicism (*Historismus*) begins to compensate for the lack of history and thus a struggle (*Kampf*) ensues. In this struggle, which is waged against aimlessness (*Ziellosigkeit*) and therefore can only be a caricature (*Zerrbild*) of the struggle, the greater groundlessness (*größere Bodenlosigkeit*), which is not bound to anything (*die an nichts gebunden*) and avails itself of everything (*alles sich dienstbar macht*), will prevail. Heidegger notes, parenthetically, that this groundlessness—in relation to which the nomadic and the parasitic intersect—is "Judaism" (*das Judentum*). Heidegger maintains, moreover, that the "actual triumph," the victory of history over what is a-historical (*der Sieg der Geschichte über das Geschichtslose*), is achieved when "what is groundless excludes itself [*wo das Bodenlose sich selbst ausschließt*] because it does not venture beyng [*weil es das Seyn nicht wagt*] but always only reckons with beings [*sondern immer nur mit dem Seienden rechnet*], and posits their calculations as what is real [*und seine Berechnungen als das Wirkliche setzt*]."[64]

Judaism is cast as the antihistorical force in modernity. As custodians of the historicism that is the hallmark of the representation of things in their machinational unessence—that is, the eclipse of being that results from the reduction of beings to calculable and interchangeable entities—the Jews emblematize the abhorrent plight of modern science and technology to relegate beings to a life experience (*Erleben*), classified under quantifiable taxonomies prone to "psychological-characterological-biological-typological dissection."[65] The language of struggle and conquest is clear indication of Heidegger's attempt to usurp and transform the Nazi lingo. Capitulating to the cultural madness of his time, Heidegger targets the Jews and marks them as illustrative of the condition that he called in the *Beiträge* "being-away" (*Weg-sein*), the exilic wandering that arises from "pressing on with *the closedness of the mystery and of being* [die Verschlossenheit des Geheimnisses und des Seins]; forgottenness of being. And this happens in *being-away* according to this sense: *to be infatuated with things, smitten with them, lost in them.*"[66] Most individuals are obsessed and enraptured with beings, and thus they experience life as closed (*Lebensnähe*), foregoing the "essential relation of Da-sein to beyng," which demands "withstanding the openness of the self-concealing" (*die Offenheit des Sichverbergens ausstehen*), the "character of *that* Da-sein which *endures* the 'there' by sheltering the truth."⁶⁷ Heidegger both strengthens and weakens the anthropocentrism of Western metaphysics by delimiting the role of the human being as the "one needed by beyng for the sake of withstanding the essential occurrence of the truth of beyng. As so needed, however, humans 'are' humans [»ist« *aber der Mensch nur Mensch*] inasmuch as they are grounded in Da-sein, i.e., inasmuch as they themselves, by creating, become the ones who ground Da-*sein*. Yet beyng is also grasped here as *appropriating event* [Er-eignis]. Both belong together: the grounding back into Da-sein and the truth of beyng as event."⁶⁸ In his weaker and more irrational moments, Heidegger stigmatized the Jews as forfeiting their status as human by misappropriating the event that is the mystery and truth of being.

The irony, however, is that the view of authentic time affirmed by Heidegger is not only not contrary to what he erroneously proffered as the mathematical-calculative perspective of the Jews, but a more accurate view of time that may be culled from Jewish sources is compatible with his avowal that repetition is the perpetuation of the identical in a manner that is always different, the return of the same that is yet to materialize in the torrent of time.⁶⁹ I would go so far as to say that the temporal underpinning of the hermeneutical conception of the oral tradition espoused by the rabbis and expanded by the kabbalists accords with Heidegger's view that a text cannot be heard anew unless it is translated, and it cannot be translated unless it is interpreted, and it cannot be interpreted unless there a return to a past that is concealed and therefore has not yet arrived.⁷⁰ Particularly germane is Heidegger's remark, "The poetry of a poet or the treatise of a thinker stands within its own proper unique word. It compels us to perceive this word again and again as if we were hearing it for the first time. These newborn words transpose us in every case to a new shore."⁷¹ Heidegger's poetic thinking shares with the rabbinic-kabbalistic hermeneutic the assumption that the uniqueness of the word triggers the need to hear it again repetitively as if it were uttered for the first time, a transporting to the new shore where one has already been. Expressed more technically, to repeat is not the continuation of what has been but the retrieval (*wieder-holen*) of the inception that is "begun again *more originally* [*der Anfang* ursprünglicher *wiederangefangen wird*], and with all the strangeness, darkness, insecurity that a genuine inception brings with it."⁷² The event of being is gauged from the standpoint of the uniqueness (*Einmaligkeit*) and singularity (*Einzigkeit*) of being itself—the aggregate that is utterly fragmentary inasmuch as "what is as a whole, as what is, itself demands a grounding in openness,"[73] and, as such, the totality is what it is in virtue of what it is to become—and hence every occurrence is a recurrence of what is yet to be in the fullness of the grounded essence of what has been.[74] The uniqueness of the singular is manifest in the repeatability of its unrepeatability, the expectation of its unexpectability. The paradox of the iteration of the inimitable at play in Heidegger is well captured by Krzysztof Ziarek: "In the end, singularity appears to carry the inscription of inescapable repetition, not simply as its shadow or companion but even as its condition of possibility. Singularity entails repetition, even demands it, because the event can claim its mark as singular only if it appears repeatable—that is, repeatedly sayable—in its uniqueness, intrinsically engaged in substitution characteristic of linguistic expression. In short, uniqueness is such only because the event's singularity can be repeated in and as its irreplaceable occurrence."[75]

Heidegger speaks often of the leap (*Sprung*) that initiates the beginning (*Anfang*) continually surpassed by the "other beginning" that must always be first, the beginning that begins before the beginning that is unfailingly second,[76] the beginning that is what is to come, wherein the last god—the god wholly other than all preceding gods—appears through thinking meditatively on the essence of godliness (*Gottwesens*) as something strange (*Befremdlichen*) and incalculable (*Unberechenbaren*),[77] the end in which "the truth of beyng must be ventured as grounding, as inventive thought of Da-sein."[78] Intriguingly reminiscent of the Jewish belief that the possibility of the Messiah's coming is predicated on the impossibility of the Messiah's arrival, the hope in the return of what is interminably still to come, Heidegger maintains that the lastness of the last god consists of the fact that god is constantly coming, which engenders a state of continual waiting. "He brings nothing, unless himself; yet even then only as the most coming of that which comes [*den Kommendsten des Kommenden*]. Ahead of himself, he bears the to-come of the future [*Zu-kunft*], his time-play-space is beyng, a time-play-space that itself waits for the god, in coming, to fulfill it and in coming to come [*im Kommen komme*]."[79]

In "Der Ursprung des Kunstwerkes," Heidegger wrote of the leap as the "suddenness of the beginning" (*Unvermittelte des Anfangs*), but the "uniqueness of what is unique to the leap" is "always a leaping-ahead

[*Vorsprung*], a leaping-ahead in which everything to come is already leapt over [*übersprungen*], even if as something veiled. Concealed within itself, the beginning contains already the end."[80] To the extent that the leap at the beginning is a leap ahead, the end can be said to be comprised in the beginning. Heidegger thus distinguishes the "genuine beginning" and that which is "primitive" on the grounds that the latter has no future "because it lacks the bestowing, grounding leap and the leap-ahead." Since the primitive has no future, it has no past of which to speak; by contrast, the beginning conserves the genuine past because it "always contains the undisclosed fullness of the extraordinary [*Ungeheuren*], and that means the strife with the ordinary [*des Streites mit dem Geheuren*]."[81] One might detect a form of temporal determinacy implied in the statements "everything to come is already leapt over" and "the beginning contains already the end." But, in fact, what Heidegger intends is just the opposite: the unpredictability of the future is upheld by the fact that the having-been in the present is grounded as what is to come, the past is molded by the future that is molded by the past. The distance between the *terminus ad quo* and the *terminus ad quem* is bridged by the creative leap, which Heidegger identifies as the poiēsis of art, an act that allows truth to arise (*entspringen*) by bringing something into being from the origin (*Ursprung*) by means of the endowing leap (*stiftenden Sprung*).[82]

It is in this sense that Heidegger, partially thinking in the wake of Hegel, can arrogate the transposal of the speculative statement that the result is the beginning: "The beginning must really be made with the result, since the beginning results from that result."[83] Nevertheless, Heidegger's assertion that the leap ahead is found in the leap at the beginning is to be distinguished from the uroboric nature of the Hegelian dialectic whereby the end is contained in the beginning as the necessary outcome, since in the end the absolute returns to itself as it was in the beginning.[84] Badiou correctly noted that buttressing this dialectical movement is the "theological circularity which, presupposing the absolute in the seeds of the beginning, leads back to this very beginning once all the stages of its effectuation, its alienation, its-going-outside-itself, and so on, are unfolded. Thus, the dead Son reintegrated into the divisible immanence of the Father *completes* the world-concept of the Christian God, which is the holiness of the Spirit."[85] For Heidegger, the realization of the beginning in the end does not presume that the end is nothing but the cyclical rotation back to the beginning so that the transcendent spirit can be finally incorporated immanently in history. The hermeneutic structure of circularity is such that the time swerve is open at both termini, and hence the end cannot be deduced from the beginning nor the beginning from the end; the reversibility of the circular linearity implies not closure or repetition in the form of a palindrome but rather an ever-changing fluctuation, the indeterminacy of the abyss or the clearing that destabilizes the model of an irreversible sequence proceeding unidirectionally from start to finish. We can say that what is to come has already been, provided we understand that what has been is perpetually what is to come. In a manner more consonant with Jewish apocalyptic sensibility, the beginning whither one returns in the end is not the beginning whence one set forth toward the end. The eschatological future is not simply a restoration of Edenic existence as if it were possible to return in the future to a state of eternity that reigned in the past outside the exigencies of time.[86] On the contrary, in reaching the end, the beginning, too, is transformed because as beginning it is meaningfully no more only to the extent that it is not yet.

From the beginning, then, we can discern the indiscernible end, albeit from an inverse perspective. That is, the end can only be imagined as the terminus that can never be terminated. In that respect, the unending end—the end that has no ending to being the end—is the mystery that marks the horizon of our demarcating the limit of language. As Hans-Jost Frey insightfully remarked,

Because the end cannot be said, saying can have no end. Where the text ends it is unfinished, because although its end has come it is still unsaid, and when the text says it, it has not yet come to an end, since it is still in the middle of saying that it has. Writing, which must always already have begun in order to be able to say that it has, must always continue in order to be able to say that it is ending. It always ends too early or too late, and therefore does not end at all, for it misses its own end.[87]

This subtle insight underscores the complex intertwining of the apophatic and the kataphatic: there is no end to speaking precisely because the end cannot be spoken. The paradox is especially pertinent in the written text. We cannot posit textual closure—a book may be sealed but the text stays open—because even at the conclusion the text is incomplete and what has been said therein remains unsaid. To speak of the unsaid does not mean to speak about the silence of not speaking but rather to speak of what is still to be spoken. Just as there is no way to speak of the beginning that has not already begun and therefore cannot end, so there is no way to speak of the end that has not already ended and therefore cannot begin. Language can begin and end, but it cannot either terminate speaking of the beginning or commence speaking of the end. From the inability to control the discourse about beginning and end, it is impossible, as Frey observed, to imagine a sense of a whole, and beginning and end are reduced to arbitrary markers.[88]

In traditional Jewish theorizing about time, the sign of the end that has commanded much attention through the generations is the eschaton, the omega that compliments the alpha of creation. I do not think it would be unreasonable to consider eschatology from a Heideggerian perspective as a form of speculating about mortality writ large, moving from the ontic-existential anxiety of the individual with the looming certainty of death to the ontological-historical trepidation of the larger human community with either the impending uncertainty of the ecological demise of the planet or the possibility of mass destruction even greater than we have witnessed heretofore. The apocalyptic secret orients one to the decisive interval in time, the future, the breaking point of the perimeter, the center of the margin, the end close at hand that persists as what is always most distant, the not yet that already is and therefore is not yet.[89] As far removed as Derrida's idea of messianicity is from traditional forms of Jewish messianism, in the following hypothetical question, and the distinction between eschatology and teleology upon which it is based, he demonstrates a profound grasp of the paradoxical corollary of the temporal comportment of the achronic future implied in the belief that the possibility of the Messiah's coming is predicated on the impossibility of the Messiah's arrival: "Is there not a messianic extremity, an *eskhaton* whose ultimate event (immediate rupture, unheard-of-interruption, untimeliness of the infinite surprise, heterogeneity without accomplishment) can exceed, *at each moment*, the final term of a *phusis*, such as work, the production, and the *telos* of any history?"[90]

The telos is indexical of a past that projects a determinate goal, a destination that closes the circuit; the end, by contrast, is a signpost of the advent of a future that is indeterminate, the coming that is always to come.⁹¹ The unveiling of the truth of the end, therefore, is endlessly beyond the end, the revelation of the revelation revealed as nothing to be revealed, the secret that there is no secret, *an apocalypse without an apocalypse*.⁹² Unbeknownst to Heidegger, ingrained in the texture of the Jewish apocalyptic is the structure of secrecy related to the mystery of the future, which originates in the past, disclosed in the present as the presence that is not present, a view that very much coincides with his own conjecture that what is yet to be reverts to what has already been, but what has already been issues from what is yet to be. Analogously, Jewish apocalyptic hope—the hope that renews itself sporadically as the hope that is deferred continuously—stems from this linear circularity, the infinite negativity of time, the impossible possibility that makes it always possible that the future that is coming threatens not to be the future that one has envisaged.⁹³ This can be profitably compared to Heidegger's own account of the unremitting and inherently futural nature of the pursuit that is part and parcel of the questioning of what is questionworthy as it pertains to the essential truth of the occurrence of being and the disclosing of the selfhood of Dasein:

Seeking is never simply a matter of *not yet* possessing [Nochnicht*haben*], deprivation. To understand it in that sense is to calculate it merely in terms of the result to be attained. Primarily and properly, seeking is an advancing into the domain in which truth opens itself or withholds itself. Seeking is intrinsically futural and is a coming into the nearness of being. Seeking brings the seekers to *themselves* for the first time, i.e., brings them into the selfhood [*Selbstheit*] of Da-sein, wherein the clearing and concealment of beings occur. Being a self is the finding that already lies *in* the seeking, the sure illumination which already gleams prior to all veneration and in virtue of which alone we are open for the resonating of what is most unique and greatest.⁹⁴

Heidegger's conclusion that the discovery—or recovery—of the self is to be sought in the seeking is notionally on a par with the Jewish messianic belief that the waiting itself is the fulfillment of the expectation, as there is no way to think of the occurrence of the messianic coming but as the occurrence of what cannot occur save in the nonoccurrence of its occurrence. The nonoccurrence in no way effects the belief in the possibility of the eruption of the future; on the contrary, insofar as that eruption cannot transpire in time except as what has not yet transpired, the nonoccurrence is, strictly speaking, what guarantees its occurrence.

Let me conclude this chapter by mentioning Heidegger's utilization of the trope of the river in Hölderlin to present an alternative to the metaphysical representation of space and time in quantifiable terms. The river yields a different way to conceptualize the spatial and temporal coordinates, the former referred to as locality (*Ortschaft*) and the latter as journey (*Wanderschaft*). The belonging together of space and time implied in this symbol accounts for the four-dimensional world of nature, that is, time as the fourth dimension added to the three dimensions of space.[95] For my purposes, I wish to emphasize that the image of the river—rendered poetically as the locality of journeying that is the journeying of locality[96]—conveys the paradoxical nature of time as the ephemerality that endures as the endurance that is ephemeral: "Time causes the passing away of what must pass away, and does so by passing away itself; yet it itself can pass away only if it persists throughout all the passing away. Time persists, consists in passing. It is, in that it constantly is not."[97] Heidegger refers to this as the "representational idea of time that characterizes the concept of 'time' which is standard throughout the metaphysics of the West." In my judgment, the poetic view of time he elicits from Hölderlin does not escape from this paradox—the image of the river communicates the idea of persisting through passing and passing through persisting, the conjunction of stasis and motion: "Time in its timing [*Zeitigend*] removes us into its threefold simultaneity [*dreifältig Gleich-Zeitiges*], moves us thence while holding out to us the disclosure of what is in the same time, the concordant oneness [*Einigkeit*] of the has-been [*Gewesen*], presence [*Anwesen*], and the present [*Gegen-Wart*] waiting the encounter. In removing us and bringing toward us, time moves on its way what simultaneity yields and throws open to it: time-space. But time itself, in the wholeness of its nature, does not move; it rests in stillness."[98]

Most important, the confluence of the fixed and the fluid conveyed by the symbol of the river betrays a striking affinity to the Jewish sensibility that the temporal flux fosters the return of the same in which the same is the replication of difference. This paradox upholds the messianic belief that the delay of the end's materialization is what secures the potency of its constant instantiation. The continual stay of the moment, in other words, the not yet that is resolutely at hand, the tomorrow that is now because it is now tomorrow, is what eternalizes the temporal and temporalizes the eternal. The exposure in the present of the secret of the end as the end of the secret—sometimes expressed as the unveiling of the truth without a garment or as the seeing of the face without a mask—bridges the breach between past and future by imparting hope in the return of what is not to come, the quintessential event of the nonevent.

Chapter Four

BEING'S TRAGEDY

Heidegger's Silence and the Ring of Solitude

> In this the gods speak and tell of what remains in keeping it silent.
> —HEIDEGGER, *HÖLDERLIN'S HYMN "THE ISTER"*

> By death! Alive!
> Speaks true who speaks shadow.
> —CELAN, "SPEAK YOU TOO"

It is often said, and not without justification, that what was most scandalous in the Heidegger affair was his refusal to address his own moral culpability for the fidelity he showed to the Nazi party as well as the more specific failure to denounce the horrors committed against the Jews and other innocent martyrs, let alone to deal effectively with the philosophical implications of the manifestation of such pernicious evil.[1] Was this, as some have argued, a calculated and deliberate silence? Unforgivingly, Lyotard wrote that the silence of Heidegger cannot be interpreted as a kind of taciturnity that communicates more than idle chatter. It is rather "a mute silence that lets nothing be heard. A leaden silence."[2] For his part, Habermas wrote, "It is not Heidegger's 'Profession of Faith in Adolf Hitler and the National Socialist Movement' (the title under which his address to the election rally of German scholars and scientists held in Leipzig on 11 November 1933 was disseminated) that calls for a judgment by those born later—who cannot know whether in a similar situation they, too, would not have failed. What is irritating is the unwillingness and the inability of this philosopher, after the end of the Nazi regime, to admit his error with so much as *one* sentence—an error fraught with political consequences. Instead, Heidegger embraces the maxim that it is not the perpetrators but the victims themselves who are guilty."[3] Pursuing a related line of argument, Babich acknowledges that "Heidegger failed to express significant sensitivity, horror, pain, remorse; Heidegger failed to confess responsibility for and complicity with the Nazi program of exterminating Jews, the murder of the Jews."[4] Even so, she reaches a surprising conclusion that shifts the focus: "If we would condemn Heidegger it cannot be for his silence where, as the path of another inquiry would show, silence, the still point between tone (caesura) and the breath (diaresis) is the very condition of full speech and best affinity. Rather what is to be continually deplored is only ... Heidegger's silencing of the significance of the silence of other languages, of other words. Heidegger's crime then is in forgetting the resonant sense or working of affinity."[5] The most disconcerting silence to emerge from the "racist humanism" attributed to Heidegger is not his own lack of speech but his muzzling of other voices.[6]

In response to Marcuse's query why he never straightforwardly decried his connection with the Nazis,[7] Heidegger replied, "You are entirely correct that I failed to provide a public, readily comprehensible counter-declaration; it would have been the end of both me and my family. On this point, Jaspers said: that we remain alive is our guilt."[8] Invoking the comment of Jaspers shows some modicum of human decency, but, on the whole, Heidegger's retort is woefully deficient and wretchedly self-centered. The same can be said about Heidegger's remark in his 1945 ruminations on the situation in 1933:

But if indeed one wants to look for those who are guilty and judge them by their guilt: is there not also a guilt incurred by failing to do what is essential? Those who even then were so endowed with the gift of prophecy that they foresaw all that came, as it came—I was not so wise—why did they wait almost ten years before opposing the threatening disaster? Why did not those who in 1933 thought they possessed such wisdom, why did not they, especially, then arouse themselves to turn everything, from the very bottom, towards the good? To be sure—it would have been difficult to gather all capable forces; difficult, too, to gradually gain influence on the movement in its entirety and its position of power—but not more difficult than the burden that we were later forced to bear. With the assumption of the rectorate I had made the attempt to save, purify, and to strengthen what was positive. ... But it was also clear to me that first of all the positive possibilities that I then saw in the movement had to be underscored and affirmed in order to prepare for a gathering of all capable forces in a manner that would be grounded not only in the facts, but in what mattered. Immediate and mere opposition would neither have been in keeping with what was then my conviction (which was never blind faith in the party), nor would it have been prudent.⁹

Even if one were to accept that it would have been dangerous or inexpedient to criticize the party in the early stages of the movement, there is hardly any rationale for the continued refusal to speak out in candor after the Nazis were defeated. Heidegger's stubbornness lends credence to Gadamer's surmise that his silence can be explained by the fact that he felt no responsibility for the extermination of the Jews, since the revolution for which he had hoped and for which he advocated, a renewal of the spiritual and moral strength of the German people, was perverted and ultimately demolished by Hitler.¹⁰

Derrida wryly noted that Heidegger's silence on the Holocaust was "as monstrous as that about which he remained silent."¹¹ Elaborating on the point in the Heidelberg conference, Derrida opined: "For I believe that most of us are in agreement on the fact that, even if one could understand, explain, excuse the engagement of 1933 and some of the consequences that came after, in a complicated and equivocal manner, the years that followed, what is *unforgivable* (this is Lacoue-Labarthe's word), what is a 'a wound for thought,' as Blanchot says, is the silence after the war, on Auschwitz."¹² In his attempt to plumb the depth of this depravity, to heed the thundering reticence of the philosophical wordsmith, Derrida embarks on what he labels a "risky hypothesis" that it was by not speaking that Heidegger offered the possibility for others to think the unthought connection between his thought and National Socialism. Had Heidegger explicitly offered an apology for his blunders, he would have likely been absolved, and there would have been closure and less of an impetus for subsequent philosophers and intellectual historians to contemplate the affinities, synchronisms of thinking, and common roots that he might have shared with Nazism. However, the legacy of Heidegger's "terrifying, perhaps unforgivable, silence" bequeaths to us the duty of doing the work and the "*injunction* to think what he did not think."¹³ Derrida goes further and vindicates Heidegger's silence on the grounds that he "did not pretend, as it would have been easy to do, to have understood what had happened and to condemn it. I believe that, perhaps, Heidegger said to himself: I will only be able to pronounce a condemnation of Nazism if I can pronounce it in a language that would not only measure up to what I have already said, but also to what happened there. And that; he was not capable of that. And this silence is perhaps an honest way of recognizing that he was not capable of that."[14]

The reserve of Heidegger is not premeditated evasiveness but rather an earnest acknowledgment that there was nothing else he could say about the gruesomeness of the Holocaust other than the obvious rebuke. The silence, therefore, confers upon others the responsibility and necessity

of reading Heidegger as he did not read himself—at least he didn't claim to. Or perhaps he did claim to, and it is there I suppose that he thus comforted himself in his silence, that he had already said, in his way, without giving in to easy statements, what, in Nazism, was bound to be corrupted. . . . He was not able to say anything more. So it is up to us, if we want to do more than say: yes, Auschwitz, it is the absolute horror, one of the absolute horrors of human history; if we can do more, it is up to us to do it. And I believe that this injunction, it is inscribed in what is most terrifying but perhaps also most valuable as a chance in the heritage left by Heidegger.[15]

Without justifying the unjustifiable or explaining the inexplicable, I will follow in this vein and suggest that Heidegger's reluctance to address Nazism and the misery inflicted on the Jews was, at least in part, a conscious attempt to uphold what he honestly believed to be the limit of language that one must face in confronting a world in which the old gods are dead and the last god has yet to be born.[16] The "future ones" (*Zukünftigen*), he wrote in an entry from the *Schwarze Hefte*, "are difficult to recognize, especially since, if they *are* indeed such, they keep silent."[17] Heidegger is drawn to silence because it is the only acceptable call to conscience, since it alone can prepare one to listen to the stillness of the beckoning hint of the withdrawing presence of the god that is present in its absence.[18] Sounding a related note in the lecture course presented at the University of Freiburg in 1937–1938, Heidegger proclaimed in a more general way that the historical event, as opposed to its historiological recounting, is enveloped in what is inaudible to most people: "The essence of truth is a happening, more real and more efficacious than all historiographical occurrences and facts, because it is their ground. What is historical in all history comes to pass in that great silence for which man only rarely has the right ear. That we know so little or even nothing of this hidden history of the essence of truth is no proof of its unreality but only evidence of our lack of reflective power."[19]

In confronting the inscrutable, a reluctance to speak may be the only valid way of speaking. Consider the daring formulation of Samuel IJsseling: "Auschwitz is perhaps a name for this unfathomable dimension, a name that must be pronounced with the same reticence with which the Jews pronounce the name of Yahweh. But often when one speaks about Heidegger's National Socialism, there seems to be little appreciation of this absolutely unfathomable dimension."[20] To be more accurate, the tradition is that devout Jews do not pronounce the Tetragrammaton at all, and not that they pronounce it reservedly, but that only strengthens the force of the analogy, as sacrilegious as it might seem. My argument is in basic agreement as well with the supposition of Rockmore that "Heidegger kept silent about the Holocaust and Nazism in general for the reason that to do so is supposedly to engage in an authentic form of genuine discourse by maintaining the standards of rigorous thought based in silence."[21] Rockmore wonders, however, if a thought that remains silent before the Holocaust because it can neither express nor grasp the calamity of that historical event can be considered authentic or rigorous.[22] Raising such an objection fails to take seriously Heidegger's insistence that the highest form of the thinking and saying of being requires the ability to keep silent.[23] The view that speech is grounded in silence was not affirmed by Heidegger as a strategy to avoid dealing with the catastrophes of Nazism. On the contrary, the latter lent further credence to a philosophical position that he cultivated independently.

De Beistegui has argued similarly that Heidegger's silence bespeaks not an insufficiency of thinking but the only ethical response capable of harboring the horror of the Shoah, an episode so singular in its victimization of the other that one can speak of it only through language imbued with silence, a language that repudiates the prospect of language.[24] In that respect, Heidegger's steadfast refusal to speak of the matter corresponds to the recurrent emphasis in his thinking regarding silence as the ground of language, as speech in the most originary sense. To sharpen this stance, it will be beneficial to contrast it to the position recently advanced by Trawny. Conceding the possibility that Heidegger's thinking moved "in domains in which there was hardly anything left to think," and thus was disposed "to say what need not have been said," Trawny avers that the limit (*Grenze*) that must be interrogated after the publication of the *Überlegungen*, the "dividing line" (*Grenzscheide*), is not the unsayable—the border of speech or the limit to thinking, the other side of which is nonsense (*Unsinn*), as Ludwig Wittgenstein expressed it[25]—but rather the crossroads (*Scheideweg*) where the sheath (*Scheiden*) separates good and evil, fostering the "difference" (*Unterschied*) that is the "decision" (*Entscheidung*).[26] I would respectfully counter that the limit of language is indeed the issue at hand, for that limit is the differentiating point that demarcates the borderline between being and nonbeing. Trawny seems closer to the point when he noted that Heidegger believed his thinking more generally—and not only his attitude toward the Jews—needed to be concealed from the public because it culminated at the edge of silence and stillness and therefore could not be divulged without the expectation of misunderstanding.[27]

Elsewhere I have discussed the matter of apophasis in Heidegger's thought, especially as it relates to his notion of poiēsis when compared to the kabbalistic approach to language.[28] The point to emphasize here is that Heidegger's lack of an adequate verbal reply to his compliance with Nazism may be a genuine application of his belief that, just as we cannot comprehend a thinker's thought unless we are attuned to the unthought (*das Ungedachte*)[29]—an attunement that involves dialogue (*Zwiesprache*) with the thinker that is not to be conceived historically if the latter is construed chronometrically[30]—so we cannot truly listen to a word that is spoken unless we hearken to the unspoken (*das Ungesprochene*). Every interpretation, Heidegger assures us, is a dialogue with a particular work or a saying contained therein, but the dialogue is pointless if it is confined to what is directly said rather than leading the interlocutors to the realm and abode of the unspoken.[31] Heidegger's perspective is captured adroitly in the following comment by Arendt in the address she offered to celebrate his eightieth birthday: "Moreover, thinking, as Hegel, in a letter to Zillmann in 1807, remarked about philosophy, is 'something solitary,' and this not only because I am alone in what Plato speaks of as the 'soundless dialogue with myself' (*Sophist* 263e), but because in this dialogue there always reverberates something 'unutterable' which cannot be brought fully to sound through language and articulated in speech, and which, therefore, is not communicable, not to others and not to the thinker himself. It is presumably this 'unsayable,' of which Plato speaks in the Seventh Letter, that makes thinking such a lonely business and yet forms the ever varied fertile soil from which it rises up and constantly renews itself."[32] As she expressed the matter in *The Human Condition*, "only solitude can become an authentic way of life in the figure of the philosopher, whereas the much more general experience of loneliness is so contradictory to the human condition of plurality that it is simply unbearable for any length of time and needs the company of God, the only imaginable witness of good works, if it is not to annihilate human existence altogether."[33] Arendt perceptively notes the link between the essence of thought as what cannot be spoken and the existential solitariness the thinker will endure, but she also correctly understood that ineffability is the quality that inspires new responses: there is no end to speaking the unspeakable. In the domain of philosophy, as opposed to the social arena of theopolitics, the yoke of solitude is the womb that bears the possibility of deep relationality.

Already in a section from *Sein und Zeit*, Heidegger avers that to keep silent is an "essential possibility of discourse." Understanding is not facilitated by speaking excessively, speaking minimally, or by keeping silent, but only by genuine discourse that comes about through authentic silence. "In order to be silent, Dasein must have something to say, that is, must be in command of an authentic and rich disclosedness [*Erschlossenheit*] of itself.... As a mode of discourse, reticence [*Verschwiegenheit*] articulates the intelligibility of Dasein so primordially that it gives rise to a genuine potentiality for hearing and to a being-with-one-another that is transparent."[34] In *Die Grundbegriffe der Metaphysik*, Heidegger extends the argument by noting that philosophizing can be considered as "something living only where it comes to language and expresses itself, although this does not necessarily imply 'communicating itself to others.'" Quite to the contrary, "once philosophizing is expressed, then it is exposed to misinterpretation, and not merely that misinterpretation which lies in the relative ambiguity and unreliability of all terminology; rather it is exposed to that essential *substantive misinterpretation* for which *ordinary understanding* inevitably falls."[35]

The philosopher is encumbered by the inevitability of misinterpretation, but it is also a badge of honor that every philosophical saying contains what is unsaid. Heidegger thus began "Platons Lehre von der Wahrheit," a text composed in 1940 on the basis of the notes for the lectures on the essence of truth offered in the winter semester of 1931–1932, by contrasting scientific knowledge (*Erkenntnisse der Wissenschaften*) as that which is "expressed in propositions and is laid before us in the form of conclusions that we can grasp and put to use," and the doctrine of a thinker (*Denker*) as "that which, within what is said, remains unsaid [*Ungesagte*], that to which we are exposed so that we might expend ourselves on it."[36] Of course, as Heidegger immediately adds, to experience and to know what a thinker left unsaid demands that we have to consider what has been said. Nevertheless, the mandate is not to attend exclusively to the said, which is hard enough, but to the unsaid in the said, the silence at the heart of all that is spoken. In *Vom Wesen der Wahrheit* (1933–1934), Heidegger writes, "*The ability to keep silent is therefore the origin and ground of language* [Das Schweigenkönnen ist also der Ursprung und Grund der Sprache]. All speaking is a breach [*Unterbrechung*] of keeping silent, a breach that does not have to be understood negatively."[37] The reasoning behind such a claim is inherently paradoxical or, in Heidegger's idiom, circular: "This circularity makes itself known now in that we are supposed to speak about keeping silent—and this is highly problematic. For whoever discourses about keeping silent is in danger of proving in the most immediate way that he neither knows nor understands keeping silent."[38]

The seemingly intractable snare of the apophatic need to speak about not speaking is exemplified in poetic language. "If indeed we consider such language," writes Heidegger, "in terms of its capacity for expression, then it is here precisely not supposed to express anything, but to leave the unsayable unsaid [*das Unsagbare ungesagt*], and to do so in and through its saying."[39] Again, we note that with respect to poetizing and, by extension, language more generally, there is a commingling of the apophatic and the kataphatic: precisely through the act of saying, the poet leaves the unsayable unsaid, not by not speaking but by speaking-not, that is, saying the unsayable in the unsaying of the sayable. Heidegger relates this to another central motif on the path of thinking concerning the concealment and veiling that are proper to the manifestness of beings that is the essence of truth as unconcealment (*alētheia*):

The mystery is not a barrier that lies on the other side of truth, but is itself the highest figure [*höchste Gestalt*] of truth; for in order to let the mystery truly be what it is—concealing preservation of authentic beyng [*verbergende Bewahrung des eigentlichen Seyns*]—the mystery must be manifest as such. A mystery that is not known in its power of veiling is no mystery. The higher our knowing concerning the veiling and the more genuine the saying of it as such, the more untouched its concealing power remains. Poetic saying of the mystery is *denial* [*Verleugnung*].[40]

To speak of the mystery as the highest configuration of truth means that every act of unconcealing is at the same time an act of concealing: what is exposed is the hiddenness of the exposure. The mystery (*das Geheimnis*) is thus defined as the *concealing preservation of authentic beyng*, that is, the withholding of being that is proper to the bestowal of being. For this mystery to be revealed as mystery, it must be revealed in its veiling power (*verhüllenden Macht*). Translated into the linguistic register, to speak of the mystery presumes the concealing power (*verbergende Macht*) that precludes the mystery from being spoken. The disclosive utterance is itself a veiling (*Verhüllung*), and in that sense, the poetic saying necessarily is a repudiation of what is said.

The essential origin of language is the ability to keep silent. Consider this striking meditation in the *Beiträge* on restraint (*Verhaltenheit*), silence (*Schweigen*), and language (*Sprache*):

Words fail us; they do so originally and not merely occasionally, whereby some discourse or assertion could indeed be carried out but is left unuttered, i.e., where the saying of something sayable or the re-saying of something already said is simply not carried through. Words do not yet come to speech at all, but it is precisely in failing us that they arrive at the first leap. This failing is the event as intimation and incursion of beyng. This failing us is the inceptual condition for the self-unfolding possibility of an original (poetic) naming of beyng.[41]

Heidegger's notion of ineffability does not imply the saying of the unsayable, if the latter is understood as something potentially sayable that is presently not spoken. What he proposed rather is the unsaying of the sayable, which is to say, the belief that every utterance falls short of articulating the words that have yet to assume the character of speech, but this failure is precisely what makes possible the poetic naming of being. Insofar as the naming cannot be severed from the nameless that defies naming, the mystery to which language can only allude, the apophatic and the kataphatic are inextricably conjoined. Thus, in a second passage from the *Beiträge*, Heidegger expounded the theme of "Beyng and its bearing silence" (*Das Seyn und seine Erschweigung*), which he calls "sigetics" (*die Sigetik*):

Bearing silence is the prudent lawfulness of the silence-bearing activity.... Bearing silence is the "logic" of philosophy inasmuch as philosophy asks the basic question out of the other beginning. Philosophy seeks the *truth of the essential occurrence* of beyng, and this truth is the intimating-resonating concealment (the mystery) of the event (the hesitant withholding).... Bearing silence arises out of the essentially occurring origin of language itself.[42]

In yet another passage from the *Beiträge*, Heidegger explains that every language of Dasein is, in essence, silence, insofar as it originates in the turning (*Kehre*), or the counterturning (*Wider-kehre*), of the event that occurs "in between the call (to the one that belongs) and the belonging (of the one that is called).... *The call* to the leap into the appropriation is the great stillness of the most concealed self-knowledge."[43]

To keep silent, therefore, is not related to the muteness (*Stummheit*) of the animal or to the absence of language (*Sprachlosigkeit*),[44] but rather to what Heidegger still considered to be the linguistic capacity unique to the human being; indeed, the "saying that bears silence is what grounds."[45] Interpreting the parable of Jesus that invokes the birds of the air and the lilies of the field (Matthew 6:26–28; Luke 12:24–27), Kierkegaard similarly observed: "For surely it is speech that places the human being above the animal, and if you like, far above the lily. But because the ability to speak is an advantage, it does not follow that there is no art in the ability to keep silent, or that it would be an inferior art. On the contrary, precisely because a human being has the ability to speak, for this very reason the ability to keep silent is an art; and precisely because this advantage of his tempts him so easily, the ability to keep silent is a great art."[46] Heidegger would not have tempered his anthropocentric bias on the basis of the parabolic invocation of the bird and the lily as the "silent teachers" who can instruct us about silence, nor would he have welcomed the theological belief that being silent and becoming nothing are the beginning of seeking God's kingdom.[47] In the main, however, Heidegger's insistence that diffidence is a mode of the ability to talk and not merely the negation (*Negativum*) of not talking (*Nichtreden*) or saying nothing is in accord with Kierkegaard. Silence is, more precisely, the "not-talking of someone who can talk," which is to say, a deliberate act of "being unwilling to talk." Hence, "by keeping silent we are often able to say something much more definite than by the most longwinded talking."[48]

BEING'S TRAGEDY

For Heidegger, the truism that "every truth has its *time*" implies that "it is a sign of education to withhold certain truths from knowledge and to keep silent about them. Truth and truth is not simply the same [*Wahrheit und Wahrheit ist nicht einfach dasselbe*]."[49] Could this *fundamental mood of reticence* (Grundstimmung der Verschwiegenheit), this *nonessence of language* (Unwesen der Sprache),[50] the letting go of representational thinking and the adoption of an imageless saying of nothing responding to the silent call of being,[51] not provide a clue to understand—even if not to defend—Heidegger's own implacable silence? This silence is equivalent to what Heidegger elicits from the lines in George's poem "Das Wort," "So I renounced and sadly see: / Where word breaks off no thing may be" (*So lernt ich traurig den verzicht: / Kein ding sei wo das wort gebricht*): the nondenial of self (*Sich-nicht-versagen*)—or the nonself denial—that instigates the poet's owning of self (*Sich-verdanken*) is expressed in the saying (*Sagen*) of thanking (*Dank*), which is the gesture of renunciation (*Verzicht*), as opposed to a refusal (*Absage*), indebted to the original utterance of the mystery of the word (*Geheimnis des Wortes*).[52]

Support for this conjecture may be elicited from the following passage in the 1943 postscript to *Was ist Metaphysik?* (1929): "Thinking, obedient to the voice of being, seeks from being the word through which the truth of being comes to language. Only when the language of historical human beings springs from the word does it ring true. Yet if it does ring true, then it is beckoned by the testimony granted it from the silent voice of hidden sources. . . . The saying of the thinker comes from a long-protected speechlessness and from the careful clarifying of the realm thus cleared."[53] An echo of the Parmenidean correlation of being and thought is discernible here, but with the emphasis placed squarely on speech as the medium through which the truth of being is manifest. However, this truth rings true only when the language of Dasein's historicity springs from that voice of being, and this, in turn, is imparted by the guarded speechlessness whence the utterance of the thinker arises. Returning to this theme in "Die Sprache" (1950), Heidegger notes that the human being can be said to speak insofar as his speech corresponds to language (*Der Mensch spricht, insofern er der Sprache entspricht*), but that correspondence must be in the form of listening (*Das Entsprechen ist Hören*), and there is no listening unless it "belongs to the behest of silence" (*dem Geheiß der Stille gehört*).[54]

The matter is repeated apodictically in a lecture delivered during the summer semester of 1952 at the University of Freiburg and eventually included in *Was Heißt Denken*? "Every primal and proper identification states something unspoken, and states it so that it remains unspoken."[55] In *Aus einem Gespräch von der Sprache*, written in 1953–1954 on the occasion of a visit by Tomio Tezuka (1903–1983) of the Imperial University of Tokyo,[56] the Japanese interlocutor asserts that dialogue should have "a character all its own, with more silence than talk," to which the Inquirer (an obvious literary cipher for Heidegger) responds, "Above all, silence about silence," which is marked as the "authentic saying" (*eigentliche Sagen*) and the "constant prologue to the authentic dialogue *of* language" (*stete Vorspiel zum eigentlichen Gespräch* von *der Sprache*).[57] In the words of Hölderlin cited by Heidegger in "Das Wesen der Sprache" (1957–1958), "This is a law of fate, that each shall know all others, / That when the silence returns there shall be language too" (*Schiksaalgesez ist diß, daß Alle sich erfahren, / Daß, wenn die Stille kehrt, auch eine Sprache sei*).[58] Perhaps even more relevant is the articulation of this theme in the 1959 lecture "Der Weg zur Sprache," arranged by the Bavarian Academy of Fine Arts and the Academy of Arts in Berlin:

To say [*Sagen*] and to speak [*Sprechen*] are not identical. A man may speak, speak endlessly, and all the time say nothing [*nichtssagend*]. Another man may remain silent, not speak at all and yet, without speaking [*Nichtsprechen*], say a great deal [*viel sagen*]. . . . Language first of all and inherently obeys the essential nature of speaking: it says [*das Sagen*]. Language speaks by saying [*Die Sprache spricht, indem sie sagt*], that is, by showing [*zeigt*]. What it says wells up from the formerly spoken [*gesprochenen*] and so far still unspoken Saying [*ungesprochenen Sage*] which pervades the design of language. . . . In our speaking [*Sprechen*], as a listening [*Hören*] to language, we say again the Saying we have heard. We let its soundless voice [*lautlose Stimme*] come to us, and then demand, reach out and call for the sound that is already kept in store for us.[59]

Just as in the case of language, the saying, which involves a "listening to the unspoken," corresponds to what is said, so too, silence, which is regarded as the "source of speaking," corresponds to the "soundless tolling of the stillness of appropriating-showing Saying [*lautlosen Geläut der Stille der ereignend-zeigenden Sage*]."[60] On the one hand, the saying cannot be captured in any verbal statement (*Aussage*); it demands that "we achieve by silence the appropriating, initiating movement [*ereignende Be-wëgung*] within the being of language [*Sprachwesen*]—and do so without talking about silence."[61] On the other hand, the renunciation (*Verzicht*) of speech—typified by the poet's relinquishing having words under control—is not just a "rejection of Saying" (*Absage an das Sagen*), or a lapse into "mere silence" (*bloßes Verstummen*), for, as self-denial (*Sichversagen*), the renunciation remains a Saying (*Sagen*) and thus "preserves the relation to the word" (*Verhältnis zum Wort*).[62] Elucidating the line from Hölderlin's "Heimkunft/An die Verwandten," "Often we must be silent; holy names are lacking" (*Schweigen müssen wir oft; es fehlen heilige Nahmen*), Heidegger offers a distilled summary of his own thinking about speech, speechlessness, and the unspoken: "Silence [*Schweigen*]—does this merely mean: to say nothing [*nichts sagen*], to remain speechless [*stumm*]? Or can only he who has something to say be truly silent? If this were the case, then he would be capable of letting the unsaid [*das Ungesagte*] appear in his speech, of letting it appear as unsaid, would, precisely through this alone, be capable of silence in the highest degree."[63]

It seems plausible that Heidegger's own silence is indicative of this twofold admonition: only by not speaking could he properly speak, only by heeding the silent voice could he respond to and thereby resay what could be heard from the saying, a word always spoken as unspoken and unspoken as spoken.[64] I would suggest that this sentiment is also underlying the passage cited in chapter 2 where he confirmed that the bloodshed of the Second World War was an illustration of the incongruous excess of evil and willfulness[65] that arose from the "nonessence of Beyng" (*Unwesen des Seyns*), also referred to as the "a-nihilation" (*Ver-nichtung*) of the "forgottenness of Being" (*Vergessenheit des Seins*) and as the "nihilating of memory" (*Nichten des Gedächtnisses*) in the event of appropriation.[66] The silence is commensurate to the horridness of the Holocaust, which is a symptom of what Hölderlin called a caesura, a radical break in history that comes about from the separation of God and human.[67]

In what undoubtedly must be considered a great incongruity, Heidegger's explanation for the evil of the Holocaust demonstrates an uncanny resemblance to one of the central doctrines of the kabbalah, first enunciated in the zoharic literature and then amplified by later kabbalists, regarding the realm of impure forces known collectively as the Other Side (*siṭra aḥara*).[68] Broadly speaking, the kabbalists oscillate between a dualistic and a monistic perspective. According to the former, the force of evil on the left constitutes a parallel realm that is antagonistic to the force of good on the right, and thus the goal must be its eradication. According to the latter, since the darkness emanates from the light and is not ontologically independent, the ideal is restoration. Logically, it would seem that the monistic model is more consistent, for even the dualistic-minded kabbalists view the unholy as originating in the holy—or, to be more precise, in the aspect of the divine that precedes the division into holy and unholy, identified variously as the *Ein Sof* itself, the *sefirah* of *Keter*, or the *parṣuf* of *Arikh Anpin*, the place where impurity does not reach inasmuch as it is transposed into its opposite—and hence the task should be reintegration and not elimination. Of the many sources that could have been cited to illustrate the point, I will mention here a lucid account offered by the Lithuanian kabbalist Solomon ben Ḥayyim Eliashiv (1841–1926). Referring to a passage in Zohar 3:133a (*Idra Rabba*), Eliashiv emphasizes that purification consists of the amelioration of the force of unholiness in its source so that the imperfection (*qilqul*) is turned into the rectification (*tiqqun*) and the transgression (*pesha*) transposed into the overflow (*shefa*). The transposition is epitomized in the verse "Who can produce a clean thing out of an unclean one" (Job 14:4), that is, the impure is itself transmuted into purity. This metamorphosis is possible only if we assume that in the infinite opposites can no longer be discriminated as opposite, that is, the opposites coexist as nonoppositional. In the same passage, however, Eliashiv reflects the tension that can be traced to kabbalistic sources from the twelfth and thirteenth centuries, insofar as he speaks of both the destruction of evil and its containment in the higher source where the binary is overcome.[69]

Irrespective of how we account for the etiology of the Other Side, the crucial point is that this mythical construct provides a psychological rationale to accept the presence of evil as an inescapable potency in history, rendered theosophically as the overabundance of judgment unmitigated by the counterbalancing force of grace. The shadowy element—whence the demonic comes to be—is not the privation of light but a smokescreen through which the light dissimulates as darkness. In what is perhaps one of the boldest expressions of the archetypal symbol, kabbalists identify the root of judgment—that which initiates the first contraction (*ha-ṣimṣum ha-ri'shon*) within infinity—as the capacity for limit lodged in the heart of the limitless, the potential for differentiation within indifference, the point imprinted in the pointless.[70] This nucleus whence the worlds are created is referred to—in the Sarugian version of Lurianic kabbalah[71] and in later Sabbatian sources[72]—by the technical designation *malkhut de-ein sof*, the kingship of the infinite, the source whence emerge the Edomite kings, who reigned before the kings of Israel, that is, judgment that precedes mercy, the shell that precedes the fruit.[73] Translated into Heideggerian parlance, the evil of the Other Side is the willful manifestation of the nonessence that belongs to the essence of being, the event of appropriation, which comprises the inexpressible that is expressive of the essentially tragic nature of being. In Heidegger's mind, likely influenced by Schelling's tragic absolute,[74] the tragedy necessitates that philosophical knowledge is only for the rare individuals who possess the courage to accept the inevitable ruin of Dasein.[75] As he elaborates in one of the diary entries from the late 1930s:

Beyng itself is "tragic"—i.e., it begins out of the downgoing qua abyss and tolerates such beginnings only as that which does justice to its truth—the knowledge of beyng is therefore always reserved to the unique ones and specifically to those of them that *necessarily* must remain unrecognizable in all historiological cognition. The limit even of genuine historical meditation therefore does not lie in the extent of the capacity for confrontation—but in the essential misrecognition which spreads over those unique ones, expanding out from a determinate circle of solitude.[76]

The passage is too intricate to unpack fully, but the strategic point is that Heidegger offers an explanation of his own retreat from and reticence with regard to the political,[77] based on the premise that being itself is inherently tragic—Das Seyn *selbst ist »tragisch«*—because the beginning is marked by a downfall (*Untergang*) and the abyssal withdrawal from the ground (*Abgrund*), and therefore knowledge thereof is reserved for the unique ones (*Einzigen*), who are unrecognizable (*Unerkennbaren*) by the metrics of historiographical knowledge (*historischen Bekanntheit*), and, even from the standpoint of historical meditation (*geschichtlichen Besinnung*), these rare individuals, who belong to a circle of solitude (*Ring der Einsamkeit*), are marked not by the capacity for confrontation (*Aus-einander-setzung*) but by an essential misrecognition (*Verkennbarkeit*).[78]

Expanding this Heideggerian insight, Schürmann noted that the "urgent task for thinking" is "to better know the tragic condition. To learn to love it."[79] On this score, Heidegger's alignment with Hitler marked the tragic denial of the awareness of the tragic nature of being, an alienation from alienation, an appropriation without expropriation.[80] Heidegger's thought here is indebted to Schelling's discussion of the possibility of the "absolute Being of absolute identity" becoming other and thereby manifesting itself as God. The freedom to do evil, which is essential to creation, has its roots in the othering of self that proceeds from the tension between the "inner ground" (*innern Grund*) and the "existence" (*Existenz*) of the One.[81] For Schelling, God alone—the one who exists (*Er selbst der Existirende*)—dwells in pure light (*reinen Lichte*), since God is the only being that is self-begotten (*sich selbst*), but the ground from which the beings that are distinguished from God emerge—the ground that is in God but not God himself—is identified as the darkness (*Dunkel*) that is the necessary inheritance of finite creatures.[82] Moreover, the possibility of evil with regard to divinity has to be assessed from the vantage point that God is not a system but a life—*Gott selbst ist kein System, sondern ein Leben*—and, insofar as all existence demands a condition of delineation so that it may become real, God's luminal existence, too, could not be real—that is, God could not assume the actuality of the absolute personality—without the condition of darkness, which does not come from God but is necessary for his existence.[83]

As Heidegger discerningly explicated Schelling's view, we should not think

> the essential project of the movement of becoming [*Werdebewegtheit*] of the Absolute in such a way that initially there is only a ground and then existence accrues to it from somewhere. Rather, both are in their own way the whole, but they are not simply simultaneous in the Absolute. Their duality [*Zweiheit*] erupts directly from the neither-nor [*Weder-Noch*] of absolute indifference [*absoluten Indifferenz*]. This primordial duality becomes an opposition [*Gegensatz*] only when the will of love enters the decidedness of being absolutely superior and lets the ground be ground. If opposition is not at all primordially "there" by itself in the Absolute, then the opposition of good and evil is certainly not there which first comes about when the creator drives himself out [*heraustreibt*] into the particularity [*Eigenheit*] of created spirit, and human freedom is realized.[84]

The becoming of the creator as an expulsion from the absolute indifference—the nonground that is neither good nor evil but the disjunction in virtue of which both are equivalent or indifferent, *gleichgültig*, literally equally valid[85]—to the differentiated selfhood is mirrored in human freedom and the becoming of the finite self. From both processes of individuation we can deduce that unity is manifest through dissonance, and thus Heidegger applies to Schelling the dictum of Heraclitus, "strife is the basic law and basic power of Being [*Grundmacht des Seyns*]. But the greatest strife is love because it arouses the deepest discord in order to be itself in conquering it."[86]

I have investigated Schelling's thought, and particularly the affinities between the indifference (*Indifferenz*) of the *Ungrund* and the equanimous oneness (*aḥdut ha-shaweh*) of the kabbalistic *Ein Sof*, elsewhere.[87] Suffice it to say at this juncture that, like the kabbalists, Schelling sought to explain the paradox of an all-encompassing One longing to give birth to itself as what is other than itself by positing a nonessence (*Nicht-Wesen*)—being in the other rather than being in itself[88]—that is coeternal with but not identical to the essence, "that which in God himself is not *He Himself*" (*was in Gott selbst nicht Er Selbst ist*).[89] The indifference of the Absolute—as opposed to nondifferentiation—thus entails the opposition of coincidence rather than the coincidence of opposition; that is, the infinite is marked by an irreducible duality (*Dualität*), doubling (*Doppelheit*), or twofoldness (*Zweiheit*)—mathematically formulated as A + B—the two principles predicated as the nonopposites (*Nichtgegensätze*) that precede the polarization into opposites and the concomitant need to efface the difference between them in the dialectical identity of the identity of nonidentity and the nonidentity of identity.[90] The critical point for our purposes is that Schelling—in a manner that resonates with kabbalistic theosophy—assumed that the pure Godhead betrays the equally primal propulsion of the masculine to bestow the self onto the other and the compulsion of the feminine to retract the self from the other,[91] the eternal Yes and the eternal No.[92] The darkness thus coexisted indivisibly with the light in the indifferent oneness of the infinite as the nonbeing of being that resists sublation into the being of nonbeing.

Heidegger was acutely influenced by Schelling's locating the origin of evil in the ground of the nonground, the force of contraction that complements the force of expansion. As Heidegger summarizes Schelling's view:

Creation is self-presentation emerging from itself in the ground. Creation presupposes the will to self-revelation [*Selbstoffenbarung*] (existence) [*Existenz*] and at the same time that in which it presents itself as in another. This other is the ground, the basis. Letting the ground operate is necessary in order that a creator be able to be a creature. Of course, the Absolute makes the ground independent of its self its own. The creature, on the other hand, never gains complete control over the ground. It shatters itself upon it and remains excluded from it and thus burdened by its gravity.... What comes from the mere ground does not come from God. But evil is the insurrection of the ground's craving [*Aufspreizung der Sucht des Grundes*], as the ground not to be one condition, but the sole condition. Because evil comes from the ground, the ground, however, belongs to the essence of beings [*Wesen des Seienden*], evil is posited in principle with the Being of beings [*Seyn des Seienden*]. Where beings as a whole are projected in the jointure of Being [*Gefüge des Seyns*], where system is thought, evil is included and implicated.[93]

From the divine perspective, the inherently tragic nature of being—the inclusion and implication of evil in the being of beings when the latter are projected as a whole in the jointure of being—serves as the source for the "eternal joy of overcoming," but, from the creature's perspective, it is experienced as the "veil of dejection [*Schleier der Schwermuth*] that is spread over all nature, the deep indestructible melancholy [*tiefe unzerstörliche Melancholie*] of all life."[94] The distinction notwithstanding, Schelling insists that even for human beings joy must have suffering, and the task is to transfigure that suffering in joy.[95] In Heidegger's rendition in the aforecited passage from the notebooks,[96] the melancholic tragedy of the ground's recoiling from the ground—reminiscent of what Hegel tellingly described as the nocturnal point of contraction[97]—is mirrored in the individual's flight from the sociopolitical arena. The knowledge of being, consequently, is limited to the individuals who remain faithful to the truth of the cataclysmic beginning and can make peace with it. Such individuals are neither recognized by the calculative nature of historiographical knowledge nor by the meditative nature of historical contemplation. Their mission is not to be sought in the ability to confront the other, but to accept the essential misrecognition that ensues from living and thinking within the ring of solitude.

In another passage from the *Schwarze Hefte*, Heidegger reiterates that the "tragic" arises out of the downfall because it assumes the task of grounding (*Gründerschaft*) in the groundless abyss (*Ab-grund*), that is, the task to ground in the absence of all grounds. The comprehension (*Auffassung*) of the tragic—obtained through the "traversal [*Durchmessung*] of its respective essential depth [*Wesenstiefe*]"—is "determined by what the tragic itself has at any time acquired of the truth of beyng [*Wahrheit des Seyns*]." Hence, the tragic is "a preeminent assignment [*ausgezeichnete Zugewiesenheit*] of the human being to the essential occurrence of beyng, in accord with the current openness of the human being for what is essential." The essential core of anything tragic demands the "unclosedness toward what is question-worthy [*Ent-schlossenheit in das Fragwürdige*]."[98] In the *Beiträge*, Heidegger noted that the age of machination is characterized by the "complete absence of questioning," which destroys all solitude. This intolerance of anything questionable can be overcome "only by an *age of that simple solitude* in which a readiness for the truth of beyng itself is prepared."[99] As Heidegger would later put it in the first lecture course he gave after a hiatus that extended from 1944 to 1951, the way of thinking (*Denk-Weg*) proceeds by a "thoughtful questioning" (*denkende Fragen*), a movement (*Be-wegung*) that is part of the "precursoriness [*Vor-läufigkeit*] of thinking," which "in turn depends on an enigmatic solitude [*rätselvollen Einsamkeit*]. . . . No thinker ever has entered into another thinker's solitude. Yet it is only from its solitude that all thinking, in a hidden mode, speaks to the thinking that comes after or that went before."[100] The paradox of thinking as a social gesture propagated in isolation is captured brilliantly in this passage: thinking wells forth from a place of solitude so overwhelming that Heidegger insists categorically that no thinker has ever entered into another thinker's solitude, but it is precisely from that place of ontological aloneness—which is to be distinguished from the ontic feeling of loneliness[101]—that the individual thinker becomes part of a community that cuts across the divide of time, relating to what has been thought in the past and what will be thought in the future.

The following comment about the task of the poet could very well be applied to Heidegger himself:

The poet—Hölderlin—stands here in solitude, and he is driven even further back into his solitude if he is now made to be timely "in the course" of "cultural politics"—without our meditating on what it is *poets* are to accomplish—; the aspect of Hölderlin's works that is richest in suggestion is therefore: the poetizing about the poet [*die Dichtung des Dichters*]. But who could fathom this without at the same time radically experiencing the plight of the abandonment by being [*Seinsverlassenheit*]? What will happen if out of this deepest ground we do not become ones who ground the overcoming [*Überwindung*] of the ground? If we do not become open and trusting enough to accomplish both: this that is most originary *and* the first step in the mastery of the immediate afflictions?[102]

In emulation of his poetic exemplar—the one whose poetry is characterized as the "first overcoming" of metaphysics[103]—Heidegger is driven deeper into solitude when confronted with the trials and tribulations of *Kulturpolitik*. Furthermore, I would suggest that he took his cue from Hölderlin and from this point forward he imagined that the main objective of his own thinking was to poeticize about poetics. This task, which can be assumed only by one who experiences the abandonment of being intensely, is also referred to paradoxically as grounding the overcoming of the ground.

One must also not forget that Heidegger, building on a passage from the pseudo-Aristotelian *Problemata*,[104] accepted the inherent connection between melancholia and creativity. To be more precise, Heidegger identifies creative achievement as a "free formative activity," but freedom is found only when there is a burden that weighs so heavily that the overall mood of the person is consumed with melancholy. Heidegger relates this general observation to the particular case of philosophy: "As a creative and essential activity of human Dasein, philosophy stands in the *fundamental attunement of melancholy* [Grundstimmung der Schwermut]. This melancholy concerns the form rather than the content of philosophizing, but it necessarily prescribes a fundamental attunement which delimits the substantive content of philosophical questioning."[105] It is reasonable to infer from these words that, for Heidegger, a vital component of the disconsolate state linked to philosophical ingenuity is the sense of subjectivity consigned to the silence of solitude, especially when in converse with other human beings. The disaffection signifies the surging rather than the ebbing of the vitality of selfhood, an occlusion that results in a more authentic display of originality and resourcefulness.[106]

Here it is useful as well to recall the remark of Rosenzweig that the "distinctive sign" of the self, the "seal of its greatness, and the mark of its weakness" is that "it is silent." The tragic hero, therefore, "has only one language that is in perfect accordance with him: precisely, silence.... By being silent, the hero dismantles the bridges that link him to God and the world, and he tears himself away from the landscapes of personality, which, through the spoken word, marks out its limits and individualizes itself in the face of others in order to climb into the icy solitude of the Self. For the Self knows nothing outside itself; it is quite simply solitary."[107] This conception of solipsism is surely objectionable on the grounds that, as Maurice Merleau-Ponty observed, solitude and communication are not "two terms of an alternative, but rather two moments of a single phenomenon." Just as reflection must always present the unreflected, so the experience of self must always present the experience of others, and if this were not the case, one could not even speak of solitude and declare the other inaccessible.[108] My sense of the other is not an inference based on perceptual or cognitive judgment, but rather part of the warp and woof of the very being of coexistence that shapes our social world, an experience of alterity that is prior to the division of experience into subjective and objective.[109] I submit that Heidegger, in spite of his emphasis on the phenomenological dimension of *Mitsein*, would have found common cause with Rosenzweig's account of the tragic hero and his escape into the solitude of silence.[110] The plausibility of this comparison is strengthened by Walter Benjamin's interpretive gloss in the *Ursprung des deutschen Trauerspiels* on Rosenzweig's observation: "Yet tragic silence, as presented in this important description, must not be thought of as being dominated by defiance alone. Rather, this defiance is every bit as much a consequence of the experience of speechlessness as a factor which intensifies the condition."[111] Far from being an act of insolence or frailty, speechlessness is a gesticulation of moral rectitude.

I propose that from this essentially reclusive manner of being underway (*unterwegs*) on the path of thought we can deduce an answer to the query that has been raised numerous times: why would Heidegger never candidly renounce his wrongdoing? Heidegger's lack of response could be explained—even though not justified—by the avowal of the disavowal concerning our ability to speak of the unspeakable misfortune. The Nazi cruelty was a specific cultural-historical instantiation of the intrinsic tragedy of existence. Heidegger tendered the question, does silence (*Verschweigung*) belong essentially to the tragic, the gift (*Geschenk*) for those who in their own time are futural (*Zukünftigen*)?[112] The answer is a definitive yes. However we psychoanalyze Heidegger's megalomania, he seems to have fancied himself as one of those individuals whose knowledge of being persuaded him not to confront opponents in the political arena but to retire into seclusion where he could ostensibly persevere in the silent detachment of meditative contemplation envisioned as pious gratitude, the thinking that is a mode of thanking the *es gibt* of being, the giving that gives without the willful subjectivity of giver or recipient.

Chapter Five

POLITICAL DISAVOWAL
Truth and Concealing the Unconcealment

> Man is the one who honors, and consequently also the one who denies, truth.
> —HEIDEGGER, *NIETZSCHE: THE WILL TO POWER AS KNOWLEDGE AND METAPHYSICS*

> All the truth in the world adds up to one big lie.
> —BOB DYLAN, "THINGS HAVE CHANGED"

Support for the conjecture with which I ended the previous chapter is to be found in Heidegger's emphasis on the inseparability of truth and untruth, a premise that is linked to his assumption that every disclosure is a concealment, every protraction is a retraction. Many have discussed these themes,[1] but not in the context of assessing his political thought, and especially as this dynamic relates to his Nazism. I shall approach the topic by discussing Heidegger's interpretation of Plato's allegory of the cave in the *Republic*, which he undertook in at least three different occasions, the lecture course *Vom Wesen der Wahrheit: Zu Platons Höhlengleichnis und Theätet* in the winter semester of 1931–1932; the lecture course *Vom Wesen der Wahrheit* in the winter semester of 1933–1934; and the essay "Platons Lehre von der Wahrheit," written in 1940 but based on the notes from the earlier lectures. In the ensuing analysis I will draw compositely upon all three texts, but, in the first instance, the focus will be on Heidegger's remarks in the section on the philosopher as liberator (*Befreier*) from the second of the aforementioned sources. Interpreting the fourth and final stage in the occurrence of truth (*Wahrheitsgeschehen*) from Plato's allegory, Heidegger focuses on the insistence in the *Republic* (516e 3–517a 6) that the one who ascends from the darkness of the cave to the daylight must descend back into the cave to assist in the liberation of the others who remain imprisoned, even though some of them would surely wish to slay such a person:

> The *killing* consists in the fact that the philosopher and his questioning are suddenly transferred into the language of the cave dwellers, that he makes himself ridiculous before them, that he falls prey to public ridicule. Therefore it belongs to the essence of the philosopher that he is *solitary* [einsam]; it lies in his way to be, in the position he has in the world. He is all the more solitary because in the cave he cannot retreat. Speaking out from solitude, he speaks at the decisive moment. He speaks with the danger that what he says may suddenly turn into its opposite. Nevertheless, the philosopher *must* climb down into the cave, but not in order to get into debates with the cave dwellers there, but only in order to seize this or that person whom he thinks he has recognized and lead him up the steep path, not through a one-time act but through the happening of history itself.[2]

Those who dwell in the cave, unlike the enlightened who escape, cannot recognize the *shadows as shadows* and hence the unconcealment (*Unverborgenheit*) of which they are capable covers up (*verdeckt*) the real unconcealment of light, the agency that alone can expose the shadowy nature of the shadow. For the prisoners, the shadows appear to be truth, what is unhidden (*Unverborgene*, Heidegger's translation of Plato's τὸ ἀληθές), but, in truth, they do not even see the shadows, since they do not apprehend either the things of which the shadows are shadows or the fire in whose luminosity the shadows are cast; indeed, they are altogether unaware of the distinction between light and darkness.[3]

The cave dweller is in a state of delusion, *Einsichtslosigkeit*, literally, lacking insight, the term that Heidegger deploys to render the Greek ἀφροσύνη, the counterconcept to φρόνησις or σωφροσύνη, Plato's words for knowledge. In the absence of *phronēsis*, everything is shadowlike (*schattenhaft*), and "there is no relationship to the *genuinely* true and unhidden."[4] By contrast, the liberator "is someone who has become free in that he looks into the light, has the illuminative view [*Lichtblick*], and thus has a surer footing in the ground of human-historical Dasein. Only then does he gain power to the violence [*Gewalt*] he must employ in liberation [*Befreiung*]." The violence, Heidegger is quick to explain, is not blind caprice or some kind of crudity, but it is rather the noble duty of dragging others into the light.[5] "The liberated one [*Freigewordene*] returns to the cave with an eye for *being*. . . . This means that he who has been filled with the illuminating view for the being of beings will make known to the cave-dwellers his thoughts on what *they*, down there, take for beings."⁶ The philosopher accomplishes this by staying true to his view of the essence (*Wesenblick*) and by disclosing to those in the cave their mistaking the shadow for being. By uncovering the shadow as shadow, the one who is emancipated reveals that the "unhidden is such that, precisely in its showing, the beings hide themselves;"⁷ that is, what is disclosed is the concealment that conceals itself in its disclosure. Consequently, an antagonism (*Gegeneinanderauftreten*) inescapably ensues between what is manifest (*Offenbaren*) for the enlightened and what is cloaked (*Verdeckenden*) for the unenlightened—the self-showing of the shadows (*Sich-zeigen der Schatten*) is exposed as a form of occlusion, but "the manifestness of beings occurs only through the *overcoming* [Überwindung] of concealing. Truth, therefore, is not just unhiddenness of beings such that the previous hiddenness is done away with, but the manifestness of beings is in itself necessarily an overcoming of a concealment."⁸ To overcome concealment, however, the concealment must be concealed, but if the concealment is concealed, the concealment inevitably would not be overcome.

In Heidegger's eccentric interpretation of Plato, to apprehend the ideas means "setting beings free" by "wrenching beings from hiddenness and overcoming their concealment." If one were to regard the ideas "as just beings of a higher order," then the deconcealment would not have occurred. From this vantage point, the liberator is the "bearer of a *differentiation* [Unterscheidung]," since he distinguishes not only between being and beings—an obvious allusion to what Heidegger later calls the ontological difference—but also between being and appearing, the unhidden and what conceals itself in the self-showing, truth and untruth. And yet the discernment of the divergence is coupled with a sense of co-belonging (*Zusammengehörigkeit*): "Only on the basis of the divorce between the true and the untrue does it become clear that the essence of truth as unhiddenness consists in the overcoming of concealing, meaning that unhiddenness contains an essential *connection* with hiddenness and concealing. . . . Untruth *belongs* to the essence of truth [*Zum Wesen der Wahrheit* gehört *die Unwahrheit*]."⁹ The belonging-together of truth and untruth as disparate implies that the surmounting of concealment happens only through a "primordial struggle against hiddenness," a struggle that entails the "*bridging over*

[Brückenschlagen] of each *towards* and *against* the other."¹⁰ As Heidegger emphasized in the 1933–1934 lectures, the philosopher realizes that "liberation cannot lead to some tranquil enjoyment and possession outside the cave, but that unconcealment happens in history, in the constant confrontation [*Auseinandersetzung*] with the false and with semblance. This leads to the fundamental insight that there is no *truth in itself* at all, but instead, truth *happens* in the innermost confrontation with *concealment* in the sense of *disguise* and *covering up*. . . . Man exists in the truth and in the untruth, in concealment and unconcealment *together*."¹¹

Turning the traditional reading of Plato's allegory of the cave on its head, Heidegger extrapolates from the text the view that emancipation occurs within the muddle of history and not by escaping to a suprasensible realm of ideas, the world of eternal forms. There is no truth but the truth that arises from friction with the semblance of truth. However, inasmuch as every person exists as part of a "historical people in community" (*geschichtliches Volk in der Gemeinschaft*), the human condition is such that there can be no semblance of truth without untruth, no access to reality (*Wirklichkeit*) without the deception (*Täuschung*) of appearance (*Schein*). The "struggle for truth" (*Kampf um die Wahrheit*), therefore, must always be a "confrontation with untruth" (*Auseinandersetzung mit der Unwahrheit*).¹² Untruth can be understood as not-truth (*Nicht-Wahrheit*) but this does not necessarily imply falsity (*Falschheit*).¹³ To grasp the essence of truth as unhiddenness requires inquiring into the untruth, and this comes about only by assuming the posture of an attack (*Angriff*), taking a stand against the enemy (*Feind*).¹⁴ But what is the nemesis of truth? Not untruth as the negation of truth but the concealment of the concealment, the hiddenness of beings that opposes truth as the unhiddenness of being.¹⁵ Through this struggle we ascertain that untruth "is not an opposite that occurs alongside (next to truth), and that must *also* and subsequently be taken into account, but the *one* question concerning the essence of truth is *in itself* the question concerning the essence of *un*-truth, for this latter belongs to the *essence* of truth."¹⁶ To attain release from being shackled to the shadows, one must be prepared to confront such resistance. The ascent from the cave thus demands violence and will likely cause strain and suffering.¹⁷

A more elaborate interpretation of the allegory of the cave, focusing on the themes of education (*paideia*) and truth as unhiddenness (*alētheia*), was offered by Heidegger in "Platons Lehre von der Wahrheit." In that context he emphasizes as well the inversion of the more predictable way to interpret Plato: "Liberation does not come about by the simple removal of the chains, and it does not consist in unbridled license; rather, it first begins as the continuous effort at accustoming one's gaze to be fixed on the firm limits of things that stand fast in their visible form. Authentic liberation is the steadiness of being oriented toward that which appears in its visible form and which is the most unhidden in this appearing. Freedom exists only as the orientation that is structured in this way."[18] Deliverance from the shadowy world of appearance comes about through disclosure of the essence of truth as unhiddenness. Truth is not the "agreement of the representation in thought with the thing itself" (*adaequatio intellectus et rei*),[19] but rather the unearthing that renders accessible whatever appears and keeps it revealed in its appearing. As Heidegger put it in the lectures from 1931–1932, the notion of truth as correctness of assertion (*Richtigkeit der Aussage*)—that is, the correspondence of idea and object—is itself grounded in the more rudimentary notion of truth as the unhiddenness of beings (*Unverborgenheit des Seienden*).[20] The idea conveyed by Heidegger is not easy to express, as it impinges on the domain of the unsayable. Every act of revealing is a concealing, for the veil cannot be unveiled unless it persists in being veiled. The utterance of truth, on this score, is not a verbal enunciation but the holding silent (*Stille halten*) that is the most propitious and attentive response to the event of being.[21] Truth is thus the mystery of the unconcealing of the concealment,[22] the opening that overcomes the hiddenness of the hidden, that is, the exposure of there being nothing but the exposure that is exposed. This is the import of Heidegger's remark, "The unhidden must be torn away from a hiddenness; it must in a sense be stolen from hiddenness" (*Das Unverborgene muß einer Verborgenheit entrissen, dieser im gewissen Sinne geraubt werden*).[23] The complete removal of all hiddenness foreshadows the awareness that there is nothing to illumine but the shadow, that the unconcealment of truth is the limit of vision.

To be sure, following Plato's narrative, Heidegger describes the ascent from the cave as a progressive adaptation of vision from darkness to light, culminating in seeing the light of the sun itself, which is to say, "to see the sun as what *gives* the light, as what gives *time*, as what *rules over* everything, and which is the ground even of what is seen in the *cave*, of the shadows and the light and the fire."[24] The language here should not obfuscate Heidegger's effort to infer the unthought from what is overtly thought in the Platonic dialogue rather than to examine its surface meaning; indeed, he states explicitly that it does not help to inquire about how Plato himself would have interpreted the allegory.²⁵ What concerns him, and what drives his philological exegesis, is to determine hermeneutically what the allegory is *saying* (*was* sagt), that is, what does the text mean for Dasein and its relation to truth as unhiddenness?²⁶ The emancipating vision consists of seeing through the shadowy character of the cave existence by perceiving the light, the highest idea of the good (ἰδέα τοῦ ἀγαθοῦ), but Heidegger proffers an idiosyncratic explanation of the Platonic ἰδέα (or εἶδος) as the "*look* [Anblick] of something *as* something. It is through these looks that individual things *present* [präsentiert] themselves as this and that, as *being-present* [anwesend]. Presence [*Anwesenheit*] for the Greeks is παρουσία, shortened as οὐσία, and means *being* [Sein]. That something *is* means that it is present [*es ist anwesend*], or better: that it *presences* [*es* west an] in the present [*Gegenwart*]. The look, ἰδέα, thus gives *what* something presences *as* [als was *ein Ding anwest*], i.e. what a thing *is*, its being [*sein* Sein]. . . . Understanding what such things mean is nothing else but the seeing of the look, the ἰδέα. In the idea we see *what* every being is and *how* it is, in short the *being* of beings [*das* Sein *des Seienden*]."²⁷

Heidegger creatively extracts from—or, if you prefer, confers upon—the quintessentially metaphysical notion of the Platonic ideas, which are located outside the cave in a noetic place (τόπος νοητός), that is, a place perceived by the mind (νοῦς) through nonsensory seeing,²⁸ his own postmetaphysical notion of being, the grounding event that makes present the being of everything that presences in the present but that cannot itself be represented as presence. This is the intent that Heidegger ascribes to Plato's referring to the ideas as τὸ ὄντως ὄν, "the being which has being [*das seiendlich Seiende*]—the being which is *in the way* that only beings can *be*: *being* [*das* Sein]."²⁹ To perceive the idea, for Heidegger, is not to contemplate an eternal form but rather to understand the being of beings, to know what belongs to a being and its unhiddenness.³⁰ This "most beingful being" (*seiendste Seiende*), the what-being (*Was-sein*) of that which genuinely exists,³¹ is identified as well as the brightness (*Helle*) and transparency (*Durchsichtigkeit*) of the light (φῶς), which Heidegger emphatically states is "not a thing, neither a property of any kind of thing . . . nothing which can be grasped hold of; it is something *intangible* [Unfaßliche], almost like nothingness [*Nichts*] and the void [*Leere*]."³² The seeing of the idea means, therefore, comprehending the being that allows beings to be recognized as the beings they are, the being that cannot be thingified, the being that is most suitably compared to nothingness and the void, the transparent light that has the character of going-through, spreading-out, and opening-up, as distinct from the staying-back and impenetrability of darkness.³³ In this regard, truth belongs most appropriately to the ideas, for they "are the most unhidden, the essentially unhidden, the primordially unhidden, because the unhiddenness of beings *originates* in them."³⁴ The ideas are the light that ensures that the concealed will become visible, and thus what is most meaningful about the ideas—their essence as truth in removing hiddenness—is their being, that which *lets beings through*, that is, the passage (*Durchlaß*) that countenances the disclosing of what is most disclosive and the lighting of what is most illuminative.³⁵ Liberation consists in the event of deconcealment (*Entbergsamkeit*), the removal of concealment, looking into the light, becoming-free (*Frei-werden*) by binding oneself (*Sich-binden*) to the ideas, letting *being* take the lead (*dem Sein die Führung überlassen*).³⁶ The essence of being human—the ground of Dasein—is to be the being that lets being be in the unhiddenness of beings, a task that is best enacted in philosophical work.³⁷ Heidegger thus translates Plato's definition of the philosopher in the *Sophist* (254a 8–b 1) as "someone concerned with perceiving [*Er-blicken*] and constantly thinking [*be-denkend*] the being of beings [*des Seins des Seienden*]."³⁸

Reiterating this insight in "Platons Lehre von der Wahrheit," Heidegger notes that the idea is the "visible form that offers a view of what is present" (*die Aussicht in das Anwesende verleihende Aussehen*), a pure shining (*reine Scheinen*) that does not let something else other than itself shine, that is, the reflexivity that shines a light on the shining of the light, the shining that is concerned only with the shining inasmuch as what shines in the shining is the shining of the shining. "The ἰδέα is that which can shine [*das Scheinsame*]. The essence of the idea consists in its ability to shine and be seen [*Schein- und Sichtsamkeit*]. This is what brings about presencing [*Anwesung*], specifically the coming to presence of what a being is in any given instance. A being becomes present in each case in its whatness [*Was-sein*]. But after all, coming to presence is the essence of being."³⁹ The seeing of this shining—casting light on the shadow so that one apprehends the shadow as light—is the upshot of the hiddenness being exposed in the unhiddenness of the unhiddenness. When the enlightened person returns to the cave, a battle will be waged because the prisoners unfailingly resist liberation.

In the lectures from 1931–1932, Heidegger emphasized that "the philosopher exposes himself to the fate of death in the cave." The death of which he speaks is not necessarily physical demise but rather the "forfeiture and rendering powerless of one's own essence." Indeed, Heidegger goes so far as to say that the powerlessness that the philosopher must confront in the spatiotemporal world is a death that is more "actual" (*wirkliche*).[40] And yet, the philosopher must appropriate that death and not withdraw from the cave. "Being-free, being a liberator, is to act together in history with those to whom one belongs in one's nature. He must remain in the cave with the prisoners, and with those who count down there as philosophers."[41] Although the philosopher by nature is solitary, the isolation should not lead to retreat from social responsibility. Thus, in "decisive moments" (*entscheidenden Augenblicken*), the philosopher must be there (*da sein*) and not give way (*nicht weichen*).[42] Having seen through the shadows, not as the adumbration of light but as the radiance itself, the task of the thinker is to disclose the disclosure by exposing the shadowiness of the shadow and thereby remove the illusion that there is reality behind the appearance. Near the conclusion of the lecture "Die Zeit des Weltbildes" (1938), Heidegger reiterated the point: "Everyday opinion sees in the shadow merely the absence of light, if not its complete denial. But, in truth, the shadow is the manifest, though impenetrable, testimony of hidden illumination. Conceiving of the shadow this way, we experience the incalculable [*Unberechenbare*] as that which escapes representation [*Vorstellung*], yet is manifest in beings [*Seienden*] and points to the hidden being [*Sein*]."[43]

That the shadow manifest in beings points to the hidden being should not be understood in metaphysical terms but rather as an undermining of the clear-cut distinction between appearance and reality. As Heidegger expressed the matter in the notes for his seminar on Nietzsche's *Vom Nutzen und Nachteil der Historie für das Leben* (1874), offered in the winter semester 1938–1939 in Freiburg: "Thus 'being' is *in itself equivocal*; it is its own mask, one thing stands for another, essentially a blend; the same holds for 'appearance'; being and appearance are always *intrinsically* blended together and, as such, in their blending are essentially related to each other. The blending itself of what is already intrinsically blended is what first constitutes—even preceding it—the 'playing' of the world game."[44] The mission of disclosing the shadow as the secreted illumination rather than the absence of light—the mask of the face that is its own mask—can only be accomplished with violence inasmuch as it goes against the nature of the cave dwelling wherein philosophy and the truth—the exposure of the untruth of the truth—are not accorded priority. Heidegger, no doubt, saw himself as the liberated prisoner, and thus he was committed to speak out of solitude only at decisive moments, all the while fearful that whatever he would say was likely to be turned into its opposite. If he had the presence of mind to articulate this trepidation during the time he was the rector and publicly supported Hitler, surely he would have been all the more apprehensive to speak at later stages of the war and after it ended in defeat.

Further corroboration for my surmise may be culled from the third of the dialogues included in the *Feldweg-Gespräche*, an imaginary conversation set in a prisoner-of-war camp in Russia and signed May 8, 1945, roughly the time that the Germans surrendered to the Western Allies and the Soviet Union. In response to the younger man's query about the possibility of recuperation, the older man asserts, "in order to comprehend what has become healing for you, I would have to know what is wounded in you. And what is not all wounded and torn apart in us?—us, for whom a blinded leading-astray of our own people is too deplorable to permit wasting a complaint on, despite the devastation that covers our native soil and its helplessly perplexed [*ratlose*] humans."[45] The allusion in this passage is obvious: Heidegger acknowledges that the acts of the Nazis were so revolting that one is not even permitted to grumble about the current bewilderment and aimlessness of the German people. The possibility for recovery seems so remote, given the fact that the Germans are "all wounded and torn apart." Heidegger's uncommunicativeness likely reflects an inner conflict, but, even more tellingly, it may represent putting into practice his contention that the situation was too deplorable to validate uttering a complaint verbally, not because of a paucity of words but because the surfeit of words is precisely what is deficient.

In an aphorism from *Aus der Erfahrung des Denkens* (1947), which begins with the depiction of a nocturnal winter storm followed by the morning landscape hushed in a blanket of snow—a metaphor that conveys the natural beauty of the bucolic setting and the moral desolation of the cultural terrain—Heidegger poetically captured the invariable deficiency of language: "Thinking's saying would be stilled in its being only by becoming unable to say that which must remain unspoken [*ungesprochen*].... What is spoken is never, and in no language, what is said [*Nie ist das Gesprochene und in keiner Sprache das Gesagte*]."[46] Philosophical poiēsis is a form of discourse that is a "saying not-saying" (*sagenden Nichtsagens*),[47] a paradoxical formulation that entails both that what is said is never quite what is spoken and that what is spoken is never quite what is said. Given the *Zeitgeist* of Nazi Germany and the postwar years, that Heidegger would have transferred this understanding of language to the political arena should come as no surprise.[48] Related to the question of Heidegger's apolitical politics, that is, the politics of political disavowal, I further presume that the conception of language as a gesture of unsaying engendered a form of esotericism, amplified by the assumption that there is no disclosure that is not concurrently a concealment, no laying bare of truth that is not entwined with untruth, no clearing of the path that is not suffused with the wreckage of the way.

The hermeneutical basis for the entanglement of truth and untruth was laid by Heidegger well before the war, as is attested in the following passage from the essay "Vom Wesen der Wahrheit" (1930): "Considered with respect to truth as disclosedness [*Entborgenheit*], concealment [*Verborgenheit*] is then un-disclosedness [*Un-entborgenheit*] and accordingly the un-truth [*Un-wahrheit*] that is most proper to the essence of truth [*Wahrheitswesen*]."[49] What Heidegger is enunciating here is his signature idea that the disclosure (*Entbergung*) of beings is simultaneously and intrinsically the concealing (*Verbergung*) of beings. "In the simultaneity [*Zugleich*] of disclosure and concealing, errancy [*Irre*] holds sway. Errancy and the concealing of what is concealed belong to the originary essence of truth."[50] Inasmuch as truth is the unveiling of what remains veiled, truth cannot be disentangled from untruth, and hence the concealing of the concealed is disclosed in the concealment of the disclosure. Momentously, Heidegger applied the mystery of errancy—the principle that freedom arises from the essential counteressence to the originary essence of truth—to the political and historical situation of Nazi Germany. Thus, he portentously wrote in *Logik als die Frage nach dem Wesen der Sprache* (1934):

Every era has its unessence [*Unwesen*], its unhistory [*Ungeschichte*]. That must be so. No light is without shadow. However, who sees only the shadows and is horrified by that has not comprehended the light. To the towering height belongs the crash. History is no obstacle-free stroll into the future.... The unessence has the peculiarity that it does not let the essence arise; that it, however, itself tries to erect by itself the semblance [*Schein*] of an essence. The unessence would be a matter of indifference, not worth the effort and easily visible at a glance, if unessence were similar in meaning with non-essence [*Nichtwesen*]. However, unessence is always the semblance of the essence, and it appeals to our craving for recognition, bewitches what we do and do not do, even with seemingly good intention. So also is true leadership [*Führung*] falsified, which then spreads as leading astray [*Verführung*].[51]

Conventionally, the expression *Unwesen* denotes mischief or nuisance, that is, an unbalanced behavior that disturbs or deforms the essential order of things and brings about a dreadful state of affairs. However, Heidegger uses it—perhaps inspired by the language of Eckhart, which he creatively misconstrues[52]—to denote the sense of de-essentialization, the withholding sway of the nonground, the ownmost singularity that is neither present nor absent, the essence that resists essentializing.[53] Bret W. Davis adroitly renders *Unwesen* as the "originary dissonant excess ... that could neither be wholly eradicated from the would-be pure tonality of a univocal origin, nor dialectically sublated into the redemptive harmony of an absolute identity."[54] To comprehend fully Heidegger's use of the term, one must be aware of the fact that he conserves something of the negative implication of its more mundane connotation, which he relates to the need to acknowledge the presence of evil in the world.

A crucial stage in his thinking about this topic can be adduced from the 1936 interpretation of Schelling's *Freiheitsschrift*, a careful analysis of which sheds light on his support of National Socialism. Heidegger extracts from Schelling's thought the supposition that our freedom "is not the decidedness [*Entschiedenheit*] for good or evil, but the decidedness for good and evil, or the decidedness for evil and good. This freedom alone brings man to the ground of his existence in such a way that lets him emerge at the same time in the unity of the will to essence [*Wesen*] and deformation of essence [*Unwesen*] aroused in him. This aroused will is spirit, and as such spirit history."[55] I submit that this is an exceptionally important passage as it articulates that human freedom entails the will to essence and nonessence, the polarity of good and evil. The essential relation of these two primal inclinations of the will implies, first, that "the presentation of appearing evil becomes at the same time the presentation of appearing good" and, second, that the concluding part of the statement, "the form of evil is in itself the form of evil and good," does not signify "an ethical, moral unity as if each time the other were only what should and should not be. Rather, appearing, emerging into beings as beings, evil in human being is at the same time an appearance of the good and vice-versa."[56] The portrayal of the nonground (*Ungrund*) as that which posits an opposition of coincidence in opposition to the coincidence of opposition, is an idea that is reminiscent of Jacob Böhme's positing of the equally omnipotent and conflictual forces of wrath and love in the divine essence,[57] which, in turn, may reflect kabbalistic teaching.[58] Be that as it may, the principle was articulated forthrightly by Schelling in *Philosophie und Religion* (1804), "It is true that ... much is already gained by having the negative, the realm of nothingness, separated from the positive realm of reality by an incisive boundary [*schneidende Gränze*] since the former could only emanate from it after this separation. Whoever holds that good can be recognized without evil commits the greatest of all errors, for in philosophy, as in Dante's poem, the path toward heaven leads through the abyss [*Abgrund*]."[59]

Heidegger is creatively modulating the "terrible solitude" of God that is at the heart of Schelling's *Naturphilosophie*. As Schelling put in the third and longest version of *Die Weltalter*:

If we take into consideration the many terrible things in nature [*Natur*] and the spiritual world [*Geisterwelt*] and the great many other things that a benevolent hand seems to cover up from us, then we could not doubt that the Godhead [*Gottheit*] sits enthroned over a world of terrors [*Welt von Schrecken*]. And God, in accordance with what is concealed in and by God [*und Gott nach dem, was in ihm und durch ihn verborgen ist*], could be called the awful [*Schreckliche*] and the terrible [*Fürchterliche*], not in a derivative fashion, but in their original sense.[60]

Strikingly, the Godhead is depicted as being enthroned over a world of terrors, but, even more dauntingly, Schelling notes that the adjectives *awful* and *terrible* can be ascribed to the divine in virtue of the negative force—a kind of dark matter—that is concealed in and by him. In the first draft of *Die Weltalter*, Schelling already spoke of the primordial being's "stultifying solitude" (*schreckliche Einsamkeit*), whence we can deduce that the divine "must fight its way through chaos for itself, utterly alone."[61] In Heidegger's translation, the negativity with which being is permeated is this dissonant surplus, the nonessence that inessentially belongs to the essence.[62] As he puts it in the *Beiträge*, "Only because beyng essentially occurs in this manner does it have nonbeing [*Nichtsein*] as its other, for this other is the other of itself. *Insofar as beyng essentially occurs as permeated with negativity, it at the same time makes possible and compels otherness.*"[63]

The sense of alterity (*Andersheit*) is the "other of itself," the otherness rooted in the uniqueness of the appertaining not (*zugehörigen Nicht*) that is the uniqueness of the other emerging from, and therefore contained within, the uniqueness of being. "The one *and* the other compel for themselves the either-or [*Entweder-Oder*] as first."[64] We grant that the first will be marked by either-or, *the one and the other*—a point that is consistent with Schelling's idea of the duality or doubling connected to the indifference of the infinite, as we discussed in the previous chapter—but how are we to make sense of the assertion that the *other is other of itself*? In what way does this constitute a legitimate sense of alterity? Can we attribute an other of itself whose otherness would not be assimilated in the identity of that self? The conjunctive *and* connotes not the juxtaposition of the different but the apposition of the same. It is at this point of unintelligibility—the unknowing that is inherent to knowing—that Heidegger draws the vital distinction between the old metaphysical thinking and the new path of inceptual thinking. The general and vacuous distinction of the one and the other is an outcome of the correlationist reasoning[65] regarding the something (*Etwas*) and the not-something (*Nicht-Etwas*) that has informed the Western metaphysical interpretation of beingness (*Seiendheit*) as ἰδέα from the Parmenidean standpoint of the equation of being and thinking. But the "not" of this negation of something—the nothingness (*das Nichts*)—is "likewise representationally groundless and empty."[66]

On the basis of these philological insights, history is portrayed as the struggle between essence and unessence, good and evil, light and shadow, preeminence and the pedestrian. Moreover, the unessence is distinguished from nonessence, since the former presents itself as the semblance of essence whereas the latter is the eradication of essence. As Heidegger formulates the principle, "Everything great and essential—and this belongs to its essence—always has beside it and before it its non-essence [*Unwesen*] as its semblance [*Scheinbares*]."[67] The unessence is the unhistorical dimension of history, if by "unhistorical" one means the negative energy that is in perpetual strife with the positive energy. To comprehend the light, one must not be dismayed by the shadows; there can be no scaling of the heights without plunging to the depths. Heidegger thus fatefully warned that true leadership invariably will be falsified and then dispersed as that which will lead others astray. Is it not reasonable to detect in these words a grim warning about the potential abuses of the Führer that were soon to become all-too-real?[68]

In the final analysis, Heidegger politically disavows the political out of the conviction that the political is rooted in and symptomatic of the historical destiny of being that is greater than—and consequently determinative of—every particular political movement.

> The desire to battle politically against political worldviews [*politischen Weltanschauungen*], indeed the desire to burden them with accidental and isolated misgivings, means to misunderstand that in them something is happening of which they themselves are not the master and of which they are only the driven and shackled exporters. This something is the abandonment by being [*Seinsverlassenheit*], an abandonment relegated to beings by beyng itself; in other words, it is the concealed refusal of the beginning and of the site of the originary decisions.... Therefore, meditation [*Besinnung*] would never think to take seriously the everyday, myopic objections against those political movements—as little as meditation can accept their accompanying "fanatical" affirmation ... as evidence of their *essential* truth.[69]

All that transpires politically is expressive of the primordial abandonment, the concealed refusal of the beginning, and thus one given to meditating on the greatness that pertains to the decision for or against being, which is always manifest through the mystery of language, adopts a dispassionate attitude to the political movements that shape the quotidian struggle for socioeconomic power.

If my hypothesis concerning Heidegger's appraisal of the political environment is plausible, then we can view it as an application of his hermeneutical assumption that untruth is an indispensable dimension of truth. In the sixth volume of the *Schwarze Hefte*, Heidegger writes that there is no pure essence of truth "because truth is always also untruth, such that something individual does not remain equal to it and precisely then least of all when it is a matter of seizing its full essence (which includes its distorted essence [*Unwesen*])."[70] The essence encompasses the unessence just as truth always includes untruth. Heidegger concludes the 1933–1934 lectures with a penetrating musing on "the essence of truth as historical man's struggle with untruth" (*Das Wesen der Wahrheit als Kampf des geschichtlichen Menschen mit der Unwahrheit*): "The *essence of truth* is the *struggle* with *untruth*, where *untruth* is *posited with the enabling of the essence of truth*. This struggle, as struggle, is always a specific struggle. Truth is always truth *for us*."[71] But how does Heidegger understand the nature of that struggle? In the continuation, he reaffirms the main theme of the rectoral address: the distinguishing feature of being human is that we are historical (*geschichtlicher*); that is, each of us "exists in the togetherness of a historical people [*im Miteinander eines geschichtlichen Volkes existiert*], with a specific *historical mission* [geschichtlichen Auftrag], and exists in the preservation of the forces that carry him forward and to which he is bound. . . . This fundamental constitution [*Grundverfassung*] is the *domain* [Bereich] within which the *struggle for the truth* [Kampf um die Wahrheit] must play itself out."[72]

Surely, the struggle of which Heidegger speaks is a clash that can be pursued only by one of a resilient comportment capable of confronting the untruth essential to the truth, the shadow that envelops the light. Heidegger thus poses the question whether the people (*Volk*), i.e., the German people, "is strong enough—whether it, in itself, has the will to itself, to stand up to the will of its own essence. It means asking whether we will grapple with this, whether we will take on as our task this knowing and will to know in their full intensity and hardness, or whether we are of the opinion that culture and spiritual life [*Kultur und Geistesleben*] are a supplement that produces itself by itself, while we look on as if it were a game."[73] The struggle is a battle for the heart of the culture and the spirit of the nation and not for geopolitical dominance, let alone the state-sponsored slaughter of millions driven by racial chauvinism and intolerance. Heidegger writes with a palpable moralistic tenor:

So we stand or fall by the *will to knowledge and spirit* [Wille zu Wissen und Geist]. Today, there is much talk of *blood and soil* [Blut und Boden] as forces that are frequently invoked. The literati, who are still around even today, have seized upon these forces. Blood and soil are indeed powerful and necessary, but they are *not sufficient* [nicht hinreichende] conditions for the Dasein of a people. Other conditions are *knowledge and spirit*, but not as an addendum to a list. Knowledge first brings a direction and path to the blood's flow, first brings to the soil the fecundity of what it can bring to term. Knowledge lets the nobility of the soil yield what the soil can bring to term.[74]

The greatness (*Größe*) of the Germans—both in terms of blood and soil—is dependent on the decision (*Entscheidung*) to create their destiny (*Schicksal*) based on prioritizing knowledge and spirit. However, insofar as this decision is made in freedom, one must be prepared to expose oneself to the danger of one's Dasein.[75]

Dasein's being, its sense of freedom, is made possible by the inexorability of the wayward, "the errancy-fugue of the clearing," which commences from and is sustained by the interplay of concealment and unconcealment in the guise of truth as the concealing of the concealment.[76] This is the import of Heidegger's remark that serves as the epigraph of chapter 1 of this book, "He who thinks greatly must err greatly" (*Wer groß denkt, muß groß irren*).[77] Thinking occurs in the clearing that is always also obfuscation, the "placelessness of error, a landscape of placelessness, an a-topography, which appears as a 'fugue' or 'conjuncture' [*Fuge*]."[78] As the clearing concomitantly opens and closes, so the conjuncture conjoins and divides and thereby enables the conjoined structure within which the appropriative event of truth eventuates as the straying of thought into the place of error, the place that is placeless, the place from which one is continually displaced. The homecoming to this place of displacement is facilitated by cultivating the mood of shyness (*die Scheu*), which, as opposed to bashfulness (*die Schüchternheit*), is not indicative of faintheartedness, fearfulness, or insecurity, but it is rather the resolve of keeping-to-oneself (*Ansichhalten*) that fosters the decisiveness to be patient. In what I consider a remarkably important passage, written in 1942, Heidegger thus concludes: "Shyness attunes the course toward poetic paths. Shyness determines that one go to the origin. It is more decisive than all violence."[79]

On one of the rare instances when the matter of the Holocaust was addressed by Heidegger, we see the degree and depth of his lingering insensitivity. In the 1949 Bremen lectures, he remarked: "Agriculture is now a mechanized food industry, in essence the same as the production of corpses in the gas chambers and extermination camps, the same as the blockading and starving of countries, the same as the production of hydrogen bombs."[80] The context for this comment is Heidegger's contrasting the peasant's tending to the field and the utilitarian proclivity, which he calls "requisitioning" (*Bestellen*).[81] The admittedly problematic estrangement from the earth, attested in the bulk production of food, is compared to various forms of technologically induced violence against humanity, including the mass murder of millions of innocent souls under the Nationalist Socialist regime.[82] One can appreciate the rationale that led Heidegger to link together the different items in this list—in his mind, economic exploitation and technological conquest are the two predominant manifestations of the spiritual deterioration of Western civilization exemplified by America and Russia.[83] The logic of his analogical thinking has merit, but his words still bespeak a callous incapacity to comprehend the magnitude of the brutality perpetrated by the Germans singularly against the Jewish people.[84] The same can be said about the following comment in *Was Heißt Denken?*:

What did the Second World War really decide? (We shall not mention here its fearful consequences for my country, cut in two.) This world war has decided nothing—if we here use "decision" in so high and wide a sense that it concerns solely man's essential fate on this earth. Only the things that have remained undecided stand out somewhat more clearly. But even here, the danger is growing again that those matters in this undecided area which are moving toward a decision, and which concern world government as a whole—that these matters, which now must be decided, will once again be forced into politico-social and moral categories that are in all respects too narrow and faint-hearted, and thus will be deprived of a possible befitting consideration and reflection.[85]

Heidegger's impassive and abstract mode of expression—even if we grant the veracity of the substance of some of his claims—exhibits an astonishing tone-deafness to the uniqueness of Jewish suffering at the hands of the Germans that intimates the collapse of the most elementary sense of empathy and civility. The parenthetical remark is so emotionally obtuse that it does not warrant any response.

However, it is worth ruminating over a second passage from the Bremen lectures where Heidegger alludes again to the genocide of the Jews: "Hundreds of thousands die in masses. Do they die? They perish. They are put down. Do they die? They become pieces of inventory of a standing reserve for the fabrication of corpses. Do they die? They are unobtrusively liquidated in annihilation camps. And even apart from such as these—millions now in China abjectly end in starvation."[86] Bracketing the curious reference at the end to the starvation of millions in China, it is obvious that the primary focus in this passage is the hardship of the Jewish victims slaughtered in the extermination camps (*Vernichtungslagern*). Three times Heidegger poses the question whether these victims died, a rhetorical ploy meant in its own feeble way to honor the martyred souls by driving home the point that they were not accorded the chance "to carry out death in its essence," which is only possible "when our essence is endeared to the essence of death." That essence is disguised by the mass production of corpses. For Heidegger, death is neither the "empty nothing" of nihilism—at least as it is commonly conceived—nor the "transition from one existence to another" of certain religious beliefs. Rather death belongs to Dasein "*as appropriated from the essence of beyng.* Thus death harbors the essence of beyng. Death is the highest refuge [*Gebirg*] of the truth of beyng itself, the refuge that in itself shelters [*birgt*] the concealment [*Verborgenheit*] of the essence of beyng and gathers together the sheltering [*Bergung*] of its essence. Thus the human is first and only capable of death when beyng itself from the truth of its essence brings the essence of the human into the ownership of the essence of beyng."[87]

According to the Heideggerian analytics of *Existenz*, for the human to exist in the most exact sense is to be in the manner that Dasein is, which is to say, to be the being constituted by the absolute contingency of the not yet of one's mortality; as being-toward-death (*Sein zum Tode*), the being that is always already ahead of itself, we appear to be the sole species mindful that the only permanence is impermanence. I will cite here one passage from the *Beiträge* that addresses the point. After asserting that the being-toward-death in *Sein und Zeit* was "thought only within 'fundamental ontology' and never conceived anthropologically or in terms of a 'worldview,'" Heidegger recasts the earlier discussion in light of his current thinking about the appropriating event of *Ereignis* as the truth of being:

The uniqueness [*Einzigkeit*] of death in human Da-sein belongs to the most original determination of Da-sein, namely, to be ap-propriated [*er-eignet*] by beyng itself in order to ground this latter in its truth (openness of self-concealing). In the unusualness and uniqueness of death, what opens up is the most unusual amid all beings, beyng itself, which essentially occurs as estrangement [*Befremdung*]. Yet in order to surmise anything at all of this most original nexus ... what had to be made visible first ... is the relation of Da-sein to death itself, i.e., the connection between resoluteness (openness) and death, i.e., the running ahead [*Vor-laufen*]. Yet this running ahead toward death is not to be made visible for the sake of attaining mere "nothingness" [*Nichts*], but just the opposite, so that openness for beyng might be disclosed—fully and out of what is most extreme ... The essential context for the projection of death is the original *futurity* [*ursprünglichen* Zukünftigkeit] of Dasein within its very essence (as that essence is understood in fundamental ontology). In the framework of the task of *Being and Time*, this primarily means that death is connected to "time," which in turn is established as the domain of the projection of the truth of beyng itself. This already shows, clearly enough for anyone who wants to participate in the questioning, that there the question of death stands in an essential relation to the *truth of beyng* [Wahrheit des Seyns] and stands *only* in that relation. Accordingly, death is not taken there, and is never taken, as the denial of beyng [*Verneinung des Seyns*] or even, qua "nothingness," as the essence of beyng [*Wesen des Seyns*]. Instead, the exact opposite is the case: death is the highest and ultimate attestation of beyng [*der Tod das höchste und äußerste Zeugnis des Seyns*].[88]

As this passage indicates, and the succeeding section of the *Beiträge* makes even clearer, Heidegger was responding to critics who understood his investigation of being-toward-death as promoting a worldview (*Weltanschauung*) that led to nihilism. Setting the record straight, Heidegger proclaims that the intent of his analysis was to enact the "ultimate measuring out [*Ausmessung*] of *temporality* [Zeitlichkeit] and thereby the move into the *space* of the truth of beyng, *the indication of time-space* [die Anzeige des Zeit-Raumes]: thus *not* in order to deny 'beyng,' but rather in order to establish the ground of its complete and essential affirmability [*Bejahbarkeit*]."[89]

The victims of the Nazi savagery were not given the opportunity to die authentically, to enact the implementation of being-toward-death that is essential to every human being, to claim their finitude as the refuge that shelters and thereby divulges the concealment of the truth of being in the world. It has been argued that the failure of Heidegger as a person and as a thinker is accentuated by the fact that he never addressed the persecution of the Jews as a philosophical problem.[90] I discussed this accusation in the previous chapter and I do not wish to rehearse my argument, but it behooves me to say that in the aforementioned passages it appears that Heidegger did try—though his effort was unquestionably minimal—to deal with the fact that the Jewish victims of the Holocaust were deprived of the nonevent of death proper to the event of Dasein's being in the world. Just as we saw in chapter 2 that Heidegger associates the topology of worldhood exclusively with Dasein, so he insists that only the human dies. Beyond the phenomenological analysis of being-toward-death in *Sein und Zeit*, Heidegger maintained this viewpoint for the duration of his years. Thus, to cite one example, he writes in the essay "Das Ding" (1950):

To die means to be capable of death as death. Only man dies. The animal perishes. It has death neither ahead of itself nor behind it. Death is the shrine of Nothing, that is, of that which in every respect is never something that merely exists, but which nevertheless presences, even as the mystery of Being itself. As the shrine of Nothing, death harbors within itself the presencing of Being. As the shrine of Nothing, death is the shelter of Being. We now call mortals mortals—not because their earthly life comes to an end, but because they are capable of death as death. Mortals are who they are, as mortals, present in the shelter of Being. They are the presencing relation to Being as Being.[91]

What makes Dasein human is the capacity to die, which for Heidegger means the capacity to be present in the shrine of nothing, the shelter of being, that which presences even as it is irreducible to something that exists—death, in other words, uncovers the meontological mystery of being that is nothing. The Jews, who perished at the hands of the Nazis, were not accorded the dignity of affirming their humanity in death and hence they were deprived of this presencing relation to the nonbeing of being realized through the being of nonbeing.

Here it is germane to recall Heidegger's incisive criticism of Nazi ideology in "Die Überwindung der Metaphysik." After having established more generally that the struggle for power "expropriates from man the possibility of ever escaping from the oblivion of Being . . . since it remains excluded from all differentiation [*Unterscheidung*], from the difference (of Being from beings), and thus from truth,"[92] Heidegger relates this "will to will"

(*Wille zum Willen*) more specifically, even though still obliquely, to what the Nazis were seeking to achieve:

> The plan itself is determined by the vacuum of the abandonment of Being [*Seinsverlassenheit*] within which the consumption of beings [*Verbrauch des Seienden*] for the manufacturing of technology, to which culture also belongs, is the only way out for man who is engrossed with still saving subjectivity in superhumanity. Subhumanity [*Untermenschentum*] and superhumanity [*Übermenschentum*] are the same thing. They belong together, just as the "below" of animality and the "above" of the *ratio* are indissolubly coupled in correspondence in the metaphysical *animal rationale*. Sub- and superhumanity are to be thought here metaphysically, not as moral value judgments.[93]

It may strike one as grossly unsympathetic that Heidegger attributes to the Nazis the same criticism he leveled against the Jews, but there is no question that the former are implicitly targeted for filling the vacuum created by the abandonment of being with promulgating the consumption of beings for the sake of manufacturing technological machination to boost the production of war. Human beings, who have become the "most important raw material" (*wichtigste Rohstoff*), are the prime subject of this consumption.[94] Evidently referring to Hitler as the one who sought to save subjectivity by appeal to the ideal of the *Übermensch*, Heidegger shrewdly points out that the superhuman and the subhuman, the victor and the victim, are one and the same. Just as animality and rationality are indissolubly linked in the Aristotelian definition of the human as the *zōon logon echon*, which translates into the Latin of the Scholastics as the *animal rationale*,[95] so, with respect to the stratification of a culture based on the distinction between the superhuman and the subhuman, not only is it the case that one cannot be understood without the other, as we would expect on the basis of a correlative logic, but, more profoundly, the belonging together renders them identical in virtue of their difference and thereby undermines the hierarchical foundation for the dominance of the superhuman over the subhuman. One is naturally inclined to believe that the leaders (*Führer*) shoulder the lion's share of the blame because they act out of the "blind rage of a selfish egotism [*selbstischen Eigensucht*]," and thus everything is purportedly arranged in "accordance with their own will." Closer scrutiny reveals, however, that the leaders themselves are the "necessary consequence of the fact that beings have entered the way of erring [*Irrnis*] in which the vacuum expands which requires a single order [*einzige Ordnung*] and safeguarding of beings [*Sicherung des Seienden*]."[96]

The ideal of leadership (*Führung*) necessitated by the hegemony of National Socialism consists in "the planning calculation [*planenden Berechnung*] of the safeguarding of the whole of beings." This calculation (*Rechnung*) is, in fact, a glaring "miscalculation" (*Verrechnung*) that "absolutely dominates the will," inasmuch as "there does not seem to be anything more besides the will than the safety of the mere drive for calculation, for which calculation is above all the first calculative rule." It follows, therefore, that the "complete release of subhumanity" corresponds to the "conditionless empowering of superhumanity," and the "drive of animality" (*Trieb der Tierheit*) is indistinguishable from the "*ratio* of humanity" (*ratio der Menschheit*).[97] Heidegger's observation that "subhumanity belongs to superhumanity," insofar as the "animal element is thoroughly subjugated in each of its forms to calculation and planning,"[98] is a broader criticism of modern society, but it surely applies as well to the Nazi machinery. The final caveat that subhumanity and superhumanity are metaphysical categories and not moral judgments is incoherent and indefensible. Heidegger's assumption that the metaphysical and the moral can be separated in this instance is not a reasonable or sustainable argument.

The ideology of Hitler and the Third Reich seems to be the object of the following reproach as well:

Uniformity [*Gleichförmigkeit*] is not the consequence, but the ground of the warlike disputes of individual intendants of the decisive leadership within the consumption [*Vernutzung*] of beings for the sake of securing order. The uniformity of beings arising from the emptiness of the abandonment of Being, in which it is only a matter of the calculable security of its order which it subjugates to the will to will, also conditions everywhere in advance of all national differences the uniformity of leadership, for which all forms of government are only one instrument of leadership among others. Since reality consists in the uniformity of calculable reckoning, man, too, must enter monotonous uniformity in order to keep up with what is real. A man without a uni-form today already gives the impression of being something unreal [*Unwirklichen*] which no longer belongs.[99]

The uniformity of beings, the predicament of humanity in modern industrial society, arises from the emptiness of the abandonment of being. The abandonment promotes the calculable security and subjugation of the will, which constitute the ground for the militaristic skirmishes spearheaded by a leadership that justifies the obliteration of beings under the pretext of securing order. The Nazis personified the maximum standardization of a statistical reckoning—precisely what Heidegger contemptibly associated with the Jewish people—to the point that the real is determined by a monotony of sameness and the one without the facade of a uniform is considered unreal.

Chapter Six

HEIDEGGER, BALAAM, AND THE DUPLICITY OF PHILOSOPHY'S SHADOW

There is also a blindness that sees.
—HEIDEGGER, *ÜBERLEGUNGEN III*, § 50

Hereby what is dark is not dissolved in a vain brightness, but rather the dark remains what is concealed and thereby itself first comes to appearance.... Thinking dwells inceptually in the essential space of a dark light.
—HEIDEGGER, *BREMEN AND FREIBURG LECTURES*

A devil enters into a pact only with persons about whom he is certain they are of a devilish essence. Just as God is still divine in his harshest smitings, so his adversary, a devil, is still devilish in his most innocent behavior. But what if the devil attained his greatest deviltry through the "arousing of remorse and grief" over his previous deeds?
—HEIDEGGER, *ÜBERLEGUNGEN XIII*, § 137

In the final chapter, I will elicit a more complex approach to assess Heidegger's commitment to National Socialism and his relation to Judaism from the kabbalistic tradition. The specific focus of my exegetical construction is the relationship that is established between Moses, the supreme prophet of Israel, and Balaam, the prototype of the non-Israelite soothsayer.[1] Perhaps inspired by the preamble to Balaam's prophecy—"Word of Balaam son of Beor, Word of the man whose eye is true, / Word of him who hears God's speech, Who obtains knowledge from the Most High, And beholds visions from the Almighty" (Numbers 24:15–16)—there developed in rabbinic circles the notion of parity between Moses and Balaam. This is illustrated in the following statement offered as a gloss on "Never again did there arise in Israel a prophet like Moses" (Deuteronomy 34:10): "In Israel none arose, but in the nations of the world there arose, and who was it? Balaam."[2] *Prima facie*, this is a remarkable claim as it contests the alleged uniqueness of the Jews related to the gift of prophecy and divine revelation.[3] Balaam represents the irrefutable outsider, who attains the status of the consummate insider, and thus problematizes the rigid distinction between external and internal.⁴ In various passages in zoharic literature, the parity is concurrently upheld and subverted, that is, the equivalence between Moses and Balaam is affirmed but also neutralized by the fact that the former is linked to the holy emanations on the right and the latter to the unholy emanations on the left. In the kabbalistic symbolism, Balaam becomes the chief magician and the protagonist of the demonic, whose activity corresponds to the theurgic efficacy exhibited by Moses.⁵

In one particularly noteworthy passage, the sharp division is challenged to some degree by the assumption that even though Balaam cleaves to the filth (*ṭinnufa*) of the Other Side, he was granted a distant glance (*istakkeluta de-meraḥiq*) at holiness through the faint glow (*nehiru daqqiq*) that surrounds the demonic, an aura that is identified with the biblical idea of the radiance (*nogah*) that encircled the great cloud and flashing fire (Ezekiel 1:4).⁶ The vision is depicted further as a meager glance (*istakkeluta zeʿeir*), a seeing of the radiance as from behind a wall (*ke-vatar kotala*) or from within the closed eye (*setimu de-eina*), which is linked to the expression *shetum ha-ayin* (Numbers 24:3), a vision that involves rotating the eyeball so that one sees a concealed light without seeing (*de-itgalgal eina we-ḥazei bar nash nehora setima we-lo ḥazei*).⁷ The example of Balaam attests, therefore, to an ontological monism that puts into question the feasibility of positing alterity in any definitive way: "There is no Other Side that does not contain the faint meager glow [*nehiru daqqiq zeʿeir*] from the side of holiness—like most dreams, where in the abundance of straw there is a grain of wheat⁸—except for those dim impudent forms [*ṭafsei deqiqin ḥaṣifin*], which are all extremely impure, and Balaam knew them all."⁹ The novel and radical repercussions of the zoharic interpretation are driven home at the conclusion of the homily where the parallelism between Moses and Balaam exceeds what is implied in the rabbinic tradition: "Praiseworthy is the portion of Moses, who is above all the supernal holy ones, and he contemplated [*istakkal*] that which no other human being in the world was given permission to contemplate. Just as Balaam saw a meager faint glow [*nehiru zeʿeir daqqiq*] as from behind a wall, from within that Other Side, so too Moses, through the supernal light that was great and copious [*nehiru illaʾah rav we-saggi*], saw below as from behind a wall, a faint darkness [*ḥashokha daqqiq*] that appeared to him, but not all the time, just as Balaam did not contemplate that glow all the time."¹⁰

The homology between Moses and Balaam assumes an interesting twist here. It is not only that Moses's knowledge and theurgic use of the godly emanations corresponds to Balaam's knowledge of and magical use of the ungodly gradations, but rather that, like Balaam, Moses himself had knowledge of the demonic. The underlying assumption is that since the demonic derives from the divine, the perfection of Moses's wisdom necessitated that he had knowledge of the unholy forces to complement his knowledge of the holy forces. Moreover, in the case of both Moses and Balaam, the vision is indirect—a seeing from behind the wall—and temporary. The symmetry is tempered, however, by the fact that the gaze of Balaam was fixed on the faint glow of holiness from the Other Side, whereas Moses contemplated the faint darkness of the Other Side from within the superfluity of the supernal light of holiness. In spite of this critical difference of vantage point, the main thrust of the passage is to narrow the chasm separating the two realms by underscoring the intertwining of light and dark. This gnosis is educed as well from Moses's inaugural theophany, "An angel of the Lord appeared to him in a blazing fire out of a bush" (Exodus 3:2). The bush of thorns symbolizes the force of unholiness and the flame of fire, in which the angel appears, the force of holiness. The image of the fire burning from within the bush thus intimates the dialectical integration of the demonic and the divine:

For all things cleave [*itdabaq*] to one another, the pure and the impure; there is no purity except through impurity. And this is the mystery of "Who can produce a clean thing out of an unclean one" (Job 14:4)—shell and kernel arise one with the other. This shell will not be eliminated or broken until the time that the dead will rise from the dust. Then the shell will be broken and light will radiate in the world without concealment from the kernel.[11]

Encapsulated in this passage is the fundamental tension, briefly discussed in chapter 4, between the monistic and the dualistic approaches to evil. If, as this zoharic text suggests, the demonic shell arises from the divine core, and there is no purity except through impurity, then the goal should be the restitution of the shell to the core and not its eradication. And yet the messianic end—presaged by the resurrection of the dead—occasions the breaking of the shell and the consequent shining of the light. Theoretically, the more cogent position would have been an effacing of the boundaries separating the domains represented respectively by Moses and Balaam, prompting the discernment that there is no outside that is not already contained in the inside as that which is outside, that the principle of inclusivity includes that which is excluded by a more inclusive exclusivity.[12]

The clash between the monistic and the dualistic approaches surfaces in another passage from the zoharic compilation. The lower crowns—the source of witchcraft—are said to be crowned from the radiance of the kingship above (*qizpa de-malkhuta di-le'eila*), i.e., the attribute of *Malkhut*, implying that the demonic has its root in the divine. This is followed, however, by a categorical denial that Balaam had any knowledge of the holiness above, for the knowledge of the holy is limited supposedly to Israel.[13] It is possible that in this context, as in some other zoharic homilies, which build on rabbinic precedent,[14] Balaam represents Jesus, a point enhanced by the fact that sorcery is associated with the *Siṭra Aḥara*, represented by Samael, the archon of Esau, generally correlated with the spiritual force of Christianity.[15] The relation of Judaism and Christianity, personified typologically as Jacob and Esau, embodies the tension of which we have been speaking. On the one hand, inasmuch as they are twins that emerged from one womb, there must be a point of contiguity between them. This perspective is epitomized by the fact that Hadar, the last of the eight primordial Edomite kings, is the only one whose wife, Meheṭabel, is mentioned (Genesis 36:39), and hence he is the beginning of the heterosexual rectification (*tiqqun*) of the Catholic ideal of celibacy represented by the first seven kings. The fact that the restoration of the imbalance through the conjunction of male and female, a posture that is more typically associated with the distinctive spiritual vocation of Israel, begins with the last of the kings of Edom significantly blurs the disparity between Jacob and Esau.[16] On the other hand, they are often described in language that conveys an irresolvable animosity. According to some passages, which exerted a significant influence on later generations, a connection is made between Balaam and Amaleq, the grandson of Esau and the archenemy of the Jewish people.[17] The conflation of the two in medieval sources resulted in an increased hostility toward Christendom.[18] A polemical edge of this sort is intended in the zoharic identification of Balaam as the chief of all the sorcerers in the world (*rav mi-kol ḥarshin de-alma*) and the attendant surmise that, on account of his contemplating (*istakkeluta*) the serpent (*naḥash*), he knew how to direct his intention to perform the divination (*naḥash*) at the propitious moment.[19]

There is one other passage that is worth mentioning, as it has particular resonance with the persona of Heidegger. The author of the pertinent homily explains that the scriptural claim (Numbers 24:16) that Balaam knew the supernal knowledge (*da'at elyon*) means that he knew the supernal power that rules over the thirty-nine gradations of impurity (*dargin di-mesa'avu*). Balaam, the "wicked one," clings (*mitdabaq*) to the maximum power of the demonic, and, as a result, "he knew the supernal knowledge." In a remarkably bold reading of the biblical verse, the zoharic author detects cynicism on the part of Balaam: "That wicked one was praising himself in a concealed way—he said truthful words [*millei qeshoṭ*] while stealing the minds [*we-ganiv da'ta*] of people of the world."[20] According to the esoteric decoding of the literal sense, *da'at elyon* signifies the knowledge of the supreme demonic force, and hence the words describing the nemesis of Israel can be considered truthful. However, embedded in the text is an intentional dissimulation, for most people would erroneously interpret the words as referring to the divine. Interpreted this way, the verse attests that Balaam praises himself in a hidden manner and, in the process, deceives the listener or, in the language of the zoharic text, steals the mind of the inhabitants of the world, for they believe that the verse is communicating that Balaam had knowledge of the Most High. The art of subterfuge is presented here as an integral characteristic of the diabolical tactic of knowing.

In the Lurianic material, this earlier symbolism is developed further, and amplified emphasis is placed on the aspect of knowledge, which is associated with Moses and, by extension, with Balaam. As Ḥayyim Viṭal (1543–1620) put it, "Balaam also was from the aspect of the shell attached to this knowledge as it is written 'and he knew the supernal knowledge' (Numbers 24:16) verily."[21] A second passage from Viṭal offers more detail to help the reader flesh out the comparison between Moses and Balaam:

Balaam is the aspect of the evil of Moses, and thus the nations of the world arose and appointed Balaam. Moses is from the supernal knowledge [*ha-da'at ha-elyon*] of *Ze'eir Anpin*, which is in the foundation of the father [*yesod de-abba*], and hence it is called "supernal." . . . You already know that Balaam is from the shell [*qelippah*] that corresponds to knowledge, and this is what is written "he knew the supernal knowledge." His sons were Jannes and Jambres,[22] and they were also from knowledge, and they were the leaders of the mixed multitude.[23]

I will not enter into a discussion of all the details concerning the mixed multitude (*erev rav*) and the legendary sons of Balaam.[24] My focus rather is on the innovative way that Viṭal interprets the older rabbinic correlation of Moses and Balaam. Moses derives from the supernal knowledge of *Zeʿeir Anpin*, the masculine configuration (*parṣuf*) that is the counterpart to the feminine configuration of *Nuqba*, whereas Balaam is from the corresponding demonic shell. In another passage, Viṭal writes that Balaam and the mixed multitude "are from the dregs and pollution of Moses our master, peace be upon him, whose soul was from the very knowledge of *Zeʿeir Anpin*, from the aspect of the consciousness of the father [*moḥin de-abba*]. There was still an admixture of the sparks of holiness in them, and hence Moses hastened with all his power to enter the mixed multitude beneath the wings of the Presence [*kanfei ha-shekhinah*]. And so we find concern with Balaam about whom the rabbis, blessed be their memory, said, 'Never again did there arise in Israel a prophet like Moses' (Deuteronomy 34:10)—in Israel none arose, but in the nations of the world there arose, and who was it? Balaam."[25]

Building on the zoharic material previously discussed, Viṭal struggles both to demarcate the difference between Moses and Balaam and to acknowledge that there is an intermingling of the divine and the demonic that destabilizes the boundaries. Most important for our purposes is the fact that the focal point of convergence and divergence is identified as the aspect of knowledge. The visionary emphasis in the midrashic equivalence of Moses and Balaam is replaced with a more gnoseological orientation. The gnosis of Moses is linked to *yesod de-abba*, the phallic foundation of the father, which is within *Zeʿeir Anpin*, and the gnosis of Balaam with the shell of that potency. However, even Balaam's gnosis has its origin in the divine gradation. Consider the language of Viṭal in another context: "Know, as we have already explained, 'Never again did there arise a prophet like Moses etc., but in the nations of the world there arose.' The matter is that just as Moses is from the supernal knowledge of the foundation of the father that is within *Zeʿeir Anpin*, so too Balaam verily. Therefore, it says that 'he knew the supernal knowledge,' for his root was from there, and thus he knew the supernal knowledge."²⁶ In the continuation, Viṭal elaborates on the comparison of Moses and Balaam by laying out in detail the various reincarnations of the soul of Moses, beginning with Seth and Abel and ending with the theophany of the burning bush when all the sparks were rectified and the shell that is attached to those souls, which is Balaam, was purified. The process is explained by Viṭal using imagery from alchemy: "Since that shell was actually from that very place, as is known 'the one as the other was God's doing' (Ecclesiastes 7:14), and corresponding to the root of the soul in purity is the one in impurity.... As we have explained, after the silver is purified and refined by the lead, which is the shell, there necessarily remains some sparks of the silver within the lead. So with respect to Balaam, there were with him some sparks of holiness from the root of Moses, and thus he merited this gradation and this comprehension."²⁷

The force of the analogy to alchemical transubstantiation is made even more explicit in another passage from Viṭal:

Balaam was the evil of Abel and Moses the good of Abel. It is known that when silver is refined by means of lead, which is the shell that draws the dregs of the silver, it is necessary that there will remain some sparks of silver mixed together with the dregs of that lead. The refiners return to refine this lead and they draw out from it all the sparks of silver. In this manner, when the good of Moses was refined from the evil of Balaam, there necessarily remained in him some good sparks from the root of Moses our master, peace be upon him, and they necessarily will go out and be purified from there by means of many deaths and reincarnations as is known.²⁸

Although the process of purification (*berur*) consists of the separation of good from evil, that very separation preserves the attachment of good to evil. The final reparation might consist of the absolute separation of the forces, but this does not alter the fact that good and evil derive from a common source. In my mind, this inconsistency in the kabbalistic teaching is never resolved. The universalism implicit in the messianic potential of the tradition is expressed through the prism of the singular that is embroiled in the friction between postulating an identity of difference, on one hand, and a difference of identity, on the other hand. Just as the baptismal formula recorded in Galatians 3:28 avows that in Christ there is an obliteration of ethnic, socioeconomic, and gender difference—neither Jew nor

Greek, neither slave nor free, neither male nor female—and the pledge that we are all one in Christ Jesus is an inclusivity that excludes its own exclusivity, that is, the capacity for alterity excludes those who might not desire to be incorporated into the body of Christ, so, too, the kabbalistic belief that only the Jewish soul can effectuate the transcendence of polarities in the *coincidentia oppositorum* of infinity logically entails that, by including the excluded in the claim to exclusivity, the exclusivity is rendered even more inclusive.

Lest there be any misunderstanding, let me state unambiguously that I have been critical of the kabbalistic axiology and the implied division of humanity into sacred Israel and profane Gentiles.[29] This simplistic—and demonstrably harmful—binarian thinking is adverse to my sensibility; even the subversion of the binary, the *othering of the other* that may be deduced from kabbalistic sources, and specifically as it relates to the crossing of boundaries implied by conversion,[30] is still too dependent on the binary, since, to overcome the binary, the binary constantly needs to be reasserted. To be sure, I am cognizant of the great effort expended by kabbalists to address the problem of difference and the effacing of boundaries in the boundless unity of the infinite. It is not clear to me, however, that the other is ever anything other than symptomatic of the same, the not-other, and this is so even when it is asserted that the capacity for limit is coiled paradoxically in the heart of the limitless. Nonetheless, as odd as it may seem, we can abstract from this crude mythological worldview a way of explaining how Heidegger could have reached the highest of heights in his mindful meditations and yet plunged to the lowest of depths in his mindless moral-political actions. Expressed homiletically, Heidegger is the twentieth-century Balaam, embodying the nefarious side of knowledge—what we might label philosophical wizardry—albeit infused with sparks of light. According to the Lurianic teaching, these sparks can be liberated from their demonic encasement only by delving into the darkness. But in its most esoteric valence the mythic drama presumes that the shards of the vessel are themselves light, and the dualism gives way to a monism such that, as Heidegger himself taught, illumination consists of exposing the radiance of the shadow as the shadow of the radiance. This resonates as well with the Schellingian theme discussed in the previous chapter concerning the nonessence that exists as the semblance of the essence, that is, the absolute indifference of good and evil that engenders the dissimulation of good in the appearance of evil and the dissimulation of evil in the appearance of good.

Heidegger's recalcitrance can be explained by the kabbalistic paradigm that problematizes the metaphysical dichotomy of the sacred and the profane and the related anthropological dichotomy of the self and the other.[31] On this score, the relationship between Moses and Balaam instructs us that there is nothing in the realm of the profane that is not rooted in the realm of the sacred and that the self is the mirror wherein the other is reflected as the mirror of the other that reflects the self. Perhaps the spark that we may liberate from the dross encasing Heidegger's thinking, consequent to his plummet into the demonic—by his own account a still useful symbol for the uncanny spirit of calculating and instituting (*die Dämonie der Berechnung und Einrichtung*)[32]—is the wisdom to discern that opposites are identical in virtue of their opposition or, in his preferred language, the belonging-together of the same. As part of the Balaam complex, Heidegger articulated views that cast a sharp distinction between Jews and non-Jews, sometimes following hackneyed stereotypes that were utilized by the Nazis. But just as the kabbalistic tradition portrayed Balaam as one who achieved in the realm of the blasphemous the same enlightenment as Moses, so we can think of Heidegger as attaining the uppermost level of knowledge by descending to the depths of depravity. In the dissoluteness, however, one can discover the pathway of amelioration. Through confrontation with what is foreign one can find one's way to what is familiar.

The paradoxical logic operative here is in accord with what Heidegger argued in *Die Frage nach der Technik* (1953): the unfolding of the essence of technology, as opposed to the instrumental and anthropological definition of technology,[33] harbors the "possible rise of the saving power."[34] These words echo the verse from Hölderlin's "Patmos" cited by Heidegger, "But where danger is, grows / The saving power also" (*Wo aber Gefahr ist, wächst / Das Rettende auch*).[35] What is the saving power of technology? This can be deduced from Heidegger's explication of the essence of technology, which is related not to the productivity determined by the Aristotelian causes, the four modes of occasioning (*Veranlassung*), but to the bringing forth (*Her-vor-bringen*) that is grounded in revealing (*Entbergen*) the realm where truth as *alētheia*, the unconcealment of the concealed, takes place.[36] Heidegger encourages us to appreciate that the commonplace understanding of technology as a means of instrumentality is itself based on the demarcation of the essential domain of technology as a mode of revealing. And what is revealed in this unconcealment? Technology is revealed to be a "setting-upon that challenges," the "ordering" that is the "standing-reserve" (*Bestand*),[37] the self-revealing also identified as the enframing (*Gestell*), the "gathering together of the setting-upon that sets upon man, i.e., challenges him forth, to reveal the actual, in the mode of ordering, as standing-reserve. Enframing means the way of revealing that holds sway in the essence of modern technology and that is itself nothing technological."[38]

Heidegger grounds his thought in a philological attunement that shares much with the creative wordplay evident in the midrashic exegesis of the rabbis: *Gestell* preserves the connotation of *Stellen* as the "producing and presenting [*Her-und Dar-stellen*], which, in the sense of *poiēsis*, lets what presences come forth into unconcealment."[39] The nontechnological essence of technology, therefore, is equated with the poetical inasmuch as both are ways of revealing, of *alētheia*, but, as is the case with all coming to presence, that which is revealed "keeps itself everywhere concealed to the last." This is the watchword of the poetic revealing (*dichterische Entbergen*): that which shines forth most purely—what Plato calls *to ekphanestaton*—remains hidden in its essential unfolding.[40] "All revealing belongs within a harboring and a concealing. But that which frees—the mystery [*Geheimnis*]—is concealed and always concealing itself. . . . Freedom is that which conceals in a way that opens to light, in whose clearing shimmers the veil that hides the essential occurrence of all truth and lets the veil appear as what veils."[41] Any attempt to evaluate the intersection of Heidegger's politics and thought without grasping his anarchic notion of truth is doomed to miss the deep ambivalence and mistrust he eventually entertained about gauging the destinality of the historical from the affairs of government adjudicated historiologically. Adorno famously argued in "Kulturkritik und Gesellschaft" (1949), "Cultural criticism finds itself faced with the final stage of the dialectic of culture and barbarism. To write poetry after Auschwitz is barbaric. And this corrodes even the knowledge of why it has become impossible to write poetry today."[42] In *Negative Dialektik* (1966) Adorno revised his earlier view, but in so doing posed an even more insufferable question: "Perennial suffering has as much right to expression as a tortured man has to scream; hence it may have been wrong to say after Auschwitz you could no longer write poems. But it is not wrong to raise the less cultural question whether after Auschwitz you can go on living—especially whether one who escaped by accident, one who by rights should have been killed, may go on living. His mere survival calls for the coldness, the basic principle of bourgeois subjectivity, without which there could have been no Auschwitz; this is the drastic guilt of him who was spared."[43] Heidegger, it seems, argued just the opposite, that in the wake of the catastrophic failures of the technologically driven ideologies—Nazism, Communism, and capitalism—poiēsis as a metapolitical gesture[44] is the sole justification for life and the only way to establish a world-picture (*Weltbild*) predicated on the metric of truth as letting *the veil appear as what veils*, that is, the unconcealment that reveals nothing but the concealing of the unconcealed.

Humanity does not control the unconcealment in which the actual shows itself or withdraws,[45] but Heidegger still ascribes to the human being a unique role in this revealing that challenges:

The unconcealment of the unconcealed has already propriated whenever it calls man forth into the modes of revealing allotted to him. When man, in his way, from within unconcealment reveals that which presences, he merely responds to the call of unconcealment, even when he contradicts it. Thus when man, investigating, observing, pursues nature as an area of his own conceiving, he has already been claimed by a way of revealing that challenges him to approach nature as an object of research [*Gegenstand der Forschung*], until even the object disappears into the objectlessness [*Gegenstandlose*] of standing-reserve.[46]

The essence of modern technology is a revealing that orders, which entails treating nature experimentally as a "calculable coherence of forces,"[47] identifiable as a "system of information,"[48] but, in that very pursuit, the object can dissolve into objectlessness. The undoing of this objectivity by being attentive to that which endures and grants mysteriously, the "sending that gathers" (*versammelnde Schicken*)[49]—the way of poiēsis—is the saving power that technology harbors in itself, the enframing that reveals the essence of technology that is not technological. The comportment vis-à-vis technology that is concomitantly affirmative and negative is called by Heidegger the releasement toward things (*die Gelassenheit zu den Dingen*).[50] The one who attains this vision is capable of seeing that the technical perspective itself demands of one to behold objects differently, to keep open to the meaning hidden in technology, which Heidegger calls the *openness to* *the mystery.*⁵¹ Anticipating this idea in the *Beiträge*, Heidegger writes that a consequence of the dominance of machination is that it "dispels and eradicates question-worthiness and brands it as downright deviltry." However, even in an age of the "complete absence of questioning," there is still "some validity to what is worthy of question and yet at the same time makes it innocuous." Heidegger identifies this as the lived experience (*Erlebnis*), which is understood as the "basic form of representation belonging to the machinational and the basic form of abiding therein." The nature of that experience is delineated as "the publicness (accessibility to everyone) of the mysterious, i.e., the exciting, provocative, stunning, and enchanting—all of which are made necessary by what is machinational."⁵²

To experience the essence of technology from the standpoint of enframing is to sojourn "within the free space of destining [*Freien des Geschickes*], a destining that in no way confines us to a stultified compulsion to push on blindly with technology or, what comes to the same, to rebel helplessly against it and curse it as the work of the devil. Quite to the contrary, when we once open ourselves expressly to the *essence* of technology we find ourselves unexpectedly taken into a freeing claim [*befreienden Anspruch*]."⁵³ Liberation from technology requires that one neither slavishly submit to nor blatantly rebel against its unrelenting power; in both scenarios we are guilty of representing technology as exclusively instrumental and we thus remain transfixed by the will to conquer it.⁵⁴ What is necessary to be liberated from the specious desire to master the mastery is to ponder the nontechnological essence of technology, which is related to the destiny of revealing (*Geschick der Entbergung*) that which is brought forth, the saving power harbored in the enframing.

Heidegger is well aware of the danger ensnared in this saving power. Insofar as the enframing is itself a form of destining, it necessarily banishes the human being into the revealing that is an ordering, and when the latter holds sway every other possibility of disclosing is driven away. "Above all, enframing conceals that revealing which, in the sense of *poiēsis*, lets what presences come forth into appearance.... Thus the challenging-enframing not only conceals a former way of revealing (bringing-forth) but also conceals revealing itself and with it that wherein unconcealment, i.e., truth, propriates."⁵⁵ However, the very enframing, which has the capability of blocking the lighting up of the poetological, also has the potential to apportion to itself a way of revealing that has its origin as a destining in bringing forth, a revealing that challenges the preponderant understanding of causality as instrumental[56] and the consequent technological impeding of the poetic such that all revealing is consumed in ordering and everything presents itself in the unconcealment of standing reserve.[57]

The essence of technology inherently bears the ambiguity that points to the duplicitous nature of the mystery of revealing that Heidegger dubs the constellation of truth (*Konstellation der Wahrheit*): "On the one hand, enframing challenges forth into the frenziedness of ordering that blocks every view into the propriative event of revealing and so radically endangers the relation to the essence of truth. On the other hand, enframing propriates for its part in the granting that lets man endure . . . that he may be the one who is needed and used for the safekeeping of the essence of truth. Thus the rising of the saving power appears."[58] The structure of the argument corresponds to the view of Heidegger discussed in the previous chapter regarding the nonessence that belongs essentially to the essence of being, the untruth that is inseparable from the truth, a perspective that resounds with the kabbalistic doctrine of the containment of the demonic in the divine, the closing of the gap between the righteous Moses and the malevolent Balaam. To separate good and evil by avoiding evil—as was the fate of Job—strengthens the evil and accords it a false sense of autonomy. The ideal of piety—typified by the patriarchs and Moses—consists rather of plumbing the depths of the demonic, for only by so doing does one unite the left and the right and thereby attain gnosis of the collapse of the identity or nonidentity of opposites that bespeaks the true unity of the Godhead.[59]

This is obviously not language with which Heidegger would have been comfortable, but it does coincide with his thinking about the essence of the nonessence and the truth of the untruth. "The *future thinker*," Heidegger insists, "must know the nonessence of beyng [Un-*wesen des Seyns*]," for the nonessence is the errancy that belongs essentially to the truth of the essence of being.[60] Amazingly, a remark in the notebooks where Heidegger mentions Jewish prophecy reinforces the connection we have made between him and Balaam. What is of particular intrigue is Heidegger's use of the image of the ass in Balaam's prophetic vision. In the biblical narrative, three times the donkey beholds the angel of the Lord placed in Balaam's way to be an adversary, first swerving from the road and going to the field, then pressing itself against the wall and squeezing Balaam's foot, and finally

HEIDEGGER, BALAAM, AND THE DUPLICITY OF PHILOSOPHY'S SHADOW

laying down beneath Balaam. In each case, Balaam beats the donkey with his stick, until God opens the mouth of the donkey so that she may appease Balaam. After acknowledging the trustworthiness of his beast, Balaam himself sees the angel and is made aware of the fact that the ass actually protected him from being killed (Numbers 22:21–35). Now let us consider Heidegger's words:

"Prophecy" is the technique of defense in the historically skillful ones. It is an instrument of the will to power. That the great prophets are Jews is a fact whose secret side has not yet been thought. (A footnote for donkeys: this observation has nothing to do with "anti-Semitism." Anti-Semitism is as foolish and as objectionable as the bloody and above all the unbloody attack on "the pagans" by Christianity. That Christianity too condemns anti-Semitism as "un-Christian" belongs to the highly developed finesse of its technology of power.)[61]

In contrast to other passages wherein the sense of *Geschichtlichkeit* is denied the Jews, here Heidegger identifies them as the historically skillful ones (*des Geschicklichen der Geschichte*) to whom is accorded the gift of prophecy, translated in Nietzschean terms as an instrument of the will to power. The secret dimension of the nexus between Jews and prophecy is in the category of what has not yet been thought. In the continuation, Heidegger provides a key to unlock this unthought mystery: "Prophecy is history directed forward [*die vorwärtsgerichtete Historie*] and therefore the technical perfection of the essence of history [*die technische Vollendung des Wesens der Historie*]."[62] The prophetic aptitude portends the proficiency of the Jews to look ahead in history, and this is portrayed as the perfection of the essence of history, albeit pejoratively associated with the "unconditional technique of history" (*die unbedingte Technik der Historie*) cultivated by journalism, which is directed forward and backward, but is relevant only to what is presumed to be presently actual (*vor- und rückwärts gerichtet und deshalb erst »gegenwärtsnah« und nur so »aktuell«*).[63]

Anticipating the potential negative reaction to stereotyping the Jews, Heidegger adds a footnote for people whom he considered asinine: his comment about Jews is not anti-Semitic. Indeed, he states unequivocally that anti-Semitism is foolish, objectionable, and even un-Christian. In the story of Balaam, the ass turns out to be the being whose vision of the divine angel protects the non-Jew; for Heidegger, the ass is the symbol of the non-Jew who thinks he is protective of the Jews but is, in fact, blind to the historical truth of Judaism and thus confuses the delineation of ethnic destiny with racism. The reader, however, is left to ponder if there is something still left unsaid—something more cryptic and perhaps sinister—in Heidegger's calling our attention to the unthought in the secrecy of Jewish prophecy as it pertains to the matter of what he elsewhere calls in the notebooks "the eschatology of beyng" (*die Eschatologie des Seyns*), that is, a discourse about the end that signifies a "reciprocal oblivion" (*der Kehr der Vergessenheit*)—the forgetting of the forgetting—gathered as the event of difference in the parting (*versammelt als das Ereignis des Unterschieds die Differenz in den Abschied*).[64] To mark the eschatology of being as "the event of the oblivion of difference" (*das Ereignis der Vergessenheit des Unter-Schieds*)[65] may be a tacit criticism of the reckoning of history in terms of progress toward a culmination, which Heidegger understood to be the inevitable—if not exclusive—consequence of the Jewish propensity for calculative machination. In the final analysis, we must ask, is the insight of Heidegger not on a par with the vision of Balaam, a wild blindness[66] that uncannily empowers one with the ability to see the semblance of the shadow of truth even as one is blinded to the semblance of the truth of one's own shadow?

Afterword
―――――――

> Every philosophy is *untimely* (untimeliness), that is, every essential philosophy thinks "against" its age, not in the sense of the discontentedness and surliness of the know-it-all, but as the unconcealing of the essence of the age and as a decision concerning its future: thinking-ahead to the essential necessities. Not an antagonism in the sense of a merely "historical" confrontation; that remains wholly incidental.
>
> —HEIDEGGER, *INTERPRETATION OF NIETZSCHE'S SECOND UNTIMELY MEDITATIONS*

Let me conclude this investigation by stating once more that I offer no apologia for Heidegger. Indubitably, there will be readers who will accuse me of doing what I emphatically announce I am not doing. No matter how insistent and clear-cut my denial, the passion surrounding Heidegger will prevent some individuals from being able to read my work without a predisposition that, oddly enough, smacks of the very absolutism, despotism, and homogenization they find so offensive about the fascist ideology Heidegger unwisely embraced at a crucial moment in his own development as a thinker. Years ago Samuel IJsseling remarked that "many of the publications in newspapers and even in the scientific journals on Heidegger's political attitudes are characterized by this rhetoric, a rhetoric of simplification, haste, and extrapolation, and that the tone of these publications is more similar to the discourse of Goebbels than to the discourse of Heidegger."[1] With the availability of new material, and especially the notebooks, the totalitarian proclivity to denounce totalitarianism has only been augmented.

The moral and intellectual blemishes of Heidegger cannot be denied, but a dogmatic rejection of dogmatism is no more acceptable than the dogmatism it rejects. Derrida already cautioned those who attack Heidegger that "in a field of problems of such gravity, every gesture that proceeds by conflation, precipitous totalization, short-circuited argumentation, simplification of statements... is politically a very grave gesture that recalls—through formulas of denegation that would deserve the detour of an analysis in their own right—the very thing against which we are supposed to be working."[2] Notwithstanding the likely futility of any attempt to thwart the probability that my work will be distorted—a likelihood maximized by the dubious democratization of expertise that is the unavoidable consequence of the digital revolution and social media[3]—I will repeat without hesitation or ambiguity that Heidegger's indiscretions and lapses in judgment were deliberate and reflect poorly on him, no matter how sublime his thinking. I would contend nonetheless that it is equally misguided to say either that Heidegger's anti-Semitic tendencies have nothing to do with his philosophy or that they are at its core. I have tried to demonstrate in this book that the matter is more complex than either of these extreme positions would indicate and that the truth, as is often the case, lies somewhere in the middle too often excluded by our logic of the excluded middle, a middle where something can be both true and not true, where the propositions that Heidegger was a defender of Nazism and that Heidegger was an opponent of Nazism are not mutually exclusive.

The enigmatic nature of Heidegger's life is well captured in the dictum attributed to Heraclitus, "They do not comprehend how a thing agrees at variance with itself: <it is> an attunement turning back <on itself>, like that of the bow and the lyre."[4] The Heraclitean notion of harmony, perhaps in response to the Pythagorean ideal of music, involves agreement and disagreement, consonance and dissonance, a point well understood by the gloss on the statement offered by Nietzsche: "Good and evil come together in the same thing after the fashion of bow and lyre."[5] *Good and evil come together in the same thing*—an assault on the law of noncontradiction. That one can be both at variance with oneself and in agreement with oneself—indeed, concord is to be sought in the discord, compliance in the struggle[6]—is a perfectly appropriate description of Heidegger's tormented meandering on the pathway of thought informed by both an exuberant embrace of National Socialism and an immense debate with it, as Lacoue-Labarthe noted, in the hope of exposing its secret essence as the culmination of a particular trajectory in the history of Western culture.[7]

The extreme reaction that Heidegger provokes is, no doubt, related to the fact that the darkness he evinced is commensurate with the light he disseminated. Moreover, in this decisively unsympathetic figure we see an image of ourselves that we may not wish to appropriate but nonetheless stubbornly reminds us that, like the poet, we cannot find our way home to the familiar except through an encounter with that which is foreign. Enrootedness is gauged from the vantage point of proximity to or remoteness from being, which is determinative of the fundamental character of human ek-istence, that is, the ecstatic inherence as the "there" that is the "clearing of being." Yet the essence of nearness is to bring near that which is kept at a distance. To be settled in place and to be an itinerant in search of place, therefore, are not polar opposites. What is nearby is concomitantly faraway, and hence the serenity of being-at-home is necessarily at the same time the turbulence of not-being-at-home. As Derrida rendered the notion of *Unheimliche* based on his subversive and hauntological reading of Marx, Heidegger, and Freud:

To welcome, we were saying then, but even while apprehending, with anxiety and the desire to exclude the stranger, to invite the stranger without accepting him or her, domestic hospitality that welcomes without welcoming the stranger, but a stranger who is already found within (*das Heimliche-Unheimliche*), more intimate with one than one is oneself, the absolute proximity of a stranger whose power is singular *and* anonymous (*es spukt*), an unnameable and neutral power, that is, undecidable, neither active nor passive, an an-identity that, *without doing anything*, invisibly occupies places belonging finally neither to us nor to it. Now all *this*, *this* about which we have failed to say anything whatsoever that is logically determinable, *this* that comes with so much difficulty to language, *this* that seems not to mean anything, *this* that puts to rout our meaning-to-say, making us speak regularly from the place where we want to say nothing, where we know clearly what we do not want to say but do not know what we would like to say, as if *this* were no longer either of the order of knowledge or will or will-to-say, well, *this* comes back, *this* returns, *this* insists in urgency, and *this* gives one to think . . . all *this*, *altogether other*, *every other*, from which the repetition compulsion arises: that every other is altogether other.[8]

If the task to be inclusive is limited exclusively, as Heidegger thought with respect to the unique destiny of the German people, to midwife the rebirth of philosophy and to poetize being, then the inclusivity fails to meet the demands of its own exclusivity. We might say, therefore, that the secret of Nazism to be uncovered from what remains to be thought in

AFTERWORD

Heidegger—the unthought that he himself did not think except as what was not yet thought—is that to eradicate the eradication of difference and to postulate a genuine sense of alterity—the rupture of interruption predicated on an affirmation of the other as the other to the same rather than as the same to the other—would depend on the inclusion of exclusiveness in the inclusiveness of the exclusion. It is never sufficient, and indeed it is potentially dangerous, to cultivate a worldview wherein inclusivity is only included in the demarcation of the exclusive.

NOTES

PREFACE: CALCULATING HEIDEGGER'S MISCALCULATION

1. The bibliography on this topic is overwhelming, and it is not feasible for me to attempt anything resembling an exhaustive list of references. For a succinct summary of Heidegger's affair with National Socialism, see Miguel de Beistegui, *The New Heidegger* (London: Continuum, 2005), pp. 155–179. Also valuable is the rich historical and phenomenological analysis of Bernhard Radloff, *Heidegger and the Question of National Socialism: Disclosure and Gestalt* (Toronto: University of Toronto Press, 2007). Radloff examines Heidegger's political and aesthetic thought in relation to the question of being, and specifically from the vantage point of the threat of formlessness emerging from technology and social upheaval. On the related question of Heidegger and the political, see Fred Dallmayr, *The Other Heidegger* (Ithaca: Cornell University Press, 1993), pp. 15–76; James F. Ward, *Heidegger's Political Thinking* (Amherst: University of Massachusetts Press, 1995), pp. 1–45. For a presentation of the subject in the form of philosophical fiction, see the illuminating novel by José Pablo Feinmann, *Heidegger's Shadow*, trans. Joshua Price and María Constanza Guzmán (Lubbock: Texas Tech University Press, 2016).
2. Richard Wolin, ed., *The Heidegger Controversy: A Critical Reader* (Cambridge: MIT Press, 1993), p. 97.
3. Jacques Derrida, Hans-Georg Gadamer, and Philippe Lacoue-Labarthe, *Heidegger, Philosophy, and Politics: The Heidelberg Conference*, ed. Mireille Calle-Gruber, trans. Jeff Fort (New York: Fordham University Press, 2016), p. 20. An earlier version appeared in Jacques Derrida, "Heidegger's Silence: Excerpts from a Talk Given on 5 February 1988," in *Martin Heidegger and National Socialism: Questions and Answers*, ed. Günther Neske and Emil Kettering, trans. Lisa Harries, French portions trans. Joachim Neugroschel (New York: Paragon House, 1990), p. 146.

4. Derrida, Gadamer, and Lacoue-Labarthe, *Heidegger, Philosophy, and Politics*, p. 23; Derrida, "Heidegger's Silence," pp. 146–147. For analysis of Derrida's discussion of Heidegger and Nazism, see Jeff Collins, *Heidegger and the Nazis* (New York: Totem, 2000), pp. 45–51. A more comprehensive study on Heidegger's influence in France is offered by Tom Rockmore, *On Heidegger's Nazism and Philosophy* (Berkeley: University of California Press, 1997), pp. 244–281; and Tom Rockmore, *Heidegger and French Philosophy: Humanism, Antihumanism, and Being* (London: Routledge, 1995). Derrida's relation to Heidegger is discussed on pp. 139–147, 159–165.
5. Jacques Derrida, "On Reading Heidegger: An Outline of Remarks to the Essex Colloquium," *Research in Phenomenology* 17 (1987): 178 (emphasis in original). A similar argument, albeit without any mention of Derrida, has been made by Slavoj Žižek, *Disparities* (London: Bloomsbury, 2016), pp. 233–238. Summing up his argument, Žižek writes, "Against the persistent call for the direct criminalization of Heidegger's thought, for his simple and direct exclusion from the academic canon, one should insist that he is a true philosophical classic. A direct criminalization of Heidegger's thought is an easy way out—it allows us to avoid the painful confrontation with the proper scandal of his Nazi engagement: how was it possible for such a great authentic philosopher to get engaged in this way?" (pp. 237–238).
6. Derrida, Gadamer, and Lacoue-Labarthe, *Heidegger, Philosophy, and Politics*, p. 36.
7. Jacques Derrida, *Points . . . Interviews, 1974–1994*, ed. Elisabeth Weber, trans. Peggy Kamuf and others (Stanford: Stanford University Press, 1995), p. 181.
8. Rockmore, *On Heidegger's Nazism*, p. 23. See, however, Dominique Janicaud, *Heidegger in France*, trans. François Raffoul and David Pettigrew (Bloomington: Indiana University Press, 2015), p. 214; Geoffrey Bennington, *Scatter 1: The Politics of Politics in Foucault, Heidegger, and Derrida* (New York: Fordham University Press, 2016), pp. 102–103n1.
9. Miguel de Beistegui, *Heidegger and the Political: Dystopias* (London: Routledge, 1998). See also the more balanced approach of Alexander S. Duff, *Heidegger and Politics: The Ontology of Radical Discontent* (Cambridge: Cambridge University Press, 2015).
10. As Derrida writes, "Since always, and more and more, I have been at once convinced of the force and of the necessity of Heidegger's questions, while at the same time I see, I won't say their insufficiency, but something in them that called—and I believe it is being very faithful to Heidegger to say this—not only for progress in questioning, but for another type of questioning, a possible counter-questioning, and possible . . . questions about the question" (Derrida, Gadamer, and Lacoue-Labarthe, *Heidegger, Philosophy, and Politics*, p. 32).
11. Derrida, *Points*, pp. 182–184.
12. Jacques Derrida, *Of Spirit: Heidegger and the Question*, trans. Geoffrey Bennington and Rachel Bowlby (Chicago: University of Chicago Press, 1989), p. 109; *De l'esprit: Heidegger et la question* (Paris: Galilée, 1987), p. 179.
13. Derrida, Gadamer, and Lacoue-Labarthe, *Heidegger, Philosophy, and Politics*, pp. 9–10.
14. Ibid., p. x.

15. Jean-Luc Nancy, *The Banality of Heidegger*, trans. Jeff Fort (New York: Fordham University Press, 2017), pp. 11–12 (emphasis in original).
16. Duff, *Heidegger and Politics*, pp. 6–7.
17. Martin Heidegger, *Ponderings VII–XI: Black Notebooks 1938–1939*, trans. Richard Rojcewicz (Bloomington: Indiana University Press, 2017), p. 320; *Überlegungen VII–XI (Schwarze Hefte 1938/39)* [GA 95] (Frankfurt: Vittorio Klostermann, 2014), p. 410.
18. Nancy, *The Banality*, p. 43. See the summary of Nancy's position offered by Jeff Fort, "Translator's Preface—Both/And: Heidegger's Equivocality," in Nancy, *The Banality*, pp. xiv–xv.
19. Nancy, *The Banality*, p. 51. See ibid., p. 40. In response to the question why Heidegger concealed his anti-Semitism in his public texts, Nancy opines: "No doubt for fear of the Nazis whose anti-Semitism he was at the same time challenging and confirming even while coupling it with anti-Nazism.... But no doubt also out of a more or less clear sense of the extreme fragility of these 'theses' with nothing holding them together except the exalted vindication of an absolute anti-subject Subject." Compare Feinmann, *Heidegger's Shadow*, p. 69: "I had begun to see Heidegger as a solitary voice of warning. Little he said had any relation with the real National Socialism.... How could Heidegger, the rural, provincial philosopher, the solitary man of the Black Forest, who smoked his pipe in silence with the peasants, be reconciled with the extreme modernity of the Führer's militarism? Was the regime's orientation toward warfare the genuine expression of the relationship between man and technology?" And see ibid., p. 70, where Heidegger is quoted as saying that the one who does violence "knows no kindness and conciliation ... no appeasement and mollification." Moreover, he is given credit for criticizing harshly "the vulgarizations of National Socialism. He declined to call them 'philosophy.' *That* was not philosophy. It was vulgarity, pure boorishness. Paradoxically, it verged into error because it claimed it spoke of *truth*" (emphasis in original).
20. Derrida, Gadamer, and Lacoue-Labarthe, *Heidegger, Philosophy, and Politics*, p. 3.
21. Steven E. Aschheim, "Introduction: Hannah Arendt in Jerusalem," in *Hannah Arendt in Jerusalem*, ed. Steven E. Aschheim (Berkeley: University of California Press, 2001), p. 11.
22. Martin Heidegger, *The Fundamental Concepts of Metaphysics: World, Finitude, Solitude*, trans. William McNeill and Nicholas Walker (Bloomington: Indiana University Press, 1995), p. 154; *Die Grundbegriffe der Metaphysik: Welt—Endlichkeit—Einsamkeit* [GA 29/30] (Frankfurt: Vittorio Klostermann, 1983), p. 232.
23. Heidegger, *The Fundamental Concepts*, p. 155; *Die Grundbegriffe*, p. 232.
24. Derrida, Gadamer, and Lacoue-Labarthe, *Heidegger, Philosophy, and Politics*, pp. 3–4.
25. Ibid., p. 29.
26. Ibid., pp. 36–37.
27. Ibid., pp. xvii–xviii.
28. Derrida, *Of Spirit*, p. 132n3; *De l'esprit*, p. 151n3.
29. Derrida, Gadamer, and Lacoue-Labarthe, *Heidegger, Philosophy, and Politics*, p. 39.

30. Martin Heidegger, *What Is Called Thinking?* trans. Fred W. Wieck and J. Glenn Gray (New York: Harper and Row, 1968), p. 54; *Was Heißt Denken?* [GA 8] (Frankfurt: Vittorio Klostermann, 2002), p. 57.
31. Heidegger, *What Is Called Thinking?* p. 76; *Was Heißt Denken?* p. 82.
32. Heidegger, *What Is Called Thinking?* p. 76 (emphasis in original); *Was Heißt Denken?* p. 82.
33. Martin Heidegger, *Parmenides*, trans. André Schuwer and Richard Rojcewicz (Bloomington: Indiana University Press, 1992), p. 11; *Parmenides* [GA 54] (Frankfurt: Vittorio Klostermann, 1992), p. 16. See also the characterization of philosophy as "the actual thinking of the to-be-thought" (*das eigentliche Denken des Zudenken*) in Martin Heidegger, *Heraklit* [GA 55] (Frankfurt: Vittorio Klostermann, 1994), p. 3, and the multifaceted discussion of the "originary to-be-thought" (*anfänglich Zu-denken*) in ibid., pp. 44–85.
34. Heidegger, *What Is Called Thinking?* p. 126; *Was Heißt Denken?* p. 130.
35. Derrida, *Points*, p. 184.
36. Ibid., p. 186.
37. The paraphrase is taken from the epigraph to the fifth volume in Martin Heidegger, *Überlegungen II–VI (Schwarze Hefte 1931–1938)* [GA 94] (Frankfurt: Vittorio Klostermann, 2014), p. 313. See now Martin Heidegger, *Ponderings II–VI: Black Notebooks 1931–1938*, trans. Richard Rojcewicz (Bloomington: Indiana University Press, 2016), p. 227. For a thorough analysis of Heidegger's notion of the last god, see Paola-Ludovica Coriando, *Der letzte Gott als Anfang: Zur ab-gründigen Zeit-Räumlichkeit des Übergangs in Heideggers "Beiträgen zur Philosophie (Vom Ereignis)"* (Munich: Wilhelm Fink, 1998).
38. Gadamer, "Like Plato in Syracuse," in Derrida, Gadamer, and Lacoue-Labarthe, *Heidegger, Philosophy, and Politics*, p. 82.
39. Marc Froment-Meurice, *Solitudes: From Rimbaud to Heidegger*, trans. Peter Walsh (Albany: State University of New York Press, 1995), pp. 197–229.
40. Ibid., p. 228. For a similar stance that resists the absolute extremes of extolling and disparaging Heidegger, see Mahon O'Brien, "Re-assessing the 'Affair': The Heidegger Controversy Revisited," *Social Science Journal* 47 (2010): 1–20.
41. See the comments of Lacoue-Labarthe in Derrida, Gadamer, and Lacoue-Labarthe, *Heidegger, Philosophy, and Politics*, pp. 37–39.
42. See Richard Wolin, *Heidegger's Children: Hannah Arendt, Karl Löwith, Hans Jonas, and Herbert Marcuse* (Princeton: Princeton University Press. 2001); *Heidegger's Jewish Followers: Essays on Hannah Arendt, Leo Strauss, Hans Jonas, and Emmanuel Levinas*, ed. Samuel Fleischacker (Pittsburgh: Duquesne University Press, 2008). One possible exception might have been Martin Buber, with whom Heidegger did maintain a personal connection. However, even in this case it is not entirely clear how much of his work, and especially on Jewish themes and figures, he read. The only source that Heidegger seems to have consulted was Buber's *Reden und Gleichnisse des Tschuang Tse*. See Heinrich W. Petzet, *Encounters and Dialogues with Martin Heidegger, 1929–1976*, trans. Parvis Emad and Kenneth Maly (Chicago: University of Chicago Press, 1993), pp. 18–19; Otto Pöggeler, *The Paths of Heidegger's Life and Thought*, trans. John Bailiff (Atlantic Highlands, NJ: Humanities Press, 1997), p. 67. Buber was more explicit about his engagement with Heidegger's thought, his most decisive intervention being *Das Problem des*

PREFACE: CALCULATING HEIDEGGER'S MISCALCULATION

Menschen (Heidelberg: Lambert Schneider, 1948), based on lectures delivered in Jerusalem in 1938 and first published in Hebrew in 1942, and *Gottesfinsternis: Betrachtungen zur Beziehung zwischen Religion und Philosophie* (Zürich: Manesse, 1953). Concerning the relationship between the two thinkers, see Emil L. Fackenheim, *To Mend the World: Foundations of Post-Holocaust Jewish Thought* (New York: Schocken, 1989), pp. 190–192; and, in more detail, Paul Mendes-Flohr, "Martin Buber and Martin Heidegger in Dialogue," *Journal of Religion* 94 (2014): 2–25. For more evidence of the encounter of Buber and Heidegger, including photographs, see now Gil Weissblei, "The German Martin and the Jewish Mordechai: A Meeting Between Buber and Heidegger, 1957," available at http://web.nli.org.il/sites/NLI/English/collections/personalsites/Israel-Germany/Division-of-Germany/Pages/Buber-Heidegger.aspx. On the debate between Heidegger and Buber centered on the question of ontology and human existence, see David Novak, "Buber's Critique of Heidegger," *Modern Judaism* 5 (1985): 125–140; Haim Gordon, *The Heidegger-Buber Controversy: The Status of the I-Thou* (Westport, CT: Greenwood, 2001); Maurice Friedman, "Buber, Heschel, and Heidegger: Two Jewish Existentialists Confront a Great German Existentialist," *Journal of Humanistic Psychology* 51 (2011): 129–134.

43. See the analysis of this topic in Marlène Zarader, *The Unthought Debt: Heidegger and the Hebraic Heritage*, trans. Bettina Bergo (Stanford: Stanford University Press, 2006). And compare the comments of Derrida on Zarader's monograph in Janicaud, *Heidegger in France*, pp. 358–359; and John Caputo, "People of God, People of Being: The Theological Presuppositions of Heidegger's Path of Thought," in *Appropriating Heidegger*, ed. James E. Faulconer and Mark A. Wrathall (Cambridge: Cambridge University Press, 2000), pp. 89–92. Caputo argues that Heidegger's narrative of being is "structurally analogous in all of its main points to the biblical model, that is to the narratives of the Jews and their God in the Tanach, but in Heidegger's narrative the Jews are *totally silenced*, one might even say *repressed*" (emphasis in original). Following Zarader's lead, Caputo concludes that, in spite of Heidegger's intentions, the Jews occupy the status of the unthought debt or what was left unsaid in his thought, and this is related especially to the emphasis in his own *Heilsgeschichte*, the rival history of salvation, on the need to respond to the inaugural call of being assigned to one people as their unique historical destiny. In much of my own work, I have tried to elucidate aspects of kabbalistic literature utilizing Heideggerian concepts. At the moment, I am completing the study *Heidegger and Kabbalah: Hidden Gnosis and the Path of Poiēsis* (Bloomington: Indiana University Press, 2019), wherein I attempt to elucidate aspects of Heidegger's thinking by juxtaposing them with kabbalistic sources. For an independent attempt to consider the inaccuracy of Heidegger's depiction of Judaism by drawing more positive analogies between his thinking and rabbinic thought, see Elad Lapidot, "Das Fremde im Denken," in *Heidegger und der Antisemitismus: Positionen im Widerstreit, mit Briefen von Martin und Fritz Heidegger*, ed. Walter Homolka and Arnulf Heidegger (Freiburg: Herder, 2016), pp. 269–276. See also Allen Scult, *Being Jewish/Reading Heidegger: An Ontological Encounter* (New York: Fordham University Press, 2004); and Allen Scult, "Forgiving 'La Dette Impensée': Being Jewish and Reading Heidegger," in *French Interpretations of Heidegger: An Exceptional Reception*, ed. David Pettigrew and François Raffoul

(Albany: State University of New York Press, 2008), pp. 231–244, and additional references to Fackenheim and Fagenblat in ch. 1n192.
44. Jean-François Lyotard, *Heidegger and "the jews,"* trans. Andreas Michel and Mark S. Roberts (Minneapolis: University of Minnesota Press, 1990), p. 3.
45. Ibid., p. 4.
46. Ibid., p. 56.
47. Babette E. Babich, "Heidegger's Jews: Inclusion/Exclusion and Heidegger's Anti-Semitism," *Journal of the British Society for Phenomenology* 47 (2016): 134. For an earlier analysis on the part of this author of Heidegger's political affiliation with Nazism, examined on the basis of the affinity between Germany and Greece, see Babette E. Babich, *Words in Blood, Like Flowers: Philosophy and Poetry, Music and Eros in Hölderlin, Nietzsche, and Heidegger* (Albany: State University of New York Press, 2006), pp. 227–241.
48. Elliot R. Wolfson, "Nihilating Nonground and the Temporal Sway of Becoming: Kabbalistically Envisioning Nothing Beyond Nothing," *Angelaki* 17 (2012): 40–41.
49. Luce Irigaray, *An Ethics of Sexual Difference*, trans. Carolyn Burke and Gillian C. Gill (Ithaca: Cornell University Press, 1993), p. 129.
50. Dominique Janicaud, *The Shadow of That Thought: Heidegger and the Question of Politics* (Evanston: Northwestern University Press, 1996), p. 11.
51. Martin Heidegger, *Discourse on Thinking*, trans. John M. Anderson and E. Hans Freund (New York: Harper and Row, 1966), p. 44; *Gelassenheit* (Stuttgart: Neske, 1959), pp. 11–12.
52. Heidegger, *Discourse on Thinking*, p. 44 (emphasis in original); *Gelassenheit*, p. 10.
53. Derrida, Gadamer, and Lacoue-Labarthe, *Heidegger, Philosophy, and Politics*, p. xx.

1. BARBARIC ENCHANTMENT

1. Alon Segev, *Thinking and Killing: Philosophical Discourse in the Shadow of the Third Reich* (Berlin: Walter de Gruyter, 2013), pp. 8–21, esp. 15–16.
2. Martin Heidegger, *Contributions to Philosophy (Of the Event)*, trans. Richard Rojcewicz and Daniela Vallega-Neu (Bloomington: Indiana University Press, 2012), § 53, p. 89; *Beiträge zur Philosophie (Vom Ereignis)* [GA 65] (Frankfurt: Vittorio Klostermann, 1989), p. 113.
3. Heidegger, *Ponderings II–VI: Black Notebooks 1931–1938*, trans. Richard Rojcewicz (Bloomington: Indiana University Press, 2016), pp. 10, 182; *Überlegungen II–VI (Schwarze Hefte 1931–1938)* [GA 94] (Frankfurt: Vittorio Klostermann, 2014), pp. 11–12, 248.
4. Heidegger, *Ponderings II–VI*, p. 13; *Überlegungen II–VI*, p. 16.
5. Heidegger, *Ponderings II–VI*, p. 18 (emphasis in original); *Überlegungen II–VI*, p. 23.
6. Hans Jonas, "Heidegger and Theology," *Review of Metaphysics* 18 (1964): 218 (emphasis in original), reprinted in Hans Jonas, *The Phenomenon of Life: Toward a Philosophical Biology* (Evanston: Northwestern University Press, 2001), p. 247.
7. Jonas, "Heidegger and Theology," p. 225; Jonas, *The Phenomenon*, p. 253.

1. BARBARIC ENCHANTMENT

8. Jonas, "Heidegger and Theology," pp. 229–230 (emphasis in original); Jonas, *The Phenomenon*, p. 258.
9. François Raffoul, "The Ex-appropriation of Responsibility," in *Heidegger in the Twenty-First Century*, ed. Tziovanis Georgakis and Paul J. Ennis (Dordrecht: Springer, 2015), pp. 83–99.
10. Reiner Schürmann, *Broken Hegemonies*, trans. Reginald Lilly (Bloomington: Indiana University Press, 2003), p. 134. See ibid., p. 584, and the passage from Schürmann cited in ch4n78.
11. Alexander S. Duff, *Heidegger and Politics: The Ontology of Radical Discontent* (Cambridge: Cambridge University Press, 2015), p. 152. See also Christopher Rickey, *Revolutionary Saints: Heidegger, National Socialism, and Antinomian Politics* (University Park: Pennsylvania State University Press, 2002), p. 176:

    In my judgment, Heidegger's national socialism arises out of the "factical ideal" that dominated his thinking from his early philosophy until his death. Thus there is no absolute separation between his thinking and his concrete politics. There was no "turn" against the ideal of National Socialism. *Being and Time* is not an apolitical text. The same commitment to an authentic religiosity that underlies his early phenomenology and his late considerations on the essence of technology also underlies his political engagement in 1933. This means that Heidegger's attachment to National Socialism is the concrete political expression of his factical ideal of authentic religiosity.

    On the Lutheran background of Heidegger's antinomian conception of an authentic religiosity, see ibid., pp. 3–4:

    Religion, understood broadly as the relationship between humans and the divine, was for Heidegger the central condition of human being. . . . It is his understanding of religion, however, that characterizes the peculiar nature of his politics. The peculiarity of his conception of the political lies in his understanding of authenticity, which rests upon a radically antinomian conception of religiosity. This antinomianism is central to the peculiar nature of Heidegger's political theology. . . . His antinomian ideal of authenticity is a modern-day legacy of the theological-political currents of the radical Reformation.

12. Karl Jaspers, *Tragedy Is Not Enough*, trans. Harald A. T. Reiche, Harry T. Moore, and Karl W. Deutsch (Boston: Beacon, 1952), p. 56. For discussion of this work as a response to Heidegger, see Andrew Cooper, *The Tragedy of Philosophy: Kant's Critique of Judgment and the Project of Aesthetics* (Albany: State University of New York Press, 2016), pp. 182–188.
13. Heidegger, *Contributions*, § 30, p. 53; *Beiträge*, p. 66.
14. Pierre Bourdieu, *The Political Ontology of Martin Heidegger*, trans. Peter Collier (Stanford: Stanford University Press, 1991), p. 68.
15. Heidegger, *Contributions*, § 250, p. 314; *Beiträge*, pp. 396–397.
16. William Franke, *A Philosophy of the Unsayable* (Notre Dame, IN: University of Notre Dame Press, 2014), p. 328.

1. BARBARIC ENCHANTMENT

17. Martin Heidegger, *Being and Time*, trans. Joan Stambaugh, revised and with a foreword by Dennis J. Schmidt (Albany: State University of New York Press, 2010), §§ 32, pp. 145–148, 63, pp. 301–302; *Sein und Zeit* (Tübingen: Max Niemeyer, 1993), pp. 150–153, 315.
18. Heidegger, *The Fundamental Concepts*, p. 187; *Die Grundbegriffe*, p. 276.
19. Martin Heidegger, *Pathmarks*, ed. William McNeill (Cambridge: Cambridge University Press, 1998), p. 151; *Wegmarken* [GA 9] (Frankfurt: Vittorio Klostermann, 1996), p. 198.
20. Martin Heidegger, *Introduction to Metaphysics*, trans. Gregory Fried and Richard Polt (New Haven: Yale University Press, 2000), p. 175; *Einführung in die Metaphysik* [GA 40] (Frankfurt: Vittorio Klostermann, 1983), p. 173.
21. Heidegger, *Pathmarks*, pp. 150–151; *Wegmarken*, pp. 197–198. On the question of ethics and its surpassing, see Duff, *Heidegger and Politics*, pp. 24–62.
22. Bourdieu, *The Political Ontology*, p. 93, citing William J. Richardson, *Through Phenomenology to Thought*, preface by Martin Heidegger, 3d ed. (The Hague: Martinus Nijhoff, 1974), p. 224n29.
23. Martin Heidegger, *Mindfulness*, trans. Parvis Emad and Thomas Kalary (London: Continuum, 2006), p. 229; *Besinnung* [GA 66] (Frankfurt: Vittorio Klostermann, 1997), p. 259. Compare Heidegger, *Ponderings VII–XI*, p. 11 (*Überlegungen VII–XI*, p. 14): "*Errancy* is the most concealed gift of truth—for in it is bestowed the essence of truth as the stewardship of the self-refusal and as the purest preservation of beyng in the unrecognizable protection of what always is. To be sure: errancy is here not 'error,' an established mistake, the failure of truth as correctness—but instead is that which belongs to the 'there'—of Da-*sein*" (emphasis in original).
24. Heidegger, *Pathmarks*, p. 152; *Wegmarken*, p. 199.
25. Martin Heidegger, *Identity and Difference*, trans. and with an introduction by Joan Stambaugh (New York: Harper and Row, 1969), p. 41; German text: p. 106.
26. Hermann Heidegger's preface to Martin Heidegger, "The Self-Assertion of the German University: Address, Delivered on the Solemn Assumption of the Rectorate of the University Freiburg, The Rectorate 1933/34: Facts and Thoughts," trans. Karsten Harries, *Review of Metaphysics* 38 (1985): 468. The original German was printed in Martin Heidegger, *Die Selbstbehauptung der Deutschen Universität: Rede, gehalten bei der feierlichen Übernahme des Rektorats der Universität Freiburg i. Br. am 27.5.1933; Das Rektorat 1933/34: Tatsachen und Gedanken* (Frankfurt: Vittorio Klostermann, 1983), pp. 5–6.
27. Heinrich W. Petzet, "Afterthoughts on the Spiegel Interview," in *Martin Heidegger and National Socialism: Questions and Answers*, ed. Günther Neske and Emil Kettering, trans. Lisa Harries, French portions trans. Joachim Neugroschel (New York: Paragon House, 1990), p. 71.
28. Jean Baudrillard, *Screened Out*, trans. Chris Turner (London: Verso, 2002), pp. 16–18.
29. Ibid., p. 19.
30. Ibid., p. 21.
31. Edith Wyschogrod, *Spirit in Ashes: Hegel, Heidegger, and Man-Made Mass Death* (New Haven: Yale University Press, 1990).
32. Richard Wolin, "National Socialism, World Jewry, and the History of Being: Heidegger's *Black Notebooks*," *Jewish Review of Books* (Summer 2014), available at

http://jewishreviewofbooks.com/articles/993/national-socialism-world-jewry-and-the-history-of- being-heideggers-black-notebooks/. See also the preface, "The Politics of Epistemology: Heidegger's Black Notebooks in Real Time," in Richard Wolin, *The Politics of Being: The Political Thought of Martin Heidegger* (New York: Columbia University Press, 2016), pp. xi–lix.

33. David F. Krell, "Heidegger's *Black Notebooks, 1931–1941,*" *Research in Phenomenology* 45 (2015): 159. See also Holger Zaborowski, "Licht und Schatten: Zur Diskussion von Heideggers *Schwarzen Heften,*" in *Heidegger und der Antisemitismus: Positionen im Widerstreit, mit Briefen von Martin und Fritz Heidegger,* ed. Walter Homolka and Arnulf Heidegger (Freiburg: Herder, 2016), pp. 428–440; Daniela Helbig, "Denktagebücher? Zur textuellen Form der *Schwarzen Hefte,*" in *Martin Heideggers "Schwarze Hefte": Eine philosophisch-politische Debatte,* ed. Marion Heinz and Sidonie Kellerer, with the collaboration of Tobias Bender (Berlin: Suhrkamp, 2016), pp. 310–325.

34. The comment appears in the unnumbered page preceding the frontispiece in *Überlegungen II–VI*. I have utilized the translation in *Ponderings II–VI*.

35. Peter Trawny, "Heidegger, 'World Judaism,' and Modernity," *Gatherings: The Heidegger Circle Annual* 5 (2015): 3–4, argues that Heidegger distinguished between an exoteric and an esoteric sphere of philosophy and thus composed works that rhetorically fit into one of these two categories. The *Schwarze Hefte* are considered to be "esoteric texts" insofar as they do not have specific addressees in mind but rather "speak purely and primarily to themselves.... Through this self-addressing, thinking folds back on itself. The abandonment of the 'public sphere' is carried out with no regard for others whatsoever. The thinking in the *Black Notebooks* speaks in a being-historical intimacy to itself. In this way the texts are never personal" (p. 4). Trawny does acknowledge that even the "esoteric initiative" of these texts does seek to communicate to an addressee in a seductive or an erotic style (pp. 4–5). I myself think it is useful to consider Heidegger's thought from an esoteric perspective, but I do not concur that it is the most felicitous term to describe the mode of thinking on display in the notebooks. On the gnostic resonances in Heidegger's thought, perhaps even constituting an esoteric form of Christian gnosis in polemical conflict with mainstream Christian theology, see Susan A. Taubes, "The Gnostic Foundations of Heidegger's Nihilism," *Journal of Religion* 34 (1954): 155–172, esp. 157. Also relevant is the thesis of Mario Enrique Sacchi, *The Apocalypse of Being: The Esoteric Gnosis of Martin Heidegger,* trans. Gabriel Xavier Martinez (South Bend: St. Augustine's Press, 2002). According to Sacchi, the esotericism in Heidegger is connected to his view that being is disclosed not through logical analysis or discursive thinking but through an *experience of affective connaturality* (p. 127) that is a form of poetic mysticism predicated on the abandonment of reason (p. 137). Saachi's thesis is summarized as follows: "Led by Hölderlin's hands, Heidegger ended up by confusing philosophy with an erratic dithyramb in order to think about things and *Sein* in the midst of the darkness of a language in which the esoteric gnosticism always comes together with the unintelligibility of ravings" (p. 133).

36. Krell, "Heidegger's *Black Notebooks,*" p. 159.

37. Richard Wolin, ed., *The Heidegger Controversy: A Critical Reader* (Cambridge: MIT Press, 1993), p. 64. See Frédéric de Towarnicki, *À la rencontre de Heidegger:*

1. BARBARIC ENCHANTMENT

Souvenirs d'un messager de la Forêt-Noire (Paris: Gallimard, 1993), p. 33, cited by Dominique Janicaud, *Heidegger in France*, trans. François Raffoul and David Pettigrew (Bloomington: Indiana University Press, 2015), p. 65. Consider the fictionalized account of this view in Feinmann, *Heidegger's Shadow*, p. 65:

> I, son, who studied with Heidegger, in Freiburg taught Rosenberg's huge racist doorstop of a book. A disciple of Heidegger can't be racist. His subject is Being, not race, not biology. Perhaps we thought that German philosophers—Heidegger's followers—were the most apt to inquire into Being. But Dasein has no race. Or it was not defined by race, nor by its blood, but only in terms of its attitude regarding Being. To inquire into Being or to forget all about it, losing oneself in the whirlpool of entities: that was what defined the authenticity or inauthenticity of Dasein.

To be sure, Feinmann duly notes that Heidegger believed that the unfolding of the German nation under the guidance of National Socialism alone could save Europe from its annihilation by bringing about a creative encounter of Dasein with science and nature (pp. 68–69), but he is correct to emphasize that the destiny of the German people connected to that unfolding is not to be defined in crude racial or biological terms. See ibid., pp. 70–71:

> And he kept saying it, in his courses on Nietzsche: the greatness, the truth that he, Martin Heidegger, sought in National Socialism was the authentic encounter between planetary technology and modern man. Germany, a national community, located at the center of Europe, in the center of the West, in the center of Being, had been called on to incarnate the Hellenic origin. This origin was in us still, and Germany, as supremacy, had to transform this *truth* into *historical fact* and *unfold* it into other nations. That was its duty since only these *historical-spiritual* forces would save not just Europe but the entire Earth from devastation.
>
> (emphasis in original)

38. Wolin, *The Heidegger Controversy*, p. 63. The position I have taken with respect to Heidegger's statements is in accord with Rickey, *Revolutionary Saints*, pp. 177–178.
39. George Steiner, *Lessons of the Masters* (Cambridge: Harvard University Press, 2003), p. 83.
40. Martin Heidegger, *Reden und Andere Zeugnisse eines Lebensweges 1910–1976* [GA 16] (Frankfurt: Vittorio Klostermann, 2000), pp. 409–415. The basic elements of Heidegger's self-defense were already laid out in the deposition he gave before Adolf Lampe in July 1945. See Antonia Grunenberg, *Hannah Arendt und Martin Heidegger: Geschichte einer Liebe* (Munich: Piper, 2006), p. 283, and the recently published English version, *Hannah Arendt and Martin Heidegger: History of a Love*, trans. Peg Birmingham, Kristina Lebedeva, and Elizabeth von Witzke Birmingham (Bloomington: Indian University Press, 2017), p. 206.
41. Heidegger, *Reden*, p. 414. For an alternative translation and discussion of this passage, see Jacques Derrida, *Psyche: Inventions of the Other*, vol. 2, ed. Peggy Kamuf and Elizabeth Rottenberg (Stanford: Stanford University Press, 2008), p. 32. Derrida

1. BARBARIC ENCHANTMENT

mistakenly identified this letter as the one addressed to the rector from November 1945. On Heidegger's distinction between the social-national and the nationalistic, see Laurence Paul Hemming, *Heidegger and Marx: A Productive Dialogue Over the Language of Humanism* (Evanston: Northwestern University Press, 2013), p. 197. And see the discussion of the political consequences of the delimitation of metaphysics in Heidegger's rectoral address in Phillipe Lacoue-Labarthe, *Typography: Mimesis, Philosophy, Politics*, ed. Christopher Fynsk, with an introduction by Jacques Derrida (Stanford: Stanford University Press, 1998), pp. 267–300. Compare Jean-Luc Nancy, *The Banality of Heidegger*, trans. Jeff Fort (New York: Fordham University Press, 2017), p. 4: "Heidegger, in his notebooks as well as in the *Beiträge (Contributions)* repudiates the racist or racial principle precisely because the first depends on the second, which for its part proceeds from a biological, naturalist, and therefore 'metaphysical' conception." See *n*43, this chapter. On the political implications of the concept of race in Heidegger's notebooks, see Susanne Lettow, "Heideggers Politik des Rassenbegriffs. Die *Schwarzen Hefte* im Kontext," in *Martin Heideggers "Schwarze Hefte,"* pp. 234–250.

42. Heidegger, *Ponderings VII–XI*, p. 320; *Überlegungen VII–XI*, p. 411. See also Martin Heidegger, *Ponderings XII–XV: Black Notebooks 1939–1941*, trans. Richard Rojcewicz (Bloomington: Indiana University Press, 2017), p. 38 (*Überlegungen XII–XV (Schwarze Hefte 1939–1941)* [GA 96] (Frankfurt: Vittorio Klostermann, 2014), p. 48):

> All racial thinking [*Rassedenken*] is modern and moves on the path of the conception of the human being as subjectum. Racial thinking consummates the subjectivism of modernity through an assimilation of corporeality into the subjectum and through the full conception of the subjectum as the humanity of the human masses. Contemporaneously with this consummation, and compelling it into its service, the empowerment of machination is carried out unconditionally. "Nationalities" [»*Volkstümer*«] are only reservations and means of power and purposes of power—but no longer and indeed still not an origin and a beginning—i.e., not essentially occurring out of the assignment to a grounding of the truth of beyng.

The comment is occasioned by Heidegger's attempt to distinguish between Bolshevism and Russo-Slavic nationality, but from the subsequent aphorism it is clear that he has the failure of National Socialism in mind:

> The German essence is again thrown back—and how often will it still be thus thrown—into an uncanny concealment and still lacks the clearness and the courage for sovereignty out of the silence of the bestowal of the supreme struggle in beyng itself, taking beyng as the preserved origin of the last god. It is not "through" the last god as "creator," but by a decision in favor of this god in the encounter of the essence of divinity and humanity that, of the human essence, there will come to be a people that endures the task of grounding the essence of truth and never finds a task beyond or beneath this one.
>
> (Heidegger, *Ponderings XII–XV*, p. 38; *Überlegungen XII–XV*, p. 48)

1. BARBARIC ENCHANTMENT

Heidegger is critical of Nazi ideology, but he still holds on to the belief in the uniqueness of the German people with respect to the task of grounding the essence of the truth of beyng. On the distinctive role accorded the Germans in the historical drama, see Heidegger, *Ponderings XII–XV*, p. 43 (*Überlegungen XII–XV*, p. 55): "The essence of the Germans, their historical destiny, is withdrawn from historiological calculation through folklore or historical lore and arises only at the moment that decides what underlies even 'world-historical' incidents and either jolts the Western human being into Da-sein or delivers him up to global machination." See ch. 2n110. Compare the aphorism entitled "On the situation" (*Zur Lage*) in Heidegger *Ponderings II–VI*, p. 171 (*Überlegungen II–VI*, p. 233): "Where a people posits itself as its own goal, egoism has expanded into the gigantic but has gained nothing with regard to domains and truth—the blindness toward beyng survives in a desolate and crude 'biologism' which promotes a swaggering in words. All this is radically un-German."

43. Derrida, *Of Spirit*, p. 74; *De l'esprit*, pp. 118–119. Compare Nancy, *The Banality*, p. 52: "in the end, the displacement of 'biological' racism into a metaphysics of race perhaps does not displace much at all."
44. Wolin, *The Heidegger Controversy*, p. 65.
45. Heidegger, *Introduction to Metaphysics*, pp. 38–39; *Einführung in die Metaphysik*, p. 39.
46. Martin Heidegger, *Nietzsche*, vol. 1: *The Will to Power as Art*, trans. David Farrell Krell (New York: Harper and Row, 1979), p. 4; *Nietzsche: Erster Band* [GA 6.1] (Frankfurt: Vittorio Klostermann, 1996), pp. 2–3.
47. Rudolf E. Kuenzli, "The Nazi Appropriation of Nietzsche," *Nietzsche-Studien* 12 (1983): 428–435; Yvonne Sherratt, *Hitler's Philosophers* (New Haven: Yale University Press, 2013), pp. 26–28, 33, 51; Robert C. Holub, *Nietzsche's Jewish Problem: Between Anti-Semitism and Anti-Judaism* (Princeton: Princeton University Press, 2016), pp. 1–30, esp. 14–16, 219n40. Compare the sober and discriminating assessment of Maurice Blanchot, *The Infinite Conversation*, trans. Susan Hansom (Minneapolis: University of Minnesota Press, 1993), p. 147:

> In several commentaries, Heidegger has indicated that such is the meaning of the overman: the overman is not the man of today elevated disproportionally, nor a species of man who would reject the human only to make the arbitrary his law and titanic madness his rule; he is not the eminent functionary of some will to power, any more than he is an enchanter destined to introduce paradisiacal bliss on earth. The overman is he who alone leads man to be what he is: the being who surpasses himself, and in whose surpassing there is affirmed the necessity of his passing.

On Blanchot's own fascination with fascism and right-wing politics, see Richard Wolin, *The Seduction of Unreason: The Intellectual Romance with Fascism from Nietzsche to Postmodernism* (Princeton: Princeton University Press, 2004), pp. 187–219.

48. Wolin, *The Heidegger Controversy*, p. 101. See ibid., p. 103, where the Nietzsche lectures are again described as "a confrontation with National Socialism." I respectfully disagree with the conclusion of Louis P. Blond, *Heidegger and*

1. BARBARIC ENCHANTMENT

Nietzsche: Overcoming Metaphysics (London: Continuum, 2010), pp. 2–3, that Heidegger's reading contaminates Nietzsche's doctrine of the will to power by associating it with Nazi ideology. The position I have taken is in accord with the conclusion reached by Blanchot, *The Infinite Conversation*, pp. 143–144; Maurice Blanchot, "Thinking the Apocalypse: A Letter from Maurice Blanchot to Catherine David," trans. Paula Wissing, *Critical Inquiry* 15 (1989): 476n2. See also the brief but incisive assessment of this matter in Philippe Lacoue-Labarthe, *Heidegger and the Politics of Poetry*, trans. Jeff Fort (Urbana: University of Illinois Press, 2007), p. 5.

49. Richard Wolin, "An Exchange of Letters," in Wolin, *The Heidegger Controversy*, pp. 162–163. See Victor Farías, *Heidegger and Nazism*, ed. Joseph Margolis and Tom Rockmore, trans. Paul Burrel and Dominic Di Bernardi (Philadelphia: Temple University Press, 1989), pp. 284–285.

50. Karl Löwith, *My Life in Germany Before and After 1933: A Report*, trans. Elizabeth King (London: Athlone, 1994), pp. 59–61. The passage is cited in Wolin, *The Heidegger Controversy*, pp. 141–143, and see Blanchot, "Thinking the Apocalypse," pp. 476–478. On Heidegger and National Socialism, see also Karl Löwith, *Martin Heidegger and European Nihilism*, ed. Richard Wolin (New York: Columbia University Press, 1995), pp. 216–225. The relationship between Heidegger and Löwith is explored in the essay by Richard Wolin, "Karl Löwith and Martin Heidegger—Contexts and Controversies: An Introduction," ibid., pp. 1–25, and Richard Wolin, *Heidegger's Children: Hannah Arendt, Karl Löwith, Hans Jonas, and Herbert Marcuse* (Princeton: Princeton University Press, 2001), pp. 71–100, 177–178.

51. Wolin, *The Heidegger Controversy*, pp. 101–102.

52. Heidegger, "The Self-Assertion," p. 483; *Die Selbstbehauptung*, p. 23. For analysis of Heidegger and National Socialism set in the context of his approach to the politics of the university, see Iain D. Thomson, *Heidegger on Ontotheology: Technology and the Politics of Education* (Cambridge: Cambridge University Press, 2005), pp. 78–140.

53. Heidegger, *Ponderings II–VI*, p. 141; *Überlegungen II–VI*, p. 193.

54. Wolin, *The Heidegger Controversy*, pp. 29–30.

55. Heidegger, *Ponderings II–VI*, p. 90 (emphasis in original); *Überlegungen II–VI*, p. 123.

56. See Christian Sommer, "Métapolitique de l'université. Le programme platonicien de Heidegger," *Les Études philosophiques* 93 (2010): 255–275.

57. Heidegger, *Ponderings II–VI*, p. 139; *Überlegungen II–VI*, p. 190.

58. Heidegger, *Ponderings II–VI*, pp. 135–136 (emphasis in original); *Überlegungen II–VI*, p. 185.

59. Heidegger, *Ponderings II–VI*, p. 103; *Überlegungen II–VI*, pp. 140–141.

60. Heidegger, *Ponderings II–VI*, p. 142; *Überlegungen II–VI*, p. 194.

61. I take issue with the conclusion of Slavoj Žižek, *Disparities* (London: Bloomsbury, 2016), p. 235: "Furthermore, Heidegger's growing reservations about the Nazi regime have nothing to do with the eventual rejection of its murderous brutality; far from denying its barbarism, Heidegger locates in it the greatness of Nazism." Žižek supports his argument by citing a portion of the text from the *Schwarze Hefte*, cited in the previous note. What he fails to consider is that the passage on

barbarism comes from the much earlier period and that comments in the notebooks from a later period indicate that Heidegger had a better and more critical sense of the barbarous nature of National Socialism.

62. Duff, *Heidegger and Politics*, pp. 164–167. See as well George Steiner, *After Babel: Aspects of Language and Translation*, 3d ed. (Oxford: Oxford University Press, 1998), pp. 313–315.
63. Heidegger, *Contributions*, § 92, p. 147; *Beiträge*, p. 187.
64. Heidegger, *Contributions*, § 278, p. 399; *Beiträge*, p. 507.
65. Heidegger, *Contributions*, § 144, p. 208; *Beiträge*, p. 264.
66. Heidegger, *Mindfulness*, p. 11; *Besinnung*, p. 15.
67. See the evidence educed for Heidegger's critique of National Socialism in Francesca Brencio, "Martin Heidegger and the Thinking of Evil: From the Original Ethics to the Black Notebooks," *Ivs Fvgit: Revista de Estudios Histórico-Jurídicos de la Corona de Aragón* 19 (2016): 115–120.
68. Heidegger, *Ponderings II–VI*, p. 254; *Überlegungen II–VI*, p. 348. For a balanced analysis of the inherently political nature of Heidegger's philosophy, and especially the question of being, see Ward, *Heidegger's Political Thinking*.
69. Wolin, *The Heidegger Controversy*, pp. 43–44 (emphasis in original).
70. Ibid., p. 45. See Steiner, *Lessons of the Masters*, pp. 177–178.
71. Heidegger, *Reden*, p. 151, partially translated in Andrew J. Mitchell, "Heidegger's Breakdown: Health and Healing Under the Care of Dr. V. E. von Gebsattel," *Research in Phenomenology* 46 (2016): 74.
72. In his note to Heidegger's 1933 speech "The University in the New Reich," Wolin, *The Heidegger Controversy*, p. 43, contrasts the approach Heidegger took at this time with his two "post festum justifications of his activities as rector," the *Das Rektorat 1933-34: Tatsachen und Gedanken* and the *Der Spiegel* interview, "Nur ein Gott kann uns noch retten," insofar as in these sources he claimed that he accepted the position only "to prevent the rampant politicization of university life," whereas in the speeches from 1933 he sponsored a more activist stance to integrate the university into the ideology of the party. In my judgment, this is a distinction without any difference because even in the later works Heidegger was acknowledging that he thought the university had an essential role in mollifying and refining Nazism.
73. Wolin, *The Heidegger Controversy*, pp. 94–95.
74. Ibid., p. 95.
75. Ibid., p. 96.
76. Ibid., p. 100.
77. It is of interest to note that the reaction of Jaspers to the rectoral address in a letter written to Heidegger on August 23, 1933, was predominantly positive. See *The Heidegger-Jaspers Correspondence (1920–1963)*, ed. Walter Biemel and Hans Saner, trans. Gary E. Aylesworth (Amherst: Humanity, 2003), p. 149. Several decades later, however, Jaspers admitted that while he interpreted that speech in the best light possible, he already distrusted Heidegger. See Karl Jaspers, *Notien zu Martin Heidegger*, ed. Hans Saner (Munich: Piper, 1978), pp. 260–261, partially translated in *The Heidegger-Jaspers Correspondence*, p. 251n2 (the reference there to no. 65 should be corrected to no. 165).

1. BARBARIC ENCHANTMENT

78. Friedrich Nietzsche, *The Will to Power*, ed. Walter Kaufmann, trans. Walter Kaufmann and R. J. Hollingdale (New York: Random House, 1967), § 420, p. 226 (emphasis in original), cited in Heidegger, *Nietzsche*, 1:3; *Nietzsche: Erster Band*, p. 1.
79. Wolin, *The Heidegger Controversy*, p. 97. The expression "new dawn" is proposed by the interviewers (Rudolph Augstein and Georg Folff) but Heidegger assented to it without any qualification. See ibid., p. 103.
80. Walter Biemel, *Martin Heidegger: An Illustrated Study* (London: Routledge and Paul, 1977), p. xii.
81. Derrida, "On Reading Heidegger," pp. 178–179. This, too, is the crux of the argument proffered by Rickey, *Revolutionary Spirits*, pp. 175–221, that even after having left the party out of a sense of dissatisfaction with the course it was taking, Heidegger kept the faith in the potential of National Socialism to stimulate an authentic religiosity in the German people based on the antinomianism of the Lutheran distinction between law and spirit. See *n*11, this chapter.
82. Bourdieu, *The Political Ontology*, pp. 3–4.
83. Ibid, pp. 2–3 (emphasis in original).
84. Hannah Arendt, *Essays in Understanding, 1930–1954*, ed. Jerome Kohn (New York: Harcourt Brace, 1994), p. 187n2. The words I cited appeared in the English version of the essay published in the *Parisian Review* 18 (1946) but not in the German version published in Hannah Arendt, *Sechs Essays* (Heidelberg: L. Schneider, 1948). Many have written on Heidegger and Arendt. See, for instance, Wolin, *Heidegger's Children*, pp. 34–38, 49–52.
85. Arendt, *Essays in Understanding*, p. 202.
86. *The Heidegger-Jaspers Correspondence*, p. 186.
87. Ibid., p. 188 (emphasis in original).
88. The English translation of the essay by Albert Hofstadter first appeared in the *New York Review of Books* 17, no. 6 (October 21, 1971), based on the German radio address recorded in New York on September 25, 1969, and then printed as "Martin Heidegger ist achtzig Jahre alt," *Merkur* 23 (1969): 893–902, and later in Hannah Arendt, *Menschen in finsteren Zeiten*, ed. and trans. Ursula Ludz (Munich: Piper, 1989), pp. 172–184. Arendt sent a written version of the address to Heidegger on his eightieth birthday, September 26, 1969. See Hannah Arendt and Martin Heidegger, *Letters, 1925–1975*, ed. Ursula Ludz, trans. Andrew Shields (Orlando: Harcourt, 2004), pp. 148–162.
89. Hannah Arendt, "Martin Heidegger at Eighty," in *Heidegger and Modern Philosophy: Critical Essays*, ed. Michael Murray (New Haven: Yale University Press, 1978), pp. 301–303. The ahistorical nature of the philosophical enterprise is affirmed by Heidegger himself. See Heidegger, *What Is Called Thinking?* trans. Fred W. Wieck and J. Glenn Gray (New York: Harper and Row, 1968), p. 131 (*Was Heißt Denken?* [GA 8] [Frankfurt: Vittorio Klostermann, 2002], p. 136): "Philosophy cannot be based on history—neither on the science of history nor on any other science. For every science rests on presuppositions which can never be established scientifically, though they can be demonstrated philosophically. All sciences are grounded in philosophy, but not *vice versa*."
90. This disclaimer seems very improbable in light of the fact that in 1931 Heidegger sent his brother Fritz a copy of Hitler's *Mein Kampf* for Christmas. It is not likely

1. BARBARIC ENCHANTMENT

he would have sent this book had he had no knowledge of its contents. See the reference to the *Hitlerbuch* in the letter from Heidegger to his brother dated December 18, 1931, in *Heidegger und der Antisemitismus*, p. 21; Adam Soboczynski and Alexander Cammann, "Heidegger and Anti-Semitism Yet Again: The Correspondence Between the Philosopher and His Brother Fritz Heidegger Exposed," *Los Angeles Review of Books*, December 25, 2016, available at https://lareviewofbooks.org/article/heidegger-anti-semitism-yet-correspondence-philosopher-brother-fritz-heidegger-exposed/.

91. I have cited the passage as it appears in Heidegger, *Introduction to Metaphysics*, p. 213. For the original German, see Heidegger, *Einführung in die Metaphysik*, p. 208.
92. The expression *diese Bewegung*—"this movement"—replaced the original N.S., an abbreviation for *Nationalsozialismus*, in the handwritten manuscript from 1935. See Thomas Sheehan, *Making Sense of Heidegger: A Paradigm Shift* (London: Rowman and Littlefield, 2015), p. 272n6.
93. Arendt, "Martin Heidegger at Eighty," p. 302n3. On Nazism and technology, see Rockmore, *On Heidegger's Nazism*, pp. 204–243.
94. Wolin, *The Heidegger Controversy*, p. 104: "It was present in my manuscript from the beginning and agreed completely with my conception of technology at that time, though not as yet with the later interpretation of the essence of technology as the 'frame' ['*das Ge-Stell*']. The reason I did not read this passage aloud was that I was convinced that my audience were understanding me correctly. The dumb ones, the spies, and the snoopers wanted to understand me otherwise, and would, no matter what." More recent scholarship does not support Heidegger's claim that the parenthetical remark was part of the original text and not added in 1953. See Hartmut Buchner, "Fragmentarisches," in *Erinnerung an Martin Heidegger*, ed. Günther Neske (Pfullingen: Neske, 1977), p. 49; Otto Pöggeler, *Martin Heidegger's Path of Thinking*, trans. Daniel Magurshak and Sigmund Barber (Atlantic Highlands, NJ: Humanities Press, 1987), p. 278; Jürgen Habermas, "Martin Heidegger: On the Publication of the Lectures of 1935," in Wolin, *The Heidegger Controversy*, pp. 191–192; Theodore Kisiel, "Heidegger's Philosophical Geopolitics in the Third Reich," in *A Companion to Heidegger's Introduction to Metaphysics*, ed. Richard Polt and Gregory Fried (New Haven: Yale University Press, 2001), p. 227; "Translator's Introduction" in Heidegger, *Introduction to Metaphysics*, p. xviin7.
95. Benjamin Aldes Wurgaft, *Thinking in Public: Strauss, Levinas, Arendt* (Philadelphia: University of Pennsylvania Press, 2016), pp. 186–187. See also the critique of Arendt's defense of Heidegger in Emil L. Fackenheim, *To Mend the World: Foundations of Post-Holocaust Jewish Thought* (New York: Schocken, 1989), pp. 170–171.
96. See the evidence adduced in Elisabeth Young-Bruehl, *Hannah Arendt: For Love of the World* (New Haven: Yale University Press, 1982), p. 247, that Heidegger "is notorious for lying about everything." The context in which this comment is evoked is Heidegger's finally disclosing to his wife the love affair with Arendt. For discussion of Arendt's critique of the unworldliness of Heidegger, see Dana R. Villa, *Arendt and Heidegger: The Fate of the Political* (Princeton: Princeton University Press, 1996), pp. 230–240.

1. BARBARIC ENCHANTMENT

97. For criticism of Arendt's defense of Heidegger, see Richard J. Bernstein, *The New Constellation: The Ethical-Political Horizons of Modernity/Postmodernity* (Cambridge: MIT Press, 1991), pp. 80–81. I note some other representative studies on Arendt and Heidegger: Lewis P. Hinchman and Sandra K. Hinchman, "In Heidegger's Shadow: Hannah Arendt's Phenomenological Humanism," *Review of Politics* 46 (1984): 183–211; Lawrence J. Biskowski, "Politics Versus Aesthetics: Arendt's Critiques of Nietzsche and Heidegger," *Review of Politics* 57 (1995): 59–89; Grunenberg, *Hannah Arendt und Martin Heidegger* (English translation: *Hannah Arendt and Martin Heidegger*); Peg Birmingham, "Heidegger and Arendt: The Birth of Political Action and Speech," in *Heidegger and Practical Philosophy*, ed. François Raffoul and David Pettigrew (Albany: State University of New York Press, 2002), pp. 191–202; Villa, *Arendt and Heidegger*, and Dana R. Villa, "Arendt and Heidegger, Again," in *Heidegger's Jewish Followers: Essays on Hannah Arendt, Leo Strauss, Hans Jonas, and Emmanuel Levinas*, ed. Samuel Fleischacker (Pittsburgh: Duquesne University Press, 2008), pp. 43–82.
98. Richard Rorty, "Taking Philosophy Seriously," *New Republic* 11 (1988): 31–34; and Richard Rorty, *Contingency, Irony, and Solidarity* (Cambridge: Cambridge University Press, 1989), p. 111.
99. See discussion in Gianni Vattimo, *Of Reality: The Purposes of Philosophy*, trans. Robert T. Valgenti (New York: Columbia University Press, 2016), pp. 5–6.
100. Karl Jaspers, *Philosophische Autobiographie* (Munich: Piper, 1977), p. 84: "Philosophie ist nicht ohne politische Konsequenzen."
101. Alain Badiou and Barbara Cassin, *Heidegger: His Life and His Philosophy*, trans. Susan Spitzer (New York: Columbia University Press, 2016), pp. 1–15. Badiou's view that the connection between Heidegger's philosophy and his political activities is only circumstantial is challenged by Cassin, who agrees that the philosophy does not derive from the politics but maintains that there is an essential connection insofar as Heidegger did engage in political speculation informed by his philosophical ideas. Cassin, and to some degree Badiou, accept Arendt's perspective that great thinkers are not necessarily politically savvy, or, in Aristotelian terms, they possess theoretical wisdom (*sophia*) but not practical intelligence (*phronesis*). On Badiou's view of the Holocaust, evil, and Heidegger's Nazism, see Peter Hallward, *Badiou: A Subject to Truth* (Minneapolis: University of Minnesota Press, 2003), pp. 262–264.
102. Hannah Arendt, *The Life of Mind*, vol. 2: *Willing* (New York: Harcourt Brace Jovanovich, 1978), pp. 172–194.
103. Ibid., p. 173. A similar position is taken by Paul Catanu, *Heidegger's Nietzsche: Being and Becoming* (Montreal: Eighth House, 2010), p. 75, and see James Miller, "Heidegger's Guilt," *Salmagundi* 109/110 (1996): 178–243.
104. Martin Heidegger, *Country Path Conversations*, trans. Bret W. Davis (Bloomington: Indiana University Press, 2010), p. 38; *Feldweg-Gespräche* [GA 77] (Frankfurt: Vittorio Klostermann, 1995), p. 59.
105. Peter S. Dillard, *Non-Metaphysical Theology After Heidegger* (New York: Palgrave Macmillan, 2016), p. 138. Compare Philippe Lacoue-Labarthe, *Heidegger, Art, and Politics: The Fiction of the Political*, trans. Chris Turner (Oxford: Basil Blackwell, 1990), p. 48:

1. BARBARIC ENCHANTMENT

> From the very point of view I have taken up ... I cannot see what logic other than a "spiritual," "historial" one governed the Extermination. The Extermination is, if you will, the product of a pure metaphysical decision and one inscribed, moreover, in the very heart of National Socialist doctrine. ... It means, in fact, and this is the point of the discussion, that when one thinks History in terms of the deployment of metaphysics, and one calls on the West, under this same heading, to face its responsibility—which Heidegger never ceased to do—one cannot maintain silence on the massacre of the Jews, in so far as it is precisely the massacre of *the Jews*.
>
> (emphasis in original)

106. Wolin, *The Heidegger Controversy*, p. 30; *Die Selbstbehauptung*, p. 10. For Heidegger's own critique of the notion of science affirmed in his rectoral address, see Heidegger, *Ponderings VII–XI*, p. 14; *Überlegungen VII–XI*, p. 18. In that context, Heidegger implicitly raised doubt about his embrace of the Nazi party in the comment,

    > Therefore even the first step toward the preparation of a transformation of beyng did not need to wait for "National Socialism," as little as that questioning claims to count as "National Socialist." Here realms are brought into relation which have no *im*mediate bearing but which at the same time mediately and in various ways press toward a decision concerning the essence and destiny of the Germans and thus press toward the fate of the West. The mere calculating of "standpoints" can find only "opposites" here, and even ones which do not at all "repay" taking heed of them, since indeed the ascendancy of the National Socialist worldview is decisive.
    >
    > (emphasis in original)

    For another criticism of the rectoral address related to locating the essential decision in the institution of the university, see Heidegger, *Ponderings VII–XI*, p. 337; *Überlegungen VII–XI*, p. 433.
107. Wolin, *The Heidegger Controversy*, p. 32; *Die Selbstbehauptung*, p. 12.
108. Wolin, *The Heidegger Controversy*, pp. 34–35; *Die Selbstbehauptung*, p. 15.
109. Heidegger, *Contributions*, § 8, p. 25; *Beiträge*, pp. 28–29. For discussion of Heidegger's *Beiträge* and Nazism, see Rockmore, *On Heidegger's Nazism*, pp. 176–203, and reference to previous scholars on p. 179. Rockmore concludes that "Heidegger's relation to Nazism exhibits a remarkable continuity between the exoteric public statements in the rectoral speech and the esoteric 'postphilosophic' view on display in the *Beiträge*" (p. 186). I agree that Heidegger did not entirely abandon the political role of his thought of being, and he continued to privilege the German people and the German language in the fulfillment of the destiny of that *Seinsgeschichte* related to the second beginning, but this fails to take into account the important modifications and shifts in his own thinking brought about by a disillusionment with the practical realities of National Socialism. To be sure, Rockmore is attentive to Heidegger's critical remarks about Nazism in the *Beiträge*, but he insists that the reservations relate to his assessment regarding the insufficiency of this ideology as a theory of being and

1. BARBARIC ENCHANTMENT

not to the significance of this movement as an assault on human dignity (pp. 187–188).

110. Martin Heidegger, *Elucidations of Hölderlin's Poetry*, trans. Keith Hoeller (Amherst: Humanity, 2000), p. 111; *Erläuterungen zu Hölderlins Dichtung* [GA 4] (Frankfurt: Vittorio Klostermann, 1996), p. 87.
111. Heidegger, *Country Path Conversations*, p. 70; *Feldweg-Gespräche*, p. 109. Many have opined on the Eckhartian term *Gelassenheit* and its influence on Heidegger. For representative studies, see John D. Caputo, *The Mystical Element in Heidegger's Thought* (Athens: Ohio University Press, 1978), pp. 39–40, 118–127; Reiner Schürmann, *Meister Eckhart, Mystic and Philosopher: Translations with Commentary* (Bloomington: Indiana University Press, 1978), pp. 16–17, 191–213; Robert Dobie, "Meister Eckhart and Heidegger on *Gelassenheit*," in *Martin Heidegger's Interpretations of Saint Augustine: Sein und Zeit und Ewigkeit*, ed. Frederick Van Fleteren (Lewiston, NY: Edwin Mellen, 2005), pp. 351–382; Richard Rojcewicz, *The Gods and Technology: A Reading of Heidegger* (Albany: State University of New York Press, 2006), pp. 214–217; Bret W. Davis, *Heidegger and the Will: On the Way to Gelassenheit* (Evanston: Northwestern University Press, 2007). See also Vincent Blok, "Massive Voluntarism or Heidegger's Confrontation with the Will," *Studia Phaenomenologica* 13 (2013): 449–465. On the attempt to think of *Gelassenheit* in Heidegger in comparison to the Taoist conception of *wu wei*, or noninterference, see Joan Stambaugh, "Heidegger, Taoism, and the Question of Metaphysics," in *Heidegger and Asian Thought*, ed. Graham Parkes (Honolulu: University of Hawaii Press, 1987), pp. 85–88.
112. Heidegger, *Contributions*, § 8, p. 25; *Beiträge*, p. 29.
113. Heidegger, *Contributions*, § 100, p. 154; *Beiträge*, p. 196.
114. Ryan Coyne, *Heidegger's Confessions: The Remains of Saint Augustine in Being and Time and Beyond* (Chicago: University of Chicago Press, 2015), p. 208.
115. Rockmore, *Heidegger and French Philosophy*, p. 185.
116. Emmanuel Levinas, *Collected Philosophical Papers*, trans. Alphonso Lingis (Dordrecht: Martinus Nijhoff, 1987), p. 52. The "profoundly pagan character of Heidegger's thought," which is understood as the deification of nature, was also emphasized by Jonas, "Heidegger and Theology," pp. 219–220 (*The Phenomenon of Life*, pp. 248–249). On Levinas's philosophy and the response to National Socialism, see Howard Caygill, *Levinas and the Political* (London: Routledge, 2002), pp. 5–48, esp. 29–40.
117. Emmanuel Levinas, *Difficult Freedom: Essays on Judaism*, trans. Seán Hand (Baltimore: Johns Hopkins University Press, 1990), p. 232.
118. Ibid., pp. 233–234.
119. Levinas is referring to the passage in Heidegger, *Being and Time*, § 22, p. 101 (*Sein und Zeit*, p. 104): "In taking care, Dasein, which is in its very being concerned about that being [*dem es in seinem Sein um dieses Sein selbst geht*], discovers beforehand the regions which are each in a decisive relevance."
120. The passage is from the prefatory note, written on March 28, 1990, appended to Emmanuel Levinas, "Reflections on the Philosophy of Hitlerism," *Critical Inquiry* 17 (1990): 63. The original French essay, "Quelques réflexions sur le philosophie de l'Hitlérisme," appeared in *Esprit* 2 (1934): 199–208.

1. BARBARIC ENCHANTMENT

121. Emmanuel Levinas, *Totality and Infinity: An Essay on Exteriority*, trans. Alphonso Lingis (Dordrecht: Kluwer Academic, 1969), p. 225; *Totalité et infini: Essai sur l'extériorité* (The Hague: Martinus Nijhoff, 1980), p. 201. See Jeffrey Andrew Barash, "In Heidegger's Shadow: Ernst Cassirer, Emmanuel Levinas, and the Question of the Political," in *Against the Grain: Jewish Intellectuals in Hard Times*, ed. Ezra Mendelsohn, Stefani Hoffman, and Richard I. Cohen (New York: Berghahn, 2014), pp. 93–103.
122. Emmanuel Levinas, *Nine Talmudic Readings*, trans. Annette Aronowicz (Bloomington: Indiana University Press, 1990), p. 25.
123. Dieter Thomä, "Heidegger und der Nationalsozialismus. In der Dunkelkammer der Seinsgeschichte," in *Heidegger-Handbuch: Leben —Werk—Wirkung*, ed. Dieter Thomä, in collaboration with Florian Grosser, Katrin Meyer, and Hans Bernhard Schmid, rev. ed. (Stuttgart: J. B. Metzler, 2013), pp. 108–133.
124. David Farrell Krell, *Intimations of Mortality: Time, Truth, and Finitude in Heidegger's Thinking of Being* (University Park: Pennsylvania State University Press, 1986), p. 111. Krell rightfully emphasizes the nondevelopmental nature of the *Kehre* in Heidegger's thinking as a "turning within the interrogation of being as a whole in the history of Western philosophy." He also astutely notes that "the attempt to catch up with the forward slippage of the matter of thought in *Being and Time*" is a "catching up that actually moves backward." See also the cautious remarks of Thomas Sheehan, "'Time and Being', 1925-7," in *Martin Heidegger: Critical Assessments*, vol. 1: *Philosophy*, ed. Christopher Macann (Routledge: London, 1992), p. 49, that the change in language that characterizes Heidegger's work in the thirties "does not make up the turn (*Kehre*) in the proper sense but is only a shift in direction (*Wendung*) within the turn. It merely evidences Heidegger's awareness that the turn from all forms of the metaphysics of stable presence into the non-metaphysics of privative absence (*lēthē*) could not be carried out within the language of the last form of metaphysics, transcendental horizonality."
125. Jürgen Habermas, *The Philosophical Discourse on Modernity: Twelve Lectures*, trans. Frederick Lawrence (Cambridge: MIT Press, 1987), p. 155. Concerning Habermas's debate with Heidegger with respect to the issue of philosophy and politics, see Cristina Lafont, "World-Disclosure and Critique: Did Habermas Succeed in Thinking with Heidegger Against Heidegger?" *Telos* 145 (2008): 161–176; Peter E. Gordon, *Continental Divide: Heidegger, Cassirer, Davos* (Cambridge: Harvard University Press, 2010), pp. 354–357. On Habermas's critique of Heidegger's embrace of Nazism, see as well Stefan Müller-Doohm, *Habermas: A Biography*, trans. Daniel Steuer (Cambridge: Polity, 2016), pp. 59–66.
126. For instance, see the view of Sidonie Kellerer, Emmanuel Faye's student, noted by Babette E. Babich, "Heidegger's Jews: Inclusion/Exclusion and Heidegger's Anti-Semitism," *Journal of the British Society for Phenomenology* 47 (2016): 134.
127. Wolin, "An Exchange of Letters," p. 162. A similar position was taken by Buber. See David Novak, "Buber's Critique of Heidegger," *Modern Judaism* 5 (1985): 134–136.
128. Herbert Marcuse, *Heideggerian Marxism*, ed. Richard Wolin and John Abromeit (Lincoln: University of Nebraska Press, 2005), pp. 165–166 (emphasis in original).
129. Ibid, pp. 169–170.

1. BARBARIC ENCHANTMENT

130. Ibid., p. 170. Regarding Marcuse's relationship to Heidegger, see Wolin, "An Exchange of Letters," pp. 152–164; Wolin, *Heidegger's Children*, pp. 135–172; John Abromeit, "Herbert Marcuse's Critical Encounter with Martin Heidegger, 1927–33," in *Herbert Marcuse: A Critical Reader*, ed. John Abromeit and W. Mark Cobb (New York: Routledge, 2004), pp. 131–151.
131. Leo Strauss, *The Rebirth of Classical Political Rationalism: An Introduction to the Thought of Leo Strauss*, selected by Thomas L. Pangle (Chicago: University of Chicago Press, 1989), p. 30. Strauss draws a comparison between Nietzsche and Heidegger by arguing that, while the former would not have sided with Hitler, there is an "undeniable kinship" between his thought and fascism (p. 31). The validity of this reading of Nietzsche cannot be pursued here.
132. Ibid., p. 29. For an illuminating analysis of Strauss's response to Heidegger, see Wurgaft, *Thinking in Public*, pp. 37–47. See also Steven B. Smith, "Destruktion or Recovery?: Leo Strauss's Critique of Heidegger," *Review of Metaphysics* 51 (1997): 345–377; Paul O'Mahoney, "Opposing Political Philosophy and Literature: Strauss's Critique of Heidegger and the Fate of the 'Quarrel Between Philosophy and Poetry,'" *Theoria: A Journal of Social and Political Theory* 58 (2011): 73–96.
133. Amos Funkenstein, *Perceptions of Jewish History* (Berkeley: University of California Press, 1993), p. 331.
134. Ibid., pp. 332–333. For a different perspective, see Grunenberg, *Hannah Arendt und Martin Heidegger*, p. 202; English translation: *Hannah Arendt and Martin Heidegger*, p. 131:

> In retrospect, one could say that Heidegger wanted to prepare an atheological ethics of Dasein in *Being and Time*. Such a gesture harbored the possibility of a transition to an ideology. If this ethics was to become effective, it had to be accomplished against the resistance of the "they," of the with-world and its thoughtlessness. He saw the chance to make a transition from the possibility of authentic Dasein to its actuality.... *Being and Time* offered neither fascist nor nationalist ideology, but rather a unique mixture of the systematic exposition of the question of Being and the attempt to extend it to the requirements of Dasein's ethics, without touching on the question of actualization. The question of *why* Heidegger made the leap from pure thinking to National Socialism cannot be reduced to a simple cause-effect relation.... Heidegger's commitment to National Socialism lay in the realm of the possible, not of the necessary.
>
> (emphasis in original)

135. Thomas Sheehan, "Heidegger and the Nazis," *New York Review of Books* 35, no. 10 (June 16, 1988): 38.
136. Löwith, *My Life*, p. 60, cited in Wolin, *The Heidegger Controversy*, p. 142. See Blanchot, "Thinking the Apocalypse," pp. 476–477; Wolin, *Heidegger's Children*, pp. 178–180.
137. Rainer Marten, "Heideggers Geist," in *Die Heidegger Kontroverse*, ed. Jürg Altwegg (Frankfurt: Athenaeum, 1988), p. 226, cited in Babette E. Babich, *Words in Blood, Like Flowers: Philosophy and Poetry, Music and Eros in Hölderlin, Nietzsche, and Heidegger* (Albany: State University of New York Press, 2006), p. 234.

1. BARBARIC ENCHANTMENT

138. Farías, *Heidegger and Nazism*.
139. Wolin, *The Politics of Being*; Wolin, *Heidegger's Children*, pp. 173–232.
140. Hugo Ott, *Martin Heidegger: A Political Life*, trans. Allan Blunden (New York: Basic Books, 1993).
141. Hans Sluga, *Heidegger's Crisis: Philosophy and Politics in Nazi Germany* (Cambridge: Harvard University Press, 1993).
142. Rockmore, *On Heidegger's Nazism*.
143. Johannes Fritsche, *Historical Destiny and National Socialism in Heidegger's Being and Time* (Berkeley: University of California Press, 1999).
144. Emmanuel Faye, "Nazi Foundations in Heidegger's Work," *South Central Review* 23 (2006): 55–66; and Emmanuel Faye, *Heidegger: The Introduction of Nazism Into Philosophy in Light of the Unpublished Seminars of 1933–1935*, trans. Michael B. Smith (New Haven: Yale University Press, 2011). For a critical assessment of Faye's work, see Thomas Sheehan, "Emmanuel Faye: The Introduction of Fraud Into Philosophy?" *Philosophy Today* 59 (2015): 367–400; and the response by Johannes Fritsche, "Absence of Soil, Historicity, and Goethe in Heidegger's *Being and Time*: Sheehan on Faye," *Philosophy Today* 60 (2016): 429–445.
145. Dominique Janicaud, *The Shadow of That Thought: Heidegger and the Question of Politics* (Evanston: Northwestern University Press, 1996), pp. 12–49.
146. Fred Dallmayr, *The Other Heidegger* (Ithaca: Cornell University Press, 1993).
147. Julian Young, *Heidegger, Philosophy, Nazism* (Cambridge: Cambridge University Press, 1997). See also Jeff Collins, *Heidegger and the Nazis* (New York: Totem, 2000), p. 32: "Given all the evidence, there can be little doubt of Heidegger's Nazi commitment. But are the charges primarily biographical? They do not prove that his philosophical works are Nazist, that they lead towards Nazism directly or indirectly or that they have Nazist effects." For a similarly skeptical perspective, see Randall Havas, "Nihilism and the Illusion of Nationalism," in *Martin Heidegger: Politics, Art, and Technology*, ed. Karsten Harries and Christoph Jamme (New York: Holmes and Meier, 1994), pp. 197–209.
148. Peter Trawny, *Heidegger and the Myth of a Jewish World Conspiracy*, trans. Andrew J. Mitchell (Chicago: University of Chicago Press, 2015). See the review essay by Johannes Fritsche, "National Socialism, Anti-Semitism, and Philosophy in Heidegger and Scheler: On Peter Trawny's *Heidegger & the Myth of a Jewish World-Conspiracy*," *Philosophy Today* 60 (2016): 583–608. For another defense of Heidegger on grounds that Nazism played a limited role in his thinking about the history of being, see Brencio, "Martin Heidegger," pp. 87–134.
149. Faye, *Heidegger*, p. 319. See discussion of this statement in Geoffrey Bennington, *Scatter 1: The Politics of Politics in Foucault, Heidegger, and Derrida* (New York: Fordham University Press, 2016), pp. 102–103.
150. Karl Löwith, "The Political Implications of Heidegger's Existentialism," in Wolin, *The Heidegger Controversy*, p. 174.
151. Heidegger, *Being and Time*, § 74, pp. 364–368; *Sein und Zeit*, pp. 382–387. The view taken by Löwith in 1939 corresponds to the argument of Ernst Cassirer, *The Myth of the State* (New Haven: Yale University Press, 1946), p. 293. After stating that Husserl's aim was to make philosophy an "exact science" established on the basis of "unshakable facts and indubitable principles," Cassirer notes that this

> tendency is entirely alien to Heidegger. He does not admit that there is something like "eternal" truth, a Platonic "realm of ideas," or a strict logical method of philosophic thought. All this is declared to be elusive. In vain we try to build up a logical philosophy; we can only give an *Existenzialphilosophie*. Such an existential philosophy does not claim to give us an objective and universally valid truth. No thinker can give more than the truth of his own existence; and this existence has a historical character.... To be thrown into the stream of time is a fundamental and inalterable feature of our human situation, We cannot emerge from this stream and we cannot change its course. We have to accept the historical conditions of our existence.

Cassirer's passage is cited and discussed by Wolin, *Heidegger's Children*, p. 176. Many have weighed in on the role of finitude in Heidegger's thinking and the rejection of transcendence. For an illuminating study on this theme, see Dennis J. Schmidt, *The Ubiquity of the Finite: Hegel, Heidegger, and the Entitlements of Philosophy* (Cambridge: MIT Press, 1988).

152. Karl Löwith, "The Political Implications of Heidegger's Existentialism," in Wolin, *The Heidegger Controversy*, p. 169. Compare Löwith, *My Life*, pp. 31–32.
153. Löwith, "The Political Implications," p. 169.
154. Ibid., p. 180.
155. Ibid., p. 182 (emphasis in original).
156. Löwith, *Martin Heidegger*, pp. 219–223 (emphasis in original).
157. Vattimo, *Of Reality*, p. 151.
158. Löwith, *My Life*, pp. 34–44.
159. Ibid., p. 38.
160. Vattimo, *Of Reality*, p. 200. Vattimo philosophically equates Heidegger's choice of Hitler's Nazism and the choice of Georg Lukács and Ernst Bloch to promote Stalin's communism.
161. The skeleton of the argument concerning *Sein und Zeit* is presented by Theodor W. Adorno, *The Jargon of Authenticity*, trans. Knut Tarnowski and Frederic Will (Evanston: Northwestern University Press, 1973), pp. 4–5:

> Throughout this work Heidegger employed "authenticity," in the context of an existential ontology, as a specifically philosophical term.... Of course in Heidegger, as in all those who followed his language, a diminished theological resonance can be heard to this very day. The theological addictions of these years have seeped into the language, far beyond the circle of those who at that time set themselves up as the elite. Nevertheless, the sacred quality of the authentics' talk belongs to the cult of authenticity rather than to the Christian cult, even where ... its language resembles the Christian. Prior to any consideration of particular content, this language molds thought. As a consequence, that thought accommodates itself to the goal of subordination even where it aspires to resist that goal. The authority of the absolute is overthrown by absolutized authority. Fascism was not simply a conspiracy—although it was that—but it was something that came to life in the course of a powerful social development. Language provides

it with a refuge. Within this refuge a smoldering evil expresses itself as though it were salvation.

See ibid., pp. 49–58, 95–96; Peter E. Gordon, *Adorno and Existence* (Cambridge: Harvard University Press, 2016), pp. 88–89. See, however, Martin Jay, "Taking on the Stigma of Inauthenticity: Adorno's Critique of Genuineness," in *Language without Soil: Adorno and Late Philosophical Modernity*, ed. Gerhard Richter (New York: Fordham University Press, 2010), pp. 17–29, esp. 18–19.

162. Wolin, *The Seduction of Unreason*, pp. 1–23.
163. Martin Heidegger, "Messkirch's Seventh Centennial," trans. Thomas J. Sheehan, *Listening* 8 (1973): 40–41. I thank Professor Sheehan for making a copy of his translation available to me.
164. Heidegger, *Contributions*, § 220, p. 273; *Beiträge*, p. 345.
165. Marcuse, *Heideggerian Marxism*, pp. 170–171.
166. Heidegger, *Überlegungen XII–XV*, p. 243; *Ponderings XII–XV*, p. 191. See Jaspers, *Philosophische Autobiographie*, p. 101, translated in *The Heidegger-Jaspers Correspondence*, pp. 249–250 (see also Grunenberg, *Hannah Arendt und Martin Heidegger*, pp. 178–179; English translation: *Hannah Arendt and Martin Heidegger*, pp. 116–117). Jaspers recounts that the last time he saw Heidegger, in Heidelberg in May 1933, he asked him what he thought about the "Jewish question" and the "vicious nonsense of the Elders of Zion," to which Heidegger replied: "But there is a dangerous international Jewish conspiracy" (*Es gibt doch eine gefährliche internationale Verbindung der Juden*). Concerning this elocution, see Eugen Fischer and Gerhard Kittel, "Das antike Weltjudentum," *Forschungen zur Judenfrage* 7 (1943): 1–236; Cornelia Schmitz-Berning, *Vokabular des Nationalsozialismus* (Berlin: Walter de Gruyter, 2007), pp. 689–693. See also Trawny, *Heidegger and the Myth*, p. 27.
167. Trawny, "Heidegger, 'World Judaism,' and Modernity," pp. 16–17; Trawny, *Heidegger and the Myth*, pp. 21, 27–30. Compare Nancy, *The Banality*, pp. 23–24.
168. Adolf Hitler, *Mein Kampf: Zwei Bände in einem Band* (Munich: Franz Eher Nachf, 1943), coined various phrases to denigrate the Jewish people, including the "international Jewish world finance," *internationale jüdische Weltfinanz* (p. 163) and the related "international financial world Jewry," *internationalen Weltfinanzjudentums* (p. 505); the "international world Jews," *internationalen Weltjuden* (pp. 498, 629, 763); and the "international world Jew," *internationale Weltjude* (pp. 521, 675); or simply the "international Jew," *internationale Jude* (p. 585). For an extensive discussion of the historical ramifications of the expression *international world Jewry*, see Jeffrey Herf, *The Jewish Enemy: Nazi Propaganda During World War II and the Holocaust* (Cambridge: Harvard University Press, 2006), pp. 50–91.
169. Wolin, *The Heidegger Controversy*, p. 63. See Marcuse, *Heideggerian Marxism*, p. 170.
170. The letter is translated by Gary L. Ulmen and published as "Heidegger and Schmitt: The Bottom Line," *Telos* 72 (1987): 132, cited in Gregory Fried, *Heidegger's Polemos: From Being to Politics* (New Haven: Yale University Press, 2000), p. 28 (the bracketed comments were added by him). The original German appears in Heidegger, *Reden*, p. 156. Concerning this text, see Geoff Waite, "Heidegger,

1. BARBARIC ENCHANTMENT

Schmitt, Strauss: The Hidden Monologue, or, Conserving Esotericism to Justify the High Hand of Violence," *Cultural Critique* 69 (2008): 122–123; and John Carlos Donado's brief comments, "Heidegger's Letter to Schmitt," posted on August 8, 2012, and available at http://www.telospress.com/heideggers-letter-to-schmitt/. For a more detailed discussion of Heidegger and Schmitt, focused on the critique of liberalism as founded in subjectivity and the question of the historicity of the political, see Radloff, *Heidegger*, pp. 256–290. On National Socialism as radical liberalism, see Alexander Schwan, "Heidegger's *Beiträge zur Philosophie* and Politics," in *Martin Heidegger: Politics, Art, and Technology*, pp. 76–78.

171. Heidegger, *Reden*, p. 156.
172. On the question of whether Heidegger's view should be labeled anti-Semitism or anti-Judaism, see Jesús Adrián Escudero, "Heidegger's *Black Notebooks* and the Question of Anti-Semitism," *Gatherings: The Heidegger Circle Annual* 5 (2015): 35–40. See also Dieter Thomä, "Wie antisemitisch ist Heidegger? Über die *Schwarzen Hefte* und die gegenwärtige Lage der Heidegger-Kritik," in *Martin Heideggers "Schwarze Hefte,"* pp. 211–233.
173. Trawny, *Heidegger and the Myth*, pp. 18–37. On the matter of historical anti-Semitism, see the remarks of Nancy, *The Banality*, pp. 14–17.
174. Marion Heinz, "Seinsgeschichte und Metapolitik," in *Martin Heideggers "Schwarze Hefte,"* pp. 122–143. Numerous scholars have discussed the role of the *Volk* in Heidegger's political philosophy. Here I mention only a small sampling: Berel Lang, *Heidegger's Silence* (Ithaca: Cornell University Press, 1996), pp. 40–44; James Phillips, *Heidegger's Volk: Between National Socialism and Poetry* (Stanford: Stanford University Press, 2005); Thomä, "Heidegger und der Nationalsozialismus," pp. 115–119; Rockmore, *On Heidegger's Nazism*, pp. 282–301; Radloff, *Heidegger*, pp. 173–209; Thomas Rohkrämer, "Heidegger, Kulturkritik und völkische Ideologie," in *Martin Heideggers "Schwarze Hefte,"* pp. 258–274. On the *völkisch* mood in Heidegger's *Zeitgeist*, see also Bourdieu, *The Political Ontology*, pp. 8–12.
175. Roberto Esposito, *Communitas: The Origin and Destiny of Community*, trans. Timothy Campbell (Stanford: Stanford University Press, 2010), p. 100.
176. Heidegger, *Contributions*, § 196, p. 252 (emphasis in original); *Beiträge*, p. 319.
177. Heidegger, *Ponderings II–VI*, p. 163; *Überlegungen II–VI*, p. 223.
178. Heidegger, *Ponderings II–VI*, p. 272; *Überlegungen II–VI*, p. 374. Regarding this passage, see Steven Crowell, "Reading Heidegger's *Black Notebooks*," in *Reading Heidegger's Black Notebooks, 1931–1941*, ed. Ingo Farin and Jeff Malpas (Cambridge: MIT Press, 2016), pp. 39–40.
179. Heidegger, *Contributions*, § 117, p. 181; *Beiträge*, p. 230.
180. See the reference cited at *n*185, this chapter.
181. Consider, for example, Heidegger's adamant denial of anti-Semitic behavior in his letter to Hannah Arendt, from sometime in the winter of 1932–1933, in Hannah Arendt and Martin Heidegger, *Letters, 1925–1975*, ed. Ursula Ludz, trans. Andrew Shields (Orlando, FL: Harcourt, 2004), pp. 52–53. The letter is reproduced and discussed by Krell, "Heidegger's *Black Notebooks*," pp. 155–157, based on the analysis in Grunenberg, *Hannah Arendt und Martin Heidegger*, pp. 165–166 (English translation: *Hannah Arendt and Martin Heidegger*, pp. 107–108). On the revisionist tendencies in Heidegger and some of his supporters, see Tom Rockmore,

1. BARBARIC ENCHANTMENT

"Heidegger and Holocaust Revisionism," in *Martin Heidegger and the Holocaust*, ed. Alan Rosenberg and Alan Milchman (Atlantic Highlands, NJ: Humanities Press, 1994), pp. 113–126.

182. Peter E. Gordon, "Heidegger in Black," *New York Review of Books*, October 9, 2014, available at http://www.nybooks.com/articles/archives/2014/oct/09/heidegger-in-black/; Gregory Fried, "The King Is Dead: Heidegger's "Black Notebooks": Gregory Fried on *Black Notebooks/Schwarze Hefte*, Vols. 94–96," *Los Angeles Review of Books*, September 13, 2104, available at http://lareviewofbooks.org/review/king-dead-heideggers-black-notebooks.

183. Heidegger, *Ponderings II–VI*, p. 144 (emphasis in original); *Überlegungen II–VI*, p. 196.

184. Philip Oltermann, "Heidegger's 'Black Notebooks' Reveal Antisemitism at Core of His Philosophy," *Guardian*, March 12, 2014, available at https:/www.theguardian.com/books/2014/mar/13/martin-heidegger-black-notebooks-reveal-nazi-ideology-antisemitism.

185. The remark is quoted from the preface to Martin Heidegger and Erhart Kästner, *Briefwechsel, 1953–1974*, ed. Heinrich W. Petzet (Frankfurt: Insel, 1986), p. 10, in Lacoue-Labarthe, *Heidegger, Art, and Politics*, p. 12. See also Miguel de Beistegui, *The New Heidegger* (London: Continuum, 2005), p. 164; John van Buren, *The Young Heidegger: Rumor of the Hidden King* (Bloomington: Indiana University Press, 1994), p. 393.

186. Silvio Vietta, *Heideggers Kritik am Nationalsozialismus und an der Technik* (Berlin: Walter de Gruyter, 1989), p. 101. A separate but relevant question is Heidegger's nervous breakdown in 1946 after his having been interrogated by the denazification committee, an important chapter that I cannot discuss here. For recent analysis, see Mitchell, "Heidegger's Breakdown."

187. *The Heidegger-Jaspers Correspondence*, p. 185 (emphasis in original). In one of the more emotionally earnest statements on Heidegger's part, he goes on to say, "When, at the end of the 1930s the worst evil set in with vile persecutions, I thought immediately about your wife."

188. Ibid., p. 186 (emphasis in original).

189. Ibid., p. 189.

190. Marcel Conche, *Heidegger résistant* (Treffort: Mégare, 1996); see as well as Marcel Conche, *Heidegger inconsideré* (Treffort: Mégare, 1997); and discussion in Janicaud, *Heidegger in France*, pp. 239–240. See also Anson Rabinbach, "The Aftermath: Reflections on the Culture and Ideology of National Socialism," in *Weimar Thought: A Contested Legacy*, ed. Peter E. Gordon and John P. McCormick (Princeton: Princeton University Press, 2013), pp. 396–397.

191. Fackenheim, *To Mend the World*, pp. 167–171.

192. Ibid., pp. 171–181. For the characterization of Heidegger's thought after the turn in the 1930s as the *Judaization of the entire history of Western philosophy*, see Emil L. Fackenheim, *Encounters Between Judaism and Modern Philosophy: A Preface to Future Jewish Thought* (New York: Schocken, 1980), p. 218, and see analysis in Michael Fagenblat, "'Heidegger' and the Jews," in *Reading Heidegger's Black Notebooks*, pp. 157–158. Fackenheim's criticism of Heidegger is explored in more depth by Ari Bursztein, "Emil Fackenheim on Heidegger and the Holocaust," *Iyyun: The Jerusalem Philosophical Quarterly* 53 (2004): 325–336.

2. NOMADISM, HOMELESSNESS, AND THE OBFUSCATION OF BEING

1. For discussion of Heidegger's antibiologism, on the one hand, and his commitment to *völkisch* identity and rootedness in the land, on the other hand, see Sonia Sikka, "Heidegger and Race," in *Race and Racism in Continental Philosophy*, ed. Robert Bernasconi with Sybol Cook (Bloomington: Indiana University Press, 2003), pp. 74–97. See also Robert Bernasconi, "Heidegger's Alleged Challenge to the Nazi Concepts of Race," in *Appropriating Heidegger* ed. James E. Faulconer and Mark A. Wrathall (Cambridge: Cambridge University Press, 2000), pp. 50-67.
2. See reference cited in ch. 1n37.
3. Martin Heidegger, *Ponderings II–VI: Black Notebooks 1938–1939*, trans. Richard Rojcewicz (Bloomington: Indiana University Press, 2017), p. 255 (emphasis in original); *Überlegungen II–VI (Schwarze Hefte 1931–1938)* [GA 94] (Frankfurt: Vittorio Klostermann, 2014), p. 350. Compare Martin Heidegger, *Ponderings XII–XV: Black Notebooks 1939-1941*, trans. Richard Rojcewicz (Bloomington: Indiana University Press, 2017), p. 43 (*Überlegungen XII–XV (Schwarze Hefte 1939-1941)* [GA 96] (Frankfurt: Vittorio Klostermann, 2014), p. 55): "When machination has secured its power so extensively, then the likewise machinationally grounded 'principles' of 'blood and soil' are proclaimed, and what ultimately comes into its own is 'science'—which makes its discoveries according to these new points of view." Implicit here is not only an attack on the Nazi idea of science based on the racial principles of blood and soil, but also, oddly enough, an attribution of machination to National Socialism, the very vice that is associated with the Jews.
4. See the nuanced discussion of this topic in Gerhard Richter, "The Debt of Inheritance Revisited: Heidegger's Mortgage, Derrida's Appraisal," *Oxford Literary Review* 37 (2015): 67–91. On the concept of race in the being-historical landscape of Heidegger's thinking, see also Peter Trawny, *Heidegger and the Myth of a Jewish World Conspiracy*, trans. Andrew J. Mitchell (Chicago: University of Chicago Press, 2015), pp. 38–46.
5. The reference is to Fragment 53 of Heraclitus according to the enumeration in the *Fragmente der Vorsokratiker*, ed. Hermann Alexander Diels and later revised by Walther Kranz. The text is derived from the citation in Hippolytus, *Refutatio* IX.9.4. See Charles H. Kahn, *The Art and Thought of Heraclitus: An Edition of the Fragments with Translation and Commentary* (Cambridge: Cambridge University Press, 1979), p. 67: "War is father of all and king of all; and some he has shown as gods, others men; some he has made slaves, others free." Compare the extensive analysis of this Heraclitean aphorism in Gregory Fried, *Heidegger's Polemos: From Being to Politics* (New Haven: Yale University Press, 2000), pp. 21–42.
6. Martin Heidegger, *Being and Truth*, trans. Gregory Fried and Richard Polt (Bloomington: Indiana University Press, 2010), p. 73; *Sein und Wahrheit* [GA 36/37] (Frankfurt: Vittorio Klostermann, 2001), p. 91. A passage such as this certainly gives us reason to question the categorical tone of the conclusion affirmed by Miguel de Beistegui, *The New Heidegger* (London: Continuum, 2005), p. 160:

> In the light of the evidence available, and having spent the last 15 years of my life reading Heidegger, I can say that I believe there is nothing in his

thinking that suggests any anti-Semitic tendencies (were this to be the case, taking his thought seriously, teaching it and writing about it would amount to nothing less than a complicity in what ought to be characterized outright as an immoral and criminal endeavour). There is, in other words, nothing in his thought that suggests he ever believed in the inferiority of the Jewish race, its threat to the German nation and European culture in general, its concerted effort to weaken the spirit of the German people or its collective guilt (whether in the death of Christ or the lamentable state of Germany under the Weimar Republic). There is nothing in common between the hatred, nastiness and sheer brutality of the anti-Semitism that ran—and, unfortunately, continues to run—deep in our Western culture, and the depth and brilliance of Heidegger's thought.

7. Emmanuel Faye, *Heidegger: The Introduction of Nazism Into Philosophy in Light of the Unpublished Seminars of 1933–1935*, trans. Michael B. Smith (New Haven: Yale University Press, 2011), pp. 168–169.
8. Ibid., p. 171. See as well Emmanuel Faye, "Antisémitisme et extermination: Heidegger, l'Œuvre intégrale et les Cahiers noirs," *Cités: Philosophie, Politique, Histoire* 61 (2015): 107–122.
9. Martin Heidegger, *What Is Called Thinking?* trans. Fred W. Wieck and J. Glenn Gray (New York: Harper and Row, 1968), p. 83; *Was Heißt Denken?* [GA 8] (Frankfurt: Vittorio Klostermann, 2002), p. 88.
10. Martin Heidegger, *Country Path Conversations*, trans. Bret W. Davis (Bloomington: Indiana University Press, 2010), pp. 157–158 (emphasis in original); *Feldweg-Gespräche* [GA 77] (Frankfurt: Vittorio Klostermann, 1995), p. 241.
11. Jacques Derrida, *Of Spirit: Heidegger and the Question*, trans. Geoffrey Bennington and Rachel Bowlby (Chicago: University of Chicago Press, 1989), p. 10; *De l'esprit: Heidegger et la question* (Paris: Galilée, 1987), p. 27. For a judicious discussion of Derrida's analysis, see David F. Krell, "Spiriting Heidegger," in *Of Derrida, Heidegger, and Spirit*, ed. David Wood (Evanston: Northwestern University Press, 1993), pp. 11–40.
12. Martin Heidegger, *Anmerkungen I–V (Schwarze Hefte 1942–1948)* [GA 97] (Frankfurt: Vittorio Klostermann, 2015), p. 20. The passage is cited with a different translation in Trawny, *Heidegger and the Myth*, p. 76. Compare as well the translation by David F. Krell, "Troubled Brows: Heidegger's *Black Notebooks*, 1942–1948," *Research in Phenomenology* 46 (2016): 317. Krell renders the critical term *Herrschaft* as hegemony; see *n*279, this chapter. Concerning this passage, see also Donatella di Cesare, "Heidegger—'Jews Self-destructed': New Black Notebooks Reveal Philosopher's Shocking Take on Shoah," February 9, 2015, http://www.corriere.it/english/15_febbraio_09/heidegger-jews-self-destructed-47cd3930-b03b-11e4-8615-d0fd07eabd28.shtml. And see Slavoj Žižek, *Disparities* (London: Bloomsbury, 2016), p. 236. On the possible intent of *Selbstvernichtung*, see Jean-Luc Nancy, *The Banality of Heidegger*, trans. Jeff Fort (New York: Fordham University Press, 2017), p. 84*n*6. Nancy astutely notes that however we explain the reference to Jewish self-annihilation, the most detestable thing is that "Heidegger never said a single word on any aspect of the anti-Semitic persecutions, which nonetheless would have deserved the same overt disdain and hostility he directed at 'biological'

2. NOMADISM, HOMELESSNESS, AND THE OBFUSCATION OF BEING

anti-Semitism." See ibid., p. 40: "Why did he remain silent, later, in the extermination of the Jews, even when he was faced with the friendly but pressing questions of Jaspers, and certainly of several others? No doubt because he refused to renounce the grand schema of *Geschichte* even if henceforth he treated it in a different way." See also ibid., p. 51, where Nancy explains the "stubborn silence" of Heidegger on the camps as the price he paid for his contention that the destruction of the Jewish people is connected to the self-suppression of the groundless, which occasions the victory of history over those lacking history.

13. The language is appropriated from Simon Epstein, "When the Demon Itself Complains of Being Demonized," in *Demonizing the Other: Antisemitism, Racism, and Xenophobia*, ed. Robert S. Wistrich (London: Routledge, 1999), pp. 236–243.
14. Heidegger, *Anmerkungen I–V*, p. 20.
15. See, however, Trawny, *Heidegger and the Myth*, pp. 76–77, who suggests that the self-annihilation referred to in this passage does not need to be understood as physical annihilation but can be understood rather as a self-annihilation of humanity, which is related primarily to technology. Regarding this motif and Heidegger's portrayal of National Socialism as an example of the technological demise of Western culture, see Silvio Vietta, *Heideggers Kritik am Nationalsozialismus und an der Technik* (Berlin: Walter de Gruyter, 1989). In this regard, it is of interest to consider the comment of Heidegger, *Ponderings II–VI*, p. 207 (*Überlegungen II–VI*, pp. 282–283): "What does it signify that the human masses are worth so little they could be annihilated in *one* stroke; is there a stricter proof of the abandonment by being [*Seinsverlassenheit*]? Who surmises the resonance of a last god in such a failure?" (emphasis in original).
16. Many scholars and philosophers have addressed this aspect of Heidegger's thinking. For two representative studies, see Babette E. Babich, "Heidegger's Philosophy of Science and the Critique of Calculation: Reflective Questioning, *Gelassenheit*, and Life," in *Heidegger on Science*, ed. Trish Glazebrook (Albany: State University of New York Press, 2012), pp. 159–192; Hassan Givsan, "Seyn und Macht. Seyn als Machenschaft, Seyn, die mythische Gewalt," in *Martin Heideggers "Schwarze Hefte": Eine philosophisch-politische Debatte*, ed. Marion Heinz and Sidonie Kellerer, with the collaboration of Tobias Bender (Berlin: Suhrkamp, 2016), pp. 78–99. In the address Heidegger gave in honor of Kreutzer, his position is somewhat attenuated as he acknowledges that calculative thinking (*rechnende Denken*) and meditative thinking (*besinnliche Denken*) are "each justified and needed in its own way." See Martin Heidegger, *Discourse on Thinking*, trans. John M. Anderson and E. Hans Freund (New York: Harper and Row, 1966), p. 46; *Gelassenheit* (Stuttgart: Neske, 1959), p. 13. Later on in the address, however, Heidegger resorts to language that is less discriminating and more unequivocally critical of the former kind of thinking, especially as it is expressed in the utilization of atomic energy. Heidegger poses the question if in the future the work of humanity can "still be expected to thrive in the fertile ground of a homeland and mount into the ether, into the far reaches of the heavens and the spirit? Or will everything now fall into the clutches of planning and calculation, of organization and automation?... The world now appears as an object open to the attacks of calculative thought, attacks that nothing is believed able any longer to resist" (Heidegger, *Discourse on Thinking*, pp. 49–50; *Gelassenheit*, pp. 16–17). A greater danger than

the third world war with a threat of an atomic catastrophe is the threat that calculative thinking will be accepted as the only way of thinking available to humankind (Heidegger, *Discourse on Thinking*, p. 56; *Gelassenheit*, p. 23).

17. Peter Trawny, "Heidegger, 'World Judaism,' and Modernity," *Gatherings: The Heidegger Circle Annual* 5 (2015): 9–10.
18. Martin Heidegger, *Contributions to Philosophy (Of the Event)*, trans. Richard Rojcewicz and Daniela Vallega-Neu (Bloomington: Indiana University Press, 2012), § 78, p. 127 (emphasis in original); *Beiträge zur Philosophie (Vom Ereignis)* [GA 65] (Frankfurt: Vittorio Klostermann, 1989), p. 163.
19. Heidegger, *Überlegungen XII–XV*, p. 46. For a different rendering, see Heidegger, *Ponderings XII–XV*, p. 37.
20. Heidegger, *Anmerkungen I–V*, p. 188. See Trawny, *Heidegger and the Myth*, pp. 70–71.
21. The term *topologischer Antisemitismus* is used by Luca di Blasi, "Vom nationalmessianischen Enthusiasmus zur antisemitischen Paranoia: Heideggers politisches Denken zwischen 1933 und 1945," in *Heidegger und der Antisemitismus: Positionen im Widerstreit, mit Briefen von Martin und Fritz Heidegger*, ed. Walter Homolka and Arnulf Heidegger (Freiburg: Herder, 2016), pp. 196–201.
22. Martin Heidegger, *Ponderings VII–XI: Black Notebooks 1938–1939*, trans. Richard Rojcewicz (Bloomington: Indiana University Press, 2017), p. 76; *Überlegungen VII–XI (Schwarze Hefte 1938/39)* [GA 95] (Frankfurt: Vittorio Klostermann, 2014), p. 97. See Eduardo Mendieta, "Metaphysical Anti-Semitism and Worldlessness: On World Poorness, World Forming, and World Destroying," in *Heidegger's Black Notebooks: Responses to Anti-Semitism*, ed. Andrew J. Mitchell and Peter Trawny (New York: Columbia University Press, 2017), pp. 36–51.
23. On the political issues surrounding the topological-geographical elements of Heidegger's thinking—especially the return to the fatherland—in light of his affiliation with Nazism, see Victor Farías, *Heidegger and Nazism*, ed. Joseph Margolis and Tom Rockmore, trans. Paul Burrel and Dominic Di Bernardi (Philadelphia: Temple University Press, 1989), pp. 170–176. See also Jeff Malpas, *Heidegger's Topology: Being, Place, World* (Cambridge: MIT Press, 2006), pp. 17–27, 283–285; and Jeff Malpas, *Heidegger and the Thinking of Place: Explorations in the Topology of Being* (Cambridge: MIT Press, 2012), pp. 137–157. For a critical assessment of Malpas, and greater emphasis placed on the inevitable interface between the temporality of space and the spatiality of time, see Miguel de Beistegui, "The Place of Place in Heidegger's Topology," *International Journal of Philosophical Studies* 19 (2011): 277–283.
24. Martin Heidegger, *Being and Time*, trans. Joan Stambaugh, revised and with a foreword by Dennis J. Schmidt (Albany: State University of New York Press, 2010), § 40, pp. 182–183; *Sein und Zeit* (Tübingen: Max Niemeyer, 1993), pp. 188–189. For an extensive discussion of this theme, see Katherine Withy, *Heidegger on Being Uncanny* (Cambridge: Harvard University Press, 2015), pp. 48–101.
25. For comparison of the Freudian *Unheimliche* as a psychological sentiment and Heidegger's *Unheimlichkeit* as an ontological dimension of Dasein, see Anneleen Masschelein, *The Unconcept: The Freudian Uncanny in Late-Twentieth-Century Theory* (Albany: State University of New York Press, 2011), pp. 139–143.

2. NOMADISM, HOMELESSNESS, AND THE OBFUSCATION OF BEING

26. Heidegger, *Ponderings II–VI*, p. 143; *Überlegungen II–VI*, p. 195. Heidegger mentioned Grimm's novel in a letter to his brother Fritz written on March 2, 1932. See *Heidegger und der Antisemitismus*, p. 27. The characterization of the Jews as a rootless people was ubiquitous in German philosophy and theology as is attested, for instance, in the depiction of Abraham in Georg Wilhelm Friedrich Hegel, *Early Theological Writings*, trans. Thomas Malcolm Knox (Philadelphia: University of Pennsylvania Press, 1971), pp. 185–189. On the feeling of nothingness and the sense of desolation and abjectness attributed to the Jews, see Georg Wilhelm Friedrich Hegel, *Lectures on the History of Philosophy*, trans. Elizabeth S. Haldane and Frances H. Simson (London: Routledge and Kegan Paul, 1968), 3:22. See also Georg Wilhelm Friedrich Hegel, *Lectures on the Philosophy of Religion*, ed. Peter C. Hodgson, trans. Robert F. Brown, Peter C. Hodgson, and J. McKellar Stewart (Berkeley: University of California Press, 1984), 1:331. See discussion in George Steiner, *The Poetry of Thought: From Hellenism to Celan* (New York: New Directions, 2011), pp. 104–105.
27. Thomas Sheehan, "Facticity and *Ereignis*," in *Interpreting Heidegger: Critical Essays*, ed. Daniel O. Dahlstrom (Cambridge: Cambridge University Press, 2011), p. 42.
28. Tomonobu Imamichi, "Philosophical Intuition of Religious Problems in Our Age," in *Contemporary Philosophy: A New Survey*, vol. 10: *Philosophy of Religion*, ed. Guttorm Fløistad (Dordrecht: Springer, 2010), pp. 30–32; Paul North, *The Yield: Kafka's Atheological Reformation* (Stanford: Stanford University Press, 2015), pp. 36–37, 43–44.
29. Martin Heidegger, *On the Essence of Language: The Metaphysics of Language and the Essencing of the Word, Concerning Herder's Treatise* On the Origin of Language, trans. Wanda Torres Gregory and Yvonne Unna (Albany: State University of New York Press, 2004), p. 46 (emphasis in original); *Vom Wesen des Sprache: Die Metaphysik der Sprache und Die Wesung des Wortes, Zu Herders Abhandlung "Über den Ursprung der Sprache"* [GA 85] (Frankfurt: Vittorio Klostermann, 1999), pp. 55–56.
30. John D. Caputo, "People of God, People of Being: The Theological Presuppositions of Heidegger's Path of Thought," in *Appropriating Heidegger*, ed. James E. Faulconer and Mark A. Wrathall (Cambridge: Cambridge University Press, 2000), p. 89 (emphasis in original).
31. Naomi Seidman, *Faithful Renderings: Jewish-Christian Difference and the Politics of Translation* (Chicago: University of Chicago Press, 2006), p. 153.
32. Martin Heidegger, *Logic as the Question Concerning the Essence of Language*, trans. Wanda Torres Gregory and Yvonne Unna (Albany: State University of New York Press, 2009), p. 69; *Logik als die Frage nach dem Wesen der Sprache* [GA 38] (Frankfurt: Vittorio Klostermann, 1998), p. 81. Mention should also be made here of Heidegger's phenomenological analysis of the Senegal Negro's experience of the lectern in the second part of the 1919 seminar *Der Idee der Philosophie und das Weltanschauungsproblem*. See Martin Heidegger, *Towards the Definition of Philosophy*, trans. Ted Sadler (London: Athlone, 2000), pp. 60–61; *Zur Bestimmung der Philosophie* [GA 56/57] (Frankfurt: Vittorio Klostermann, 1987), pp. 71–72. Under the pretext of examining the notion of an "environmental experience" (*Umwelterlebnis*), Heidegger acknowledges that his seeing of the lectern is different

2. NOMADISM, HOMELESSNESS, AND THE OBFUSCATION OF BEING

from the Senegalese Negro (*Senegalneger*) who has been transplanted to Germany from his hut. He insists nonetheless that there are "universally valid propositions," which would also be valid for the experience of the black man from Senegal, referred to as "unscientific" (*nichtwissenschaftliche*) but not "culture-less" (*kulturlose*). From Heidegger's standpoint, even if the Senegalese sees the lectern as a "bare something," the experience still has meaning (*Bedeutung*) for him, and thus it is "a moment of signification" (*ein bedeutungshaftes Moment*). In the final analysis, the character of the "instrumental strangeness" (»*zeuglichen Fremdseins*«) experienced phenomenologically by the Senegalese and the meaningful character of the lectern experienced phenomenologically by the German "are in their essence absolutely identical." Regarding this passage, see John van Buren, *The Young Heidegger: Rumor of the Hidden King* (Bloomington: Indiana University Press, 1994), p. 260; Geoffrey Bennington, *Scatter 1: The Politics of Politics in Foucault, Heidegger, and Derrida* (New York: Fordham University Press, 2016), pp. 62–64, and especially p. 64n13. Regarding the division of the human species by Joseph Goebbels into those who are noble and those who are parasitic, which includes Africans, referred to as savages, and the Jews, see Epstein, "When the Demon Itself Complains," p. 239.

33. Heidegger, *Logic,* pp. 71–73 (emphasis in original); *Logik,* pp. 83–86. See Bettina Bergo, "'Sterben Sie?' The Problem of Dasein and 'Animals' . . . of Various Kinds," in *Heidegger's Black Notebook*s, pp. 52–73.

34. Martin Heidegger, *Pathmarks,* ed. William McNeill (Cambridge: Cambridge University Press, 1998), p. 248; *Wegmarken* [GA 9] (Frankfurt: Vittorio Klostermann, 1996), p. 326. For a critique of Heidegger's position, see Michael Marder, *Plant-Thinking: A Philosophy of Vegetal Life* (New York: Columbia University Press, 2013), pp. 129–130.

35. Heidegger, *Pathmarks,* p. 248; *Wegmarken,* p. 326.

36. Heidegger, *Pathmarks,* p. 249; *Wegmarken,* p. 326.

37. See, however, the translator's note in Martin Heidegger, *The End of Philosophy,* trans. Joan Stambaugh (New York: Harper and Row, 1973), p. 84: "The text contains notes on the overcoming of metaphysics from the years 1936 to 1946. Their major part was selected as a contribution to the Festschrift for Emil Pretorius; one section (XXVI) appeared in the Barlachheft of the state theater at Darmstadt 1951 (editor: Egon Vietta)."

38. Heidegger, *The End of Philosophy,* p. 104; *Vorträge und Aufsätze* [GA 7] (Frankfurt: Vittorio Klostermann, 2000), p. 91.

39. Martin Heidegger, *Mindfulness,* trans. Parvis Emad and Thomas Kalary (London: Continuum, 2006), p. 160; *Besinnung* [GA 66] (Frankfurt: Vittorio Klostermann, 1997), p. 182.

40. Heidegger, *Mindfulness,* p. 160; *Besinnung,* p. 182. Many have weighed in on the issue of the status of the animal in Heidegger. Especially relevant to my argument are the critiques of Derrida, *Of Spirit,* pp. 47–57; *De l'espirit,* pp. 75–90. See also Jacques Derrida, *The Animal That Therefore I Am,* ed. Marie-Louise Mallet, trans. David Wills (New York: Fordham University Press, 2008), pp. 141–160; William McNeill, *The Time of Life: Heidegger and Ēthos* (Albany: State University of New York Press, 2006), pp. 1–51; Mark Tanzer, "Heidegger on Animality and Anthropocentrism," *Journal of the British Society for Phenomenology* 47 (2016): 18–32. For

2. NOMADISM, HOMELESSNESS, AND THE OBFUSCATION OF BEING

discussion of the shift toward a more conciliatory and less anthropocentric view, see Andrew J. Mitchell, "Heidegger's Later Thinking of Animality: The End of World Poverty," *Gatherings: The Heidegger Circle Annual* 1 (2011): 74–85, and see Yoav Kenny, "The Geneses of the Animal and the Ends of Man: The Animalistic Origins of Derrida's Writings," *Epoché* 20 (2016): 497–516, esp. 506–511.

41. Heidegger, *Being and Time*, §68, p. 330; *Sein und Zeit*, p. 346. For discussion of this passage, see Derrida, *The Animal That Therefore I Am*, p. 22.
42. Compare Heidegger, *Ponderings VII–XI*, pp. 228–229 (*Überlegungen VII–XI*, p. 293):

> The *historiological animal* [historische Tier] must finally arrive at the calculation and justification of its animality and of the needs and instincts of that animality and this at a reciprocal interpenetration of historiology-technology with animality. The human being becomes thereby more and more accustomed to taking his goals from the acts of possessing and satisfying.... The *historiological animal* does not know the essence of power—because this animal—in subjection to metaphysics—understands power as a being (present-at-hand force)—rather than as the preservation of beyng itself, and that preservation can overthrow nothing, because it is itself the field of all thrownness.
>
> (emphasis in original)

43. Philippe Burrin, "Nazi Antisemistism: Animalization and Demonization," in *Demonizing the Other*, pp. 223–235.
44. Heidegger, *What Is Called Thinking?* p. 136 (emphasis in original); *Was Heißt Denken?* p. 141.
45. Peter E. Gordon, "Heidegger in Purgatory," in Martin Heidegger, *Nature, History, State 1933–1934*, ed. and trans. Gregory Fried and Richard Polt (London: Bloomsbury, 2013), pp. 85–107.
46. Derrida, *Of Spirit*, p. 134n3; *De l'esprit*, pp. 152–153n3.
47. Derrida, *Of Spirit*, p. 134n3; *De l'esprit*, p. 152n3.
48. Derrida, *The Animal That Therefore I Am*, pp. 38–39.
49. Emmanuel Levinas, *Difficult Freedom: Essays on Judaism*, trans. Seán Hand (Baltimore: Johns Hopkins University Press, 1990), p. 153.
50. Ibid. In his condemnation of Heidegger, Levinas accepts the latter's anthropocentric demarcation of language as something distinctively human, a position that has been roundly criticized in more contemporary animal studies and discussions of the posthuman. See, for example, Donovan O. Schaefer, *Religious Affects: Animality, Evolution, and Power* (Durham: Duke University Press, 2015), pp. 178–205. It is of interest to recall in this context the view expressed by Martin Buber, *I and Thou*, trans. Walter Kaufmann (New York: Scribner's, 1970), p. 144; *Ich und Du* (Heidelberg: Lambert Schneider, 1997), p. 115:

> The eyes of an animal have the capacity of a great language. Independent, without any need of the assistance of sounds and gestures, most eloquent when they rest entirely in their glance, they express the mystery in its natural captivity, that is, in the anxiety of becoming. This state of the mystery is known only to the animal, which alone can open it up to us—for this

2. NOMADISM, HOMELESSNESS, AND THE OBFUSCATION OF BEING

state can only be opened up and not revealed. The language in which this is accomplished is what it says: anxiety—the stirring of the creature between the realms of plantlike security and spiritual risk. This language is the stammering of nature under the initial grasp of spirit, before language yields to spirit's cosmic risk which we call man. But no speech will ever repeat what the stammer is able to communicate.

In contrast to Heidegger, Buber proffered a nonanthropocentric understanding of language and of anxiety. For a collection of essays that explores the relationship of human speech, language, and the communication of animals from the perspective of evolutionary neurobiology, see Johan J. Bolhuis and Martin Everaert, eds., *Birdsong, Speech, and Language: Exploring the Evolution of Mind and Brain* (Cambridge: MIT Press, 2013).

51. Heidegger, *Nature*, pp. 55–56.
52. Numerous scholars have written on these themes in Heidegger. For two comprehensive analyses, see Robert Mugerauer, *Heidegger and Homecoming: The Leitmotif in the Later Writings* (Toronto: University of Toronto Press, 2008); Brendan O'Donoghue, *A Poetics of Homecoming: Heidegger, Homelessness and the Homecoming Venture* (Newcastle: Cambridge Scholars, 2011). For an analysis of this theme from a gender perspective, see Iris Marion Young, "House and Home: Feminist Variations on a Theme," in *Feminist Interpretations of Martin Heidegger*, ed. Nancy J. Holland and Patricia Huntington (University Park: Pennsylvania State University Press, 2001), pp. 252–288.
53. Gordon, "Heidegger in Purgatory," pp. 96–98. See Sander L. Gilman, "Cosmopolitan Jews vs. Jewish Nomads: Sources of a Trope in Heidegger's *Black Notebooks*," in *Heidegger's Black Notebooks*, pp. 18–35.
54. Jesús Adrián Escudero, "Heidegger's *Black Notebooks* and the Question of Anti-Semitism," *Gatherings: The Heidegger Circle Annual* 5 (2015): 29–35. See as well Pierre Bourdieu, *The Political Ontology of Martin Heidegger*, trans. Peter Collier (Stanford: Stanford University Press, 1991), pp. 49–50; Robert Metcalf, "Rethinking 'Bodenständigkeit' in the Technological Age," *Research in Phenomenology* 42 (2012): 49–66. Peter Blickle, *Heimat: A Critical Theory of the German Idea of Homeland* (Rochester: Camden House, 2002), provides a good background for Heidegger's various reflections on this topic.
55. Heidegger, *Being and Time*, § 12, p. 56; *Sein und Zeit*, p. 56. See Derrida, *Of Spirit*, pp. 24–25; *De l'esprit*, pp. 44–46; *The Animal That Therefore I Am*, pp. 153–154.
56. Heidegger, *Being and Time*, § 70, p. 350 (emphasis in original); *Sein und Zeit*, pp. 367–368.
57. Martin Heidegger, "Why Do I Stay in the Provinces?" (1934), in *Heidegger: The Man and The Thinker*, ed. Thomas Sheehan (Chicago: Precedent, 1981), p. 28. The German text was first published in *Der Alemanne* on March 7, 1934.
58. Heidegger, *Ponderings VII–XI*, p. 81; *Überlegungen VII–XI*, p. 104.
59. Heidegger, *Ponderings VII–XI*, pp. 8–9 (emphasis in original); *Überlegungen VII–XI*, pp. 10–11.
60. Carl G. Jung, "Zur gegenwärtigen Lage der Psychotherapie," *Zentralblatt für Psychotherapie und ihre Grenzgebiete* 7 (1934): 1–16. The English version "The State of Psychotherapy Today" is included in Carl G. Jung, *Civilization in Transition*, 2d

2. NOMADISM, HOMELESSNESS, AND THE OBFUSCATION OF BEING

ed., trans. R. F. C. Hull [CW 10] (Princeton: Princeton University Press, 1970), pp. 157–173.
61. Ibid., pp. 165–166.
62. Ibid., p. 165.
63. Ibid., p. 166.
64. Ibid.
65. For a more extensive explanation of National Socialism in terms of the archetype of the collective unconscious, see Jung, *Civilization*, pp. 237–238. On the question of Jung, Nazism, and anti-Semitism, see Andrew Samuels, *The Political Psyche* (London: Routledge, 1993), pp. 287–316, esp. 292–293; Richard Wolin, *The Seduction of Unreason: The Intellectual Romance with Fascism from Nietzsche to Postmodernism* (Princeton: Princeton University Press, 2004), pp. 63–88. Particularly noteworthy is the exchange between Erich Neumann and Jung over the references to Jews and Nazism in his lecture "Zur gegenwärtigen Lage der Psychotherapie" in Carl G. Jung and Erich Neumann, *Analytical Psychology in Exile: The Correspondence of C. G. Jung and Erich Neumann*, ed. Martin Liebscher, trans. Heather McCartney (Princeton: Princeton University Press, 2015), pp. 10–15, 51–59. Of the many interesting things that Jung writes in his response (August 12, 1934), I note his surmise that the "psychic necessity of Zionism" arose from the activation of the pagan archetype of the collective unconscious linked to the soil. See the analysis of Jung's view on Jews and Nazism in Elisabeth Roudinesco, *Freud: In His Time and Ours*, trans. Catherine Porter (Cambridge: Harvard University Press, 2016), pp. 367–372.
66. What I offer here is a brief summary of the final chapter in a monograph I am presently writing, *Heidegger and Kabbalah: Hidden Gnosis and the Path of Poiēsis*. I have taken the liberty to repeat some of my analysis verbatim but in this context I am not pursuing the comparison of Heidegger to the similar patterns in kabbalistic literature.
67. Richard Wolin, ed., *The Heidegger Controversy: A Critical Reader* (Cambridge: MIT Press, 1993), p. 29; *Die Selbstbehauptung der Deutschen Universität: Rede, gehalten bei der feierlichen Übernahme des Rektorats der Universität Freiburg i. Br. am 27.5.1933; Das Rektorat 1933/34: Tatsachen und Gedanken* (Frankfurt: Vittorio Klostermann, 1983), p. 9.
68. Wolin, *The Heidegger Controversy*, p. 29; *Die Selbstbehauptung*, p. 9.
69. Wolin, *The Heidegger Controversy*, p. 30; *Die Selbstbehauptung*, p. 10.
70. Wolin, *The Heidegger Controversy*, p. 31 (emphasis in original; translation modified); *Die Selbstbehauptung*, p. 11.
71. Martin Heidegger, *Introduction to Metaphysics*, trans. Gregory Fried and Richard Polt (New Haven: Yale University Press, 2000), p. 40; *Einführung in die Metaphysik* [GA 40] (Frankfurt: Vittorio Klostermann, 1983), pp. 40–41. The bracketed words were added in the 1953 edition.
72. Theodor W. Adorno, *Notes to Literature*, vol. 1, ed. Rolf Tiedemann, trans. Shierry Weber Nicholsen (New York: Columbia University Press, 1991), p. 192. See Alexander García Düttmann, "Without Soil: A Figure in Adorno's Thought," in *Language Without Soil: Adorno and Late Philosophical Modernity*, ed. Gerhard Richter (New York: Fordham University Press, 2010), pp. 10–16.
73. See Barbara Cassin, *Nostalgia: When Are We Ever at Home?* trans. Pascale-Anne Brault (New York: Fordham University Press, 2016), pp. 41–63. Arendt's view of

nostalgia is contrasted with that of Heidegger on pp. 49–52. Cassin accepts that Heidegger's conception of the homeland cannot be reduced to the nationalism of National Socialism (p. 50), but she insists nonetheless that his ontological notion of the homeland is still tied to the specificity of the German language (p. 51). This is correct insofar as, for Heidegger, homelessness is a function of the reduction of language to a means of communication and the consequent obscuring of its true essence as the opening in which beings come to presence through the self-concealing revealing of being. I would stipulate, however, that language, for Heidegger, is never divorced from the land of Germany, and in that sense I do not agree with Cassin's conclusion that the ontological is to be distinguished from the political. On homelessness, wordlessness, and alienation as conditions of the withdrawal of the political in modernity, see as well Dana R. Villa, *Arendt and Heidegger: The Fate of the Political* (Princeton: Princeton University Press, 1996), pp. 10–11, 171–174, 188–201, 226–227.

74. The passage that influenced Agamben is Gershom Scholem, "The Name of God and the Linguistic Theory of the Kabbala," *Diogenes* 80 (1972): 193–194. Part of the text is cited, although without proper bibliographical information.
75. Giorgio Agamben, *The Fire and the Tale*, trans. Lorenzo Chiesa (Stanford: Stanford University Press, 2017), pp. 68–71.
76. Ibid., p. 70.
77. Villa, *Arendt and Heidegger*, p. 253. See also Pol Vandevelde, *Heidegger and the Romantics: The Literary Invention of Meaning* (New York: Routledge, 2012), pp. 85–139, esp. 118–125.
78. See Richard Polt, "The Secret Homeland of Speech: Heidegger on Language, 1933–1934," in *Heidegger and Language*, ed. Jeffrey Powell (Bloomington: Indiana University Press, 2013), pp. 63–85, esp. 70–76. See also Blickle, *Heimat*, pp. 7–8, 65, 139–141.
79. Blickle, *Heimat*, p. 115.
80. Martin Heidegger, *Hölderlin's Hymns "Germania" and "The Rhine,"* trans. William McNeill and Julia Ireland (Bloomington: Indiana University Press, 2014), p. 4; *Hölderlins Hymnen "Germanien" und "Der Rhein"* [GA 39] (Frankfurt: Vittorio Klostermann, 1999), p. 4.
81. Heidegger, *Hölderlin's Hymns*, p. 119; *Hölderlins Hymnen*, p. 134.
82. Heidegger, *Hölderlin's Hymns*, p. 123; *Hölderlins Hymnen*, p. 139.
83. Heidegger, *Hölderlin's Hymns*, p. 108; *Hölderlins Hymnen*, p. 120.
84. Heidegger, *Hölderlin's Hymns*, p. 108; *Hölderlins Hymnen*, p. 120.
85. Heidegger, *Hölderlin's Hymns*, p. 109 (emphasis in original); *Hölderlins Hymnen*, p. 121.
86. Martin Heidegger, "Hebel—Friend of the House," trans. Bruce V. Foltz and Michael Heim, *Contemporary German Philosophy* 3 (1983): 99 (emphasis in original); *Aus der Erfahrung des Denkens 1910–1976* [GA 13] (Frankfurt: Vittorio Klostermann, 2002), p. 148.
87. Martin Heidegger, *Poetry, Language, Thought*, trans. Albert Hofstadter (New York: Harper and Row, 1971), pp. 191–192; *Unterwegs zur Sprache* [GA 12] (Frankfurt: Vittorio Klostermann, 1985), p. 11.
88. Heidegger, *Hölderlin's Hymns*, pp. 61–62; *Hölderlins Hymnen*, p. 67.

2. NOMADISM, HOMELESSNESS, AND THE OBFUSCATION OF BEING

89. Martin Heidegger, *Elucidations of Hölderlin's Poetry*, trans. Keith Hoeller (Amherst: Humanity, 2000), p. 44; *Erläuterungen zu Hölderlins Dichtung* [GA 4] (Frankfurt: Vittorio Klostermann, 1996), p. 26.
90. See the passage concerning Augustine from the Beuron lecture cited by Ryan Coyne, *Heidegger's Confessions: The Remains of Saint Augustine in* Being and Time *and Beyond* (Chicago: University of Chicago Press, 2015), p. 164: "This profound not-knowing [*Nichtwissen*] [time] is that *deep questionability* in which I first question that which is worthy of being questioned, so that what is worthy of being questioned only *is* because I can and do question" (emphasis in original).
91. Ibid., pp. 166–167.
92. Heidegger, *Poetry, Language, Thought*, p. 222; *Vorträge und Aufsätze*, p. 200.
93. Heidegger, *Poetry, Language, Thought*, p. 218; *Vorträge und Aufsätze*, p. 196.
94. Philippe Lacoue-Labarthe, "Poetry's Courage," in *Walter Benjamin and Romanticism*, ed. Beatrice Hanssen and Andrew Benjamin (London: Continuum, 2002), pp. 163–179, esp. 165 and 167. The essay appears in a different translation in Philippe Lacoue-Labarthe, *Heidegger and the Politics of Poetry*, trans. Jeff Fort (Urbana: University of Illinois Press, 2007), pp. 60–81, and see esp. pp. 63 and 66. See, however, p. 104, where the expression "theologico-poetic" is applied to Benjamin in contrast to the expression "theologico-political," which is applied to Heidegger.
95. Jennifer Anna Gosetti-Ferencei, *Heidegger, Hölderlin, and the Subject of Poetic Language: Towards a New Poetics of Dasein* (New York: Fordham University Press, 2004), p. 49.
96. Polt, "The Secret Homeland," p. 76. The formulation "inner truth and greatness" of the Nazi movement was used by Heidegger in *Einführung in die Metaphysik*; see ch. 1nn91–92. See also Judith Wolfe, *Heidegger and Theology* (London: Bloomsbury, 2014), p. 101:

> The main claim I will stake in this chapter is that in the early 1930s, Heidegger's de-theologized eschatology began to intersect with an eschatological consciousness that had shaped German self-understanding since the Romantic era, and was also being appropriated by Nazi leaders and intellectuals. However, though Heidegger temporarily thought to be finding in Nazism a spiritual ally—a movement bold enough to realize the intellectual ambition he was projecting—he was soon disappointed by the crass, militant apocalypticism into which the eschatological tradition of Fichte, Hegel and Hölderlin was here being shaped, and dissociated himself from the party programme in favour of an apophatic eschatology centered on a very different reading of Hölderlin.

97. Heidegger, *Introduction to Metaphysics*, pp. 167–168; *Einführung in die Metaphysik*, p. 166. The bracketed words were added in the 1953 edition.
98. Heidegger, *Introduction to Metaphysics*, pp. 182–183; *Einführung in die Metaphysik*, p. 180.
99. Lacoue-Labarthe, *Heidegger and the Politics of Poetry*. The author's main argument is summarized on p. 40: "Heidegger's commentary on Hölderlin—which is at bottom what authorizes, retrospectively, the possibility of speaking of an 'age of poets'—is more concerned with the Mytheme than with the Poem (and that it

2. NOMADISM, HOMELESSNESS, AND THE OBFUSCATION OF BEING

is, to say it as clearly as possible, a forced attempt at *remythologization*)." This remythologization is what both distinguished Heidegger from the Nazis and made him the thinker of the essence of National Socialism (see "Translator's Introduction," p. xii). On Heidegger's political-theology, see also Christian Sommer, "'Diktat des Seyns'. Zwölf Anmerkungen zu Heideggers politisch-theologischer Mythologie," in *Heidegger und der Antisemitismus*, pp. 353–362.

100. Heidegger, *Hölderlin's Hymns*, p. 195; *Hölderlins Hymnen*, p. 214. Compare Heidegger, *Ponderings XII–XV*, p. 47 (*Überlegungen XII–XV*, p. 60): "Hölderlin is the poet of that unique decision—and thus he is someone unique—incomparable; as a poet he founds in advance the essence of this decision, without thinking of it as a decision pertaining to the history of beyng—yet his poetizing is already an overcoming of all metaphysics. That can be known only thoughtfully and is also worthy of knowledge only for thinking. The word of this poet and the essence of the word."
101. See reference cited in *n*66, this chapter.
102. Lacoue-Labarthe, *Heidegger and the Politics of Poetry*, p. 4. See the analysis of Lacoue-Labarthe's criticism of Heidegger in Villa, *Arendt and Heidegger*, pp. 250–254. Compare also the attempt to situate Heidegger in a more panoramic view regarding German intellectuals of his time who were driven to an ideological core, which served as the matrix of a generic fascism that encompassed but was not exclusive to Nazism, in Matthew Feldman, "Between *Geist* and *Zeitgeist*: Martin Heidegger as Ideologue of 'Metapolitical Fascism,'" *Politics, Religion, and Ideology* 6 (2005): 175–198.
103. Heidegger, *Hölderlin's Hymns*, pp. 194–195; *Hölderlins Hymnen*, pp. 213–214. Compare Heidegger, *Ponderings VII–XI*, p. 42; *Überlegungen VII–XI*, p. 56.
104. Heidegger, *Hölderlin's Hymns*, p. 195; *Hölderlins Hymnen*, p. 214. Concerning this passage, see Lacoue-Labarthe, "Poetry's Courage," pp. 163–164; and Lacoue-Labarthe, *Heidegger and the Politics of Poetry*, pp. 60–61.
105. I concur with the conclusion of James F. Ward, *Heidegger's Political Thinking* (Amherst: University of Massachusetts Press, 1995), p. 207: "Politics thought and brought about in and through Hölderlin, the most genuine German politics, is a politics that no longer belongs to everyday chatter; as essential politics, it is great politics."
106. Heidegger, *Hölderlin's Hymns*, p. 109; *Hölderlins Hymnen*, p. 121.
107. Andrew Cooper, *The Tragedy of Philosophy: Kant's Critique of Judgment and the Project of Aesthetics* (Albany: State University of New York Press, 2016), p. 174.
108. Martin Heidegger, *Off the Beaten Track*, ed. and trans. Julian Young and Kenneth Haynes (Cambridge: Cambridge University Press, 2002), p. 46; *Holzwege* [GA 5] (Frankfurt: Vittorio Klostermann, 1977), pp. 61–62.
109. See reference in ch. 1*n*41. See Maurice Blanchot, "Thinking the Apocalypse: A Letter from Maurice Blanchot to Catherine David," trans. Paula Wissing, *Critical Inquiry* 15 (1989): 478: "By saying he preferred the national to nationalism, he was not using one word in place of another; this preference is also at the basis of his thought and expresses his deep attachment to the land, that is, the homeland (*Heimat*), his stance in favor of local and regional roots . . . and his loathing for urban life." A more satisfactory analysis, which takes into account the "contradictory ambition" on Heidegger's part that led him "to make a symbolic union of two

2. NOMADISM, HOMELESSNESS, AND THE OBFUSCATION OF BEING

polar opposites," is offered by Bourdieu, *The Political Ontology*, p. 52: "Thus his idea of a godless theology informing an initiatory academy, is an attempt to reconcile the esoteric elitism of small circles like the *George-Kreis*, from which he borrows his models of intellectual achievement (such as Hölderlin, rediscovered by Norbert von Hellingrath, or Reinhardt's *Parmenides*), with the ecological mystique of the *Jugendbewegung* or of Steiner's anthroposophy, which preach a return to rural simplicity and sobriety, forest walks, natural food, and hand-woven garments."

110. Heidegger, *Ponderings VII–XI*, p. 24; *Überlegungen VII–XI*, p. 31. Compare Heidegger, *Ponderings II–VI*, p. 123 (*Überlegungen II–VI*, p. 168): "If a truth lies in the power of 'race' (of the native-born one), will and should the Germans then lose their historical essence—abandon it—organize it away—or will they not have to bring it to the supreme tragic denouement? Instead of which, those who are now bred are shortsighted and oblivious!" And Heidegger, *Ponderings II–VI*, pp. 126–127 (*Überlegungen II–VI*, p. 173): "The many: ones who now speak 'about' race [*Rasse*] and indigenousness [*Bodenständigkeit*] and who mock themselves in their every word and action and demonstrate that they 'possess' nothing of all this, leaving aside the question of whether they actually *are* well-bred [*rassig*] and indigenous" (emphasis in original). The criticism of Germans under the sway of the Nazis also seems to be implied in Heidegger, *Ponderings XII–XV*, p. 213 (*Überlegungen XII–XV*), p. 269): "What if a people forces its own essential volition into starvation? Then this people has lost its historical beginning and, along with that, itself. Then this people can neither win nor lose a war." See the passage from the notebooks cited in ch. 1n42.
111. Heidegger, *Pathmarks*, p. 257; *Wegmarken*, pp. 337–338.
112. Heidegger, *Pathmarks*, p. 257; *Wegmarken*, p. 338.
113. Heidegger, *Pathmarks*, p. 257; *Wegmarken*, p. 338. See Lacoue-Labarthe, *Heidegger and the Politics of Poetry*, pp. 35–36.
114. Karl Löwith, *Martin Heidegger and European Nihilism*, ed. Richard Wolin (New York: Columbia University Press, 1995), p. 220. And see now Peter Trawny, "The Universal and Annihilation: Heidegger's Being-Historical Anti-Semitism," in *Heidegger's Black Notebooks*, pp. 1–17, esp. p. 5: "Within the sphere of Heidegger's thinking, a universal ontology must be able to transcend the realm of the ontic. Beings must be able to be abandoned in a 'surpassing' toward being. In this sense, only being can be universal. It is precisely this thought, however, that Heidegger employs differently in the history of being. 'Being' is reserved topographically for the Greeks and Germans; it is, so to speak, dispersed into the narrative of the history of being. In contrast, beings—as pursued solely and exclusively by machination—become 'universal' quantities." For Heidegger, the destinal dwelling of thinking is located always in the singular people that occupies a singular homeland; the universal, by contrast, assumes the character of the international quality exemplified by the sciences and technology.
115. Martin Heidegger, *Hölderlin's Hymn "The Ister*," trans. William McNeill and Julia Davis (Bloomington: Indiana University Press, 1996), p. 153; *Hölderlins Hymne "Der Ister"* [GA 53] (Frankfurt: Vittorio Klostermann, 1993), p. 191.
116. Heidegger, *Hölderlin's Hymn*, p. 153n 2; *Hölderlins Hymne*, p. 191n2.
117. Heidegger, *Introduction to Metaphysics*, p. 159; *Einführung in die Metaphysik*, p. 158.

2. NOMADISM, HOMELESSNESS, AND THE OBFUSCATION OF BEING

118. Alejandro A. Vallega, *Heidegger and the Issue of Space: Thinking on Exilic Grounds* (University Park: Pennsylvania State University Press, 2003). See also Richard Capobianco, *Engaging Heidegger* (Toronto: University of Toronto Press, 2010), pp. 52–69; O'Donoghue, *A Poetics of Homecoming*, pp. 105–165.
119. Heidegger, *Hölderlin's Hymn*, p. 125; *Hölderlins Hymne*, p. 155.
120. Paul Celan, *Selected Poems and Prose of Paul Celan*, trans. John Felstiner (New York: Norton, 2001), pp. 74–75.
121. Heidegger, *Hölderlin's Hymn*, p. 72; *Hölderlins Hymne*, p. 89.
122. Heidegger, *Hölderlin's Hymn*, p. 75; *Hölderlins Hymne*, p. 92.
123. For Heidegger, this term is closely aligned with *Zusammengehörigkeit*, the belonging-together of that which persists as disparate. See Heidegger, *Hölderlin's Hymn*, p. 68; *Hölderlins Hymne*, p. 83.
124. Withy, *Heidegger*, pp. 121–122.
125. Heidegger, *Pathmarks*, p. 151; *Wegmarken*, p. 197.
126. Heidegger, *Hölderlin's Hymn*, p. 77; *Hölderlins Hymne*, p. 95.
127. Heidegger, *Off the Beaten Track*, p. 31; *Holzwege*, p. 41.
128. Heidegger, *Ponderings II–VI*, p. 160; *Überlegungen II–VI*, p. 219.
129. Jacques Lacan, *Anxiety: The Seminar of Jacques Lacan, Book X*, ed. Jacques-Alain Miller, trans. Adrian R. Price (Cambridge: Polity, 2014), p. 47; *Le Séminaire de Jacques Lacan, livre X: L'angoisse*, ed. Jacques-Alain Miller (Paris: Seuil, 2004), p. 60. See Masschelein, *The Unconcept*, p. 55.
130. Lacan, *Anxiety*, p. 47.
131. Ibid., p. 42.
132. Ibid., p. 40. It is of interest to contrast Lacan's perspective with Philippe Lacoue-Labarthe, *Typography:Mimesis, Philosophy, Politics*, ed. Christopher Fynsk (Stanford: Stanford University Press, 1998), pp. 92–94:

> But nothing is too strong here, and all means are permitted in "capturing" the mimetician. The main thing, perhaps, is to render him, in effect, *unheimlich*, as the image in the mirror, the doubt, the living being made into a thing (the animated inanimate)—or even (why not?) as that other kind of double that deceives regarding its "life": the mechanical doll or automaton.... In the face of the *Unheimliche*—the improper—mastery becomes possible only by taking it still further, by outdoing it with the *Unheimliche*. This is what speculation is.

See ibid., p. 195:

> The absence of repetition, by consequence, reveals only the unrevealable, gives rise only to the improbable, and throws off the perceived and well-known. *Nothing* occurs: in effect, the *Unheimliche*—the most uncanny and most unsettling prodigy. For in its undecidability, the *Unheimliche* has to do not only with castration . . . the return of the repressed or infantile anxiety; it is also that which causes the most basic narcissistic assurance . . . to vacillate, in that the differentiation between the imaginary and the real, the fictive and the non-fictive, comes to be effaced (and mimesis, consequently, "surfaces").
>
> (emphasis in original)

2. NOMADISM, HOMELESSNESS, AND THE OBFUSCATION OF BEING

133. Consider Lacan's words, *Anxiety*, p. 8:

> There is also someone else whom I didn't put in the series and of whom I will say . . . that it's in reference to him that the philosophers who observe us, at the point we're coming to in this, can ask themselves—*will the analysis measure up to what we make of anxiety*? There stands Heidegger. With my play on the word *jeter*, it was precisely to him and his originative dereliction that I was closest. Being-unto-death . . . which is the inroad by which Heidegger . . . leads us to his enigmatic examination of an entity's Being . . . is a *lived* reference. He named it, it is fundamental, and it's to do with everyone, with *one*, with the omnitude of everyday human life, it is *care*. Of course, in this capacity, this reference cannot, any more than care itself, be in the least bit foreign to us.
>
> (emphasis in original)

My approach is compatible with the attempt to interpret the notion of *Unheimlichkeit* in Marx, Heidegger, and Freud offered by Jacques Derrida, *Specters of Marx: The State of the Debt, the Work of Mourning, and the New International*, trans. Peggy Kamuf, Bernd Magnus, and Stephen Cullenberg (New York: Routledge, 1994), pp. 173–174. Lacan frequently mentioned Heidegger in his seminars and even translated the essay on Fragment 50 of Heraclitus, published in *La Psychanalyse* 1 (1956): 59–79. See Jacques Lacan, *The Seminar of Jacques Lacan, Book III: The Psychoses, 1955–1956*, ed. Jacques-Alan Miller, trans. Russell Grigg (New York: Norton, 1993), p. 124; Elisabeth Roudinesco, *Jacques Lacan*, trans. Barbara Bray (New York: Columbia University Press, 1997), pp. 229–230; Silvia Lippi, "Héraclite, Lacan: du logos au significant," *Recherches en Psychanalyse* 9 (2010): 55–62; Dominique Janicaud, *Heidegger in France*, trans. François Raffoul and David Pettigrew (Bloomington: Indiana University Press, 2015), p. 453n121; David F. Krell, "Is There a Heidegger—or, for That Matter, a Lacan—Beyond All Gathering? διαφερόμενον in Heidegger's 'Logos: Heraclitus B 50' as a Possible Response to Derrida's Disquiet," in *Heidegger and Language*, ed. Jeffrey Powell (Bloomington: Indiana University Press, 2013), pp. 201–223. The intellectual relationship between Heidegger and Lacan has been discussed by various scholars. See, for example, Edward S. Casey and J. Melvin Woody, "Hegel, Heidegger, Lacan: The Dialectic of Desire," in *Interpreting Lacan*, ed. Joseph H. Smith and William Kerrigan (New Haven: Yale University Press, 1983), pp. 75–112; William J. Richardson, "Psychoanalysis and the Being-Question," in *Interpreting Lacan*, pp. 139–159; Richard Boothby, *Death and Desire: Psychoanalytic Theory in Lacan's Return to Freud* (New York: Routledge, 1991), pp. 203–221; Gabriel Riera, "Abyssal Grounds: Lacan and Heidegger on Truth," *Qui Parle* 9 (1996): 61–76; Roudinesco, *Jacques Lacan*, pp. 219–231; William Egginton, *The Philosopher's Desire: Psychoanalysis, Interpretation, and Truth* (Stanford: Stanford University Press, 2007), pp. 65, 110–112; Slavoj Žižek, *Less Than Nothing: Hegel and the Shadow of Dialectical Materialism* (London: Verso, 2012), pp. 859–903; Jacques Derrida, *Heidegger: The Question of Being and History*, ed. Thomas Dutoit, trans. Geoffrey Bennington (Chicago: University of Chicago Press, 2016), p. 56. Regarding the personal interactions of Heidegger and Lacan, see Elisabeth Roudinesco, *Jacques Lacan & Co.: A History of*

2. NOMADISM, HOMELESSNESS, AND THE OBFUSCATION OF BEING

Psychoanalysis in France, 1925–1985, trans. Jeffrey Mehlman (Chicago: University of Chicago Press, 1990), pp. 298–299.
134. Heidegger, *Hölderlin's Hymn,* p. 49; *Hölderlins Hymne,* pp. 60–61. See the discussion of the theme of homecoming through otherness in Fred Dallmayr, *The Other Heidegger* (Ithaca: Cornell University Press, 1993), pp. 149–180. See also Gosetti-Ferencei, *Heidegger,* pp. 125–128.
135. Heidegger, *Hölderlin's Hymn,* p. 99; *Hölderlins Hymne,* p. 123. See the analysis of *to deinon* and *unheimlich* in Withy, *Heidegger,* pp. 108–112.
136. Heidegger, *Hölderlin's Hymn,* p. 103; *Hölderlins Hymne,* pp. 127–128.
137. Heidegger, *Hölderlin's Hymn,* pp. 57–59; *Hölderlins Hymne,* pp. 71–72.
138. Heidegger, *Hölderlin's Hymn,* pp. 103–104; *Hölderlins Hymne,* p. 129.
139. Heidegger, *Hölderlin's Hymn,* p. 105; *Hölderlins Hymne,* pp. 130–131. See O'Donoghue, *A Poetics of Homecoming,* pp. 155–159.
140. Heidegger, *Hölderlin's Hymn,* p. 125; *Hölderlins Hymne,* p. 155.
141. Heidegger, *Elucidations,* pp. 111–112; *Erläuterungen,* p. 87.
142. Heidegger, *Hölderlin's Hymn,* p. 125; *Hölderlins Hymne,* p. 156.
143. Heidegger, *Elucidations,* p. 79; *Erläuterungen,* p. 57.
144. Heidegger, *Elucidations,* p. 79; *Erläuterungen,* p. 57. See Withy, *Heidegger,* pp. 112–120.
145. For the rendering of Hölderlin's use of the term *das Ungeheure* as the non-ordinary (*Nicht-geheuren*), see Heidegger, *Hölderlin's Hymn,* pp. 69–71; *Hölderlins Hymne,* pp. 85–87; and see the comment of Lacoue-Labarthe, *Heidegger and the Politics of Poetry,* p. 96n14.
146. Martin Heidegger, *Parmenides,* trans. André Schuwer and Richard Rojcewicz (Bloomington: Indiana University Press, 1992), pp. 118–120; *Parmenides* [GA 54] (Frankfurt: Vittorio Klostermann, 1992), pp. 175–178.
147. The literature on Heidegger and language is enormous, and I will cite here a modest sampling of relevant studies: Joseph J. Kockelmans, *On Heidegger and Language* (Evanston: Northwestern University Press, 1972); Robert Bernasconi, *The Question of Language in Heidegger's History of Being* (Atlantic Highlands, NJ: Humanities Press, 1985); Andrew Inkpin, *Disclosing the World: On the Phenomenology of Language* (Cambridge: MIT Press, 2016).
148. As Heidegger put it in the *Introduction to Metaphysics,* p. 161 (*Einführung in die Metaphysik,* p. 160), the unhomely does not countenance the possibility of being at home, but this being out of sorts accounts for the over-whelming (*Über-wältigende*), the overstepping of the limits of the homely that may result in violence.
149. Miguel de Beistegui, *Heidegger and the Political: Dystopias* (London: Routledge, 1998), pp. 87–113; and de Beistegui, *The New Heidegger,* p. 176n14; Cooper, *The Tragedy,* pp. 180–181. On poetic dwelling and the homeland, see Ward, *Heidegger's Political Thinking,* pp. 205–259. See also the wide-ranging discussion on the relation between the gesture of saying and the experience of becoming at home in Mugerauer, *Heidegger and Homecoming,* pp. 370–445, and compare Kai Hammermeister, "Heimat in Heidegger and Gadamer," *Philosophy and Literature* 24 (2000): 312–326.
150. Heidegger, *Poetry, Language, Thought,* p. 161; *Vorträge und Aufsätze,* p. 163.
151. Heidegger, *Poetry, Language, Thought,* p. 161 (emphasis in original); *Vorträge und Aufsätze,* pp. 163–164.

2. NOMADISM, HOMELESSNESS, AND THE OBFUSCATION OF BEING

152. Heidegger, *Poetry, Language, Thought*, p. 146; *Vorträge und Aufsätze*, p. 148.
153. The lecture was first published in *Hebbel Jahrbuch*, ed. Ludwig Koopmann and Erich Trunz (Heide: Westholsteinische Verlagsanstalt Boyens, 1960), pp. 27–50, and was then reprinted several times, including in Heidegger, *Aus der Erfahrung*, pp. 155–180.
154. Heidegger, *Aus der Erfahrung*, p. 180. See Mugerauer, *Heidegger and Homecoming*, p. 444.
155. See Trawny, *Heidegger and the Myth*, pp. 47–54.
156. Heidegger, *Elucidations*, p. 48 (emphasis in original); *Erläuterungen*, pp. 29–30.
157. Georg Wilhelm Friedrich Hegel, *The Science of Logic*, ed. and trans. George di Giovanni (Cambridge: Cambridge University Press, 2010), p. 12; *Wissenschaft der Logik* [Hauptwerke 3] (Hamburg: Felix Meiner, 2015), p. 11.
158. Georg Wilhelm Friedrich Hegel, *System of Ethical Life (1802/3) and First Philosophy of Spirit (Part III of the System of Speculative Philosophy 1803/4)*, ed. and trans. Henry S. Harris and Thomas M. Knox (Albany: State University of New York Press, 1979), pp. 244–245 (emphasis in original). See the analysis of Hegel's views on language, with special focus on the Herderian influence, in Michael N. Forster, *German Philosophy of Language: From Schlegel to Hegel and Beyond* (Oxford: Oxford University Press, 2011), pp. 143–177.
159. Georg Wilhelm Friedrich Hegel, *Encyclopedia of the Philosophical Sciences in Basic Outline, Part I: Science of Logic*, ed. and trans. Klaus Brinkmann and Daniel O. Dahlstrom (Cambridge: Cambridge University Press, 2010), pp. 52–53 (emphasis in original). Compare Georg Wilhelm Friedrich Hegel, *Lectures on the Philosophy of Spirit 1827–8*, trans. Robert R. Williams (Oxford: Oxford University Press, 2007), p. 225; *Enzyklopädie der philosophischen Wissenschaften im Grundrisse (1830)* [Hauptwerke 6] (Hamburg: Felix Meiner, 2015), pp. 64–65.
160. Jacques Derrida, *Acts of Religion*, ed. Gil Anidjar (New York: Routledge, 2002), pp. 152–153 (emphasis in original). On the German appropriation of the ancient Greeks, see O'Donoghue, *A Poetics of Homecoming*, pp. 57–103.
161. My comments are indebted to the discussion of Cohen's view, including a brief comparison to Heidegger, in Robert Erlewine, *Judaism and the West: From Hermann Cohen to Joseph Soloveitchik* (Bloomington: Indiana University Press, 2016), pp. 19–20. Derrida himself goes on to say that, in spite of the difference in substance and style between Heidegger and Cohen, the synergy they affirm with respect to Greek and German is related to "an interpretation of the sense of being" (*Acts of Religion*, p. 153). See also Trawny, *Heidegger and the Myth*, p. 15.
162. De Beistegui, *Heidegger and the Political*, pp. 110–113.
163. Martin Heidegger, *The Essence of Human Freedom: An Introduction to Philosophy*, trans. Ted Sadler (London: Continuum, 2002), pp. 35–36 (emphasis in original); *Vom Wesen der menschlichen Freiheit: Einleitung in die Philosophie* [GA 31] (Frankfurt: Vittorio Klostermann, 1994), pp. 50–51. It is of interest that, in the accompanying note at the end of this passage, Heidegger refers to Meister Eckhart and Hegel as the two examples to illustrate the point that the German language has a philosophical character comparable to the Greek. See Heidegger, *The Essence of Human Freedom*, p. 36n2; *Vom Wesen der menschlichen Freiheit* p. 51n3.
164. Heidegger, *Ponderings II–VI*, p. 21 (emphasis in original); *Überlegungen II–VI*, p. 27. For an alternate translation, see Trawny, *Heidegger and the Myth*, p. 14.

Trawny's comment that this passage is "seemingly from out of the blue" is not defensible as the textual evidence that he himself supplies attests.

165. Heidegger, *Elucidations*, p. 112 (emphasis in original); *Erläuterungen*, p. 87. See Andrzej Warminski, "Monstrous History: Heidegger Reading Hölderlin," in *The Solid Letter: Readings of Friedrich Hölderlin*, ed. Aris Fioretos (Stanford: Stanford University Press, 1999), pp. 201–214; Ward, *Heidegger's Political Thinking*, pp. 209–210.
166. Heidegger, *Elucidations*, p. 112; *Erläuterungen*, p. 88.
167. Heidegger, *Hölderlin's Hymn*, p. 124; *Hölderlins Hymne*, p. 154.
168. Heidegger, *Hölderlin's Hymn*, p. 54; *Hölderlins Hymne*, p. 67. The point is repeated in Heidegger, *Hölderlin's Hymn*, p. 124; *Hölderlins Hymne*, p. 154. See Ward, *Heidegger's Political Thinking*, pp. 221–222.
169. Heidegger, *Hölderlin's Hymn*, p. 54; *Hölderlins Hymne*, pp. 67–68. See the detailed analysis of the themes of *Heimat*, *Heimkunft*, the holy, and poetic language in Arthur Anthony Grugan, "Thought and Poetry: Language as Man's Homecoming. A Study of Martin Heidegger's Question of Being and Its Ties to Friedrich Hölderlin's Experience of the Holy," Ph.D. dissertation, Duquesne University, 1972, pp. 100–156.
170. Heidegger, *Hölderlin's Hymn*, pp. 54–55; *Hölderlins Hymne*, p. 68.
171. Heidegger, *Hölderlin's Hymn*, p. 55; *Hölderlins Hymne*, p. 69.
172. Heidegger, *Hölderlin's Hymn*, pp. 65–66 (emphasis in original); *Hölderlins Hymne*, pp. 79–80. By contrast, see Heidegger, *Überlegungen XII–XV*, p. 239, where he expresses his disapproval of the "reorganization" and the "prostitution" of the German language and a new colloquial speech related to so-called German knowledge (*deutschen Wissenschaft*). Heidegger complains that since this involves the education (*Bildung*) of non-Germanic peoples (*außerdeutsche Völker*), it can no longer be considered as the *German* language (*keine* deutsche *Sprache mehr*) but is rather a form of an international jargon or vernacular (*internationalen Gaunersprache*). The text is translated in Heidegger, *Ponderings XII–XV*, pp. 188–189.
173. Peter Warnek, "Translating *Innigkeit*: The Belonging Together of the Strange," in *Heidegger and the Greeks: Interpretive Essays*, ed. Drew A. Hyland and John Panteleimon Manoussakis (Bloomington: Indiana University Press, 2006), pp. 57–82.
174. Heidegger, *Hölderlin's Hymn*, p. 66; *Hölderlins Hymne*, p. 81. With respect to this issue, Heidegger is heir to the romantic notion that the German people are the bearers of European culture through translation. See Pol Vandevelde, "Translation as a Mode of Poetry: Heidegger's Reformulation of the Romantic Project," in *Phenomenology and Literature: Historical Perspectives and Systematic Accounts*, ed. Pol Vandevelde (Würzburg: Königshausen & Neumann, 2010), pp. 93–113; Vandevelde, *Heidegger and the Romantics*, pp. 42–43.
175. Heidegger, *Hölderlin's Hymn*, p. 66; *Hölderlins Hymne*, p. 81.
176. For a compatible argument, see Bret W. Davis, "Heidegger on the Way from Onto-Historical Ethnocentrism to East-West Dialogue," *Gatherings: The Heidegger Circle Annual* 6 (2016): 130–156.
177. Heidegger, *Parmenides*, p. 12; *Parmenides*, p. 17.
178. Heidegger, *Parmenides*, p. 12; *Parmenides*, p. 18. Here, too, we can note an interesting affinity between Heidegger and Rosenzweig. Compare Franz Rosenzweig, "Scripture and Luther," in Martin Buber and Franz Rosenzweig, *Scripture and*

2. NOMADISM, HOMELESSNESS, AND THE OBFUSCATION OF BEING

Translation, trans. Lawrence Rosenwald with Everett Fox (Bloomington: Indiana University Press, 1994), p. 56: "For the voice of the Bible is not to be enclosed in any space—not in the inner sanctum of a church, not in the linguistic sanctum of a people, not in the circle of the heavenly images moving above a nation's sky. Rather this voice seeks again and again to resound from outside—from outside this church, this people, this heaven.... If somewhere it has become a familiar, customary possession, it must again and anew, as a foreign and unfamiliar sound, stir up the complacent satedness of its alleged possessor from outside." See Peter E. Gordon, "Rosenzweig and Heidegger: Translation, Ontology, and the Anxiety of Affiliation," *New German Critique* 77 (1999): 113–148; and Peter E. Gordon, *Rosenzweig and Heidegger: Between Judaism and German Philosophy* (Berkeley: University of California Press, 2003), pp. 267–274. On translation as a process of defamiliarization and embrace of the foreign, see Leora Batnitzky, "Translation as Transcendence: A Glimpse Into the Workshop of the Buber-Rosenzweig Bible Translation," *New German Critique* 70 (1997): 87–116, esp. 92 and 116. There is clearly a structural similarity between Rosenzweig's approach to translation of the voice of the Hebrew Bible as that which cannot be restricted to any place and his rejection of Zionism. See Leora Batnitzky, *Idolatry and Representation: The Philosophy of Franz Rosenzweig Reconsidered* (Princeton: Princeton University Press, 2000), p. 141: "Rosenzweig's theory of translation is consonant with his argument that Jews themselves must return to their strange, foreign pathos, both for their own sake and for the sake of the redemption of the world. For Rosenzweig, this meant an embrace of a decidedly diaspora Judaism."
179. Warnek, "Translating *Innigkeit*," pp. 61–62 (emphasis in original).
180. Heidegger, *Elucidations*, p. 112; *Erläuterungen*, p. 87.
181. Heidegger, *Elucidations*, pp. 112–113; *Erläuterungen*, p. 88.
182. Heidegger, *Elucidations*, p. 42; *Erläuterungen*, pp. 23–24.
183. The lecture is included in *Reden und Andere Zeugnisse eines Lebensweges 1910–1976* [GA 16] (Frankfurt: Vittorio Klostermann, 2000), pp. 574–582, but I will cite the German text provided by Sheehan together with his translation (see the following note). For an earlier rendering of this text, see Martin Heidegger, "Homeland," trans. Thomas F. O'Meara, *Listening* 6 (1971): 231–238. The lecture is discussed in detail by Mugerauer, *Heidegger and Homecoming*, pp. 479–487.
184. Martin Heidegger, "Messkirch's Seventh Centennial," trans. Thomas J. Sheehan, *Listening* 8 (1973): 48–51.
185. Heidegger, *Discourse on Thinking*, p. 48; *Gelassenheit*, p. 15.
186. Heidegger, "Messkirch's Seventh Centennial," pp. 42–43.
187. Ibid., pp. 44–45.
188. Compare Richard Rojcewicz, *The Gods and Technology: A Reading of Heidegger* (Albany: State University of New York Press, 2006), p. 222:

> Autochthony is equivalent to Heidegger's concept of dwelling in the homeland (*die Heimat*). The authentic homeland for humans is not a certain country or other, not Germany, not Greece, but is instead a matter of attending to Being. Its main requirement is that Being disclose itself to us.... As Heidegger points out, those who remain in their native places, in a physical sense, may be just as uprooted, just as homeless, as those who

have been transplanted. That is because to be close to home, to be on one's home ground, to be autochthonous, is not a matter of physical location. It is a matter of what we heed.

I concur that Heidegger moved away from a strictly topological understanding of the homeland by emphasizing that to be at home is dependent on attunement to being, but I do not agree that he severed this sense of attunement completely from the particular space of Germany. The homeland, or the fatherland, may be identified more generally as being (see n85, this chapter, a passage referred to by Rojcewicz, ibid., p. 236n3), but this does not mean that the specific geographical identification of that homeland is abolished.

189. Heidegger, "Messkirch's Seventh Centennial," pp. 48–49. For a fuller analysis of this topic, see Charles Bambach, "Heidegger, Technology, and the Homeland," *Germanic Review: Literature, Culture, Theory* 78 (2003): 267–282; and Charles Bambach, *Heidegger's Roots: Nietzsche, National Socialism, and the Greeks* (Ithaca: Cornell University Press, 2003), pp. 12–68.

190. Novalis, *Novalis: Philosophical Writings*, trans. Margaret Mahony Stoljar (Albany: State University of New York Press, 1997), p. 135.

191. Martin Heidegger, *The Fundamental Concepts of Metaphysics: World, Finitude, Solitude*, trans. William McNeill and Nicholas Walker (Bloomington: Indiana University Press, 1995), p. 5 (emphasis in original); *Die Grundbegriffe der Metaphysik: Welt—Endlichkeit—Einsamkeit* [GA 29/30] (Frankfurt: Vittorio Klostermann, 1983), pp. 7–8. For an analysis of this passage, see Jacques Derrida, *The Beast and the Sovereign*, vol. 2, ed. Michel Lisse, Marie-Louise Mallet, and Ginette Michaud, trans. Geoffrey Bennington (Chicago: University of Chicago Press, 2011), pp. 29–30, 32–33, 37, 94–98; Cassin, *Nostalgia*, p. 51. See also Vandevelde, *Heidegger and the Romantics*, p. 12.

192. Heidegger, *The Fundamental Concepts*, pp. 5–6 (emphasis in original); *Die Grundbegriffe*, p. 8.

193. Heidegger, *Discourse on Thinking*, p. 49; *Gelassenheit*, p. 16.

194. Heidegger, "Messkirch's Seventh Centennial," pp. 42–43.

195. Ibid., pp. 46–47.

196. Ibid., pp. 48–49.

197. Ibid., pp. 50–52.

198. See Martin Heidegger, *The Principle of Reason*, trans. Reginald Lilly (Bloomington: Indiana University Press, 1991), pp. 89–90; *Der Satz vom Grund* [GA 10] (Frankfurt: Vittorio Klostermann, 1997), p. 133; Heidegger, *Pathmarks*, p. 309; *Wegmarken*, p. 409; *Identity and Difference*, trans. Joan Stambaugh (New York: Harper and Row, 1969), p. 29, German text, p. 92; *Country Path Conversations*, p. 25; *Feldweg-Gespräche*, p. 39. For discussion of this theme, see Michael Roth, *The Poetics of Resistance: Heidegger's Line* (Evanston: Northwestern University Press, 1996), pp. 19–24, 27–28.

199. Heidegger, "Messkirch's Seventh Centennial," pp. 52–53. I have modified Sheehan's translation of *Zugehörigkeit* from "oneness" to "affiliation." The latter term, in my judgment, better conveys the sense of the same but different.

200. Mugerauer, *Heidegger and Homecoming*, p. 485.

2. NOMADISM, HOMELESSNESS, AND THE OBFUSCATION OF BEING

201. Heidegger, *Introduction to Metaphysics*, p. 60; *Einführung in die Metaphysik*, p. 61.
202. Trawny, *Heidegger and the Myth*, pp. 14–16.
203. Martin Heidegger, *Four Seminars: Le Thor 1966, 1968, 1969, Zähringen 1973*, trans. Andrew Mitchell and François Raffoul (Bloomington: Indiana University Press, 2003), p. 37; *Seminare* [GA 15] (Frankfurt: Vittorio Klostermann, 2005), p. 330.
204. Heinrich W. Petzet, *Encounters and Dialogues with Martin Heidegger, 1929–1976*, trans. Parvis Emad and Kenneth Maly (Chicago: University of Chicago Press, 1993), p. 34.
205. Martin Heidegger, *Zum Ereignis-Denken* [GA 73.1] (Frankfurt: Vittorio Klostermann, 2013), p. 755. For an alternate interpretation of this passage, see Trawny, "Heidegger, 'World Judaism,' and Modernity," pp. 12–13.
206. Jacob Taubes, *Occidental Eschatology*, trans. with a preface by David Ratmoko (Stanford: Stanford University Press, 2009), pp. 24–25, argues that the exilic state of the Jews, their lack of being rooted in the land, or adhering to a state, are not exceptional but rather are part of a larger spiritual heritage of the so-called Aramaic Orient. A similar portrayal of the Jews is offered by other thinkers, on occasion with a decidedly anti-Zionist or post-Zionist slant. For instance, see George Steiner, "Our Homeland, the Text," *Salmagundi* 66 (1985): 4–25; and the rejoinder by Sidra DeKoven Ezrahi, "Our Homeland, the Text . . . Our Text the Homeland: Exile and Homecoming in Modern Jewish Imagination," *Michigan Quarterly Review* 31 (1992): 463–497; and Sidra DeKoven Ezrahi, *Booking Passage: Exile and Homecoming in the Modern Jewish Imagination* (Berkeley: University of California Press, 2000). For a relatively recent attempt to celebrate the diasporic nature of Jewish existence in rabbinic culture, see Daniel Boyarin, *A Traveling Homeland: The Babylonian Talmud as Diaspora* (Philadelphia: University of Pennsylvania, 2015).
207. Trawny, "Heidegger, 'World Judaism,' and Modernity," p. 12, linked Heidegger's description of the worldlessness of the Jews and their detachment to the traditional ideal of the Jewish Diaspora, which he, incorrectly in my view, connects to the Heideggerian trope of "disintegration" (*Zerstörung*). The bias implied in viewing the diasporic life of the Jews as a form of destruction is so obvious that it does not merit a rejoinder. Consider as well the parenthetical remark of Žižek, *Disparities*, p. 236: "And, incidentally, since this 'Jewish worldliness,' their lack of roots in a *Boden*, is counteracted by the Israeli government's endeavour to make out of Israel a proper *Heimat* for the Jewish people, maybe today's Israel would find full approval of Heidegger as an attempt to decriminalize Jewishness." Putting politics aside, this comment lacks historical perspective as the claim of the Jews to this land is not exclusive to the aspirations of modern Zionism. Even the most strident opponents to this ideology still maintain an inherent connection between the Jewish people and the land of Israel.
208. Heidegger, *The Fundamental Concepts*, pp. 176–184; *Die Grundbegriffe*, pp. 261–264. Concerning these Heideggerian theses, see Derrida, *Of Spirit*, pp. 11–12; *De l'esprit*, pp. 28–29.
209. Heidegger, *Introduction to Metaphysics*, p. 47; *Einführung in die Metaphysik*, p. 48. For analysis of this passage, see Derrida, *Of Spirit*, pp. 47–60; *De l'esprit*, pp. 75–94.

2. NOMADISM, HOMELESSNESS, AND THE OBFUSCATION OF BEING

210. Shlomo Avineri, "The Fossil and the Phoenix: Hegel and Krochmal on the Jewish Volksgeist," in *History and System: Hegel's Philosophy of History*, ed. Robert L. Perkins (Albany: State University of New York Press, 1984), pp. 47–48.
211. Heidegger, *Überlegungen XII–XV*, p. 262, translated in Trawny, "Heidegger, 'World Judaism,' and Modernity," p. 15. See as well Trawny, *Heidegger and the Myth*, pp. 30–33. For a different rendering, see Heidegger, *Ponderings XII–XV*, p. 208.
212. One is reminded of the equally revolting response that Heidegger offered to Marcuse:

> To the serious legitimate charges that you express "about a regime that murdered millions of Jews, that made terror into an everyday phenomenon, and that turned everything that pertains to the ideas of spirit, freedom, and truth into its bloody opposite," I can merely add that if instead of "Jews" you had written "East Germans" ... then the same holds true for one of the allies, with the difference that everything that had occurred since 1945 has become public knowledge, while the bloody terror of the Nazis in point of fact had been kept a secret from the German people.
> (Richard Wolin, "An Exchange of Letters," in Wolin, *The Heidegger Controversy*, p. 163)

Marcuse's response exposes the pitiful feebleness of Heidegger's words:

> You write that everything that I say about the extermination of the Jews applies just as much to the Allies, if instead of "Jews" one were to insert "East Germans." With this sentence don't you stand outside of the dimension in which a conversation between men is even possible—outside of Logos? For only outside of the dimension of logic is it possible to explain, to relativize [*auszugleichen*], to "comprehend" a crime by saying that others would have done the same thing. Even further: how is it possible to equate the torture, the maiming, and the annihilation of millions of men with the forcible relocation of population groups who suffered none of these outrages (apart perhaps from several exceptional instances)? From a contemporary perspective, there seems already to be a night and day difference in humanity and inhumanity in the difference between Nazi concentration camps and the deportations and internments of the postwar years.
> (Ibid., p. 164)

213. Babette E. Babich, "Heidegger's Jews: Inclusion/Exclusion and Heidegger's Anti-Semitism," *Journal of the British Society for Phenomenology* 47 (2016): 138–139.
214. Adolf Hitler, *Mein Kampf: Zwei Bände in einem Band* (Munich: Franz Eher Nachf, 1943), pp. 333–335, rejects the commonplace assumption that since the Jews did not have a state with territorial boundaries, they are to be considered nomads. In truth, the Jew is not a nomad but a parasite, inasmuch as the nomadic entails a definite attitude toward work that serves as the basis of a later cultural development. This element, which is characteristic of the original state of the Aryan, is lacking in the Jews, who live parasitically off the substance of others and have no

2. NOMADISM, HOMELESSNESS, AND THE OBFUSCATION OF BEING

culture of their own. They deceptively deny that they are a people with racial qualities and pretend that they are primarily a religious community (*Religionsgemeinschaft*) that can assimilate into their host nations, albeit with a special denomination (*Konfession*). The Jew, writes Hitler, is deprived of the "idealistic spirit" (*idealistische Gesinnung*), which is the essential prerequisite for cultural formation (p. 330).

215. Ibid., pp. 330–331.
216. Gordon, *Rosenzweig and Heidegger*, pp. 210–214. For some other representative studies on Rosenzweig's attitude to Zionism, see Ehud Luz, "Zionism and Messianism in the Thought of Franz Rosenzweig," *Jerusalem Studies in Jewish Thought* 2 (1983): 472–489 (Hebrew); Rivka Horwitz, "Franz Rosenzweig and Gershom Scholem on Zionism and the Jewish People," *Jewish History* 6 (1992): 99–111; Batnitzky, *Idolatry and Representation*, pp. 188–206; Mara Benjamin, "Building a Zion in German(y): Franz Rosenzweig on Yehudah Halevi," *Jewish Social Studies: History, Culture, Society* 13 (2007): 127–154, esp. 141–148.
217. I am here indebted to the formulation of Gordon, *Rosenzweig and Heidegger*, p. 213:

> Rosenzweig's idea of blood-community is not meant in a racial (or even "ethnic") sense. One might call it ontological, since it speaks to the basic temporal conditions that allow for the Jews to be who they are. The Jewish people are for Rosenzweig a blood-community that lives "in its own redemption" because of a self-grounded temporality that it wields independent of its surroundings and as part of its "ownmost" constitution. Because the Jewish people is constituted in its essence by blood alone, Jewish identity is temporally self-sufficient.

218. Franz Rosenzweig, *The Star of Redemption*, trans. Barbara Galli (Madison: University of Wisconsin Press, 2000), p. 318; *Der Mensch und sein Werk: Gesammelte Schriften II. Der Stern der Erlösung* (The Hague: Martinus Nijhoff, 1976), p. 332.
219. Rosenzweig, *The Star*, pp. 348–349; *Der Stern*, pp. 364–366.
220. Rosenzweig, *The Star*, p. 348; *Der Stern*, p. 364.
221. Rosenzweig, *The Star*, p. 348; *Der Stern*, p. 365.
222. Rosenzweig, *The Star*, p. 351; *Der Stern*, p. 368.
223. Gordon, *Rosenzweig and Heidegger*, p. 213.
224. See Franz Rosenzweig, *Die "Gritli"-Briefe: Briefe an Margrit Rosenstock-Huessy*, ed. Inken Rühle and Reinhold Mayer (Tübingen: Bilam, 2002), p. 236 (letter dated February 12, 1919): "Es ist etwas Unheimliches um das Blut. Aber sie was überhaupt unheimlich; sie selbst." The passage was mentioned by Gordon, *Rosenzweig and Heidegger*, p. 214n31.
225. Rosenzweig, *The Star*, p. 237; *Der Stern*, p. 246. I have modified the translation slightly.
226. Rosenzweig, *The Star*, p. 319; *Der Stern*, p. 333.
227. Rosenzweig, *The Star*, p. 319; *Der Stern*, p. 333.
228. Rosenzweig, *The Star*, p. 319; *Der Stern*, p. 333.
229. Rosenzweig, *The Star*, p. 321; *Der Stern*, p. 335.

2. NOMADISM, HOMELESSNESS, AND THE OBFUSCATION OF BEING

230. Barbara Galli, *Franz Rosenzweig and Jehuda Halevi: Translating, Translations, and Translators* (Montreal: McGill-Queen's University Press, 1995), p. 177, cited and analyzed in Elliot R. Wolfson, *Giving Beyond the Gift: Apophasis and Overcoming Theomania* (New York: Fordham University Press, 2014), pp. 66–67.
231. Rosenzweig, *The Star*, p. 263; *Der Stern*, p. 273.
232. Maurice Blanchot, *The Space of Literature*, trans. Ann Smock (Lincoln: University of Nebraska Press, 1982), p. 237.
233. Paul Celan, "Mikrolithen sinds, Steinchen". *Die Prosa aus dem Nachlaß: Kritische Ausgabe*, ed. Barbara Wiedemann and Bertrand Badiou (Frankfurt: Suhrkamp, 2005), p. 95: "Echte Dichtung ist antibiographisch. Die Heimat des Dichters ist sein Gedicht, sie wechselt von einem Gedicht zum andern." For the English version, see Paul Celan, "From 'Microliths,'" trans. Pierre Joris, *Poetry Magazine* (January 2017), available at https://www.poetryfoundation.org/poetrymagazine/articles/detail/91659.
234. On the notion of Jewish *Unheimlichkeit* in Rosenzweig's thinking, see Leora Batnitzky, "Rosenzweig's Aesthetic Theory and Jewish *Unheimlichkeit*," *New German Critique* 77 (1999): 87–122; Batnitzky, *Idolatry and Representation*, pp. 83–104; "Franz Rosenzweig on Translation and Exile," *Jewish Studies Quarterly* 14 (2007): 138–141; Louis P. Blond, "Franz Rosenzweig: Homelessness in Time," *New German Critique* 37 (2010): 27–58. See also Susan Shapiro, "The Uncanny Jew: A Brief History of an Image," *Judaism* 46 (1997): 63–78.
235. Alexander Altmann, "Franz Rosenzweig on History," in *The Philosophy of Franz Rosenzweig*, ed. Paul Mendes-Flohr (Hanover: University Press of New England, 1988), pp. 124–137. See also Paul Mendes-Flohr, "Franz Rosenzweig and the Crisis of Historicism," in *The Philosophy of Franz Rosenzweig*, pp. 138–161; Amos Funkenstein, "An Escape from History: Rosenzweig on the Destiny of Judaism," *History and Memory* 2 (1990): 117–135; David N. Myers, *Resisting History: Historicism and Its Discontents in German-Jewish Thought* (Princeton: Princeton University Press, 2003), pp. 68–101.
236. Emmanuel Levinas, "The Trace of the Other," in *Deconstruction in Context: Literature and Philosophy*, ed. Mark C. Taylor (Chicago: University of Chicago Press, 1986), pp. 348–349 (emphasis in original). For discussion of this passage, see Jacques Derrida, *Writing and Difference*, trans. Alan Bass (Chicago: University of Chicago Press, 1978), pp. 320–321n92; Jacques Derrida, *Adieu to Emmanuel Levinas*, trans. Pascale-Anne Brault and Michael Naas (Stanford: Stanford University Press, 1999), pp. 128–129n12; Derrida, *The Beast and the Sovereign*, pp. 95–96. Derrida offers a more extensive analysis of Levinas's concept of work in "At This Very Moment in This Work Here I Am," trans. Ruben Berezdivin, in *Re-Reading Levinas*, ed. Robert Bernasconi and Simon Critchley (Bloomington: Indiana University Press, 1991), pp. 11–48. On Levinas's use of Abraham's peregrinations in exile from his birthplace as a critique of Heidegger's idea of enrootedness in the soil, see Ephraim Meir, "The Meaning of the Abrahamic Adventure in Levinas's Thought," in *Levinas Faces Biblical Figures*, ed. Yael Lin (Lanham, MD: Lexington, 2014), pp. 21–23. See also Howard Caygill, *Levinas and the Political* (London: Routledge, 2002), p. 67.
237. Levinas, *Difficult Freedom*, p. 233.

2. NOMADISM, HOMELESSNESS, AND THE OBFUSCATION OF BEING

238. A concise summary of Levinas's view was offered by Derrida, *Adieu*, p. 66. Assessing the notion of a Torah that precedes the Sinaitic epiphany, Derrida writes:

> A hospitality beyond all revelation. It is not a question, for Levinas, of calling into question the election of Israel, its unicity or its universal exemplarity, but, quite to the contrary, a question of recognizing a universal message for which it has responsibility before or independently of the place and the event of the gift of the law: human universality, humanitarian hospitality uprooted from a singularity of the event that would then become empirical, or at the most allegorical, perhaps only "political" in a very restricted sense of this term that will have to be clarified.

For critical assessment of Levinas's view, see Caygill, *Levinas*, pp. 79–93, 162–194; Judith Butler, *Parting Ways: Jewishness and the Critique of Zionism* (New York: Columbia University Press, 2012), pp. 38–48, esp. 42–43; and the defense of Levinas's political thought, including his Zionism, offered by Michael L. Morgan, *Discovering Levinas* (Cambridge: Cambridge University Press, 2007), pp. 20–32, 395–414; and in much greater detail in Michael L. Morgan, *Levinas's Ethical Politics* (Bloomington: Indiana University Press, 2016). Butler's presentation of Levinas is discussed in detail on pp. 323–347.
239. Levinas, *Difficult Freedom*, pp. 263–264.
240. Emmanuel Levinas, *Proper Names*, trans. Michael B. Smith (Stanford: Stanford University Press, 1996), pp. 44–45. See Michael Fagenblat, "The Thing That Scares Me Most: Heidegger's Anti-Semitism and the Return to Zion," *Journal for Cultural and Religious Theory* 14 (2014): 21-22.
241. Emmanuel Levinas, *Of God Who Comes to Mind*, trans. Bettina Bergo (Stanford: Stanford University Press, 1998), p. 193n6. See also the essay "Promised Land or Permitted Land" in Emmanuel Levinas, *Nine Talmudic Readings*, trans. Annette Aronowicz (Bloomington: Indiana University Press, 1990), pp. 51–69, esp. 56: "the explorers go toward this land so that this land will be shamed, so that the worshippers of this land—for example, the Zionists of that time—will be shamed. They have decided, in the name of truth, to confound the Zionists. Please excuse these anachronisms, these excesses of language. We are among ourselves, we are among intellectuals, that is, among people to whom one tells the whole truth." Concerning this passage, see Caygill, *Levinas*, p. 194; Morgan, *Levinas's Ethical Politics*, pp. 320–321.
242. Levinas, *Proper Names*, p. 44.
243. Gordon, *Rosenzweig and Heidegger*, p. 227. On the similarity between Heidegger's notion of the homeland as a place to which one can draw near but never attain—a philosophic critique of National Socialism—and Rosenzweig's rejection of Zionism, see Fagenblat, "The Thing," p. 21.
244. Mugerauer, *Heidegger and Homecoming*, pp. 93–136. On Heidegger's engagement with Hölderlin, see also Holger Helting, *Heideggers Auslegung von Hölderlins Dichtung des Heiligen: Ein Beitrag zur Grundlagenforschung der Daseinanalyse* (Berlin: Duncker & Humblot, 1999), and Gosetti-Ferencei, *Heidegger*, pp. 61–98.
245. Reiner Schürmann, *Meister Eckhart, Mystic and Philosopher: Translations with Commentary* (Bloomington: Indiana University Press, 1978), p. 210.

2. NOMADISM, HOMELESSNESS, AND THE OBFUSCATION OF BEING

246. Heidegger, *Ponderings VII–XI*, p. 254; *Überlegungen VII–XI*, p. 326.
247. In light of Heidegger's castigation of Husserl's philosophical aptitude, it is of interest to consider the contrary view expressed in the following stanza in Scholem's poem "Amtliches Lehrgedicht der Philosophischen Fakultät der Haupt- und Staats-Universität Muri," dated December 5, 1927 and dedicated to Walter Benjamin, in Gershom Scholem, *The Fullness of Time: Poems*, trans. Richard Sieburth (Jerusalem: Ibis, 2003), pp. 74–75: "Wer helig ist und hochmodern / Zugleich, hält es mit Husserl gern. / Doch hört man ein Gerücht im Land / Daß Heidegger ihn nicht verstand" ("Whoever is ultramodern and ascetic / Will find Husserl most sympathetic. / Though there is a rumor going through the land / He was someone Heidegger could never understand").
248. Heidegger, *Überlegungen XII–XV*, pp. 46–47. For an alternate translation, see Heidegger, *Ponderings XII–XV*, p. 37. See, by contrast, Heidegger's remarks about Husserl in the *Die Spiegel* interview, Wolin, *The Heidegger Controversy*, p. 98. Heidegger declares that the controversy with Husserl had nothing to do with Nazism and was limited strictly to philosophical matters. The passage in the diary indicates, however, that Heidegger included Husserl's thought under the taxon of the computational logic allegedly exclusive to the Jews. Heidegger's explanation in the interview (pp. 98–99) for the removal of the dedication to Husserl in the fifth edition of *Sein und Zeit* (1941) seems plausible to me in light of the fact that the note of appreciation was not excised from the text. I also find credible Heidegger's denial of having prevented Husserl from having access to the university libraries. Also noteworthy is Heidegger's comment, "It was a human failing that [at Husserl's sickbed or at the time of his death] I did not express once more my gratitude and my admiration. And for that I asked Frau Husserl's forgiveness in writing" (p. 100). On Heidegger's relationship to Husserl, see Trawny, *Heidegger and the Myth*, pp. 21–22, 55–63.
249. Hitler, *Mein Kampf*, pp. 54–56, 60, 64, 68, 121, 134, 372, 628. For an exhaustive analysis of the "question of being" and the "Jewish question," see Donatella di Cesare, *Heidegger e gli ebrei: I "Quaderni neri"* (Torino: Bollati Boringhieri, 2014), pp. 83–220.
250. Martin Heidegger, *Der Anfang der Abendländischen Philosophie: Auslegung des Anaximander und Parmenides* [GA 35] (Frankfurt: Vittorio Klostermann, 2012), p. 1; Martin Heidegger, *The Beginning of Western Philosophy: Interpretation of Anaximander and Parmenides*, trans. Richard Rojcewicz (Bloomington: Indiana University Press, 2015), p. 1.
251. Compare Heidegger, *Ponderings VII–XI*, p. 124 (*Überlegungen VII–XI*, p. 161), where the illegitimate pursuit of sociology, whereby the folkish principle (*völkische Prinzip*) is subsumed under the sovereignty of society (*Gesellschaft*), is linked to Jews and Catholics. By contrast, National Socialism is credited for stamping out *sociology* as a term.
252. Heidegger, *Contributions*, § 116, p. 180; *Beiträge*, p. 228.
253. Heidegger, *Contributions*, § 269, p. 380; *Beiträge*, p. 483. See Holger Zaborowski, "Metaphysics, Christianity, and the 'Death of God' in Heidegger's *Black Notebooks* (1931–1941)," in *Reading Heidegger's Black Notebooks*, ed. Ingo Farin and Jeff Malpas (Cambridge: MIT Press, 2016), pp. 195–204.

2. NOMADISM, HOMELESSNESS, AND THE OBFUSCATION OF BEING

254. Heidegger, *Ponderings VII–XI*, pp. 233–234 (emphasis in original); *Überlegungen VII–XI*, p. 299.
255. Heidegger, *Anmerkungen I–V*, pp. 157–158.
256. See Hugo Ott, "Heidegger's Catholic Origins: The Theological Philosopher," in *Martin Heidegger: Politics, Art, and Technology*, pp. 18–33. On the residual of theology in Heidegger's thought, see George Kovacs, *The Question of God in Heidegger's Phenomenology* (Evanston: Northwestern University Press, 1990); Frank Schalow, *Heidegger and the Quest for the Sacred: From Thought to the Sanctuary of Faith* (Dordrecht: Kluwer Academic, 2001); Ben Vedder, *Heidegger's Philosophy of Religion: From God to the Gods* (Pittsburgh: Duquesne University Press, 2007); Sylvain Camilleri, *Phénoménologie de la religion et herméneutique théologique dans la pensée du jeune Heidegger: Commentaire analytique des Fondements philosophiques de la mystique médiévale (1916–1919)* (Dordrecht: Springer, 2008); Benjamin D. Crowe, *Heidegger's Religious Origins: Destruction and Authenticity* (Bloomington: Indiana University Press, 2006); Benjamin D. Crowe, *Heidegger's Phenomenology of Religion: Realism and Cultural Criticism* (Bloomington: Indiana University Press, 2008); Judith Wolfe, *Heidegger's Eschatology: Theological Horizons in Martin Heidegger's Early Work* (Oxford: Oxford University Press, 2013); Judith Wolfe, *Heidegger and Theology*; and see other sources cited in Wolfson, *Giving*, pp. 352–353n391.
257. Martin Heidegger, *Nietzsche*, vol. 1: *The Will to Power as Art*, trans. David F. Krell (New York: Harper and Row, 1979), p. 10; *Nietzsche: Erster Band* [GA 6.1] (Frankfurt: Vittorio Klostermann, 1996), p. 8.
258. Friedrich Nietzsche, *The Will to Power*, ed. Walter Kaufmann, trans. Walter Kaufmann and R. J. Hollingdale (New York: Random House, 1967), § 916, p. 484.
259. Heidegger, *Nietzsche, Volume I*, p. 5; *Nietzsche: Erster Band*, p. 4.
260. Martin Heidegger, *Schelling's Treatise on the Essence of Human Freedom*, trans. Joan Stambaugh (Athens: Ohio University Press, 1985), pp. 50–51 (emphasis in original); *Schelling: Vom Wesen der menschlichen Freiheit (1809)* [GA 42] (Frankfurt: Vittorio Klostermann, 1988), pp. 87–88. I have taken the liberty to amend Stambaugh's translation based on the original German text. For discussion of Heidegger's deconstruction of metaphysics as ontotheology, see Iain D. Thomson, *Heidegger on Ontotheology: Technology and the Politics of Education* (Cambridge: Cambridge University Press, 2005), pp. 7–43.
261. Heidegger, *Off the Beaten Track*, p. 58; *Holzwege*, p. 76.
262. Heidegger, *Introduction to Metaphysics*, pp. 165–166; *Einführung in die Metaphysik*, p. 164. On the political implications of this passage as it relates to Nazism, see Lacoue-Labarthe, *Heidegger and the Politics of Poetry*, pp. 3–6.
263. Heidegger, *Being and Time*, § 76, p. 373 (emphasis in original); *Sein und Zeit*, p. 392.
264. Heidegger, *Off the Beaten Track*, p. 47; *Holzwege*, pp. 62–63.
265. Heidegger, *Nietzsche, Volume I*, p. 6; *Nietzsche: Erster Band*, p. 4.
266. For citation and analysis of some of the relevant Derridean texts on this topic, see Wolfson, *Giving*, pp. 161–162. See also Elliot R. Wolfson, "Skepticism and the Philosopher's Keeping Faith," in *Jewish Philosophy for the Twenty-First Century: Personal Reflections*, ed. Hava Tirosh-Samuelson and Aaron W. Hughes (Leiden:

Brill, 2014), pp. 482–484. It is of interest to consider the tantalizing remark of Michel Henry, *Marx: A Philosophy of Human Reality*, trans. Kathleen McLaughlin (Bloomington: Indiana University Press, 1983), p. 71:

> Because it refers to nature, the Hegelian dialectic allows the trace of its real origin to appear in itself. This origin is not to be found in Platonism. It is always after the fact, and only in order to confirm what it considers to be self-evident that German thought refers to ancient philosophy and, for example, to Plato. The original character of the German dialectic can be seen, precisely, in its specific origin, which lies in medieval alchemy, where intuitions or illuminations, research, and work reach their culmination in the circle of thinkers and philosophers grouped around Paracelsus.

It lies beyond the scope of this project to explore this fascinating suggestion, but I think it puts into sharp relief Heidegger's single-minded—and somewhat disingenuous—effort to locate the origin of German thinking in the pre-Socratic thinkers of ancient Greece.

267. Derrida, *Of Spirit*, p. 64; *De l'esprit*, p. 104.
268. Derrida, *Of Spirit*, pp. 68–72; *De l'esprit*, pp. 109–116. A similar argument is advanced by Lacoue-Labarthe, *Heidegger and the Politics of Poetry*, pp. 6–7. John D. Caputo, "Toward a Postmodern Theology of the Cross: Augustine, Heidegger, Derrida," in *Postmodern Philosophy and Christian Thought*, ed. Merold Westphal (Bloomington: Indiana University Press, 1999), pp. 221–222, contrasts Derrida's view of language as a "mark of dispossession" with Heidegger's idea of "the language of the *Heimat*, Germany's or Being's, where speaking is empowered by autochthony, by the gathering together of the essential power of the *Volk* or *Sprache* from which one speaks." In the main, I concur with this distinction, but I would argue that the matter is more complex. The shared claim of Heidegger and Derrida that language unveils by veiling draws them closer together conceptually.
269. The expression *ontologischen Antisemitismus* is used by Donatella di Cesare, "Heidegger, das Sein und die Juden," *Information Philosophie*, February 2014, p. 8. For the related expression *metaphysische Antisemitismus*, see Donatella di Cesare, "Das Sein und der Jude: Heideggers metaphysischer Antisemitismus," in *Heidegger, die Juden, noch einmal*, ed. Peter Trawny and Andrew J. Mitchell (Frankfurt: Vittorio Klostermann, 2015), pp. 66–71; Donatella di Cesare, "Heideggers metaphysischer Antisemitismus," in *Heidegger und der Antisemitismus*, pp. 212–219; and Donatella di Cesare, "Heidegger's Metaphysical Anti-Semitism," in *Reading Heidegger's Black Notebooks*, pp. 187–190. See the essay of Mendieta cited in n22, this chapter. For a critique of this taxonomy, see Francesca Brencio, "Martin Heidegger and the Thinking of Evil: From the Original Ethics to the Black Notebooks," *Ivs Fvgit: Revista de Estudios Histórico-Jurídicos de la Corona de Aragón* 19 (2016): 100–111; and see the discussion of *l'antisemitismo metafisico* in Sonia Caporossi, "Il *silenzio* di Heidegger e la sua ricezione in Italia: una proposta di lettura," in *La pietà del pensiero. Heidegger e i Quaderni Neri*, ed. Francesca Brencio (Rome: Aguaplano, 2015), pp. 91–97. But see the comment of Lacoue-Labarthe cited in ch. 1n105.
270. A similar point with substantial textual corroboration has been made by Brencio, "Martin Heidegger," pp. 94–99. See also her "'Heidegger, una patata bollente':

2. NOMADISM, HOMELESSNESS, AND THE OBFUSCATION OF BEING

L'antisemitismo fra critica alla cristianità e *Seinsgeschichtlichkeit*," in *La pietà del pensiero*, pp. 107–186. I concur with the need to contextualize the statements about Jews and Jewry in the whole of Heidegger's notebooks, including especially his detailed criticism of Christianity, but I am uncertain of Brencio's conclusion, "Martin Heidegger," p. 99, that the portrait of the metaphysical Jew is not at the core of Heidegger's interest and hence it is inaccurate to view individual Jews as metaphysical subjects in the manner that many interpreters of his path have suggested. It is prudent to distance Heidegger from the actual atrocities of the Holocaust, but there is enough textual evidence to validate the claim that his anti-Jewish sentiment is related to the calculative-technological thinking he linked to the metaphysical oblivion of being, and therefore it is reasonable to conclude that he did champion a form of ontological anti-Judaism whereby Jews were imagined to be metaphysical subjects. In this matter, I agree with the judicious assessment of Heidegger's interpretation of the relationship between machination and world Jewry offered by Trawny, *Heidegger and the Myth*, p. 33:

> On the one hand he attributed to "world Judaism" a privileged place as the internationally acting representative of technology. On the other hand, this would all belong to the same history. In this "battle," the success of those who proclaim and achieve "world domination" is "no less relevant than the fate of those most ground down." All would still be "at the level of metaphysics" and would thus remain "excluded from anything different." The Jews would be just a further configuration of the metaphysical topology.

For a different analysis of Heidegger's complicated relationship to Christianity, see Nancy, *The Banality*, pp. 32–38, 63–73.

271. Trawny, *Heidegger and the Myth*, p. 76. The thematic link between the "two perils" (*zwei Gefahren*) of Marxism and Judaism was also exploited by Hitler, *Mein Kampf*, p. 20. See the expanded ramblings on the "Jewish Dialectic" (*Jüdische Dialektik*) and "Marxism as the Destroyer of Culture" (*Marxismus als Zerstörer der Kultur*), ibid., pp. 65–70. And see ibid., pp. 162, 170. On the diminishing of the intellectual divide between American capitalism and Soviet socialism in Heidegger and several other German intellectuals during the years of the Second World War and its aftermath, see the comments in Carlo Galli, *Janus's Gaze: Essays on Carl Schmitt*, ed. Adam Sitze, trans. Amanda Minervini (Durham: Duke University Press, 2015), pp. 117–118.
272. The expression is rendered in Nancy, *The Banality*, p. 10, "the type of human modality," and see p. 16, and the extensive philological note, p. 82n1.
273. Heidegger, *Überlegungen XII–XV*, p. 243; *Ponderings XII–XV*, p. 191. See Trawny, *Heidegger and the Myth*, p. 19; Michael Fagenblat, "'Heidegger' and the Jews," in *Reading Heidegger's Black Notebooks*, pp. 147–151; di Cesare, "Das Sein und der Jude," pp. 55–56; and di Cesare, "Heidegger's Metaphysical Anti-Semitism," pp. 181–182; Nancy, *The Banality*, pp. 10–11.
274. Nancy, *The Banality*, p. 19. Compare the stereotypical denunciation of American culture in Heidegger, *Ponderings XII–XV*, p. 213 (*Überlegungen XII–XV*, p. 269): "Americanism is the organization of the unconditional meaninglessness of 'existence,' joined to the prospect of an enhanced 'standard of living' (electric heating and cooling of homes, increase in automobile ownership, rise in the

2. NOMADISM, HOMELESSNESS, AND THE OBFUSCATION OF BEING

number of moviegoers and of other 'economic-technological-cultural' amenities of 'life')."

275. Heidegger, *What Is Called Thinking?* p. 244; *Was Heißt Denken?* p. 247.
276. Heidegger, *What Is Called Thinking?* pp. 79–80; *Was Heißt Denken?* p. 85–86.
277. Heidegger, *Logic as the Question*, p. 73; *Logik als die Frage*, p. 86.
278. See n12, this chapter.
279. Krell, "Troubled Brows," pp. 315–316, renders *aus der Judenschaft* as "from all that is Judaic," noting that this is the first appearance of this expression in the notebooks in place of the more frequent *das Judentum* or *die jüdische Welt*. Krell further suggests that the term carries the connotation of Jewish hegemony and thus parallels the term *Herrschaft* that Heidegger applies to the Jews in the same context. See n12, this chapter. See the extensive remarks on the historical usage and connotation of the word *Judenschaft* offered by Krell, ibid., p. 316n3.
280. Heidegger, *Anmerkungen I–V*, p. 20. For an alternate translation and analysis, see Trawny, "Heidegger, 'World Judaism,' and Modernity," pp. 11–12; and Trawny, *Heidegger and the Myth*, pp. 72–73. For another translation and analysis, see Krell, "Troubled Brows," pp. 315–316.
281. Heidegger, *Contributions*, § 19, p. 44; *Beiträge*, p. 54. Heidegger refers to Nietzsche's idea of the slave revolt in morals to verify the contention concerning the Jewish origin of Christianity. On occasion, Heidegger speaks of the Judeo-Christian tradition, for example, when he writes about the Christian-Jewish (*christlich-jüdische*) doctrines of the human being. See Heidegger, *Ponderings II–VI*, p. 345; *Überlegungen II–VI*, p. 475.
282. Krell, "Troubled Brows," pp. 316–317.
283. Hitler, *Mein Kampf*, p. 329, described the Jew as cunning (*gescheit*). On the cleverness (*Schlauheit*) and craftiness (*Hinterlist*) of the Jew, see ibid., pp. 338, 478, 596, 758. On p. 335 Hitler notes that the parasitic nature of Judaism (see n214, this chapter) leads to a life of dissimulation, which is supported by the quote attributed to Schopenhauer that the Jew is the "great master of lying" (*große Meister im Lügen*). As is well known, this stereotype has much older roots in Western thought.
284. See Trawny, *Heidegger and the Myth*, pp. 19, 45–46.
285. Heidegger, *Überlegungen XII–XV*, p. 56. For an alternative translation, see Heidegger, *Ponderings XII–XV*, p. 44. See the discussion of this passage in Nancy, *The Banality*, pp. 16–17. The misguided view concerning the Jewish propensity for a mathematical-calculative perspective seems to be at play in the critique of Cassirer in Martin Heidegger, *The Piety of Thinking: Essays by Martin Heidegger*, trans. James G. Hart and John C. Maraldo (Bloomington: Indiana University Press, 1977), p. 33. Heidegger argues that Cassirer's idea of mythic consciousness and "the absence of a clear delineation between dreaming and waking experiences, between the imagined and the perceived, between the original and the copy, between the word (signification) and the thing, between wished-for and actual possession, between living and dead," is neo-Kantian insofar as the "analysis of the mythic form of thought begins with a general description of the way in which objects stand over against mythic consciousness. The object-consciousness of mathematical physics as understood by the Kantian interpretation of Hermann Cohen serves as a guide to the characterization: There is an active forming of a

passively given 'chaos of sensation' into a 'cosmos.'" The mathematical physics is traced to Cohen's understanding of Kant!
286. Nancy, *The Banality*, p. 20.
287. Heidegger, *Ponderings VII–XI*, pp. 75–76; *Überlegungen VII–XI*, pp. 96–97.
288. For an extensive discussion of the Augustinian idea of Jewish witness, see Jeremy Cohen, *Living Letters of the Law: Ideas of the Jew in Medieval Christianity* (Berkeley: University of California Press, 1999), pp. 19–145.
289. Nancy, *The Banality*, p. 45.
290. Ibid., pp. 24–25.
291. Ibid., pp. 36–37.
292. Villa, *Arendt and Heidegger*, pp. 246–253.
293. Ibid., p. 250.
294. Martin Heidegger, "Critical Comments on Karl Jaspers's *Psychology of Worldviews*," in *Becoming Heidegger: On the Trail of His Early Occasional Writings, 1910–1927*, ed. Theodore Kisiel and Thomas Sheehan (Evanston: Northwestern University Press, 2007), p. 119 (emphasis in original); *Wegmarken*, pp. 4–5. In the version in *Wegmarken*, the date given for the review is 1919–1921, but I have followed the suggestion of Kisiel and Sheehan, *Becoming Heidegger*, p. 110, that the correct date is 1920–1921.

3. JEWISH TIME AND THE ECLIPSE OF HISTORICAL DESTINY

1. Martin Heidegger, *The Phenomenology of Religious Life*, trans. Matthias Fritsch and Jennifer Anna Gosetti-Ferencei (Bloomington: Indiana University Press, 2004), pp. 83–89; *Phänomenologie des religiösen Lebens* [GA 60] (Frankfurt: Vittorio Klostermann, 1995), pp. 116–125. The discussion here develops my previous analyses of this Heideggerian text in Elliot R. Wolfson, *Giving Beyond the Gift: Apophasis and Overcoming Theomania* (New York: Fordham University Press, 2014), pp. 101–102, 231–232; and Elliot R. Wolfson, "Not Yet Now: Speaking of the End and the End of Speaking," in *Elliot R. Wolfson: Poetic Thinking*, ed. Hava Tirosh-Samuelson and Aaron W. Hughes (Leiden: Brill, 2015), pp. 148–152. For other discussions of this text, see Thomas J. Sheehan, "Heidegger's 'Introduction to the Phenomenology of Religion,' 1920–21," in *A Companion to Heidegger's "Being and Time,"* ed. Joseph Kockelmans (Washington, DC: University Press of America, 1986), pp. 40–62; Giorgio Agamben, *The Time That Remains: A Commentary on the Letter to the Romans* (Stanford: Stanford University Press, 2005), pp. 33–34; Ben Vedder, *Heidegger's Philosophy of Religion: From God to the Gods* (Pittsburgh: Duquesne University Press, 2007), pp. 51–59; Sylvain Camilleri, *Phénoménologie de la religion et herméneutique théologique dans la pensée du jeune Heidegger: Commentaire analytique des Fondements philosophiques de la mystique médiévale (1916–1919)* (Dordrecht: Springer, 2008), pp. 457–464; Joachim L. Oberst, *Heidegger on Language and Death: The Intrinsic Connection in Human Existence* (London: Continuum, 2009), pp. 17–47, esp. 28–36; Justin D. Klassen, "Heidegger's Paul and Radical Orthodoxy on the Structure of Christian Hope," in *Paul,*

3. JEWISH TIME AND THE ECLIPSE OF HISTORICAL DESTINY

Philosophy, and the Theopolitical Vision: Critical Engagements with Agamben, Badiou, Žižek, and Others, ed. Douglas Harink (Eugene: Cascade, 2010), pp. 64–89; Simon Critchley, *The Faith of the Faithless: Experiments in Political Theology* (London: Verso, 2012), pp. 166–194; Simon Critchley, "You Are Not Your Own: On the Nature of Faith," in *Paul and the Philosophers*, ed. Ward Blanton and Hent de Vries (New York: Fordham University Press, 2013), pp. 224–255; Judith Wolfe, *Heidegger's Eschatology: Theological Horizons in Martin Heidegger's Early Work* (Oxford: Oxford University Press, 2013), pp. 61–65; Benjamin D. Crowe, "Heidegger and the Apostle Paul," in *Paul in the Grip of the Philosophers: The Apostle and Contemporary Continental Philosophy*, ed. Peter Frick (Minneapolis: Fortress, 2013), pp. 39–56; Ryan Coyne, *Heidegger's Confessions: The Remains of Saint Augustine in* Being and Time *and Beyond* (Chicago: University of Chicago Press, 2015), pp. 17–52; Ezra Delahaye, "Heidegger on Religious Faith: The Development of Heidegger's Thinking About Faith Between 1920 and 1928," in *Rethinking Faith: Heidegger Between Nietzsche and Wittgenstein*, ed. Antonio Cimino and Gert-Jan van der Heiden (New York: Bloomsbury, 2017), pp. 146–152; Gert-Jan van der Heiden, "The Experience of Contingency and the Attitude to Life: Nietzsche and Heidegger on Paul," in *Rethinking Faith*, pp. 161–177. On the influence of Pauline anthropology on Heidegger, see also Antonio Cimino, "Paul as a Challenge for Contemporary Philosophers: Nietzsche, Heidegger and Agamben," in *Rethinking Faith*, pp. 183–196.

2. Heidegger, *The Phenomenology of Religious Life*, p. 83; *Phänomenologie des religiösen Lebens*, pp. 116–117.
3. Martin Heidegger, "Critical Comments on Karl Jaspers's *Psychology of Worldviews*," in *Becoming Heidegger: On the Trail of His Early Occasional Writings, 1910–1927*, ed. Theodore Kisiel and Thomas Sheehan (Evanston: Northwestern University Press, 2007), p. 142.
4. Thomas Sheehan, "Introduction: Heidegger, the Project and the Fulfillment," in *Heidegger: The Man and The Thinker*, ed. Thomas Sheehan (Chicago: Precedent, 1981), p. xv (emphasis in original). On the importance of *Vollzugssinn* in Heidegger's thought, see also Sheehan, "Heidegger's 'Introduction,'" pp. 50–52, and, more recently, Gianni Vattimo, *Of Reality: The Purposes of Philosophy*, trans. Robert T. Valgenti (New York: Columbia University Press, 2016), pp. 36–47. And compare Schürmann's assessment in Simon Critchley and Reiner Schürmann, *On Heidegger's Being and Time*, ed. Steven Levine (London: Routledge, 2008), p. 57: "Heidegger's point of departure is the notion of the subject as 'process' (*Vollzug*).... Dasein is thrown into the world, but there is no thrower. In its process (*Vollzug*), the subject, considered in itself, is now utterly finite."
5. Heidegger, *The Phenomenology of Religious Life*, p. 83; *Phänomenologie des religiösen Lebens*, pp. 116–117.
6. Heidegger, *The Phenomenology of Religious Life*, p. 57; *Phänomenologie des religiösen Lebens*, p. 82.
7. Heidegger, *The Phenomenology of Religious Life*, p. 89; *Phänomenologie des religiösen Lebens*, pp. 124–125.
8. Martin Heidegger, *Being and Time,* trans. Joan Stambaugh, revised and with a foreword by Dennis J. Schmidt (Albany: State University of New York Press, 2010), § 72, p. 358; *Sein und Zeit* (Tübingen: Max Niemeyer, 1993), pp. 375–376.

3. JEWISH TIME AND THE ECLIPSE OF HISTORICAL DESTINY

9. Heidegger, *Being and Time*, § 80, p. 392; *Sein und Zeit*, p. 411.
10. Martin Heidegger, *The Concept of Time*, trans. William McNeill (Oxford: Blackwell, 1992), p. 17.
11. Ibid., p. 18.
12. Martin Heidegger, *On the Way to Language*, trans. Peter D. Hertz (New York: Harper and Row, 1971), p. 176; *Unterwegs zur Sprache* [GA 12] (Frankfurt: Vittorio Klostermann, 1985), p. 53. See also Heidegger, *Being and Time*, § 81, pp. 400–406; *Sein und Zeit*, pp. 420–428; *The Basic Problems of Phenomenology*, trans. Albert Hofstadter (Bloomington: Indiana University Press, 1982), pp. 233–234; *Die Grundprobleme der Phänomenologie* [GA 24] (Frankfurt: Vittorio Klostermann, 1997), pp. 330–331; *What Is Called Thinking?* trans. Fred W. Wieck and J. Glenn Gray (New York: Harper and Row, 1968), pp. 101–102; *Was Heißt Denken?* [GA 8] (Frankfurt: Vittorio Klostermann, 2002), pp. 104–105. See n69, this chapter.
13. Martin Heidegger, *Schelling's Treatise on the Essence of Human Freedom*, trans. Joan Stambaugh (Athens: Ohio University Press, 1985), p. 167. Heidegger's comment about his interpretation of Schelling can be extended to his thinking more generally: "Perhaps in the long run we cannot distinguish between historiographical (*historisch*) explanation and historical (*geschichtlich*) thinking, but we shall keep one thing in mind. The historical thinking attempted here cannot be subsumed either under philosophical-historical explanation nor under 'systematic' reflection nor under a combination of both" (an excerpt from manuscripts, copied by Fritz Heidegger, in preparation for an advanced seminar on Schelling in the summer semester, 1941).
14. Heidegger, *On the Way to Language*, p. 54; *Unterwegs zur Sprache*, p. 146. And compare the description of true time as "the arrival of that which has been," which is not the past but "the gathering of essential being," in Heidegger, *On the Way to Language*, p. 176; *Unterwegs zur Sprache*, p. 53.
15. Martin Heidegger, *Basic Questions of Philosophy: Selected 'Problems' of 'Logic,'* trans. Richard Rojcewicz and André Schuwer (Bloomington: Indiana University Press, 1994), pp. 37–38; *Grundfragen der Philosophie: Ausgewählte "Probleme" der "Logik"* [GA 45] (Frankfurt: Vittorio Klostermann, 1992), p. 40.
16. Heidegger, *Being and Time*, § 65, p. 314; *Sein und Zeit*, p. 329.
17. Heidegger, *Being and Time*, § 65, pp. 312–313 (emphasis in original); *Sein und Zeit*, p. 327.
18. Heidegger, *Being and Time*, § 65, p. 314; *Sein und Zeit*, p. 329.
19. Martin Heidegger, *The Fundamental Concepts of Metaphysics: World, Finitude, Solitude*, trans. William McNeill and Nicholas Walker (Bloomington: Indiana University Press, 1995), p. 145; *Die Grundbegriffe der Metaphysik: Welt—Endlichkeit—Einsamkeit* [GA 29/30] (Frankfurt: Vittorio Klostermann, 1983), p. 218.
20. Heidegger, *Being and Time*, § 72, p. 359; *Sein und Zeit*, p. 376.
21. Martin Heidegger, *Introduction to Metaphysics*, trans. Gregory Fried and Richard Polt (New Haven: Yale University Press, 2000), pp. 46–47 (emphasis in original); *Einführung in die Metaphysik* [GA 40] (Frankfurt: Vittorio Klostermann, 1983), pp. 47–48. The matter is examined thoroughly in Jeffrey Andrew Barash, *Martin Heidegger and the Problem of Historical Meaning* (New York: Fordham University Press, 2003).

3. JEWISH TIME AND THE ECLIPSE OF HISTORICAL DESTINY

22. Martin Heidegger, *Contributions to Philosophy (Of the Event)*, trans. Richard Rojcewicz and Daniela Vallega-Neu (Bloomington: Indiana University Press, 2012), § 273, p. 387; *Beiträge zur Philosophie (Vom Ereignis)* [GA 65] (Frankfurt: Vittorio Klostermann, 1989), p. 492.
23. Heidegger, *Contributions*, § 273, pp. 387–388; *Beiträge*, pp. 492–493.
24. Heidegger, *Contributions*, § 273, p. 388 (emphasis in original); *Beiträge*, pp. 493–494.
25. Heidegger, *Contributions*, § 273, p. 389; *Beiträge*, p. 494.
26. Heidegger, *The Concept of Time*, trans. McNeill, p. 20.
27. Heidegger, *Being and Time*, § 6, p. 19 (emphasis in original); *Sein und Zeit*, pp. 19–20. See Jean Greisch, *Ontologie et Temporalité: Esquisse d'une interprétation intégrale de Sein und Zeit* (Paris: Presses Universitaires de France, 1994), pp. 352–382; Françoise Dastur, *Heidegger and the Question of Time*, trans. François Raffoul and David Pettigrew (Atlantic Highlands, NJ: Humanities Press, 1998), pp. 38–51.
28. Martin Heidegger, *Hölderlin's Hymns "Germania" and "The Rhine,"* trans. William McNeill and Julia Ireland (Bloomington: Indiana University Press, 2014), p. 122; *Hölderlins Hymnen "Germanien" und "Der Rhein"* [GA 39] (Frankfurt: Vittorio Klostermann, 1999), p. 139.
29. On Heidegger's resistance to and subversion of system, see Gary Shapiro, "Subversion of System/Systems of Subversion," in *Writing the Politics of Difference*, ed. Hugh J. Silverman (Albany: State University of New York Press, 1991), pp. 1–11; John McCumber, "Essence and Subversion in Hegel and Heidegger," in *Writing the Politics of Difference*, pp. 13–29; Elliot R. Wolfson, "Zeitliche Entzweiung und offenes System. Die Atonalität der Kabbala und Heideggers anfängliches Denken," in *Martin Heidegger: die Falte der Sprache*, ed. Michael Friedman and Angelika Seppi (Vienna: Turia and Kant, 2017), pp. 121–167.
30. Martin Heidegger, *Pathmarks*, ed. William McNeill (Cambridge: Cambridge University Press, 1998), p. 255; *Wegmarken* [GA 9] (Frankfurt: Vittorio Klostermann, 1996), p. 335.
31. Sheehan, "Heidegger's 'Introduction,'" pp. 52–59. For a more detailed analysis of this dimension of Heidegger's thinking about time, see Wolfson, "Not Yet Now," pp. 128–142.
32. Martin Heidegger, *Zum Wesen des Sprache und Zur Frage nach der Kunst* [GA 74] (Frankfurt: Vittorio Klostermann, 2010), p. 112.
33. Heidegger, *The Concept of Time*, trans. McNeill, p. 21.
34. Heidegger, *The Phenomenology of Religious Life*, pp. 83–84; *Phänomenologie des religiösen Lebens*, p. 117. The discussion of Heidegger's earlier phenomenology of the eschatological and messianic views, attributed respectively to Christianity and Judaism, is based on Wolfson, "Not Yet Now," pp. 146–156.
35. Heidegger, *The Phenomenology of Religious Life*, p. 73 (translation modified); *Phänomenologie des religiösen Lebens*, p. 104.
36. Heidegger, *The Phenomenology of Religious Life*, p. 66; *Phänomenologie des religiösen Lebens*, p. 95.
37. Heidegger, *The Phenomenology of Religious Life*, p. 84; *Phänomenologie des religiösen Lebens*, p. 117. Travis Kroeker, "Living 'As If Not': Messianic Becoming or the Practice of Nihilism?" in *Paul, Philosophy, and the Theopolitical Vision*, p. 40n8, commented on the conceptual kinship between Heidegger's interpretation

3. JEWISH TIME AND THE ECLIPSE OF HISTORICAL DESTINY

of Paul's notion of "having become" and Badiou's emphasis on becoming a subject. I would add that another similarity relates to the primacy accorded the now of the singularity of the event, or as Alain Badiou, *Saint Paul: The Foundation of Universalism*, trans. Ray Brassier (Stanford: Stanford University Press, 2003), p. 59, puts it, "every truth is marked by an indestructible *youthfulness*" (emphasis in original). I read Badiou's idea of the evental truth as a further secularization of Heidegger's interpretation of Pauline eschatology and the hope engendered by waiting for the second coming. Consider the following summary given in an interview with Fabien Tarby in Alain Badiou, *Philosophy and the Event*, trans. Louise Burchill (Cambridge: Polity, 2014), p. 12: "In every situation, there are processes faithful to an event that has previously taken place. It's not a matter, then, of desperately awaiting a miraculous event but, rather, of following through to the very end, to the utmost degree, what you've been able to extract from the previous event and of being as prepared as possible, therefore, to take in subjectively what will inevitably come about. For me, truth is an undertaking; it is a process made possible by the event. The event is only there as a source of possibilities." For a sustained critique of Badiou's approach to Paul, see Stephen Fowl, "A Very Particular Universalism: Badiou and Paul," in *Paul, Philosophy, and the Theopolitical Vision*, pp. 119–134.

38. Heidegger, *The Phenomenology of Religious Life*, p. 57; *Phänomenologie des religiösen Lebens*, p. 82.
39. Heidegger, *The Phenomenology of Religious Life*, p. 83; *Phänomenologie des religiösen Lebens*, p. 116.
40. Heidegger, *The Phenomenology of Religious Life*, pp. 73, 85; *Phänomenologie des religiösen Lebens*, pp. 104, 119.
41. Norbert Fischer, "Was ist Ewigkeit? Ein Denkanstoß Heideggers und eine Annäherung an die Antwort Augustins," in *Martin Heidegger's Interpretations of Saint Augustine: Sein und Zeit und Ewigkeit*, ed. Frederick Van Fleteren (Lewiston, NY: Edwin Mellen, 2005), pp. 155–184; Coyne, *Heidegger's Confessions*, pp. 157–193, esp. 176–183. See also C. Agustín Corti, *Zeitproblematik bei Martin Heidegger und Augustinus* (Würzburg: Königshausen & Neumann, 2006), pp. 224–292.
42. Elliot R. Wolfson, *Alef, Mem, Tau: Kabbalistic Musings on Time, Truth, and Death* (Berkeley: University of California Press, 2006), pp. 176–177. My approach should be contrasted with Emil L. Fackenheim, *To Mend the World: Foundations of Post-Holocaust Jewish Thought* (New York: Schocken, 1989), pp. 149–150, who distinguishes the two thinkers on the grounds that Rosenzweig affirms a sense of eternity in the midst of time, whereas Heidegger rejects this possibility, considering the historicity of the human condition exclusively from the perspective of temporality. See, however, Karl Löwith, "F. Rosenzweig and M. Heidegger on Temporality and Eternity," *Philosophy and Phenomenological Research* 3 (1942): 53–77. For the revised version, see Karl Löwith, *Nature, History, and Existentialism*, ed. Arnold Levison (Evanston: Northwestern University Press, 1966), pp. 51–78, and the German version with significant variations, Karl Löwith, "M. Heidegger und F. Rosenzweig. Ein Nachtrag zu 'Sein und Zeit,'" *Zeitschrift für philosophische Forschung* 12 (1958): 161–187.
43. Martin Heidegger, *Ponderings VII–XI: Black Notebooks 1938–1939*, trans. Richard Rojcewicz (Bloomington: Indiana University Press, 2017), p. 93 (emphasis in

3. JEWISH TIME AND THE ECLIPSE OF HISTORICAL DESTINY

original); *Überlegungen VII–XI (Schwarze Hefte 1938/39)* [GA 95] (Frankfurt: Vittorio Klostermann, 2014), p. 120. Compare Heidegger, *Contributions*, § 100, p. 154; *Beiträge*, pp. 196–197.

44. Heidegger, *The Fundamental Concepts*, p. 151; *Die Grundbegriffe*, p. 226.
45. Heidegger, *Schelling's Treatise*, p. 112; *Schelling: Vom Wesen*, p. 195.
46. Heidegger, *Schelling's Treatise*, p. 113 (emphasis in original); *Schelling: Vom Wesen*, p. 197.
47. Martin Heidegger, *Sein und Zeit* [GA 2] (Frankfurt: Vittorio Klostermann, 1977), p. 5na, cited and translated in Dermot Moran, "Dasein as Transcendence in Heidegger and the Critique of Husserl," in *Heidegger in the Twenty-First Century*, ed. Tziovanis Georgakis and Paul J. Ennis (Dordrecht: Springer, 2015), p. 41. For an alternative rendering, see the Stambaugh translation of Heidegger, *Being and Time*, p. 36.
48. Heidegger, *The Concept of Time*, trans. McNeill, p. 1. The scriptural citation is from Galatians 4:4. Heidegger copied this introduction in the article with the same name, "Der Begriff der Zeit," also written in 1924. See Martin Heidegger, *The Concept of Time*, trans. Ingo Farin with Alex Skinner (London: Continuum, 2011), p. 37.
49. Heidegger, *The Concept of Time*, trans. McNeill, pp. 1–2.
50. Heidegger, *Hölderlin's Hymns*, p. 52; *Hölderlins Hymnen*, pp. 54–55. Compare Heidegger, *Contributions*, § 58, p. 96 (*Beiträge*, p. 121):

> On this basis, then, the erroneous representation of the high and the "highest" in the monstrous form of record-breaking performances; purely quantitative increase, blindness to *the truly momentary, which is not the transient, but is what opens up eternity*. With respect to speed, however, the eternal is the mere endurance of the same, the empty "and so on and on"; the genuine unrest of the battle remains concealed, and in its place has stepped the restlessness of constantly more ingenious activity, which is pushed forward by the dread of becoming bored with oneself.
>
> (emphasis added)

51. Heidegger, *Hölderlin's Hymns*, p. 52; *Hölderlins Hymnen*, p. 55.
52. Heidegger, *Hölderlin's Hymns*, p. 53; *Hölderlins Hymnen*, pp. 55–56.
53. Heidegger, *Hölderlin's Hymns*, p. 53; *Hölderlins Hymnen*, p. 56.
54. Heidegger, *Contributions*, § 238, p. 293 (emphasis in original); *Beiträge*, p. 371.
55. Compare the discussion of the parousia in Jean-Yves Lacoste, "The Phenomenality of Anticipation," in *Phenomenology and Eschatology: Not Yet in the Now*, ed. Neal DeRoo and John Panteleimon Manoussakis (Surrey: Ashgate, 2008), pp. 15–33.
56. Heidegger, *The Phenomenology of Religious Life*, p. 73; *Phänomenologie des religiösen Lebens*, p. 105. By contrast, compare Jacob Taubes, *Occidental Eschatology*, trans. David Ratmoko (Stanford: Stanford University Press, 2009) pp. 69–70:

> The hiatus between the Resurrection and the Parousia is so great that a situation of constant expectation [*steten Harrens*], characteristic of the Jewish Apocalypse, is mirrored in Christianity. The Revelation to John is evidence of this change. In the early Church it certainly was already treated

with suspicion as being "Jewish," and Luther placed it on a par with the Fourth Book of Ezra.... The Revelation to John thus fits into the series of noncanonical apocalypses, which all involve Christian interpolations around a Jewish core.

57. Gershom Scholem, *The Messianic Idea and Other Essays on Jewish Spirituality* (New York: Schocken, 1971), pp. 1–4. See the criticism by Jacob Taubes, "The Price of Messianism," in *Essential Papers on Messianic Movements and Personalities in Jewish History*, ed. Marc Saperstein (New York: New York University Press, 1992), pp. 551–557. Taubes argued that it is necessary to remove the "road-block of interiorization which Scholem has erected to preserve in a dogmatic fashion an 'essential' difference between the '-isms'—Judaism and Christianity," so that "a more coherent reading of the inner logic of the Messianic idea becomes possible. Internalization, or opening the inward realm, belongs essentially to the career of that 'idea,' if such an idea should have a career at all in an unredeemed world" (p. 553). It is merely an "illusion" to think that redemption "happens on the stage of history. For every attempt to bring about redemption on the level of history without a transfiguration of the Messianic idea leads straight into the abyss" (p. 557). I concur with Taubes's comments, but he ignores the fact that Scholem himself articulates a similar sentiment when he concludes that "in Judaism the Messianic idea has compelled a *life lived in deferment*, in which nothing can be done definitively, nothing can be irrevocably accomplished. One may say, perhaps, the Messianic idea is the real anti-existentialist idea.... This makes for the greatness of Messianism, but also for its constitutional weakness. Jewish so-called *Existenz* possesses a tension that never finds true release; it never burns itself out. And when in our history it does discharge, then it is foolishly decried (or, one might say, unmasked) as 'pseudo-Messianism'" (*The Messianic Idea*, p. 35). This tragic dimension of Scholem's understanding of Jewish messianism has been rightly emphasized by David Biale, *Gershom Scholem: Kabbalah and Counter-History* (Cambridge: Harvard University Press, 1979), pp. 148–170, and more recently by Martin Kavka, "Reading Messianically with Gershom Scholem," in *Rethinking the Messianic Idea in Judaism*, ed. Michael L. Morgan and Steven Weitzman (Bloomington: Indiana University Press, 2015), pp. 407–408. Also relevant here is Biale's argument that Scholem, under the influence of Gustav Landauer's political anarchism, envisioned Zionism as a "counter-nationalism" and that his primary interest was not establishing a Jewish state but rather in creating a new community of Jews. See David Biale, "Scholem und der moderne Nationalismus," in *Gershom Scholem: Zwischen den Disziplinen*, ed. Peter Schäfer and Gary Smith (Frankfurt: Suhrkamp, 1995), pp. 259, 263. For a different approach, see Yossef Schwartz, "Gustav Landauer and Gerhard Scholem: Anarchy and Utopia," in *Gustav Landauer: Anarchist and Jew*, ed. Paul Mendes-Flohr and Anya Mali in collaboration with Hanna Delf von Wolzogen (Berlin: Walter de Gruyter, 2015), pp. 185–187. Taubes's criticism of Scholem is analyzed by Moshe Idel, *Messianic Mystics* (New Haven: Yale University Press, 1998), pp. 240–241. For Idel's own critical assessment of Scholem's perspective, see ibid., pp. 18–21. See also Thomas Macho, "Zu Frage nach dem Preis des Messianismus. Der intellektuelle Bruch zwischen Gershom Scholem und Jacob Taubes als Erinnerung ungelöster Probleme des Messianismus," in

3. JEWISH TIME AND THE ECLIPSE OF HISTORICAL DESTINY

Gershom Scholem: Literatur und Rhetorik, ed. Stéphane Mosès (Cologne: Böhlau, 2000), pp. 133–152.
58. Heidegger, *The Phenomenology of Religious Life*, p. 81; *Phänomenologie des religiösen Lebens*, p. 114. Heidegger's presentation of Christian eschatology and his interpretation of Paul has been reiterated by Agamben, *The Time That Remains*, pp. 61–62, although he does not distinguish the Jewish and Christian perspectives as sharply as Heidegger. Agamben emphasizes that Paul's technical term for the messianic event is *ho nyn kairos*, the time of the now, which is not the end of time that will happen in the future but the time of the end that is experienced as the interminable waiting in the present. Messianic time is thus defined as "*the time that time takes to come to an end*, or, more precisely, the time we take to bring to an end, to achieve our representation of time. This is not the line of chronological time ... nor the instant of its end ... nor is it a segment cut from chronological time; rather, it is operational time pressing within the chronological time, working and transforming it from within; it is the time we need to make time end: *the time that is left us*" (pp. 67–68). The seventh day emblematizes messianic time because the Sabbath "is not another day, homogenous to others; rather, it is that innermost disjointedness within time through which one may—by a hairsbreadth—grasp time and accomplish it" (p. 72). See Eleanor Kaufman, "The Saturday of Messianic Time: Agamben and Badiou on the Apostle Paul," in *Paul and the Philosophers*, 297–309; Ryan L. Hansen, "Messianic or Apocalyptic? Engaging Agamben on Paul and Politics," in *Paul, Philosophy, and the Theopolitical Vision*, 198–223; Alain Gignac, "Agamben's Paul: Thinker of the Messianic," in *Paul in the Grip of the Philosophers*, 165–192.
59. Stéphane Mosès, "Walter Benjamin and Franz Rosenzweig," *Philosophical Forum* 15 (1983–1984): 188–205, esp. 200–202; Stéphane Mosès, *The Angel of History: Rosenzweig, Benjamin, Scholem*, trans. Barbara Harshav (Stanford: Stanford University Press, 2009), pp. 56–57; Pierre Bouretz, *Witness for the Future: Philosophy and Messianism*, trans. Michael Smith (Baltimore: Johns Hopkins University Press, 2010), pp. 138–147.
60. See references cited in ch. 2nn219–220.
61. Emmanuel Levinas, *Beyond the Verse: Talmudic Readings and Lectures*, trans. Gary D. Mole (London: Athlone, 1994), p. 143.
62. Emmanuel Levinas, *God, Death, and Time*, trans. Bettina Bergo (Stanford: Stanford University Press, 2000), p. 139. See analysis in Wolfson, *Giving*, pp. 113–120.
63. The language here reflects the view of Steven Schwarzschild, *The Pursuit of the Ideal: Jewish Writings of Steven Schwarzschild*, ed. Menachem Kellner (Albany: State University of New York Press, 1990), pp. 209–211, previously cited and discussed in Wolfson, *Giving*, p. 116. See also Wolfson, "Not Yet Now," p. 154n101.
64. Heidegger, *Ponderings VII–XI*, pp. 75–76; *Überlegungen VII–XI*, pp. 96–97. For an earlier critique of historicism and its fundamental opposition to the teleological-critical method of philosophy, see Martin Heidegger, *Towards the Definition of Philosophy*, trans. Ted Sadler (London: Athlone, 2000), p. 32; *Zur Bestimmung der Philosophie* [GA 56/57] (Frankfurt: Vittorio Klostermann, 1987), p. 39.
65. Heidegger, *Ponderings VII–XI*, p. 200; *Überlegungen VII–XI*, p. 258. In that context, Heidegger pejoratively refers to Jewish psychoanalysis (*jüdische »Psychoanalyse«*). Compare Martin Heidegger, *Überlegungen XII–XV (Schwarze Hefte 1939–1941)*

3. JEWISH TIME AND THE ECLIPSE OF HISTORICAL DESTINY

[GA 96] (Frankfurt: Vittorio Klostermann, 2014), p. 218, where the psychoanalysis of the Jew "Freud" (*die Psychoanalyse des Juden »Freud«*) is described as "pure nihilism" (*reine Nihilismus*) insofar as it is a "way of 'thought,' which, in advance, permits no 'being' at all" (*die überhaupt im voraus kein »Sein« zuläßt*). An English translation of the whole passage is now available in Martin Heidegger, *Ponderings XII–XV: Black Notebooks 1939-1941*, trans. Richard Rojcewicz (Bloomington: Indiana University Press, 2017), p. 171. See discussion in David F. Krell, "Heidegger's *Black Notebooks, 1931–1941*," *Research in Phenomenology* 45 (2015): 137–138. Elisabeth Roudinesco, *Freud: In His Time and Ours*, trans. Catherine Porter (Cambridge: Harvard University Press, 2016), p. 372, compares the passage of Heidegger about Freud and Jewish nihilism to the view on Jews espoused by Jung:

> Just as Jung excluded diaspora Jews from any access to "Jewish individuation," Heidegger excluded Jews from thinking humanity, reducing them to the morass of instincts. In both cases, the anti-Semitism that did not want to speak its name claimed to be eliminating the Jewish mind from the world scene, inasmuch as that mind was thought to have given rise to a specifically Jewish doctrine. For Jung, psychoanalysis lacked an "archetypical ground"; for Heidegger it was a nihilism bearing the name of the Jew Freud. Jung and Heidegger had in common their adherence to a sort of anti-Judeo-Christian and polytheistic theology.

66. Heidegger, *Contributions*, § 177, p. 238 (emphasis in original); *Beiträge*, p. 301.
67. Heidegger, *Contributions*, § 177, p. 238 (emphasis in original); *Beiträge*, p. 301.
68. Heidegger, *Contributions*, § 195, p. 252 (emphasis in original); *Beiträge*, p. 318.
69. Heidegger, *Contributions*, § 28, p. 52, § 39, p. 65; *Beiträge*, pp. 65, 81–82. This analysis is a continuation of the phenomenological account of anxiety in Heidegger, *Being and Time*, § 68, p. 328 (*Sein und Zeit*, p. 343) as that which "brings one back to thrownness *as something to be possibly repeated. And thus it also reveals the possibility of an authentic potentiality-of-being that must, as something futural in repetition, come back to the thrown There. Bringing before the possibility of repetition is the specific ecstatic mode of the attunement of the having-been that constitutes anxiety*" (emphasis in original). Also relevant here is the characterization of the "double visage" (*eigentümliches Doppelgesicht*) of the now according to Aristotle in Heidegger, *The Basic Problems*, pp. 247–248 (*Die Grundprobleme*, pp. 349–351):

> Time is held together within itself by the now; time's specific continuity is rooted in the now. But conjointly, with respect to the now, time is divided, articulated into the no-longer-now, the earlier, and the not-yet-now, the later. It is only with respect to the now that we can conceive of the then and at-the-time, the later and the earlier. The now that we count in following a motion is *in each instance a different now*. To de nun dia to kineisthai to pheromenon aiei heteron, on account of the transition of the moving thing the now is always another, an advance from one place to the other. In each now the now is a different one, but still each different now is, as now, always now. The ever different nows are, *as different*, nevertheless always exactly

the same, namely, now. Aristotle summarizes the peculiar nature of the now and thus of time—when he interprets time purely by way of the now... that is, in each now it is now; its *essentia*, its what, is always *the same* (tauto)—and nevertheless every now is, by its nature, different in each now... nowness, being-now [*Jetztsein*], is always *otherness, being-other* [Anderssein]... the now is in a certain way always the same and in a certain way never the same. The now articulates and bounds time with respect to its earlier and later. On the one hand it is indeed always the same, but then it is never the same.... This constitutes its always being-now, its otherhood [*Andersheit*]. But what it always already was as that which it is, namely, now—that is the same."

(emphasis in original)

Notwithstanding Heidegger's criticism of Aristotle's mathematical understanding of time as the measure of bodies in motion, the paradox of the now as the locus of sameness and difference—the now is always the same because always different and always different because always the same—had a profound influence on his thinking about time in all periods of his life.

70. Heidegger, *What Is Called Thinking?* pp. 175–176; *Was Heißt Denken?* p. 180. See as well the text cited in ch. 2n177.
71. Martin Heidegger, *Parmenides*, trans. André Schuwer and Richard Rojcewicz (Bloomington: Indiana University Press, 1992), p. 12; *Parmenides* [GA 54] (Frankfurt: Vittorio Klostermann, 1992), p. 18.
72. Heidegger, *Introduction to Metaphysics*, p. 41 (emphasis in original); *Einführung in die Metaphysik*, p. 42. On the paradox of the repetition of the origin in Heidegger, see Paola Marrati, *Genesis and Trace: Derrida Reading Husserl and Heidegger* (Stanford: Stanford University Press, 2005), pp. 109–113. On the "politics of repetition" in Heidegger, see Miguel de Beistegui, *Thinking with Heidegger: Displacements* (Bloomington: Indiana University Press, 2003), pp. 49–60. See also Calvin O. Schrag, "Heidegger on Repetition and Historical Understanding," *Philosophy East and West* 20 (1970): 287–295; Alexander S. Duff, *Heidegger and Politics: The Ontology of Radical Discontent* (Cambridge: Cambridge University Press, 2015), pp. 176–182. On repetition and the experience of poetic language, see William S. Allen, *Ellipsis: Of Poetry and the Experience of Language After Heidegger, Hölderlin, and Blanchot* (Albany: State University of New York Press, 2007), pp. 25–57; and the analysis of linguistic repetition as theological revelation in Christian epic from Dante to Joyce in William Franke, *Poetry and Apocalypse: Theological Disclosures of Poetic Language* (Stanford: Stanford University Press, 2009), pp. 97–123.
73. Martin Heidegger, *Off the Beaten Track*, ed. and trans. Julian Young and Kenneth Haynes (Cambridge: Cambridge University Press, 2002), p. 48; *Holzwege* [GA 5] (Frankfurt: Vittorio Klostermann, 1977), p. 64.
74. Heidegger, *Contributions*, § 29, p. 53; *Beiträge*, p. 66.
75. Krzysztof Ziarek, "On Heidegger's *Einmaligkeit* Again: The Single Turn of the Event," *Gatherings: The Heidegger Circle Annual* 6 (2016): 91.
76. Heidegger, *Contributions*, § 117, p. 180; *Beiträge*, pp. 228–229.

3. JEWISH TIME AND THE ECLIPSE OF HISTORICAL DESTINY

77. Heidegger, *Contributions*, § 254, p. 322; *Beiträge*, p. 407. Compare Heidegger, *Ponderings VII–XI*, p. 47 (*Überlegungen VII–XI*, p. 62): "The incalculable—is not a being and occurs 'only' as beyng itself, with which all calculation can 'do nothing' [lit., 'begin nothing'], not because beyng is worthless for a beginning, but because calculation and explanation never grasp the beginning."
78. Heidegger, *Contributions*, § 117, p. 181; *Beiträge*, p. 230. See Tracy Colony, "Given Time: The Question of Futurity in Heidegger's *Contributions to Philosophy*," *Heythrop Journal* 50 (2009): 284–292.
79. Martin Heidegger, *The History of Beyng*, trans. William McNeill and Jeffrey Powell (Bloomington: Indiana University Press, 2015), p. 179; *Die Geschichte des Seyns* [GA 69] (Frankfurt: Vittorio Klostermann, 1998), p. 211.
80. Heidegger, *Off the Beaten Track*, p. 48; *Holzwege*, p. 64. For a different approach to this passage, see Philippe Lacoue-Labarthe, *Heidegger and the Politics of Poetry*, trans. Jeff Fort (Urbana: University of Illinois Press, 2007), pp. 8–9, and compare the alternate version of this passage cited on p. 97n17.
81. Heidegger, *Off the Beaten Track*, p. 48; *Holzwege*, p. 64.
82. Heidegger, *Off the Beaten Track*, p. 49; *Holzwege*, pp. 65–66.
83. Martin Heidegger, *Identity and Difference*, trans. Joan Stambaugh (New York: Harper and Row, 1969), p. 53; German text, p. 120.
84. See Ryan Johnson, "Thinking the Abyss of History: Heidegger's Critique of Hegelian Metaphysics," *Gatherings: The Heidegger Circle Annual* 6 (2016): 51–68, esp. 62–65.
85. Alain Badiou, *Theory of the Subject*, trans. Bruno Bosteels (London: Continuum, 2009), p. 19 (emphasis in original).
86. Steven S. Schwarzschild, "An Introduction to the Thought of R. Isaac Hutner," *Modern Judaism* 5 (1985): 244. For more on Schwarzschild's messianic thinking, see Wolfson, "Not Yet Now," pp. 154–156.
87. Hans-Jost Frey, *Interruptions*, trans. Georgia Albert (Albany: State University of New York Press, 1996), p. 23.
88. Ibid., p. 24.
89. Elliot R. Wolfson, "Gazing Beneath the Veil: Apocalyptic Envisioning the End," in *Reinterpreting Revelation and Tradition: Jews and Christians in Conversation*, ed. John T. Pawlikowski, O.S.M. and Hayim Goren Perelmuter (Franklin, WI: Sheed and Ward, 2000), pp. 83–86.
90. Jacques Derrida, *Specters of Marx: The State of the Debt, the Work of Mourning, and the New International*, trans. Peggy Kamuf (New York: Routledge, 1994), p. 37 (emphasis in original).
91. Jacques Derrida, "Of an Apocalyptic Tone: Recently Adopted in Philosophy," *Semeia* 23 (1982): 85.
92. Ibid., p. 94.
93. For a more conventional account of the intermingling of hope and despair in the apocalyptic imagination, see Franke, *Poetry and Apocalypse*, p. 15: "The extreme imagery of apocalyptic is undoubtedly an expression of despair, but it is a despair that is connected with hope, a despair in the historical order that is continuous with a hope for its transcendence into a radically new order of existence. Not the images themselves, but their impact on the present in opening it to the

3. JEWISH TIME AND THE ECLIPSE OF HISTORICAL DESTINY

future by interpretive projection, constitutes the final import of apocalyptic representations."

94. Heidegger, *Contributions*, § 250, p. 315 (emphasis in original); *Beiträge*, p. 398.
95. Heidegger, *Hölderlin's Hymns*, pp. 43–44; *Hölderlins Hymnen*, pp. 52–53.
96. Heidegger, *Hölderlin's Hymns*, p. 43; *Hölderlins Hymnen*, p. 52. See Julian Young, "Poets and Rivers: Heidegger on Hölderlin's 'Der Ister,'" in *Heidegger Reexamined*, vol. 3: *Art, Poetry, and Technology*, ed. Hubert Dreyfus and Mark Wrathall (New York: Routledge, 2002), pp. 79–104.
97. Heidegger, *What Is Called Thinking?* p. 99; *Was Heißt Denken?* p. 103.
98. Heidegger, *On the Way to Language*, p. 106; *Unterwegs zur Sprache*, pp. 201–202. It is possible that with respect to the understanding of time as the concomitant conjoining and disjoining of the contraries of motion and immobility, Heidegger was influenced as well by Taoist thought. In the letter Heidegger wrote to Paul Shih-yi Hsiao on October 9, 1947, printed and translated in Paul Shih-yi Hsiao, "Heidegger and Our Translation of the *Tao Te Ching*," in *Heidegger and Asian Thought*, ed. Graham Parkes (Honolulu: University of Hawaii Press, 1987), pp.102–103, he notes that he has contemplated the passage "Who can be still and out of stillness and through it move something on to the Way so that it comes to shine forth?" Heidegger glosses this text in his own philosophical idiom, "Who is able through making still to bring something into Being?" On the comparison of Heidegger and Taoism, see Graham Parkes, "Thoughts on the Way: *Being and Time* via Lao-Chuang," in *Heidegger and Asian Thought*, pp. 105–144, and Lin Ma, *Heidegger on East-West Dialogue: Anticipating the Event* (New York: Routledge, 2008), pp. 119–143.

4. BEING'S TRAGEDY

1. Many have weighed in on this topic. See Berel Lang, "Heidegger's Silence and the Jewish Question," in *Martin Heidegger and the Holocaust*, ed. Alan Rosenberg and Alan Milchman (Atlantic Highlands, NJ: Humanities Press, 1994), pp. 1–18; and Berel Lang, *Heidegger's Silence* (Ithaca: Cornell University Press, 1996). See the comments of Jean-Luc Nancy cited in ch. 2*n*12. For more references, see *n*16, this chapter.
2. Jean-François Lyotard, *Heidegger and "the jews,"* trans. Andreas Michel and Mark S. Roberts (Minneapolis: University of Minnesota Press, 1990), p. 52.
3. Jürgen Habermas, *The Philosophical Discourse on Modernity: Twelve Lectures*, trans. Frederick G. Lawrence (Cambridge: MIT Press, 1987), p. 155.
4. Babette E. Babich, *Words in Blood, Like Flowers: Philosophy and Poetry, Music and Eros in Hölderlin, Nietzsche, and Heidegger* (Albany: State University of New York Press, 2006), p. 237.
5. Ibid., p. 239.
6. Ibid., p. 233. Babich's terminology is based on Rainer Marten's essay "Ein rassistisches Konzept von Humanität," *Badische Zeitung*, December 19/20 (1987).
7. Richard Wolin, "An Exchange of Letters," in *The Heidegger Controversy: A Critical Reader* (Cambridge: MIT Press, 1993), pp. 160–161.
8. Ibid., pp. 162–163.

4. BEING'S TRAGEDY

9. Martin Heidegger, "The Self-Assertion of the German University: Address, Delivered on the Solemn Assumption of the Rectorate of the University Freiburg; The Rectorate 1933/34: Facts and Thoughts," trans. Karsten Harries, *Review of Metaphysics* 38 (1985): 486; *Die Selbstbehauptung der Deutschen Universität: Rede, gehalten bei der feierlichen Übernahme des Rektorats der Universität Freiburg i. Br. am 27.5.1933; Das Rektorat 1933/34: Tatsachen und Gedanken* (Frankfurt: Vittorio Klostermann, 1983), p. 26.
10. Jacques Derrida, Hans-Georg Gadamer, and Philippe Lacoue-Labarthe, *Heidegger, Philosophy, and Politics: The Heidelberg Conference*, ed. Mireille Calle-Gruber, trans. Jeff Fort (New York: Fordham University Press, 2016), p. 12. For the fuller argument, see Hans-Georg Gadamer, "Like Plato in Syracuse," ibid., p. 81. See also the critical intervention regarding Heidegger's silence about the extermination camps made by Micha Brumlik, ibid., pp. 48–49. An equally unforgiving stance concerning Heidegger's reticence is taken by Maurice Blanchot, "Thinking the Apocalypse: A Letter from Maurice Blanchot to Catherine David," trans. Paula Wissing, *Critical Inquiry* 15 (1989): 478–479.
11. Jacques Derrida, "On Reading Heidegger: An Outline of Remarks to the Essex Colloquium," *Research in Phenomenology* 17 (1987): 173.
12. Derrida, Gadamer, and Lacoue-Labarthe, *Heidegger, Philosophy, and Politics*, p. 34. For an earlier version, see Jacques Derrida, "Heidegger's Silence: Excerpts from a Talk Given on 5 February 1988," in *Martin Heidegger and National Socialism: Questions and Answers*, ed. Günther Neske and Emil Kettering, trans. Lisa Harries, French portions trans. Joachim Neugroschel (New York: Paragon House, 1990,) p. 147.
13. Derrida, Gadamer, and Lacoue-Labarthe, *Heidegger, Philosophy, and Politics*, p. 35 (emphasis in original); Derrida, "Heidegger's Silence," p. 147.
14. Derrida, Gadamer, and Lacoue-Labarthe, *Heidegger, Philosophy, and Politics*, p. 35; Derrida, "Heidegger's Silence," p. 148.
15. Derrida, Gadamer, and Lacoue-Labarthe, *Heidegger, Philosophy, and Politics*, pp. 35–36; Derrida, "Heidegger's Silence," p. 148. For an entirely different approach, which presumes Heidegger's silence and lack of apology or self-defense are related to the fact that there was no change in his thinking and hence nothing for which to repent, see Alain Badiou and Barbara Cassin, *Heidegger: His Life and His Philosophy*, trans. Susan Spitzer (New York: Columbia University Press, 2016), pp. 19–20.
16. William Vaughan, "Heidegger *silentio*," in *Martin Heidegger and the Holocaust*, pp. 70–101. See also Dominique Janicaud, *The Shadow of That Thought: Heidegger and the Question of Politics* (Evanston: Northwestern University Press, 1996), pp. 4–6, 85–105; Tom Rockmore, *On Heidegger's Nazism and Philosophy* (Berkeley: University of California Press, 1997), pp. 200–203; and Tom Rockmore, "Heidegger and Holocaust Revisionism," in *Martin Heidegger and the Holocaust*, pp. 120–122; Christoph von Wolzogen, "Heideggers Schweigen. Zur Rede 'Edmund Husserl zum siebenzigsten Geburtstag,'" *Heidegger und der Nationalsozialismus, II: Interpretationen*, ed. Alfred Denker and Holger Zaborowski [*Heidegger-Jahrbuch* 5] (Freiburg: Karl Alber, 2009), pp. 382–396. Utilizing the talk that Heidegger gave on the occasion of Husserl's seventieth birthday, which contained a citation about language and philosophy from Plato's *Seventh Letter*, Wolzogen

argues that Heidegger's political silence could be understood as his adaptation of the idea that the ascent to the realm of forms must result in silence. I offer a different construal of the apophatic limits of language in Heidegger, but there is something common to our approaches, and neither of us claims that an explanation should be construed as a justification for Heidegger's actions or the reticence that followed in their wake. On silence as authentic discourse, see Alexander S. Duff, *Heidegger and Politics: The Ontology of Radical Discontent* (Cambridge: Cambridge University Press, 2015), pp. 156–159. For a different attempt to rationalize Heidegger's silence philosophically, see Rainer Alisch, "Heidegger's 'Silence' About the Holocaust: An Attempt at a Reconstruction," in *Martin Heidegger and the Holocaust*, pp. 127–149, esp. 135–141. See also Marc Froment-Meurice, *Solitudes: From Rimbaud to Heidegger*, trans. Peter Walsh (Albany: State University of New York Press, 1995), pp. 213–215, who defends Heidegger against the charge of anti-Semitism on the grounds that no word for "Jew" is to be found in his thought—an idea he supports on the basis of Heidegger's own analysis of language and its limits—nor was he knowledgeable of any Jewish language, and consequently, he had no need to resolve the Jewish question. Moreover, on account of the diasporic nature of Jewish history, there is no specific name, country, land, or peoplehood linked to the Jews and thus they belie any rootedness or logocentrism. I will refrain from a detailed response, but the more recent textual evidence from Heidegger's *Black Notebooks* indicates that he was engaged with the Jewish question quite explicitly and indeed at times utilizing images that are far from neutral or disengaged. My hesitancy notwithstanding, there is a point of contiguity between Froment-Meurice's approach and my own inasmuch as we both link Heidegger's silence about the Holocaust to his understanding of the silence demanded by a caesura in history in virtue of which one's relationship to language is radically altered. For an altogether different explanation that downplays the extent to which Heidegger was silent, see Julian Young, *Heidegger, Philosophy, Nazism* (Cambridge: Cambridge University Press, 1997), pp, 204–205. And see Sonia Caporossi, "Il *silenzio* di Heidegger e la sua ricezione in Italia: una proposta di lettura," in *La pietà del pensiero: Heidegger e i Quaderni Neri*, ed. Francesca Brencio (Rome: Aguaplano, 2015), pp. 67–105.

17. Martin Heidegger, *Ponderings II–VI: Black Notebooks 1931–1938*, trans. Richard Rojcewicz (Bloomington: Indiana University Press, 2016), p. 266 (emphasis in original); *Überlegungen II–VI (Schwarze Hefte 1931–1938)* [GA 94] (Frankfurt: Vittorio Klostermann, 2014), p. 365.
18. Walter Brogan, "Listening to the Silence: Reticence and the Call of Conscience in Heidegger's Philosophy," in *Heidegger and Language*, ed. Jeffrey Powell (Bloomington: Indiana University Press, 2013), pp. 32–45.
19. Martin Heidegger, *Basic Questions of Philosophy: Selected "Problems" of "Logic,"* trans. Richard Rojcewicz and André Schuwer (Bloomington: Indiana University Press, 1994), pp. 41–42.
20. Samuel IJsseling, "Heidegger and Politics," in *Ethics and Danger: Essays on Heidegger and Continental Thought*, ed. Arleen B. Dallery and Charles E. Scott with P. Holley Roberts (Albany: State University of New York Press, 1992), p. 5.
21. Rockmore, "Heidegger and Holocaust Revisionism," p. 122.
22. Rockmore, *On Heidegger's Nazism*, p. 203.

4. BEING'S TRAGEDY

23. Martin Heidegger, *Ponderings VII–XI: Black Notebooks 1938–1939*, trans. Richard Rojcewicz (Bloomington: Indiana University Press, 2017), p. 130; *Überlegungen VII–XI (Schwarze Hefte 1938/39)* [GA 95] (Frankfurt: Vittorio Klostermann, 2014), p. 169.
24. Miguel de Beistegui, *Heidegger and the Political: Dystopias* (London: Routledge, 1998), pp. 146–157, esp. 147–148.
25. Ludwig Wittgenstein, *Tractatus Logico-Philosophicus*, trans. Charles K. Ogden (London: Routledge, 1995), p. 27. See Elliot R. Wolfson, *Language, Eros, Being: Kabbalistic Hermeneutics and Poetic Imagination* (New York: Fordham University Press, 2005), pp. 289–291; Timothy D. Knepper, "Ineffability Investigations: What the Later Wittgenstein Has to Offer to the Study of Ineffability," *International Journal for Philosophy of Religion* 65 (2009): 65–76. On the ineffability of semantics in Wittgenstein's approach to the accountability of grammar to reality, see Felicity McCutcheon, *Religion Within the Limits of Language Alone: Wittgenstein on Philosophy and Religion* (Aldershot: Ashgate, 2001), pp. 99–101. For comparative analyses of the topic of silence or the unsayable in the thought of Heidegger and Wittgenstein, see Peter J. McCormick, "Saying and Showing in Heidegger and Wittgenstein," *Journal of the British Society of Phenomenology* 3 (1972): 27–35; Peter J. McCormick, *Heidegger and the Language of the World: An Argumentative Reading of the Later Heidegger's Meditations on Language* (Ottawa: University of Ottawa Press, 1976), pp. 157–171; Steven L. Bindeman, *Heidegger and Wittgenstein: The Poetics of Silence* (Lanham: University Press of America, 1981); and Nikita Dhawan, *Impossible Speech: On the Politics of Silence and Violence* (Sankt Augustin: Academia, 2007), pp. 122–197. On Heidegger and Wittgenstein, see also Wolfson, *Language*, pp. 15–16, and other studies cited on p. 410nn128–129; William Franke, *Poetry and Apocalypse: Theological Disclosures of Poetic Language* (Stanford: Stanford University Press, 2009), p. 40. See as well my remarks in Wolfson, *Language*, p. 419n211; and the slightly revised position in Elliot R. Wolfson, "Skepticism and the Philosopher's Keeping Faith," in *Jewish Philosophy for the Twenty-First Century: Personal Reflections*, ed. Hava Tirosh-Samuelson and Aaron W. Hughes (Leiden: Brill, 2014), pp. 506–508. Regarding a comparative analysis of this topic, see Herman Philipse, "Heidegger and Wittgenstein on External World Skepticism," in *Wittgenstein and Heidegger*, ed. David Egan, Stephen Reynolds, and Aaron James Wendland (New York: Routledge, 2013), pp. 116–132.
26. Peter Trawny, *Freedom to Fail: Heidegger's Anarchy*, trans. Ian Alexander Moore and Christopher Turner (Cambridge: Polity, 2015), pp. 3–4. The passage Trawny refers to is the very playful and somewhat enigmatic aphorism in Martin Heidegger, *Zum Ereignis-Denken* [GA 73.2] (Frankfurt: Vittorio Klostermann, 2013), p. 904: "Das Scheiden in Gut und Böse | Unterschied—*die Entscheidung* Grenzscheide — | — Grenze | Scheideweg Ent-scheidung — | Ver-söhnung |. *ursprüngliche Sammlung und Wahrung.*"
27. Peter Trawny, *Heidegger and the Myth of a Jewish World Conspiracy*, trans. Andrew J. Mitchell (Chicago: University of Chicago Press, 2015), p. 6. On Heidegger's subversion of language as a "private soliloquy," bordering on silence, as a deliberate attempt to be misunderstood, see the comments of George Steiner, *Grammars of Creation: Originating in the Gifford Lectures for 1990* (New Haven: Yale University Press, 2001), p. 152.

28. The matter is pursued in depth in the seventh chapter, "Disclosive Language: Poiēsis and the Apophatic Occlusion of the Occlusion," in Elliot R. Wolfson, *Heidegger and Kabbalah: Hidden Gnosis and the Path of Poiēsis* (Bloomington: Indiana University Press, 2019).
29. See preface at n30.
30. Martin Heidegger, *What Is Called Thinking?* trans. Fred W. Wieck and J. Glenn Gray (New York: Harper and Row, 1968), p. 77; *Was Heißt Denken?* [GA 8] (Frankfurt: Vittorio Klostermann, 2002), p. 83.
31. Heidegger, *What Is Called Thinking?* p. 178; *Was Heißt Denken?* p. 182. See Michael Roth, *The Poetics of Resistance: Heidegger's Line* (Evanston: Northwestern University Press, 1996), pp. 63, 70–71, 75–77, 81–83.
32. Hannah Arendt, "Martin Heidegger at Eighty," in *Heidegger and Modern Philosophy: Critical Essays*, ed. Michael Murray (New Haven: Yale University Press, 1978), pp. 298–299.
33. Hannah Arendt, *The Human Condition*, 2d ed. (Chicago: University of Chicago Press, 1996), p. 76.
34. Martin Heidegger, *Being and Time*, trans. Joan Stambaugh, revised and with a foreword by Dennis J. Schmidt (Albany: State University of New York Press, 2010), § 34, p. 159; *Sein und Zeit* (Tübingen: Max Niemeyer, 1993), p. 165. For an attempt to identify Derrida's notion of friendship, *différance*, and the critique of presence as a politicized echo of Heidegger's emphasis on hearing the other and the *unheimliche* spacing of Dasein's call-structure, see Sinéad Hogan, "Hearing Heidegger: Proximities and Readings," in *Heidegger in the Twenty-First Century*, ed. Tziovanis Georgakis and Paul J. Ennis (Dordrecht: Springer, 2015), pp. 101–117.
35. Martin Heidegger, *The Fundamental Concepts of Metaphysics: World, Finitude, Solitude*, trans. William McNeill and Nicholas Walker (Bloomington: Indiana University Press, 1995), pp. 291–292 (emphasis in original); *Die Grundbegriffe der Metaphysik: Welt—Endlichkeit—Einsamkeit* [GA 29/30] (Frankfurt: Vittorio Klostermann, 1983), p. 422.
36. Martin Heidegger, *Pathmarks*, ed. William McNeill (Cambridge: Cambridge University Press, 1998), p. 155; *Wegmarken* [GA 9] (Frankfurt: Vittorio Klostermann, 1996), p. 203.
37. Martin Heidegger, *Being and Truth*, trans Gregory Fried and Richard Polt (Bloomington: Indiana University Press, 2010), p. 84 (emphasis in original); *Sein und Wahrheit* [GA 36/37] (Frankfurt: Vittorio Klostermann, 2001), p. 107. On Heidegger's view that silence is the basis of language, see Richard Polt, "The Secret Homeland of Speech: Heidegger on Language, 1933–1934," in *Heidegger and Language*, ed. Jeffrey Powell (Bloomington: Indiana University Press, 2013), pp. 65–70. It is of interest to recall in this context Heidegger's coinage of the expression *Entgegenschweigen*, "remaining silent," in his last letter to Celan. See Steiner, *Grammars of Creation*, p. 203.
38. Heidegger, *Being and Truth*, p. 85; *Sein und Wahrheit*, p. 107.
39. Martin Heidegger, *Hölderlin's Hymns "Germania" and "The Rhine,"* trans. William McNeill and Julia Ireland (Bloomington: Indiana University Press, 2014), p. 108; *Hölderlins Hymnen "Germanien" und "Der Rhein"* [GA 39] (Frankfurt: Vittorio Klostermann, 1999), p. 119.
40. Heidegger, *Hölderlin's Hymns*, p. 108; *Hölderlins Hymnen*, p. 119.

4. BEING'S TRAGEDY

41. Martin Heidegger, *Contributions to Philosophy (Of the Event)*, trans. Richard Rojcewicz and Daniela Vallega-Neu (Bloomington: Indiana University Press, 2012), § 13, p. 30; *Beiträge zur Philosophie (Vom Ereignis)* [GA 65] (Frankfurt: Vittorio Klostermann, 1989), p. 36.
42. Heidegger, *Contributions*, §§ 37–38, pp. 62–63 (emphasis in original); *Beiträge*, pp. 78–79. See Emilio Brito, *Heidegger et l'hymne du sacré* (Leuven: Leuven University Press, 1999), pp. 103–113; David R. Law, "Negative Theology in Heidegger's *Beiträge zur Philosophie*," *International Journal for Philosophy of Religion* 48 (2000): 139–156, esp. 145–146; Jean-François Ænishanslin, "La logique, la pensée, le silence. Un style en transition," in *Heideggers* Beiträge zur Philosophie: *Internationales Kolloquium vom 20.-22.Mai 2004 an der Universität Lausanne (Schweiz)*, ed. Emmanuel Mejía and Ingeborg Schüßler (Frankfurt: Vittorio Klostermann, 2009), pp. 359–366, esp. 364–365; Krzysztof Ziarek, *Language After Heidegger* (Bloomington: Indiana University Press, 2013), pp. 142–174, esp. 149–150.
43. Heidegger, *Contributions*, § 255, p. 323 (emphasis in original); *Beiträge*, pp. 407–408.
44. Jacques Derrida, *The Animal That Therefore I Am*, ed. Marie-Louise Mallet, trans. David Wills (New York: Fordham University Press, 2008), p. 19.
45. Heidegger, *Contributions*, § 38, p. 64; *Beiträge*, p. 80.
46. Søren Kierkegaard, *The Lily of the Field and the Bird of the Air: Three Godly Discourses*, trans. Bruce H. Kirmmse (Princeton: Princeton University Press, 2016), p. 16.
47. Ibid., p. 17: "You shall in the deepest sense make yourself nothing, become nothing before God, learn to keep silent. In this silence is the beginning, which is *first* to seek God's kingdom. . . . The beginning is not that with which one begins but is that to which one comes, and one comes to it backward. Beginning is this art of *becoming* silent, for there is no art in keeping silent as nature is" (emphasis in original). Heidegger similarly conceives of the beginning as that which lays ahead and not behind, that is, the future to which one returns, but of course he would have removed from this conception the theological elements that were central to Kierkegaard.
48. Heidegger, *Being and Truth*, pp. 85–86; *Sein und Wahrheit*, pp. 108–109.
49. Martin Heidegger, *The Essence of Truth: On Plato's Cave Allegory and Theaetetus*, trans. Ted Sadler (New York: Continuum, 2002), p. 25 (emphasis in original); *Vom Wesen der Wahrheit: Zu Platons Höhlengleichnis und Theätet* [GA 34] (Frankfurt: Vittorio Klostermann, 1988), p. 32.
50. Heidegger, *Being and Truth*, p. 88; *Sein und Wahrheit*, p. 111.
51. Daniela Vallega-Neu, "Heidegger's Reticence: From *Contributions* to *Das Ereignis* and Toward *Gelassenheit*," *Research in Phenomenology* 45 (2015): 1–32.
52. Martin Heidegger, *On the Way to Language*, trans. Peter D. Hertz (New York: Harper and Row, 1971), p. 152; *Unterwegs zur Sprache* [GA 12] (Frankfurt: Vittorio Klostermann, 1985), p. 221. On representation and renunciation in Heidegger's reading of the poem of George "Das Wort," see McCormick, *Heidegger*, pp. 9–16.
53. Heidegger, *Pathmarks*, p. 237; *Wegmarken*, p. 309.
54. Heidegger, *Unterwegs zur Sprache*, p. 30. For an alternative translation, see Martin Heidegger, *Poetry, Language, Thought*, trans. Albert Hofstadter (New York: Harper and Row, 1971), p. 207.
55. Heidegger, *What Is Called Thinking?* p. 196; *Was Heißt Denken?* p. 199.

4. BEING'S TRAGEDY

56. Heidegger, *On the Way to Language*, p. 199. See Lin Ma, *Heidegger on East-West Dialogue: Anticipating the Event* (New York: Routledge, 2008), pp. 19–23; and the text of Tomio Tezuka, "Eine Stunde mit Heidegger," in *Japan und Heidegger: Gedenkschrift der Stadt Meßkirch zum hundertsten Geburtstag Martin Heideggers*, ed. Hartmut Buchner (Sigmaringen: Thorbecke, 1989), pp. 173–180; English version in Reinhard May, *Heidegger's Hidden Sources: East Asian Influences on His Work*, trans. Graham Parkes (London: Routledge, 1996), pp. 59–64. Also pertinent is the study by Tetsuaki Kotoh, "Language and Silence: Self-Inquiry in Heidegger and Zen," in *Heidegger and Asian Thought*, ed. Graham Parkes (Honolulu: University of Hawaii Press, 1987), pp. 201–211.
57. Heidegger, *On the Way to Language*, pp. 52–53; *Unterwegs zur Sprache*, p. 144.
58. Heidegger, *On the Way to Language*, p. 78; *Unterwegs zur Sprache*, p. 172.
59. Heidegger, *On the Way to Language*, pp. 122, 124; *Unterwegs zur Sprache*, pp. 241, 243–244. For a theological casting of this aspect of Heidegger's thinking, see Jean-Louis Chrétien, *The Call and the Response*, trans. Anne A. Davenport (New York: Fordham University Press, 2004), pp. 27–30. *Inter alia*, Chrétien notes the affinity between Heidegger's notion of speech as a response or correspondence to the word that has been spoken and Levinas's notion of epiphany as the Saying that one receives. For a similar attempt to decrease the divide between Heidegger and Levinas on this point, see Elliot R. Wolfson, *Giving Beyond the Gift: Apophasis and Overcoming Theomania* (New York: Fordham University Press, 2014), pp. 123–135.
60. Heidegger, *On the Way to Language*, p. 131; *Unterwegs zur Sprache*, p. 251.
61. Heidegger, *On the Way to Language*, pp. 134–135; *Unterwegs zur Sprache*, p. 255.
62. Heidegger, *On the Way to Language*, p. 147; *Unterwegs zur Sprache*, p. 216.
63. Martin Heidegger, *Elucidations of Hölderlin's Poetry*, trans. Keith Hoeller (Amherst: Humanity, 2000), p. 216; *Erläuterungen zu Hölderlins Dichtung* [GA 4] (Frankfurt: Vittorio Klostermann, 1996), p. 189.
64. Consider the candid and startling comment in the conversation on November 6, 1951, published as the appendix to the Zurich Seminar in Martin Heidegger, *Seminare* [GA 15] (Frankfurt: Vittorio Klostermann, 2005), p. 426: "Ich habe in meiner 30–35 jährigen Lehrtätigkeit nur ein bis zweimal von meinen Sachen gesprochen." It is surely an extraordinarily disheartening admission to say that one has spoken only once or twice in three decades of teaching about things that mattered the most.
65. Bret W. Davis, *Heidegger and the Will: On the Way to Gelassenheit* (Evanston: Northwestern University Press, 2007), pp. 289–298.
66. Martin Heidegger, *Country Path Conversations*, trans. Bret W. Davis (Bloomington: Indiana University Press, 2010), p. 158; *Feldweg-Gespräche* [GA 77] (Frankfurt: Vittorio Klostermann, 1995), p. 241.
67. Vaughan, "Heidegger *silentio*," pp. 74–75. See also Janicaud, *The Shadow*, pp. 89–94.
68. Isaiah Tishby, *The Wisdom of the Zohar: An Anthology of Texts*, trans. David Goldstein (Oxford: Oxford University Press, 1989), pp. 447–474; Gershom Scholem, *On the Mystical Shape of the Godhead: Basic Concepts in the Kabbalah*, ed. Jonathan Chipman, trans. Joachim Neugroschel (New York: Schocken, 1991), pp. 56–87; Elliot R. Wolfson, "Left Contained in the Right: A Study in Zoharic Hermeneutics," *Association for Jewish Studies Review* 11 (1986): 27–52; and Elliot

4. BEING'S TRAGEDY

R. Wolfson, "Light Through Darkness: The Ideal of Human Perfection in the Zohar," *Harvard Theological Review* 81 (1988): 73–95. Revised versions of these two essays appear in Elliot R. Wolfson, *Luminal Darkness: Imaginal Gleanings from Zoharic Literature* (Oxford: Oneworld, 2007), pp. 1–55. For two more recent studies that engage the problem of evil and the Other Side in zoharic literature, see Nathaniel Berman, "'Improper Twins': The Ambivalent 'Other Side' in the Zohar and Kabbalistic Tradition," Ph.D. thesis, University College, London, 2014; Oded Yisraeli, "Cain as the Scion of Satan: The Evolution of a Gnostic Myth in the *Zohar*," *Harvard Theological Review* 109 (2016): 56–74.

69. Solomon ben Ḥayyim Eliashiv, *Leshem Shevo we-Aḥlamah: Haqdamot u-She'arim* (Jerusalem: Aaron Barzanai, 2006), p. 57. On the future obliteration of the evil impulse, see Solomon ben Ḥayyim Eliashiv, *Leshem Shevo we-Aḥlamah: Sefer ha-De'ah* (Jerusalem: Aaron Barzanai, 2005), pt. 2, p. 392.

70. Solomon ben Ḥayyim Eliashiv, *Leshem Shevo we-Aḥlamah: Ḥeleq ha-Be'urim* (Jerusalem: Aaron Barzanai, 2011), pt. 1, p. 27.

71. Joseph Solomon Delmedigo, *Novelot Ḥokhmah* (Basle, 1631), 151b.

72. Yehuda Liebes, *On Sabbateanism and Its Kabbalah: Collected Essays* (Jerusalem: Bialik Institute, 1995), pp. 308–309n71 (Hebrew).

73. Eliashiv, *Leshem Shevo we-Aḥlamah: Ḥeleq ha-Be'urim*, pt. 1, p. 20; and Solomon ben Ḥayyim Eliashiv, *Leshem Shevo we-Aḥlamah: Sefer ha-Kelalim* (Jerusalem: Aaron Barzanai, 2010), p. 217.

74. David F. Krell, *The Tragic Absolute: German Idealism and the Languishing of God* (Bloomington: Indiana University Press, 2005).

75. Heidegger, *Ponderings VII–XI*, p. 281 (*Überlegungen VII–XI*, p. 359): "The courage for philosophy is the knowledge of the necessary downgoing of Da-sein [*notwendigen Untergang des Da-seins*]. Philosophy, since it can be borne only in the disposition of such courage, shares with everything essential (everything appertaining to the grounding of the truth of beyng) the privilege of rarity. Philosophy does not stand related to the 'intelligentsia' or the 'believers' or those who calculate or the never-too-populous throng."

76. Heidegger, *Ponderings VII–XI*, p. 325 (emphasis in original); *Überlegungen VII–XI*, p. 417. For an alternative translation, see David F. Krell, *Ecstasy, Catastrophe: Heidegger from Being and Time to the Black Notebooks* (Albany: State University of New York Press, 2015), p. 161.

77. On the critique of the political, see Dieter Thomä, "Heidegger und der Nationalsozialismus. In der Dunkelkammer der Seinsgeschichte," in *Heidegger-Handbuch: Leben—Werk—Wirkung*, rev. ed., ed. Dieter Thomä (Stuttgart: J. B. Metzler, 2013), pp. 126–128.

78. My position is in accord with the argument of Reiner Schürmann, "A Brutal Awakening to the Tragic Condition of Being: On Heidegger's *Beiträge zur Philosophie*," in *Martin Heidegger: Politics, Art, and Technology*, ed. Karsten Harries and Christoph Jamme (New York: Holmes and Meier, 1994), pp. 89–105. Summarizing his thesis, Schürmann writes, "The hubristic blindness that had led to the statement, 'The *Führer* himself alone is the German reality of today and of tomorrow as well as its law,' turns into the tragic blindness that sees the retraction of death in the very attraction for life; that sees concealment in unconcealment and expropriation in appropriation; or again (but these are not Heidegger's words), the

singularization to come in any phenomenal economy; hence, in terms of the law, the transgression in every hegemonic legislation" (p. 104). Schürmann refers to this notion of the singular as anarchic isomorphism, which is always translated into the universal representation of an archic isomorphism. On the archic and anarchic isomorphism, see as well Reiner Schürmann, *Broken Hegemonies,* trans. Reginald Lilly (Bloomington: Indiana University Press, 2003), pp. 541–546. The centrality of the tragic in Heidegger's understanding of being is noted by Schürmann, ibid., p. 30: "The tragic truth that names the differend serves as a vehicle to discover the originary strategies in being, strategies Heidegger describes as thrusts and withdrawals without genus between appropriation and expropriation." And ibid., p. 551: "What is abyssal, finally, is the tragic contrariety itself that through all these strategies Heidegger seeks to rehabilitate in being, beyond theticism.... The renunciation of all names that lay down the law and the subsequent affirmation of tragic being remains without precedent in the doctrines of first conditions. The event, then, equals originary dissension."

79. Schürmann, *Broken Hegemonies,* p. 345.
80. Ibid., p. 676n30.
81. Friedrich Wilhelm Joseph Schelling, *Philosophical Investigations Into the Essence of Human Freedom,* trans. Jeff Love and Johannes Schmidt (Albany: State University of New York Press, 2006), p. 28; *Philosophische Untersuchungen über das Wesen menschlichen Freiheit und die damit zusammenhängenden Gegenstände* in Friedrich Wilhelm Joseph Schelling, *Sämmtliche Werke,* ed. Karl Friedrich August Schelling (Stuttgart: Cotta, 1860), 7:358.
82. Schelling, *Philosophical Investigations,* p. 29; *Philosophische Untersuchungen,* p. 360.
83. Schelling, *Philosophical Investigations,* pp. 62–63; *Philosophische Untersuchungen,* p. 399.
84. Martin Heidegger, *Schelling's Treatise on the Essence of Human Freedom,* trans. Joan Stambaugh (Athens: Ohio University Press, 1985), p. 162 (translation slightly modified); *Schelling: Vom Wesen der menschlichen Freiheit (1809)* [GA 42] (Frankfurt: Vittorio Klostermann, 1988), p. 280.
85. Schelling, *Philosophical Investigations,* p. 69; *Philosophische Untersuchungen,* p. 407. See Krell, *The Tragic Absolute,* p. 95. On the synonymy of "equivalence" (*Gleichgültigkeit*) and "indifference" (*Indifferenz*), see Friedrich Wilhelm Joseph Schelling, *The Ages of the World (Fragment) from the Handwritten Remains, Third Version (c. 1815),* trans. Jason M. Wirth (Albany: State University of New York Press, 2000), p. 25; *Die Weltalter,* in Friedrich Wilhelm Joseph Schelling, *Sämmtliche Werke,* ed. Karl Friedrich August Schelling (Stuttgart: Cotta, 1861), 8:236.
86. Heidegger, *Schelling's Treatise,* p. 162; *Schelling: Vom Wesen,* p. 281.
87. Wolfson, *Language,* pp. 99–105. I have reexamined this matter in chapter 3, "Heidegger's Seyn/Nichts and the Kabbalistic Ein Sof," in Wolfson, *Heidegger and Kabbalah.* For reference to other treatments of the influence of kabbalah on Schelling, see Wolfson, *Language,* pp. 392–393n2. To the sources mentioned there, one might add Jürgen Habermas, "The German Idealism of the Jewish Philosophers (1961)," in *Philosophical-Political Profiles,* trans. Frederick G. Lawrence (Cambridge: MIT Press, 1983), pp. 21–43; and Jürgen Habermas, "Dialectical Idealism in Transition to Materialism: Schelling's Idea of a Contraction of God and

4. BEING'S TRAGEDY

Its Consequences for the Philosophy of History," in *The New Schelling*, ed. Judith Norman and Alistair Welchman (London: Continuum, 2004), pp. 43–89, esp. 53–61; Christoph Schulte, "Zimzum bei Schelling," in *Kabbala und Romantik*, ed. Eveline Goodman-Thau, Gert Mattenklott, and Christoph Schulte (Tubingen: Max Niemeyer, 1994), pp. 97–118; and Christoph Schulte, *Zimzum: Gott und Weltursprung* (Berlin: Suhrkamp, 2014), pp. 296–323; Paul Franks, "Inner Anti-Semitism or Kabbalistic Legacy? German Idealism's Relationship to Judaism," *International Yearbook of German Idealism* 7 (2010): 254–279; and Paul Franks, "Rabbinic Idealism and Kabbalistic Realism: Jewish Dimensions of Idealism and Idealist Dimensions of Judaism," in *The Impact of Idealism: The Legacy of Post-Kantian German Thought*, vol. 4: *Religion*, ed. Nicholas Boyle, Liz Disley, and Nicholas Adams (Cambridge: Cambridge University Press, 2013), pp. 219–245, esp. 237–238.
88. Friedrich Wilhelm Joseph Schelling, *Philosophy and Religion (1804)*, trans. Klaus Ottmann (Putnam, CT: Spring, 2010), p. 33; *Philosophie und Religion*, in Friedrich Wilhelm Joseph Schelling, *Sämmtliche Werke 1804*, ed. Karl Friedrich August Schelling (Stuttgart: Cotta, 1860), 6:45. For a more recent edition, see Friedrich Wilhelm Joseph Schelling, *Philosophie und Religion*, ed. Alfred Denker and Holger Zaborowski (Munich: Karl Alber, 2008), pp. 36–37.
89. Schelling, *Philosophical Investigations*, p. 28 (emphasis in original); *Philosophische Untersuchungen*, p. 359.
90. Schelling, *Philosophical Investigations*, pp. 68–69; *Philosophische Untersuchungen*, p. 407. For citation and analysis of these sources as well as some other texts from Schelling, see Elliot R. Wolfson, "Achronic Time, Messianic Expectation, and the Secret of the Leap in Habad," in *Habad Hasidism: History, Thought, Image*, ed. Jonatan Meir and Gadi Sagiv (Jerusalem: Zalman Shazar, 2016), pp. 57–73 (English section).
91. Schelling, *The Ages*, p. 6; *Die Weltalter*, pp. 211–212.
92. Schelling, *The Ages*, p. 85; *Die Weltalter*, p. 313.
93. Heidegger, *Schelling's Treatise*, p. 160; *Schelling: Vom Wesen*, pp. 277–278.
94. Schelling, *Philosophical Investigations*, pp. 62–63; *Philosophische Untersuchungen*, p. 399. See Krell, *The Tragic Absolute*, pp. 102–103. Heidegger, *Schelling's Treatise*, p. 160 (*Schelling: Vom Wesen*, p. 278), connects Schelling's description of the human experience of nature with what he presumed to be Aristotle's view regarding the melancholic nature of creative people, thinkers, and statesmen. See *n*104, this chapter.
95. Schelling, *Philosophical Investigations*, p. 63; *Philosophische Untersuchungen*, p. 399.
96. See reference in *n*76, this chapter.
97. Catherine Clément, *Syncope: The Philosophy of Rapture*, trans. Sally O'Driscoll and Deirdre M. Mahoney (Minneapolis: University of Minnesota Press, 1994), pp. 62–63; Francesca Brencio, "'The Nocturnal Point of the Contraction': Hegel and Melancholia," in *Melancholia: The Disease of the Soul*, ed. Dariusz Skorzewski and Andrzej Wiercinski (Lublin: Wydawnictwo KUL, 2014), pp. 149–167.
98. Heidegger, *Ponderings VII–XI*, p. 326; *Überlegungen VII–XI*, p. 418. For an alternate translation, see Krell, *Ecstasy*, pp. 161–162.
99. Heidegger, *Contributions*, § 51, p. 87 (emphasis in original); *Beiträge*, p. 109. On the juxtaposition of simplicity (*Einfache*) and solitude (*Einsamkeit*), see Heidegger, *Ponderings VII–XI*, p. 29; *Überlegungen VII–XI*, pp. 37–38.

4. BEING'S TRAGEDY

100. Heidegger, *What Is Called Thinking?* p. 169; *Was Heißt Denken?* p. 174.
101. See Heidegger, *Ponderings II–VI*, p. 45 (*Überlegungen II–VI*, p. 59): "Only if and only as long as this originary *aloneness* [Alleinheit] of Dasein is experienced can true community [*Gemeinschaft*] grown indigenously; only thus is to be overcome all publicness of those who have come together and are driven together" (emphasis in original). Compare Martin Heidegger, "Why Do I Stay in the Provinces?" (1934), in *Heidegger: The Man and the Thinker*, ed. Thomas Sheehan (Chicago: Precedent, 1981), p. 28: "People in the city often wonder whether one gets lonely up in the mountains among the peasants for such long and monotonous periods of time. But it isn't loneliness, it is solitude. In large cities one can easily be as lonely as almost nowhere else. But one can never be in solitude there. Solitude has the peculiar and original power not of isolating us but of projecting our whole existence out into the vast nearness of the presence [*Wesen*] of all things."
102. Heidegger, *Ponderings II–VI*, p. 247 (emphasis in original); *Überlegungen II–VI*, p. 340.
103. Heidegger, *Ponderings II–VI*, p. 311; *Überlegungen II–VI*, p. 428.
104. The final form of the thirty-eight books contained in the *Problemata* is considered to be pseudo-Aristotelian, but there is a growing consensus that some of the material in the compilation developed from an authentic Peripatetic core. See Ann Blair, "The *Problemata* as a Natural Philosophical Genre," in *Natural Particulars: Nature and the Disciplines in Renaissance Europe*, ed. Anthony Grafton and Nancy Siraisi (Cambridge: MIT Press, 1999), pp. 171–204; Pieter de Leemans and Michèle Goyens, "Introduction," in *Aristotle's* Problemata *in Different Times and Tongues*, ed. Pieter de Leemans and Michèle Goyens (Leuven: Leuven University Press, 2006), pp. ix–xvi; István Bodnar, "The *Problemata physica*: An Introduction," in *The Aristotelian* Problemata Physica*: Philosophical and Scientific Investigations*, ed. Robert Mayhew (Leiden: Brill, 2015), pp. 1–9.
105. Heidegger, *The Fundamental Concepts*, pp. 182–183; *Die Grundbegriffe*, pp. 270–271. See Espen Hammer, "Being Bored: Heidegger on Patience and Melancholy," *British Journal for the History of Philosophy* 12 (2004): 277–295, esp. 292–293. See also Ilit Ferber, *Philosophy and Melancholy: Benjamin's Early Reflections on Theater and Language* (Stanford: Stanford University Press, 2013), pp. 5–8. As Ferber describes her project, "This book adopts Heidegger's framework and proposes to establish melancholy as a fundamental mood of philosophical disclosure. In setting aside the attraction to the more subjective nature of melancholy, it scrutinizes the hidden traces of the melancholic mood in the structure of metaphysics and ontology. It attempts to unpack the concept of melancholy outside its customary usage and to think of it as a philosophical, structural edifice—as one of the states of mind governing philosophy itself" (p. 8). I concur with this reading of Heidegger and also embrace it as a constructive prism through which to view the philosophical temperament. See my discussion in "Not Yet Now," pp. 171–180. For further analysis of the role of mood as determinative of the structure of subjectivity, see Ilit Ferber, "Leibniz's Monad: A Study in Melancholy and Harmony," in *Philosophy's Moods: The Affective Grounds of Thinking*, ed. Hagi Kenaan and Ilit Ferber (Dordrecht: Springer, 2011), pp. 53–68, esp. 54–57; and Ilit Ferber, "*Stimmung*: Heidegger and Benjamin," in *Sparks Will Fly: Benjamin and Heidegger*, ed.

Andrew Benjamin and Dimitris Vardoulakis (Albany: State University of New York Press, 2015), pp. 67–93.

106. I am responding to Max Pensky, *Melancholy Dialectics: Walter Benjamin and the Play of Mourning* (Amherst: University of Massachusetts Press, 1993), pp. 62–63. What I have argued with respect to Heidegger can be ascribed as well to Benjamin. Pensky's attributing a negative valence to melancholy follows the more typical assessment, as we find, for instance, in Sigmund Freud, "Mourning and Melancholia," in *The Standard Edition of the Complete Psychological Works of Sigmund Freud*, trans. James Strachey (London: Hogarth, 1957), 14:244: "The distinguishing mental features of melancholia are a profoundly painful dejection, cessation of interest in the outside world, loss of the capacity of love, inhibition of all activity, and a lowering of the self-regarding feelings to a degree that finds utterance in self-reproaches and self-revilings, and culminates in a delusional expectation of punishment."
107. Franz Rosenzweig, *The Star of Redemption*, trans. Barbara Galli (Madison: University of Wisconsin Press, 2000), pp. 85–86; *Der Mensch und sein Werk: Gesammelte Schriften II. Der Stern der Erlösung* (The Hague: Martinus Nijhoff, 1976), pp. 83–84. On Rosenzweig's privileging of silence and the apophatic vision, see Wolfson, *Giving*, pp. 34–89, esp. 67, 69–83.
108. Maurice Merleau-Ponty, *Phenomenology of Perception*, trans. Donald A. Landes (London: Routledge, 2012), p. 376.
109. Claude Romano, *At the Heart of Reason*, trans. Michael B. Smith and Claude Romano (Evanston: Northwestern University Press, 2015), pp. 456–457.
110. For a feminist critique of Heidegger's portrayal of Dasein as the solitary male hero, coupled with an attempt to reinterpret some of his ideas nonfoundationally, see Mechthild Nagel, "Thrownness, Playing-in the-World, and the Question of Authenticity," in *Feminist Interpretations of Martin Heidegger*, ed. Nancy J. Holland and Patricia Huntington (University Park: Pennsylvania State University Press, 2001), pp. 289–306.
111. Walter Benjamin, *The Origin of German Tragic Drama*, introduction by George Steiner (London: Verso, 1998), p. 108.
112. Heidegger, *Ponderings VII–XI*, p. 326; *Überlegungen VII–XI*, p. 418.

5. POLITICAL DISAVOWAL

1. Marvin Farber, "Heidegger on the Essence of Truth," *Philosophy and Phenomenological Research* 18 (1958): 523–532; John M. Anderson, "Truth, Process, and Creature in Heidegger's Thought," in *Heidegger and the Quest for Truth*, ed. with an introduction by Manfred S. Frings (Chicago: Quadrangle, 1968), pp. 28–61; Joan Stambaugh, *The Finitude of Being* (Albany: State University of New York Press, 1992), pp. 13–30; Ernst Tugendhat, *Der Wahrheitsbegriff bei Husserl und Heidegger* (Berlin: Walter de Gruyter, 1967), pp. 389–393, 396–399, 402–403; Ernst Tugendhat, "Heidegger's Idea of Truth," in Richard Wolin, ed., *The Heidegger Controversy: A Critical Reader* (Cambridge: MIT Press, 1993), pp. 245–263; and discussion in Santiago Zabala, *The Hermeneutic Nature of Analytic Philosophy: A Study*

of *Ernst Tugendhat* (New York: Columbia University Press, 2008), pp. 25–44; Daniel O. Dahlstrom, *Heidegger's Concept of Truth* (Cambridge: Cambridge University Press, 1994), pp. 182, 214, 223–231, 238–240, 291–292, 300–301, 314–315, 322–325, 389–392, 397–407, 431–432; Frederick A. Olafson, "Being, Truth, and Presence in Heidegger's Thought," *Inquiry* 41 (1998): 45–64; John Sallis, "Interrupting Truth," in *Heidegger Toward the Turn: Essays on the Work of the 1930s*, ed. James Risser (Albany: State University of New York Press, 1999), pp. 19–30; Rodolphe Gasché, "Tuned to Accord: On Heidegger's Concept of Truth," in *Heidegger Toward the Turn*, pp. 31–49; Miguel de Beistegui, *Truth and Genesis: Philosophy as Differential Ontology* (Bloomington: Indiana University Press, 2004), pp. 122–130, 142–146, 153–154; Mark A. Wrathall, "Heidegger, Truth, and Reference," *Inquiry* 45 (2002): 217–228; Mark A. Wrathall, "Heidegger on Plato, Truth, and Unconcealment: The 1931–32 Lecture on *The Essence of Truth*," *Inquiry* 47 (2004): 443–463; Mark A. Wrathall, *Heidegger and Unconcealment: Truth, Language, and History* (Cambridge: Cambridge University Press, 2011), pp. 11–39; Francisco J. Gonzalez, *Plato and Heidegger: A Question of Dialogue* (University Park: Pennsylvania State University Press, 2009), pp. 225–255; Louis P. Blond, *Heidegger and Nietzsche: Overcoming Metaphysics* (London: Continuum, 2010), pp. 79–98; László Tengelyi, "Transformations in Heidegger's Conception of Truth Between 1927 and 1930," in *Variations on Truth: Approaches in Contemporary Phenomenology*, ed. Pol Vandevelde and Kevon Hermberg (London: Continuum, 2011), pp. 94–108.

2. Martin Heidegger, *Being and Truth*, trans. Gregory Fried and Richard Polt (Bloomington: Indiana University Press, 2010), p. 141 (emphasis in original); *Sein und Wahrheit* [GA 36/37] (Frankfurt: Vittorio Klostermann, 2001), pp. 182–183. For an examination of Heidegger's interpretation of the Platonic allegory, see Mary-Jane Rubenstein, *Strange Wonder: The Closure of Metaphysics and the Opening of Awe* (New York: Columbia University Press, 2008), pp. 47–56. An analysis in a Gadamerian register is given by Abdul Rahinm Afaki, "The Cave, the Lifeworld and the Tradition: The Transcendence-Immanence Contrast Perspective," *Analecta Husserliana* 117 (2014): 111–134. See also Pol Vandevelde, "Heidegger's Fluid Ontology in the 1930s: The Platonic Connection," in *Variations on Truth*, pp. 109–126, esp. 116–122.

3. Martin Heidegger, *The Essence of Truth: On Plato's Cave Allegory and Theaetetus*, trans. Ted Sadler (New York: Continuum, 2002), pp. 20–21; *Vom Wesen der Wahrheit: Zu Platons Höhlengleichnis und Theätet* [GA 34] (Frankfurt: Vittorio Klostermann, 1988), p. 26.

4. Heidegger, *The Essence of Truth*, p. 27 (emphasis in original); *Vom Wesen der Wahrheit*, p. 36.

5. Heidegger, *The Essence of Truth*, p. 59; *Vom Wesen der Wahrheit*, pp. 81–82.

6. Heidegger, *The Essence of Truth*, p. 64 (emphasis in original); *Vom Wesen der Wahrheit*, p. 88.

7. Heidegger, *The Essence of Truth*, p. 65; *Vom Wesen der Wahrheit*, p. 89.

8. Heidegger, *The Essence of Truth*, p. 65 (emphasis in original); *Vom Wesen der Wahrheit*, p. 90.

9. Heidegger, *The Essence of Truth*, p. 66 (emphasis in original); *Vom Wesen der Wahrheit*, pp. 91–92. It is possible that with regard to the matter of truth and untruth, Heidegger is influenced by Kierkegaard. See Elliot R. Wolfson, *Giving*

5. POLITICAL DISAVOWAL

  Beyond the Gift: Apophasis and Overcoming Theomania (New York: Fordham University Press, 2014), p. 45 and the sources discussed on pp. 313–314*n*91.
10. Heidegger, *The Essence of Truth*, p. 66 (emphasis in original); *Vom Wesen der Wahrheit*, p. 92.
11. Heidegger, *Being and Truth*, p. 142 (emphasis in original); *Sein und Wahrheit*, p. 184.
12. Heidegger, *Being and Truth*, p. 142; *Sein und Wahrheit*, p. 184–185.
13. On the distinction between untruth (*Unwahrheit*) and falsity (*Falschheit*), compare Heidegger, *Parmenides*, trans. André Schuwer and Richard Rojcewicz (Bloomington: Indiana University Press, 1992), pp. 26–27; *Parmenides* [GA 54] (Frankfurt: Vittorio Klostermann, 1992), pp. 38–40.
14. Heidegger, *The Essence of Truth*, p. 92; *Vom Wesen der Wahrheit*, pp. 126–127.
15. Heidegger, *The Essence of Truth*, p. 91; *Vom Wesen der Wahrheit*, p. 125.
16. Heidegger, *The Essence of Truth*, p. 92 (emphasis in original); *Vom Wesen der Wahrheit*, p. 127.
17. Heidegger, *The Essence of Truth*, p. 32; *Vom Wesen der Wahrheit*, p. 42.
18. Martin Heidegger, *Pathmarks*, ed. William McNeill (Cambridge: Cambridge University Press, 1998), p. 170; *Wegmarken* [GA 9] (Frankfurt: Vittorio Klostermann, 1996), p. 222.
19. Heidegger, *Pathmarks*, p. 168; *Wegmarken*, p. 218.
20. Heidegger, *The Essence of Truth*, p. 26; *Vom Wesen der Wahrheit*, p. 34.
21. Krzysztof Ziarek, *Language After Heidegger* (Bloomington: Indiana University Press, 2013), p. 142.
22. Martin Heidegger, *Zollikon Seminars: Protocols—Conversations—Letters*, ed. Medard Boss, trans. with notes and afterwords by Franz Mayr and Richard Askay (Evanston: Northwestern University Press, 2001), p. 171.
23. Heidegger, *Pathmarks*, p. 171; *Wegmarken*, p. 223.
24. Heidegger, *The Essence of Truth*, p. 32 (emphasis in original); *Vom Wesen der Wahrheit*, p. 43.
25. Heidegger, *The Essence of Truth*, p. 33; *Vom Wesen der Wahrheit*, p. 45.
26. Heidegger, *The Essence of Truth*, p. 34; *Vom Wesen der Wahrheit*, p. 45.
27. Heidegger, *The Essence of Truth*, p. 38 (emphasis in original); *Vom Wesen der Wahrheit*, pp. 51–52. See Vandevelde, "Heidegger's Fluid Ontology," p. 118. On Heidegger and the Platonic *to agathon*, see Ted Sadler, *Heidegger and Aristotle: The Question of Being* (London: Athlone, 1996), pp. 133–140, esp. 136–137. On the one hand, Sadler acknowledges that Heidegger's analysis of the Platonic *to agathon* is "clearly reminiscent of his own way of speaking about truth and Being as 'event.'" On the other hand, Heidegger refuses to accept that with this notion "Plato was reaching beyond the 'truth of beings' to a more primordial *aletheia*." This more primordial truth, or, as Heidegger understands the term, this more primordial unconcealment, is related to the description of the good as *epekeina tēs ousias*, beyond beingness. The matter is more complex insofar as the import of the ontological difference is to clear the space to think being equiprimordially with the nothing, and in this equiprimordiality being is, so to speak, beyond being.
28. Heidegger, *The Essence of Truth*, p. 69; *Vom Wesen der Wahrheit*, p. 95.
29. Heidegger, *The Essence of Truth*, p. 49; *Vom Wesen der Wahrheit*, p. 67.
30. Heidegger, *The Essence of Truth*, p. 64; *Vom Wesen der Wahrheit*, p. 89.

5. POLITICAL DISAVOWAL

31. Heidegger, *The Essence of Truth*, p. 50; *Vom Wesen der Wahrheit*, p. 68.
32. Heidegger, *The Essence of Truth*, p. 40; *Vom Wesen der Wahrheit*, p. 53.
33. Heidegger, *The Essence of Truth*, p. 40; *Vom Wesen der Wahrheit*, p. 55.
34. Heidegger, *The Essence of Truth*, p. 48 (emphasis in original); *Vom Wesen der Wahrheit*, p. 66.
35. Heidegger, *The Essence of Truth*, p. 51; *Vom Wesen der Wahrheit*, pp. 69–70.
36. Heidegger, *The Essence of Truth*, p. 53; *Vom Wesen der Wahrheit*, p. 73.
37. Heidegger, *The Essence of Truth*, p. 57; *Vom Wesen der Wahrheit*, p. 78.
38. Heidegger, *The Essence of Truth*, p. 60; *Vom Wesen der Wahrheit*, p. 82.
39. Heidegger, *Pathmarks*, p. 173; *Wegmarken*, p. 225.
40. Heidegger, *The Essence of Truth*, p. 61; *Vom Wesen der Wahrheit*, p. 84.
41. Heidegger, *The Essence of Truth*, p. 62; *Vom Wesen der Wahrheit*, p. 85.
42. Heidegger, *The Essence of Truth*, p. 63; *Vom Wesen der Wahrheit*, p. 86.
43. Martin Heidegger, *Off the Beaten Track*, ed. and trans. Julian Young and Kenneth Haynes (Cambridge: Cambridge University Press, 2002), p. 85; *Holzwege* [GA 5] (Frankfurt: Vittorio Klostermann, 1977), p. 112.
44. Martin Heidegger, *Interpretation of Nietzsche's Second Untimely Meditation*, trans. Ulrich Haase and Mark Sinclair (Bloomington: Indiana University Press, 2016), p. 170 (emphasis in original).
45. Martin Heidegger, *Country Path Conversations*, trans. Bret W. Davis (Bloomington: Indiana University Press, 2010), p. 133; *Feldweg-Gespräche* [GA 77] (Frankfurt: Vittorio Klostermann, 1995), p. 206.
46. Martin Heidegger, *Poetry, Language, Thought*, trans. Albert Hofstadter (New York: Harper and Row, 1971), p. 11; *Aus der Erfahrung des Denkens 1910–1976* [GA 13] (Frankfurt: Vittorio Klostermann, 2002), p. 83.
47. Martin Heidegger, *Identity and Difference*, trans. Joan Stambaugh (New York: Harper and Row, 1969), p. 142. I have modified Stambaugh's translation of *sagenden Nichtsagen* as "telling silence" (p. 73).
48. See the analysis in Geoff Waite, "Heidegger, Schmitt, Strauss: The Hidden Monologue, or, Conserving Esotericism to Justify the High Hand of Violence," *Cultural Critique* 69 (2008): 113–144.
49. Heidegger, *Pathmarks*, p. 148; *Wegmarken*, p. 193.
50. Heidegger, *Pathmarks*, p. 151; *Wegmarken*, p. 198.
51. Martin Heidegger, *Logic as the Question Concerning the Essence of Language*, trans. Wanda Torres Gregory and Yvonne Unna (Albany: State University of New York Press, 2009), p. 97; *Logik als die Frage nach dem Wesen der Sprache* [GA 38] (Frankfurt: Vittorio Klostermann, 1998), pp. 116–117.
52. Eckhart uses the expression *unwesene* to describe the state of nonbeing in which God acts prior to creation. See *Meister Eckhart: Die deutschen und lateinischen Werke*, vol. 1: *Meister Eckharts Predigten*, ed. and trans. Josef Quint (Stuttgart: W. Kohlhammer, 1958), p. 145 (Pr. 9): "Got würket über wesene in der wîte, dâ er sich geregen mac, er würket in unwesene; ê denne wesene wære, dô worhte got; er worhte wesen, dô niht wesen enwas." English translation in *The Complete Mystical Works of Meister Eckhart*, ed. and trans. Maurice O'C. Walshe, revised by Bernard McGinn (New York: Herder and Herder, 2009), p. 342: "God works beyond being, in breadth, where He can move, and He works in nonbeing: before there was being, God was working: He wrought being where no being was." In a

5. POLITICAL DISAVOWAL

second passage from the same sermon, Eckhart argued that the soul's power to remember by envisioning things that are not present mimics God's ability to work in nonbeing. See *Meister Eckharts Predigten*, p. 151 (Pr. 9): "Ein ander kraft ist in der sêle, dâ mite si gedenket. Disiu kraft bildet in sich diu dinc, diu niht gegenwertic ensint... und mit dirre kraft würket diu sêle in unwesene und volget gote, der in unwesene würket." English translation in *The Complete Mystical Works of Meister Eckhart*, p. 343: "There is another power in the soul, with which she remembers. This power is able to picture in itself things which are not present... and with *this* power the soul works in nonbeing and follows God, who works in nonbeing" (emphasis in original). I detect the influence of the second of these passages in the brief aphorism on *"A-nihilation—and Forgetfulness of Being"* (Ver-nichtung—und Seinsvergessenheit) in Heidegger, *Country Path Conversations*, p. 158 (*Feldweg-Gespräche*, pp. 241–242):

> Allowing oneself to become absorbed into the nihilating [*Nichten*] of one's ownmost concealed essence, that is, into the forgottenness of being in the form of the presumption of its effect in objectification. The nihilating of memory in the event of appropriation [*Ereignis*]. *Forgottenness* and *subjectivity* (*subjectivity*: humanity, nationality, bestiality, brutality), but in a concealed manner belonging to the truth of beyng. But still in the nonessence [*Unwesen*] not to be denied as memory in the event of appropriation— namely, as the willing of the will to will.
>
> (emphasis in original)

I have altered Davis's translation of *Unwesen* as "terrible non-essence" because I think this confounds Heidegger's intent. For the rationale of this rendering, see ibid., p. 158*n*16. A Heideggerian interpretation of the Eckhartian terminology is offered by Reiner Schürmann, *Meister Eckhart, Mystic and Philosopher: Translations with Commentary* (Bloomington: Indiana University Press, 1978), p. 86:

> Conversely, *unwesene* is reserved by Meister Eckhart for that essential coming forth which, at the same time, retreats into concealment, that is, into the darkness in which the acting of the mind is united to the acting of God.... In a certain sense, *unwesene* could be translated by "nothingness"; but as it expresses the abolition of the positivity of being, it points, so to speak, not beneath but beyond being, as the ὑπὲρ-ὄν of the Neoplatonists. In the *unwesene* of the Godhead, the activity of the ground of the mind is identical with the actuality of God. *Unwesene*, then, does not apply to creatures.

See also Sonya Sikka, *Forms of Transcendence: Heidegger and Medieval Mystical Theology* (Albany: State University of New York Press, 1997), p. 115.

53. Andrew J. Mitchell, "Contamination, Essence, and Decomposition: Heidegger and Derrida," in *French Interpretations of Heidegger: An Exceptional Reception*, ed. David Pettigrew and François Raffoul (Albany: State University of New York Press, 2008), pp. 135–140. See, however, Peter Trawny, *Freedom to Fail: Heidegger's Anarchy*, trans. Ian Alexander Moore and Christopher Turner (Cambridge: Polity, 2015), p. 10.

54. Bret W. Davis, *Heidegger and the Will: On the Way to Gelassenheit* (Evanston: Northwestern University Press, 2007), p. 283. For discussion of the different ways to understand *Unwesen*, see ibid., p. 364n7.
55. Martin Heidegger, *Schelling's Treatise on the Essence of Human Freedom*, trans. Joan Stambaugh (Athens: Ohio University Press, 1985), p. 156; *Schelling: Vom Wesen der menschlichen Freiheit (1809)* [GA 42] (Frankfurt: Vittorio Klostermann, 1988), p. 270.
56. Heidegger, *Schelling's Treatise*, p. 156; *Schelling: Vom Wesen*, p. 271.
57. The topic is repeated in many of Böhme's compositions, but I will cite here one of the clearer formulations: Jacob Boehme, *Six Theosophic Points and Other Writings* (Ann Arbor: University of Michigan Press, 1958), p. 18:

> The will which is called Father, which has freedom in itself, so generates itself in Nature, that it is susceptible of Nature, and that it is the universal part of Nature. The terror of its Nature is a kindler of fire. For when the dark anguish, as the very fervent, stern being, receives freedom in itself, it is transformed in the terror, in freedom, into a flash, and the flash embraces freedom or gentleness. Then the sting of death is broken; and there rises in Nature the other will of the Father, which he drew prior to Nature in the mirror of wisdom, viz. his heart of love, the desire of love, the kingdom of joy.

Robert H. Paslick, "The Ontological Context of Gadamer's 'Fusion': Boehme, Heidegger, and Non-Duality," *Man and World* 18 (1985): 412–413, interprets Böhme's theosophy dialectically in Lurianic terms:

> Now no manifestation can occur until this ungrounded will is grounded; and it can be grounded only by positing that which is not itself. But since there exists nothing outside the divine spirit, *it must clear a space within itself*, which is in itself but is not itself. This space is what Boehme calls nature, the dark world of the divine ground, similar to an unreflecting mirror into whose darkness the spirit sacrifices its freedom in its anguished yearning to reveal itself.... The desire to manifest demands the creation of real darkness without which the light of manifestation cannot be seen. But the *severe contraction*, by which the dark world is formed in the free spirit, arouses in it the raging desire to escape this prisonhouse of darkness. Of course there is no escape. The paradox is unresolvable. The light which desires to be manifest must desire equally strongly both the creation and the endurance of the darkness which makes manifestation possible. Thus the life process consists in continually overcoming a darkness which can never be completely overcome.
>
> (emphasis added)

58. For some representative studies on Böhme and the kabbalah, see Wilhelm August Schulze, "Jacob Boehme und die Kabbala," *Judaica* 11 (1955): 12–29; John Yost Stoudt, *Jacob Boehme: His Life and Thought* (New York: Seabury, 1957), pp. 22, 88, 89n17, 96, 115; Ernest B. Koenker, "Grund and Ungrund in Jacob Boehme," *Philosophy Today* 15 (1971): 45–51, esp. 46–47; Ernst Benz, *The Mystical Sources of*

5. POLITICAL DISAVOWAL

German Romantic Philosophy, trans. Blair R. Reynolds and Eunice M. Paul (Allison Park, PA: Pickwick, 1983), pp. 47–58; John Schulitz, *Jakob Böhme und die Kabbalah: Eine vergleichende Werkanalyse* (Frankfurt: Peter Lang, 1993); Susanne Edel, "Kabbala in der Theosophie Jacob Böhmes und in der Metaphysik Leibnizens," in *Religion und Religiosität im Zeitalter des Barock*, ed. Dieter Breuer (Wiesbaden: Harrassowitz, 1995), 2:845–856; Susanne Edel, *Die individuelle Substanz bei Böhme und Leibniz: Die Kabbala als tertium comparationis für eine rezeptionsgeschichtliche Untersuchung* (Stuttgart: Franz Steiner, 1995); Susanne Edel, "Métaphysique des idées et mystique des lettres: Leibniz, Böhme et la Kabbale prophétique," *Revue de l'Histoire des Religions* 213 (1996): 443–466; Cyril O'Regan, *Gnostic Apocalypse: Jacob Boehme's Haunted Narrative* (Albany: State University of New York Press, 2002), pp. 193–209; Wilhelm Schmidt-Biggemann, "Jakob Bohme und die Kabbala," in *Christliche Kabbala*, ed. Wilhelm Schmidt-Biggemann (Ostfildem: Jan Thorbecke, 2003), pp. 157–181; Sibylle Rusterholz, "Elemente der Kabbala bei Jacob Böhme," in *Mystik und Schriftkommentierung*, ed. Günther Bonheim and Petra Kattner (Berlin: Weissensee, 2007), pp. 15–45; Andrew Weeks, *Boehme: An Intellectual Biography of the Seventeenth-Century Philosopher and Mystic* (Albany: State University of New York Press, 1991), pp. 106, 116, 147, 200, 204–205; and Andrew Weeks,"Radical Reformation and the Anticipation of Modernism in Jacob Boehme," in *An Introduction to Jacob Boehme: Four Centuries of Thought and Reception*, ed. Ariel Hessayon and Sarah Apetrei (New York: Routledge, 2014), p. 52. See also Elliot R. Wolfson, *Language, Eros, Being: Kabbalistic Hermeneutics and Poetic Imagination* (New York: Fordham University Press, 2005), pp. 8, 197, 471n435, 485–486n180, and references to other scholars cited on pp. 423n259 and 468n392. On the more specific relationship between Böhme and Christian kabbalah, see Wilhelm Schmidt-Biggemann, "The Christian Kabbala: Joseph Gikatilla (1247–1305), Johannes Reuchlin (1455–1522), Paulus Ricius (d. 1541), and Jacob Böhme (1575–1624)," in *The Language of Adam, Die Sprache Adams*, ed. Allison Coudert (Wiesbaden: Harrassowitz, 1999), pp. 81–121; Wilhelm Schmidt-Biggemann, *Philosophia Perennis: Historical Outlines of Western Spirituality in Ancient, Medieval and Early Modern Thought* (Dordrecht: Springer, 2004), pp. 117–128, 187–192; Leigh T. I. Penman, "Boehme's Intellectual Networks and the Heterodox Milieu of His Theosophy, 1600–1624," in *An Introduction to Jacob Boehme*, pp. 66–71. The influence of Böhme on Schelling has been noted by various scholars. For instance, see Ernst Benz, *Schellings theologische Geistesahnen* (Wiesbaden: F. Steiner, 1955); Robert F. Brown, *The Later Philosophy of Schelling: The Influence of Boehme on the Works of 1809–1815* (Lewisburg: Bucknell University Press, 1977); Christoph Schulte, "F. W. J. Schellings Ausleihe von Hand- und Druckschriften," *Zeitschrift für Religion und Geistesgeschichte* 45 (1993): 267–277; Jean-Louis Vieillard-Baron, "Schelling et Jacob Böhme: Les Recherches de 1809 et la lecture de la *Lettre pastorale*," *Les Études philosophiques* 2 (1999): 223–242. For comparative studies on Böhme and Heidegger, see Paslick, "The Ontological Context," pp. 405–422, esp. 409–412; Hans-Joachim Friedrich, *Der Ungrund der Freiheit in Denken von Böhme, Schelling und Heidegger* (Stuttgart: Frommann-Holzboog, 2009); Mark A. Peckler, "Imagination, Religious Practice, and World Transformations: Sophia, Heidegger, and Jacob Böhme's *The Way to Christ*," Ph.D. dissertation, University of Denver and Iliff School of

Theology, 2009. See also the passing remark of Jürgen Habermas, "Martin Heidegger: On the Publication of the Lectures of 1935," in Richard Wolin, ed., *The Heidegger Controversy: A Critical Reader* (Cambridge: MIT Press, 1993), pp. 195–196.

59. Friedrich Wilhelm Joseph Schelling, *Philosophy and Religion (1804)*, trans. Klaus Ottmann (Putnam, CT: Spring, 2010), p. 31; Friedrich Wilhelm Joseph Schelling, *Philosophie und Religion*, in Friedrich Wilhelm Joseph Schelling, *Sämmtliche Werke 1804*, ed. Karl Friedrich August Schelling (Stuttgart: Cotta, 1860), 6:42–43. For a more recent edition, see Friedrich Wilhelm Joseph Schelling, *Philosophie und Religion*, ed. Alfred Denker and Holger Zaborowski (Munich: Karl Alber, 2008), p. 35.
60. Friedrich Wilhelm Joseph Schelling, *The Ages of the World (Fragment) from the Handwritten Remains, Third Version (c. 1815)*, trans. Jason M. Wirth (Albany: State University of New York Press, 2000), p. 49; Friedrich Wilhelm Joseph Schelling, *Die Weltalter*, in Friedrich Wilhelm Joseph Schelling, *Sämmtliche Werke*, ed. Karl Friedrich August Schelling (Stuttgart: Cotta, 1861), 8:268.
61. Friedrich Wilhelm Joseph Schelling, *Die Weltalter in den Urfassungen von 1811 und 1813 (Nachlaßband)*, ed. Manfred Schröter (Munich: Beck, 1946), p. 43, as translated in Jason M. Wirth, *Schelling's Practice of the Wild: Time, Art, Imagination* (Albany: State University of New York Press, 2015), p. 58.
62. See Martin Heidegger, *Überlegungen VII–XI (Schwarze Hefte 1938/39)* [GA 95] (Frankfurt: Vittorio Klostermann, 2014), p. 430, where *Bildung* is said to comprise both *Wesen* and *Unwesen*. Notably, the latter is equated with *Unbildung*. See Martin Heidegger, *Ponderings VII–XI: Black Notebooks 1938-1939*, trans. Richard Rojcewicz (Bloomington: Indiana University Press, 2017), p. 335: "*Refinement* [Bildung], in its essence [*Wesen*] (developed formation of 'life') *and* in its distorted essence [*Unwesen*] ('affectation'), is not a need and is a phenomenon of modernity. . . . The modern age of refinement becomes transformed into the age of 'education' and thus necessarily turns into the age of *unrefinement* [Unbildung]. Unrefinement is not a *preliminary* stage of refinement; it is rather a *consequence* of refinement" (emphasis in original).
63. Martin Heidegger, *Contributions to Philosophy (Of the Event)*, trans. Richard Rojcewicz and Daniela Vallega-Neu (Bloomington: Indiana University Press, 2012), § 146, p. 210 (emphasis in original); *Beiträge zur Philosophie (Vom Ereignis)* [GA 65] (Frankfurt: Vittorio Klostermann, 1989), p. 267.
64. Heidegger, *Contributions*, § 146, p. 210 (emphasis in original); *Beiträge*, p. 267.
65. See Quentin Meillassoux, *After Finitude: An Essay on the Necessity of Contingency*, trans. Ray Brassier (London: Continuum, 2008), p. 5: "Correlationism consists in disqualifying the claim that it is possible to consider the realms of subjectivity and objectivity independently of one another. Not only does it become necessary to insist that we never grasp an object 'in itself,' in isolation from its relation to its subject, but it also becomes necessary to maintain that we can never grasp a subject that would not always-already be related to an object."
66. Heidegger, *Contributions*, § 146, pp. 210–211; *Beiträge*, pp. 267–268.
67. Heidegger, *Being and Truth*, p. 87; *Sein und Wahrheit*, p. 111.
68. For a different interpretation, see Geoffrey Bennington, *Scatter 1: The Politics of Politics in Foucault, Heidegger, and Derrida* (New York: Fordham University Press, 2016), p. 101: "However tempting it might be to read the last sentence here in context as bearing the trace of Heidegger's recent resignation as rector of

Freiburg University... it is undeniable that this issue of *Führung* connects directly with Heidegger's political decisions at this time and his continued apparently enthusiastic support for the Nazi regime and the so-called *Führerprinzip* in the courses from the following year." This explanation does not seem preferable to me since it does not consider that Heidegger states explicitly that true leadership will be falsified and will lead astray.

69. Heidegger, *Ponderings VII–XI*, pp. 247-248 (emphasis in original); *Überlegungen VII–XI*, pp. 317-318.
70. Martin Heidegger, *Ponderings II–VI: Black Notebooks 1931–1938*, trans. Richard Rojcewicz (Bloomington: Indiana University Press, 2016), p. 343; *Überlegungen II–VI (Schwarze Hefte 1931–1938)* [GA 94] (Frankfurt: Vittorio Klostermann, 2014), p. 473.
71. Heidegger, *Being and Truth*, p. 200 (emphasis in original); *Sein und Wahrheit*, p. 262.
72. Heidegger, *Being and Truth*, pp. 200–201 (emphasis in original); *Sein und Wahrheit*, p. 263.
73. Heidegger, *Being and Truth*, p. 201; *Sein und Wahrheit*, p. 263.
74. Heidegger, *Being and Truth*, p. 201 (emphasis in original); *Sein und Wahrheit*, p. 263.
75. Heidegger, *Being and Truth*, p. 201; *Sein und Wahrheit*, p. 264.
76. Trawny, *Freedom to Fail*, pp. 28–29.
77. Heidegger, *Poetry, Language, Thought*, p. 9; *Aus der Erfahrung*, p. 81.
78. Trawny, *Freedom to Fail*, p. 5. My own language here is indebted to Trawny.
79. Martin Heidegger, *Elucidations of Hölderlin's Poetry*, trans. Keith Hoeller (Amherst: Humanity, 2000), p. 153; *Erläuterungen zu Hölderlins Dichtung* [GA 4] (Frankfurt: Vittorio Klostermann, 1996), p. 131.
80. Martin Heidegger, *Bremen and Freiburg Lectures: Insight Into That Which Is and Basic Principles of Thinking*, trans. Andrew J. Mitchell (Bloomington: Indiana University Press, 2012), p. 27; *Bremer und Freiburger Vorträge* [GA 79] (Frankfurt: Vittorio Klostermann, 1994), p. 27.
81. Heidegger, *Bremen and Freiburg Lectures*, p. 26; *Bremer und Freiburger Vorträge*, p. 27.
82. See Mahon O'Brien, *Heidegger, History, and the Holocaust* (London: Bloomsbury Academic, 2015), pp. 24–41.
83. See Martin Heidegger, *Introduction to Metaphysics*, trans. Gregory Fried and Richard Polt (New Haven: Yale University Press, 2000), p. 40; *Einführung in die Metaphysik* [GA 40] (Frankfurt: Vittorio Klostermann, 1983), pp. 40–41. As Leo Strauss rightly noted, *The Rebirth of Classical Political Rationalism: An Introduction to the Thought of Leo Strauss*, selected and introduced by Thomas L. Pangle (Chicago: University of Chicago Press, 1989), p. 42, for Heidegger, America and Soviet Russia are "metaphysically the same."
84. See the analysis of both passages in Berel Lang, *Heidegger's Silence* (Ithaca: Cornell University Press, 1996), pp. 16–19.
85. Martin Heidegger, *What Is Called Thinking?* trans. Fred W. Wieck and J. Glenn Gray (New York: Harper and Row, 1968), pp. 66–67; *Was Heißt Denken?* [GA 8] (Frankfurt: Vittorio Klostermann, 2002), p. 71.
86. Heidegger, *Bremen and Freiburg Lectures*, p. 53; *Bremer und Freiburger Vorträge*, p. 56.

87. Heidegger, *Bremen and Freiburg Lectures*, p. 53 (emphasis in original); *Bremer und Freiburger Vorträge*, p. 56.
88. Heidegger, *Contributions*, § 161, pp. 222–223; *Beiträge*, pp. 283–284.
89. Heidegger, *Contributions*, § 162, pp. 223–224; *Beiträge*, pp. 284–285.
90. Miguel de Beistegui, *The New Heidegger* (London: Continuum, 2005), pp. 163–164.
91. Heidegger, *Poetry, Language, Thought*, pp. 178–179; *Vorträge und Aufsätze* [GA 7] (Frankfurt: Vittorio Klostermann, 2000), p. 180. Similar language is used by Heidegger in two 1951 lectures, "Bauen Wohnen Denken" (*Poetry, Language, Thought*, p. 150; *Vorträge und Aufsätze*, p. 152) and "... dichterisch wohnet der Mensch ..." (*Poetry, Language, Thought*, p. 222; *Vorträge und Aufsätze*, p. 200).
92. Martin Heidegger, *The End of Philosophy*, trans. Joan Stambaugh (New York: Harper and Row, 1973), p. 102; *Vorträge und Aufsätze*, p. 89.
93. Heidegger, *The End of Philosophy*, p. 103; *Vorträge und Aufsätze*, p. 90.
94. Heidegger, *The End of Philosophy*, p. 104; *Vorträge und Aufsätze*, p. 91.
95. Compare Heidegger, *Ponderings II–VI*, p. 270 (*Überlegungen II–VI*, p. 370). Commenting on the "total European situation in its movements and countermovements," Heidegger notes "that a reversion to the previous 'metaphysics' is setting in everywhere and that the human is revived as *animal rationale*—as the rational animal (race and reason)." For discussion of Heidegger's analysis of the definition of the human as the rational animal, see Matthew Calarco, *Zoographies: The Question of the Animal from Heidegger to Derrida* (New York: Columbia University Press, 2008), pp. 43–53; Andrew J. Mitchell, *The Fourfold: Reading the Late Heidegger* (Evanston: Northwestern University Press, 2015), pp. 213–223.
96. Heidegger, *The End of Philosophy*, p. 105 (translation slightly altered); *Vorträge und Aufsätze*, p. 92.
97. Heidegger, *The End of Philosophy*, pp. 105–106 (translation slightly altered); *Vorträge und Aufsätze*, pp. 92–93.
98. Heidegger, *The End of Philosophy*, p. 106; *Vorträge und Aufsätze*, p. 93.
99. Heidegger, *The End of Philosophy*, p. 108; *Vorträge und Aufsätze*, p. 95.

6. HEIDEGGER, BALAAM, AND THE DUPLICITY OF PHILOSOPHY'S SHADOW

1. The first section of Michael Fagenblat, "'Heidegger and the Jews,'" in *Reading Heidegger's Black Notebooks, 1931–1941*, ed. Ingo Farin and Jeff Malpas (Cambridge: MIT Press, 2016), pp. 145–147, is entitled "Balaam's Ass." The rationale for choosing this title to frame the discussion of Heidegger's anti-Semitism is offered in the last paragraph of the section:

    If Heidegger lost his way, if he got the wrong people, earth and blood, the errancy at the same time betrays his proximity to the very Jews he anathematized. Like Balaam's ass, he "strayed from the way and went into the field" (Num. 22:23) when the Angel of Yhwh confronted him on the road— the angel of Yhwh, which Heidegger could even be forgiven for having mistaken for *die Schicken des Seyns*. And if he "strayed from the way" and was "thrashed thrice" for his trouble, we now find ourselves, like Balaam,

6. HEIDEGGER, BALAAM, AND THE DUPLICITY OF PHILOSOPHY'S SHADOW

sitting on the donkey's back in "a narrow place, where there was no way to turn either to the right or to the left" (Num. 22:26). The prophetic ass once spoke, and good readers always laughed; this one kept his silence but for some notebooks. Decent folk think it is no laughing matter—not the silence, not the notebooks, and not the narrow place in which we, who are also straying, find ourselves.

(pp. 146–147)

My emphasis is on another aspect of the Balaam character. The symbolic association of Heidegger and Balaam first arose in the context of a conversation I had many years ago with Asher Crispe, who was a doctoral student of mine at the time.

2. *Sifre on Deuteronomy*, ed. Louis Finkelstein (New York: Jewish Theological Seminary of America, 1969), sec. 357, p. 430. For other rabbinic references, see Louis Ginzberg, *The Legends of the Jews*, 7 vols. (Philadelphia: Jewish Publication Society of America, 1968), 6:125n727. For the figure of Balaam in rabbinic and early Christian Literature, see Jay Braverman, "Balaam in Rabbinic and Early Christian Traditions," in *Joshua Finkel Festschrift*, ed. Sidney B. Hoenig and Leon D. Stitskin (New York: Yeshiva University Press, 1974), pp. 41–50; Judith R. Baskin, *Pharaoh's Counsellors: Job, Jethro, and Balaam in Rabbinic and Patristic Tradition* (Chico: Scholars Press, 1983), pp. 74–114. See also the reference to Urbach cited in n14, this chapter. On the status of Balaam and Moses in the rabbinic, zoharic, and Lurianic corpora, see the extensive analysis in Shaul Magid, *From Metaphysics to Midrash: Myth, History, and the Interpretation of Scripture in Lurianic Kabbala* (Bloomington: Indiana University Press, 2008), pp. 143–195. My focus here is far more limited than the intricate details of Lurianic cosmology and anthropology, including the doctrine of metempsychosis, discussed by Magid.

3. Elliot R. Wolfson, *Venturing Beyond: Law and Morality in Kabbalistic Mysticism* (Oxford: Oxford University Press, 2006), pp. 43–44.

4. Magid, *From Metaphysics to Midrash*, pp. 150–151.

5. Zohar 2:21b–22a. For a list of other sources, see Elliot R. Wolfson, *Luminal Darkness: Imaginal Gleanings from Zoharic Literature* (Oxford: Oneworld, 2007), pp. 19–20 n18, 215n36; and Wolfson, *Venturing Beyond*, pp. 43–44n112, 140–141n46. Compare the text of Gikatilla cited in Wolfson, *Venturing Beyond*, p. 100. I respectfully disagree with Magid's conclusion, *From Metaphysics to Midrash*, p. 160, that the zoharic authors do not primarily view the midrashic equation of Moses and Balaam "in terms of prophecy but rather in terms of leadership (Moses—Israel, Balaam—gentiles)." The point accentuated in various zoharic homilies is the analogy between the theurgy of Moses and the magic of Balaam. The key difference is that Moses, as other faithful prophets, beholds the divine glory, whereas Balaam gazes through his witchcraft only at the lower crowns. See Zohar 3:207b.

6. The notion of the four shells of the demonic that surround the Shekhinah is derived from Ezekiel 1:4, the "stormy wind" (*ruaḥ se'arah*), "great cloud" (*anan gadol*), "flashing fire" (*esh mitlaqqaḥat*), and "radiance" (*nogah*). The last of these is the subtlest shell and the one closest to the core of holiness. For references, see Wolfson, *Venturing Beyond*, pp. 99n331 and 104n359.

7. For discussion of the vision of the closed eye in zoharic texts, see Elliot R. Wolfson, *Through a Speculum That Shines: Vision and Imagination in Medieval Jewish*

Mysticism (Princeton: Princeton University Press, 1994), pp. 380–383. See also Wolfson, *Venturing Beyond*, p. 219n113.

8. Based on the statement attributed to Simeon ben Yoḥai in Babylonian Talmud, Berakhot 55a, "Just as wheat cannot be without straw, so there be no dream without nonsense." For discussion of this talmudic dictum, which is an explication of Jeremiah 23:28, and its interpretation in several zoharic homilies and later kabbalistic texts, see Elliot R. Wolfson, *A Dream Interpreted Within a Dream: Oneiropoiesis and the Prism of Imagination* (New York: Zone, 2011), pp. 189–197.
9. Zohar 2:69a–b.
10. Ibid., 2:69b.
11. Ibid.
12. Magid, *From Metaphysics to Midrash*, p. 167, reaches a similar conclusion, but, as he duly notes, his thinking builds on my own speculation regarding the status of the other in kabbalistic lore. Especially relevant is my notion of "othering the other," wherein the boundaries are affirmed to be negated. See Wolfson, *Venturing Beyond*, pp. 129–185. The effacing of boundaries is exemplified by the process of conversion. See the summary of the zoharic account (ibid., p. 171):

> The phenomenon of conversion involves the ultimate reversal, for what appears to be so obviously distinct—the priest's daughter married to a foreign man—is undermined by the zoharic exegesis. It is nevertheless the case that the reversal itself is occasioned by a dichotomous orientation wherein the soul of the Jew is depicted as the daughter of the divine and the body of the Christian as the unclean foreskin that must be removed and discarded. Even if it is the case that the mystical insight helps one see that the foreskin and core are not radically other, as we may have initially thought, the normative framework that facilitates the vision is one in which the dichotomy is posited.

For a more elaborate discussion of conversion in zoharic kabbalah, see Wolfson, *Luminal Darkness*, pp. 264–271. Magid, *From Metaphysics to Midrash*, pp. 168–169, also emphasizes conversion as a model of the crossing of boundaries, but in his analysis of the Lurianic material there is the additional element of reincarnation. Even closer to Magid's language of the destabilizing of the inside/outside dichotomy is my interpretation of Kafka's parable "Before the Law" in Wolfson, *Venturing Beyond*, pp. 252–253:

> This is the lesson the priest set out to teach K. through the parable: the obsessive desire to get out from under the authority of law is equivalent to the intractable urge to enter the door through which one would access the law that cannot be accessed. The man is outside the law not because he wants to go in, as one critic expressed the matter, but precisely because he is already inside, that is, the inside is the vantage-point from which he imagines that he is outside.... The relentless quest to enter indicates that one has never exited; being outside is what it is to be inside. Denial of access to the law, therefore, is invitation to enter before the law, the hermeneutical act of re/covery, that is, re/turning to where one has continuously never been.

6. HEIDEGGER, BALAAM, AND THE DUPLICITY OF PHILOSOPHY'S SHADOW

And see p. 257:

The darkness of Kafka's vision dazzles the mind in its befuddling light refracted as it is in the prism of paradox. To close the door of the law, to bring closure to the law, would be to remove the means by which one trespasses the law, but entry through the door of law would necessitate discarding the law. To be before the law, one must stand outside the law, for the door of the law is open as long as there is no access to the law. To get beyond the law, however, one must go through the law, for the point of departure is the point of entry, the way out the way in. No one heeds the law like the outlaw.

13. Zohar 1:167a–b. For a slightly different interpretation of this passage, see Magid, *From Metaphysics to Midrash*, p. 162.
14. Ephraim E. Urbach, *The World of the Sages: Collected Studies* (Jerusalem: Magnes, 1988), pp. 537–555 (Hebrew), and see discussion of Urbach's argument in Magid, *From Metaphysics to Midrash*, pp. 151–153. See also Baskin, *Pharaoh's Counsellors*, pp. 91–93; Wolfson, *Venturing Beyond*, pp. 44n112, 56n167, 140n44.
15. Wolfson, *Luminal Darkness*, pp. 189–190. On the image of Balaam as Christ in zoharic literature, see now Ellen D. Haskell, *Mystical Resistance: Uncovering the Zohar's Conversations with Christianity* (New York: Oxford University Press, 2016), pp. 66–106.
16. Zohar 1:223b, 3:135a–b, 142a, 292a. See Elliot R. Wolfson, *Language, Eros, Being: Kabbalistic Hermeneutics and Poetic Imagination* (New York: Fordham University Press, 2005), pp. 311, 386–387, 567n122; and other sources cited in Wolfson, *A Dream*, pp. 429–430n177.
17. Zohar 2:195a, 3:194a, 281b (*Ra'aya Meheimna*).
18. Elliott Horowitz, *Reckless Rites: Purim and the Legacy of Jewish Violence* (Princeton: Princeton University Press, 2006), pp. 125–129.
19. Zohar 3:112b. On Balaam's attachment to the place of impurity (*atar di-mesa'ava*) represented symbolically as the wicked serpent (*ḥivya bisha*), see Zohar 2:195a. See also Zohar 2:264a. On the comparison of Balaam to a serpent on account of his traveling alone, see Zohar 1:170a.
20. Zohar 3:194a. For a different interpretation of Balaam's knowing the supernal knowledge (Numbers 24:16), see Zohar 3:208b. In that context, this knowledge consists of Balaam's being able to determine through sorcery the moment when judgment looms over the world. This explanation is based on Babylonian Talmud, Berakhot 7a, where the scriptural verse is interpreted as Balaam possessing the knowledge to determine the precise moment in which God gets angry.
21. Ḥayyim Viṭal, *Eṣ Ḥayyim* (Jerusalem: Aharon Barzanai, 2004), 32:2, 36b.
22. Regarding these names of the two magicians, who were opponents of Moses, later identified as the sons of Balaam, see Ginzberg, *The Legends of the Jews*, 5:407n80, 425n161; 6:127n740, 144n854.
23. Ḥayyim Viṭal, *Sha'ar ha-Pesuqim* (Jerusalem: Sitrei Ḥayyim, 2013), p. 264.
24. For a thorough discussion of the *erev rav* understood as the "other" Israel and identified historically with the conversos, see Magid, *From Metaphysics to Midrash*, pp. 75–110. On Balaam and the *erev rav*, see ibid., pp. 168–170.
25. Viṭal, *Sha'ar ha-Pesuqim*, p. 204.

26. Ḥayyim Viṭal, *Liqquṭei Torah* (Jerusalem: Yeshivat Qol Yehudah, 1995), p. 224.
27. Ibid.
28. Viṭal, *Shaʿar ha-Pesuqim*, p. 265.
29. Wolfson, *Venturing Beyond*, pp. 17–128.
30. Ibid., pp. 129–185. See *n*12, this chapter.
31. Long after this chapter was completed I came across the following anecdotal comment by Slavoj Žižek, *Disparities* (London: Bloomsbury, 2016), p. 238: "When I asked a Heideggerian Jewish friend of mine how Heidegger could remain a key reference for him in view of his anti-Semitism and Nazi sympathies, he mentioned an old Jewish wisdom according to which there are some deep, traumatic insights that can only be formulated by a diabolical person." No source is given for this wisdom and I am not familiar with any dictum that articulates matters in precisely this fashion. However, the argument I have offered in this chapter has affinity with the sentiment expressed in this remark.
32. Martin Heidegger, *Ponderings VII–XI: Black Notebooks 1938–1939*, trans. Richard Rojcewicz (Bloomington: Indiana University Press, 2017), p. 53; *Überlegungen VII–XI (Schwarze Hefte 1938/39)* [GA 95] (Frankfurt: Vittorio Klostermann, 2014), p. 70.
33. Martin Heidegger, *Basic Writings*, rev. ed., ed. David Farrell Krell (London: Harper Perennial, 2008), pp. 312–313; *Vorträge und Aufsätze* [GA 7] (Frankfurt: Vittorio Klostermann, 2000), pp. 8–9.
34. Heidegger, *Basic Writings*, p. 337; *Vorträge und Aufsätze*, p. 33. My thinking here has been influenced by the remarks of Aurélien Barrau in Jean-Luc Nancy and Aurélien Barrau, *What's These Worlds Coming To?* trans. Travis Holloway and Flor Méchain (New York: Fordham University Press, 2015), pp. 72–73.
35. Heidegger, *Basic Writings*, p. 333; *Vorträge und Aufsätze*, p. 29. The English version is from Friedrich Hölderlin, *Poems and Fragments*, trans. Michael Hamburger (Ann Arbor: University of Michigan Press, 1966), pp. 462–463.
36. Heidegger, *Basic Writings*, pp. 318–319; *Vorträge und Aufsätze*, pp. 13–14.
37. Heidegger, *Basic Writings*, p. 322; *Vorträge und Aufsätze*, p. 17.
38. Heidegger, *Basic Writings*, p. 325; *Vorträge und Aufsätze*, p. 21.
39. Heidegger, *Basic Writings*, p. 326; *Vorträge und Aufsätze*, pp. 21–22.
40. Heidegger, *Basic Writings*, pp. 327, 340; *Vorträge und Aufsätze*, pp. 23, 36.
41. Heidegger, *Basic Writings*, p. 330; *Vorträge und Aufsätze*, p. 26.
42. Theodor W. Adorno, *Prisms*, trans. Samuel and Shierry Weber (Cambridge: MIT Press, 1983), p. 34.
43. Theodor W. Adorno, *Negative Dialectics*, trans. E. B. Ashton (New York: Seabury, 1973), pp. 362–363.
44. The expression *metapolitics* is used by Peter Trawny, *Heidegger and the Myth of a Jewish World Conspiracy*, trans. Andrew J. Mitchell (Chicago: University of Chicago Press, 2015), p. 112*n*12. See also the reference to Heinz cited in ch. 1*n*174.
45. Heidegger, *Basic Writings*, p. 323; *Vorträge und Aufsätze*, p. 18.
46. Heidegger, *Basic Writings*, p. 324; *Vorträge und Aufsätze*, p. 19.
47. Heidegger, *Basic Writings*, p. 326; *Vorträge und Aufsätze*, p. 22.
48. Heidegger, *Basic Writings*, p. 328; *Vorträge und Aufsätze*, p. 24.
49. Heidegger, *Basic Writings*, p. 329; *Vorträge und Aufsätze*, p. 25.
50. Martin Heidegger, *Discourse on Thinking*, trans. John M. Anderson and E. Hans Freund (New York: Harper and Row, 1966), p. 54; *Gelassenheit* (Stuttgart: Neske,

1959), p. 25. See Gregory Tropea, *Religion, Ideology, and Heidegger's Concept of Falling* (Atlanta: Scholars Press, 1987), pp. 95–113, esp. 106–110.
51. Heidegger, *Discourse on Thinking*, p. 55; *Gelassenheit*, p. 26. See Richard Rojcewicz, *The Gods and Technology: A Reading of Heidegger* (Albany: State University of New York Press, 2006), pp. 174–178, 218–226.
52. Heidegger, *Contributions to Philosophy (Of the Event)*, trans. Richard Rojcewicz and Daniela Vallega-Neu (Bloomington: Indiana University Press, 2012), § 51, p. 87; *Beiträge zur Philosophie (Vom Ereignis)* [GA 65] (Frankfurt: Vittorio Klostermann, 1989), p. 109.
53. Heidegger, *Basic Writings*, pp. 330–331 (emphasis in original); *Vorträge und Aufsätze*, p. 26.
54. Heidegger, *Basic Writings*, p. 337; *Vorträge und Aufsätze*, p. 33.
55. Heidegger, *Basic Writings*, pp. 332–333; *Vorträge und Aufsätze*, p. 28.
56. Heidegger, *Basic Writings*, p. 335; *Vorträge und Aufsätze*, p. 31.
57. Heidegger, *Basic Writings*, p. 339; *Vorträge und Aufsätze*, p. 34.
58. Heidegger, *Basic Writings*, p. 338; *Vorträge und Aufsätze*, p. 34.
59. Wolfson, *Luminal Darkness*, pp. 22–23n45, 34–43.
60. Heidegger, *Ponderings VII–XI*, p. 6 (emphasis in original); *Überlegungen VII–XI*, p. 7. I have modified the translation of Un-*wesen* from "*distorted* essence" to "nonessence."
61. Martin Heidegger, *Anmerkungen I–V (Schwarze Hefte 1942–1948)* [GA 97] (Frankfurt: Vittorio Klostermann, 2015), p. 159. I have availed myself of the translation in David F. Krell, "Troubled Brows: Heidegger's *Black Notebooks*, 1942–1948," *Research in Phenomenology* 46 (2016): 319.
62. Heidegger, *Anmerkungen I–V*, p. 159.
63. Ibid.
64. Ibid., p. 284.
65. Ibid., p. 290.
66. The phrase "wild blindness" (*wilde Blindheit*) is used by Martin Heidegger, *Ponderings II–VI: Black Notebooks 1931–1938*, trans. Richard Rojcewicz (Bloomington: Indiana University Press, 2016), p. 50 (*Überlegungen II–VI (Schwarze Hefte 1931–1938)* [GA 94] (Frankfurt: Vittorio Klostermann, 2014), p. 66), together with "flight into faith" (*Flucht in den Glauben*) as possible responses to the break with philosophizing. The blindness is further glossed as "rationalizing and technologizing" (*Rationalisierung und Technisierung*). See Trawny, *Heidegger and the Myth*, pp. 10–11.

AFTERWORD

1. Samuel IJsseling, "Heidegger and Politics," in *Ethics and Danger: Essays on Heidegger and Continental Thought*, ed. Arleen B. Dallery and Charles E. Scott, with P. Holley Roberts (Albany: State University of New York Press, 1992), pp. 4–5.
2. Jacques Derrida, Hans-Georg Gadamer, and Philippe Lacoue-Labarthe, *Heidegger, Philosophy, and Politics: The Heidelberg Conference*, ed. Mireille Calle-Gruber, trans. Jeff Fort (New York: Fordham University Press, 2016), p. 17.
3. It is worth recalling the judicious and prescient assessment of Martin Heidegger, *The Essence of Truth: On Plato's Cave Allegory and Theaetetus*, trans. Ted Sadler

(New York: Continuum, 2002), pp. 61–62 (*Vom Wesen der Wahrheit: Zu Platons Höhlengleichnis und Theätet* [GA 34] [Frankfurt: Vittorio Klostermann, 1988], pp. 84–85):

> But let us leave this question of whether or not philosophers exist today. The matter cannot in any case be decided by discussions in magazines and newspapers or on radio; it is quite outside any decision in the public realm.... Today, the poisoning would consist in the philosopher being pushed into the circle of those who are interesting and about whom one writes and gossips, those in whom, within a few years, certainly no one will any longer be interested. For one can interest oneself only in something new, and only as long as others do so too.

4. Charles H. Kahn, *The Art and Thought of Heraclitus: An Edition of the Fragments with Translation and Commentary* (Cambridge: Cambridge University Press, 1979), p. 195.
5. Friedrich Nietzsche, *The Pre-Platonic Philosophers*, ed. and trans. Greg Whitlock (Urbana: University of Illinois Press, 2001), p. 66.
6. See the discussion of harmony as "struggling-apart" in Martin Heidegger and Eugene Fink, *Heraclitus Seminar, 1966/67*, trans. Charles H. Seibert (University: University of Alabama Press, 1979), pp. 158–159.
7. Derrida, Gadamer, and Lacoue-Labarthe, *Heidegger, Philosophy, and Politics*, pp. 37–38.
8. Jacques Derrida, *Specters of Marx: The State of the Debt, the Work of Mourning, and the New International*, trans. Peggy Kamuf (New York: Routledge, 1994), pp. 172–173 (emphasis in original).

BIBLIOGRAPHY

Abromeit, John. "Herbert Marcuse's Critical Encounter with Martin Heidegger, 1927–33." In *Herbert Marcuse: A Critical Reader*, ed. John Abromeit and W. Mark Cobb, 131–151. New York: Routledge, 2004.
Adorno, Theodor W. *The Jargon of Authenticity*. Trans. Knut Tarnowski and Frederic Will. Evanston: Northwestern University Press, 1973.
——. *Negative Dialectics*. Trans. E. B. Ashton. New York: Seabury, 1973.
——. *Notes to Literature*, vol. 1. Ed. Rolf Tiedemann, trans. Shierry Weber Nicholsen. New York: Columbia University Press, 1991.
——. *Prisms*. Trans. Samuel and Shierry Weber. Cambridge: MIT Press, 1983.
Ænishanslin, Jean-François. "La logique, la pensée, le silence. Un style en transition." In *Heideggers* Beiträge zur Philosophie: *Internationales Kolloquium vom 20.–22. Mai 2004 an der Universität Lausanne (Schweiz)*, ed. Emmanuel Mejía and Ingeborg Schüßler, 359–366. Frankfurt: Vittorio Klostermann, 2009.
Afaki, Abdul Rahinm. "The Cave, the Lifeworld and the Tradition: The Transcendence-Immanence Contrast Perspective." *Analecta Husserliana* 117 (2014): 111–134.
Agamben, Giorgio. *The Fire and the Tale*. Trans. Lorenzo Chiesa. Stanford: Stanford University Press, 2017.
——. *The Time That Remains: A Commentary on the Letter to the Romans*. Stanford: Stanford University Press, 2005.
Alisch, Rainer. "Heidegger's 'Silence' About the Holocaust: An Attempt at a Reconstruction." In *Martin Heidegger and the Holocaust*, ed. Alan Rosenberg and Alan Milchman, 127–149. Atlantic Highlands, NJ: Humanities Press, 1994.
Allen, William S. *Ellipsis: Of Poetry and the Experience of Language After Heidegger, Hölderlin, and Blanchot*. Albany: State University of New York Press, 2007.
Altmann, Alexander. "Franz Rosenzweig on History." In *The Philosophy of Franz Rosenzweig*, ed. Paul Mendes-Flohr, 124–137. Hanover, NH: University Press of New England, 1988.

BIBLIOGRAPHY

Anderson, John M. "Truth, Process, and Creature in Heidegger's Thought." In *Heidegger and the Quest for Truth*, ed. with an introduction by Manfred S. Frings, 28–61. Chicago: Quadrangle, 1968.

Arendt, Hannah. *Essays in Understanding, 1930–1954*. Ed. Jerome Kohn. New York: Harcourt Brace, 1994.

———. *The Human Condition*, 2d ed. Introduction by Margaret Canovan. Chicago: University of Chicago Press, 1996.

———. *The Life of Mind*, vol. 2: *Willing*. New York: Harcourt Brace Jovanovich, 1978.

———. "Martin Heidegger at Eighty." In *Heidegger and Modern Philosophy: Critical Essays*, ed. Michael Murray, 293–303. New Haven: Yale University Press, 1978.

———. "Martin Heidegger ist achtzig Jahre alt." *Merkur* 23 (1969): 893–902.

———. *Menschen in finsteren Zeiten*. Ed. and trans. Ursula Ludz. Munich: Piper, 1989.

———. *Sechs Essays*. Heidelberg: L. Schneider, 1948.

Arendt, Hannah, and Martin Heidegger. *Letters, 1925–1975*. Ed. Ursula Ludz, trans. Andrew Shields. Orlando, FL: Harcourt, 2004.

Aschheim, Steven E. "Introduction: Hannah Arendt in Jerusalem." In *Hannah Arendt in Jerusalem*, ed. Steven E. Aschheim, 1–15. Berkeley: University of California Press, 2001.

Avineri, Shlomo. "The Fossil and the Phoenix: Hegel and Krochmal on the Jewish Volksgeist." In *History and System: Hegel's Philosophy of History*, ed. Robert L. Perkins, 47–63. Albany: State University of New York Press, 1984.

Babich, Babette E. "Heidegger's Jews: Inclusion/Exclusion and Heidegger's Anti-Semitism." *Journal of the British Society for Phenomenology* 47 (2016): 133–156.

———. "Heidegger's Philosophy of Science and the Critique of Calculation: Reflective Questioning, *Gelassenheit*, and Life." In *Heidegger on Science*, ed. Trish Glazebrook, 159–192. Albany: State University of New York Press, 2012.

———. *Words in Blood, Like Flowers: Philosophy and Poetry, Music and Eros in Hölderlin, Nietzsche, and Heidegger*. Albany: State University of New York Press, 2006.

Badiou, Alain. *Philosophy and the Event*. Trans. Louise Burchill. Cambridge: Polity, 2014.

———. *Saint Paul: The Foundation of Universalism*. Trans. Ray Brassier. Stanford: Stanford University Press, 2003.

———. *Theory of the Subject*. Trans. and with an introduction by Bruno Bosteels. London: Continuum, 2009.

Badiou, Alain, and Barbara Cassin. *Heidegger: His Life and His Philosophy*. Trans. Susan Spitzer, introduction by Kenneth Reinhard. New York: Columbia University Press, 2016.

Bambach, Charles. "Heidegger, Technology, and the Homeland." *Germanic Review: Literature, Culture, Theory* 78 (2003): 267–282.

———. *Heidegger's Roots: Nietzsche, National Socialism, and the Greeks*. Ithaca: Cornell University Press, 2003.

Barash, Jeffrey Andrew. "In Heidegger's Shadow: Ernst Cassirer, Emmanuel Levinas, and the Question of the Political. In *Against the Grain: Jewish Intellectuals in Hard Times*, ed. Ezra Mendelsohn, Stefani Hoffman, and Richard I. Cohen, 93–103. New York: Berghahn, 2014.

———. *Martin Heidegger and the Problem of Historical Meaning*. New York: Fordham University Press, 2003.

BIBLIOGRAPHY

Baskin, Judith R. *Pharaoh's Counsellors: Job, Jethro, and Balaam in Rabbinic and Patristic Tradition*. Chico, CA: Scholars Press, 1983.
Batnitzky, Leora. "Franz Rosenzweig on Translation and Exile." *Jewish Studies Quarterly* 14 (2007): 131–143.
——. *Idolatry and Representation: The Philosophy of Franz Rosenzweig Reconsidered*. Princeton: Princeton University Press, 2000.
——. "Rosenzweig's Aesthetic Theory and Jewish *Unheimlichkeit*." *New German Critique* 77 (1999): 87–122.
——. "Translation as Transcendence: A Glimpse Into the Workshop of the Buber-Rosenzweig Bible Translation." *New German Critique* 70 (1997): 87–116.
Baudrillard, Jean. *Screened Out*. Trans. Chris Turner. London: Verso, 2002.
Benjamin, Mara. "Building a Zion in German(y): Franz Rosenzweig on Yehudah Halevi." *Jewish Social Studies: History, Culture, Society* 13 (2007): 127–154.
Benjamin, Walter. *The Origin of German Tragic Drama*. Introduction by George Steiner. London: Verso, 1998.
Bennington, Geoffrey. *Scatter 1: The Politics of Politics in Foucault, Heidegger, and Derrida*. New York: Fordham University Press, 2016.
Benz, Ernst. *The Mystical Sources of German Romantic Philosophy*. Trans. Blair R. Reynolds and Eunice M. Paul. Allison Park, PA: Pickwick, 1983.
——. *Schellings theologische Geistesahnen*. Wiesbaden: F. Steiner, 1955.
Bergo, Bettina. "'Sterben Sie?' The Problem of Dasein and 'Animals'... of Various Kinds." In *Heidegger's Black Notebooks: Responses to Anti-Semitism*, ed. Andrew J. Mitchell and Peter Trawny, 52–73. New York: Columbia University Press, 2017.
Berman, Nathaniel. "'Improper Twins': The Ambivalent 'Other Side' in the Zohar and Kabbalistic Tradition." Ph.D. dissertation, University College, London, 2014.
Bernasconi, Robert. "Heidegger's Alleged Challenge to the Nazi Concepts of Race." In *Appropriating Heidegger*, ed. James E. Faulconer and Mark A. Wrathall, 50–67. Cambridge: Cambridge University Press, 2000.
——. *The Question of Language in Heidegger's History of Being*. Atlantic Highlands, NJ: Humanities Press, 1985.
Bernstein, Richard J. *The New Constellation: The Ethical-Political Horizons of Modernity/Postmodernity*. Cambridge: MIT Press, 1991.
Biale, David. *Gershom Scholem: Kabbalah and Counter-History*. Cambridge: Harvard University Press, 1979.
——. "Scholem und der moderne Nationalismus." In *Gershom Scholem: Zwischen den Disziplinen*, ed. Peter Schäfer and Gary Smith, 257–274. Frankfurt: Suhrkamp, 1995.
Biemel, Walter. *Martin Heidegger: An Illustrated Study*. London: Routledge and Paul, 1977.
Bindeman, Steven L. *Heidegger and Wittgenstein: The Poetics of Silence*. Lanham, MD: University Press of America, 1981.
Birmingham, Peg. "Heidegger and Arendt: The Birth of Political Action and Speech." In *Heidegger and Practical Philosophy*, ed. François Raffoul and David Pettigrew, 191–202. Albany: State University of New York Press, 2002.
Biskowski, Lawrence J. "Politics Versus Aesthetics: Arendt's Critiques of Nietzsche and Heidegger." *Review of Politics* 57 (1995): 59–89.

Blair, Ann. "The *Problemata* as a Natural Philosophical Genre." In *Natural Particulars: Nature and the Disciplines in Renaissance Europe*, ed. Anthony Grafton and Nancy Siraisi, 171–204. Cambridge: MIT Press, 1999.

Blanchot, Maurice. *The Infinite Conversation*. Trans. and with a foreword by Susan Hansom. Minneapolis: University of Minnesota Press, 1993.

———. *The Space of Literature*. Trans. Ann Smock. Lincoln: University of Nebraska Press, 1982.

———. "Thinking the Apocalypse: A Letter from Maurice Blanchot to Catherine David." Trans. Paula Wissing, *Critical Inquiry* 15 (1989): 475–480.

Blickle, Peter. *Heimat: A Critical Theory of the German Idea of Homeland*. Rochester, NY: Camden House, 2002.

Blok, Vincent. "Massive Voluntarism or Heidegger's Confrontation with the Will." *Studia Phaenomenologica* 13 (2013): 449–465.

Blond, Louis P. "Franz Rosenzweig: Homelessness in Time." *New German Critique* 37 (2010): 27–58.

———. *Heidegger and Nietzsche: Overcoming Metaphysics*. London: Continuum, 2010.

Bodnar, István. "The *Problemata physica*: An Introduction." In *The Aristotelian* Problemata Physica: *Philosophical and Scientific Investigations*, ed. Robert Mayhew, 1–9. Leiden: Brill, 2015.

Boehme, Jacob. *Six Theosophic Points and Other Writings*. Introduction by Nicholas Berdyaev. Ann Arbor: University of Michigan Press, 1958.

Bolhuis, Johan J., and Martin Everaert, eds. *Birdsong, Speech, and Language: Exploring the Evolution of Mind and Brain*. Cambridge: MIT Press, 2013.

Boothby, Richard. *Death and Desire: Psychoanalytic Theory in Lacan's Return to Freud*. New York: Routledge, 1991.

Bourdieu, Pierre. *The Political Ontology of Martin Heidegger*. Trans. Peter Collier. Stanford: Stanford University Press, 1991.

Bouretz, Pierre. *Witness for the Future: Philosophy and Messianism*. Trans. Michael Smith. Baltimore: Johns Hopkins University Press, 2010.

Boyarin, Daniel. *A Traveling Homeland: The Babylonian Talmud as Diaspora*. Philadelphia: University of Pennsylvania, 2015.

Braverman, Jay. "Balaam in Rabbinic and Early Christian Traditions." In *Joshua Finkel Festschrift*, ed. Sidney B. Hoenig and Leon D. Stitskin, 41–50. New York: Yeshiva University Press, 1974.

Brencio, Francesca. "'Heidegger, una patata bollente': L'antisemitismo fra critica alla cristianità e *Seinsgeschichtlichkeit*." In *La pietà del pensiero: Heidegger e i Quaderni Neri*, ed. Francesca Brencio, 107–186. Rome: Aguaplano, 2015.

———. "Martin Heidegger and the Thinking of Evil: From the Original Ethics to the Black Notebooks." *Ivs Fvgit: Revista de Estudios Histórico-Jurídicos de la Corona de Aragón* 19 (2016): 87–134.

———. "'The Nocturnal Point of the Contraction': Hegel and Melancholia." In *Melancholia: The Disease of the Soul*, ed. Dariusz Skorzewski and Andrzej Wiercinski, 149–167. Lublin: Wydawnictwo KUL, 2014.

Brito, Emilio. *Heidegger et l'hymne du sacré*. Leuven: Leuven University Press, 1999.

Brogan, Walter. "Listening to the Silence: Reticence and the Call of Conscience in Heidegger's Philosophy." In *Heidegger and Language*, ed. Jeffrey Powell, 32–45. Bloomington: Indiana University Press, 2013.

BIBLIOGRAPHY

Brown, Robert F. *The Later Philosophy of Schelling: The Influence of Boehme on the Works of 1809–1815*. Lewisburg: Bucknell University Press, 1977.
Buber, Martin. *Das Problem des Menschen*. Heidelberg: Lambert Schneider, 1948.
———. *Gottesfinsternis: Betrachtungen zur Beziehung zwischen Religion und Philosophie*. Zurich: Manesse, 1953.
———. *I and Thou*. Trans. with a prologue and notes by Walter Kaufmann. New York: Scribner's, 1970.
———. *Ich und Du*. Heidelberg: Lambert Schneider, 1997.
Buchner, Hartmut. "Fragmentarisches." In *Erinnerung an Martin Heidegger*, ed. Günther Neske, 47–51. Pfullingen: Neske, 1977.
Burrin, Philippe. "Nazi Antisemistism: Animalization and Demonization." In *Demonizing the Other: Antisemitism, Racism, and Xenophobia*, ed. Robert S. Wistrich, 223–235. London: Routledge, 1999.
Bursztein, Ari. "Emil Fackenheim on Heidegger and the Holocaust." *Iyyun: The Jerusalem Philosophical Quarterly* 53 (2004): 325–336.
Butler, Judith. *Parting Ways: Jewishness and the Critique of Zionism*. New York: Columbia University Press, 2012.
Calarco, Matthew. *Zoographies: The Question of the Animal from Heidegger to Derrida*. New York: Columbia University Press, 2008.
Camilleri, Sylvain. *Phénoménologie de la religion et herméneutique théologique dans la pensée du jeune Heidegger: Commentaire analytique des Fondements philosophiques de la mystique médiévale (1916–1919)*. Dordrecht: Springer, 2008.
Capobianco, Richard. *Engaging Heidegger*. Toronto: University of Toronto Press, 2010.
Caporossi, Sonia. "Il *silenzio* di Heidegger e la sua ricezione in Italia: una proposta di lettura." In *La pietà del pensiero: Heidegger e i Quaderni Neri*, ed. Francesca Brencio, 67–105. Rome: Aguaplano, 2015.
Caputo, John D. "People of God, People of Being: The Theological Presuppositions of Heidegger's Path of Thought." In *Appropriating Heidegger*, ed. James E. Faulconer and Mark A. Wrathall, 85–100. Cambridge: Cambridge University Press, 2000.
———. *The Mystical Element in Heidegger's Thought*. Athens: Ohio University Press, 1978.
———. "Toward a Postmodern Theology of the Cross: Augustine, Heidegger, Derrida." In *Postmodern Philosophy and Christian Thought*, ed. Merold Westphal, 202–225. Bloomington: Indiana University Press, 1999.
Casey, Edward S., and J. Melvin Woody. "Hegel, Heidegger, Lacan: The Dialectic of Desire." In *Interpreting Lacan*, ed. Joseph H. Smith and William Kerrigan, 75–112. New Haven: Yale University Press, 1983.
Cassin, Barbara. *Nostalgia: When Are We Ever at Home?* Trans. Pascale-Anne Brault. New York: Fordham University Press, 2016.
Catanu, Paul. *Heidegger's Nietzsche: Being and Becoming*. Montreal: Eighth House, 2010.
Caygill, Howard. *Levinas and the Political*. London: Routledge, 2002.
Celan, Paul. "From 'Microliths.'" Trans. Pierre Joris. *Poetry Magazine* (January 2017). Available at https://www.poetryfoundation.org/poetrymagazine/articles/detail/91659.

——. "Mikrolithen sinds, Steinchen." Die Prosa aus dem Nachlaß: Kritische Ausgabe. Ed. with a commentary by Barbara Wiedemann and Bertrand Badiou. Frankfurt: Suhrkamp, 2005.

——. Selected Poems and Prose of Paul Celan. Trans. John Felstiner. New York: Norton, 2001.

Chrétien, Jean-Louis. The Call and the Response. Trans. Anne A. Davenport. New York: Fordham University Press, 2004.

Cimino, Antonio. "Paul as a Challenge for Contemporary Philosophers: Nietzsche, Heidegger and Agamben." In Rethinking Faith: Heidegger Between Nietzsche and Wittgenstein, ed. Antonio Cimino and Gert-Jan van der Heiden, 179–201. New York: Bloomsbury, 2017.

Clément, Catherine. Syncope: The Philosophy of Rapture. Trans. Sally O'Driscoll and Deirdre M. Mahoney, foreword by Verena Andermatt Conley. Minneapolis: University of Minnesota Press, 1994.

Cohen, Jeremy. Living Letters of the Law: Ideas of the Jew in Medieval Christianity. Berkeley: University of California Press, 1999.

Collins, Jeff. Heidegger and the Nazis. New York: Totem, 2000.

Colony, Tracy. "Given Time: The Question of Futurity in Heidegger's Contributions to Philosophy." Heythrop Journal 50 (2009): 284–292.

Conche, Marcel. Heidegger inconsideré. Treffort: Mégare, 1997.

——. Heidegger résistant. Treffort: Mégare, 1996.

Cooper, Andrew. The Tragedy of Philosophy: Kant's Critique of Judgment and the Project of Aesthetics. Albany: State University of New York Press, 2016.

Coriando, Paola-Ludovica. Der letzte Gott als Anfang: Zur ab-gründigen Zeit-Räumlichkeit des Übergangs in Heideggers "Beiträgen zur Philosophie (Vom Ereignis)." Munich: Wilhelm Fink, 1998.

Corti, C. Agustín. Zeitproblematik bei Martin Heidegger und Augustinus. Würzburg: Königshausen & Neumann, 2006.

Coyne, Ryan. Heidegger's Confessions: The Remains of Saint Augustine in Being and Time and Beyond. Chicago: University of Chicago Press, 2015.

Critchley, Simon. The Faith of the Faithless: Experiments in Political Theology. London: Verso, 2012.

——. "You Are Not Your Own: On the Nature of Faith." In Paul and the Philosophers, ed. Ward Blanton and Hent de Vries, 224–255. New York: Fordham University Press, 2013.

Critchley, Simon, and Reiner Schürmann. On Heidegger's Being and Time. Ed. Steven Levine. London: Routledge, 2008.

Crowe, Benjamin D. "Heidegger and the Apostle Paul." In Paul in the Grip of the Philosophers: The Apostle and Contemporary Continental Philosophy, ed. Peter Frick, 39–56. Minneapolis: Fortress, 2013.

——. Heidegger's Phenomenology of Religion: Realism and Cultural Criticism. Bloomington: Indiana University Press, 2008.

——. Heidegger's Religious Origins: Destruction and Authenticity. Bloomington: Indiana University Press, 2006.

Crowell, Steven. "Reading Heidegger's Black Notebooks." In Reading Heidegger's Black Notebooks, 1931–1941, ed. Ingo Farin and Jeff Malpas, 29–44. Cambridge: MIT Press, 2016.

BIBLIOGRAPHY

Dahlstrom, Daniel O. *Heidegger's Concept of Truth*. Cambridge: Cambridge University Press, 1994.
Dallmayr, Fred. *The Other Heidegger*. Ithaca: Cornell University Press, 1993.
Dastur, Françoise. *Heidegger and the Question of Time*. Trans. François Raffoul and David Pettigrew. Atlantic Highlands, NJ: Humanities Press, 1998.
Davis, Bret W. *Heidegger and the Will: On the Way to Gelassenheit*. Evanston: Northwestern University Press, 2007.
——. "Heidegger on the Way from Onto-Historical Ethnocentrism to East-West Dialogue." *Gatherings: The Heidegger Circle Annual* 6 (2016): 130–156.
De Beistegui, Miguel. *Heidegger and the Political: Dystopias*. London: Routledge, 1998.
——. *The New Heidegger*. London: Continuum, 2005.
——. "The Place of Place in Heidegger's Topology." *International Journal of Philosophical Studies* 19 (2011): 277–283.
——. *Thinking with Heidegger: Displacements*. Bloomington: Indiana University Press, 2003.
——. *Truth and Genesis: Philosophy as Differential Ontology*. Bloomington: Indiana University Press, 2004.
Delahaye, Ezra. "Heidegger on Religious Faith: The Development of Heidegger's Thinking About Faith Between 1920 and 1928." In *Rethinking Faith: Heidegger Between Nietzsche and Wittgenstein*, ed. Antonio Cimino and Gert-Jan van der Heiden, 145–160. New York: Bloomsbury, 2017.
De Leemans, Pieter, and Michèle Goyens. "Introduction." In *Aristotle's* Problemata *in Different Times and Tongues*, ed. Pieter de Leemans and Michèle Goyens, ix–xvi. Leuven: Leuven University Press, 2006.
Delmedigo, Joseph Solomon. *Novelot Ḥokhmah*. Basle, 1631.
Derrida, Jacques. *Acts of Religion*, ed. with an introduction by Gil Anidjar. New York: Routledge, 2002.
——. *Adieu to Emmanuel Levinas*. Trans. Pascale-Anne Brault and Michael Naas. Stanford: Stanford University Press, 1999.
——. *The Animal That Therefore I Am*. Ed. Marie-Louise Mallet, trans. David Wills. New York: Fordham University Press, 2008.
——. "At This Very Moment in This Work Here I Am." Trans. Ruben Berezdivin. In *Re-reading Levinas*, ed. Robert Bernasconi and Simon Critchley, 11–48. Bloomington: Indiana University Press, 1991.
——. *The Beast and the Sovereign*, vol. 2. Ed. Michel Lisse, Marie-Louise Mallet, and Ginette Michaud, trans. Geoffrey Bennington. Chicago: University of Chicago Press, 2011.
——. *De l'esprit: Heidegger et la question*. Paris: Galilée, 1987.
——. *Heidegger: The Question of Being and History*. Ed. Thomas Dutoit, with the assistance of Marguerite Derrida, trans. Geoffrey Bennington. Chicago: University of Chicago Press, 2016.
——. "Heidegger's Silence: Excerpts from a Talk Given on 5 February 1988." In *Martin Heidegger and National Socialism: Questions and Answers*, ed. Günther Neske and Emil Kettering, trans. Lisa Harries, French portions trans. Joachim Neugroschel, introduction by Karsten Harries, 145–148. New York: Paragon House, 1990.
——. "Of an Apocalyptic Tone: Recently Adopted in Philosophy." *Semeia* 23 (1982): 63–97.

———. *Of Spirit: Heidegger and the Question.* Trans. Geoffrey Bennington and Rachel Bowlby. Chicago: University of Chicago Press, 1989.

———. "On Reading Heidegger: An Outline of Remarks to the Essex Colloquium." *Research in Phenomenology* 17 (1987): 171–185.

———. *Points... Interviews, 1974–1994.* Ed. Elisabeth Weber, trans. Peggy Kamuf and others. Stanford: Stanford University Press, 1995.

———. *Psyche: Inventions of the Other,* vol. 2. Ed. Peggy Kamuf and Elizabeth Rottenberg. Stanford: Stanford University Press, 2008.

———. *Specters of Marx: The State of the Debt, the Work of Mourning, and the New International.* Trans. Peggy Kamuf, with an introduction by Bernd Magnus and Stephen Cullenberg. New York: Routledge, 1994.

Derrida, Jacques, Hans-Georg Gadamer, and Philippe Lacoue-Labarthe. *Heidegger, Philosophy, and Politics: The Heidelberg Conference,* ed. Mireille Calle-Gruber, trans. Jeff Fort, preface by Jean-Luc Nancy. New York: Fordham University Press, 2016.

De Towarnicki, Frédéric. *À la rencontre de Heidegger: Souvenirs d'un messager de la Forêt- Noire.* Paris: Gallimard, 1993.

Dhawan, Nikita. *Impossible Speech: On the Politics of Silence and Violence.* Sankt Augustin: Academia, 2007.

Di Blasi, Luca. "Vom nationalmessianischen Enthusiasmus zur antisemitischen Paranoia: Heideggers politisches Denken zwischen 1933 und 1945." In *Heidegger und der Antisemitismus: Positionen im Widerstreit, mit Briefen von Martin und Fritz Heidegger,* ed. Walter Homolka and Arnulf Heidegger, 190–201. Freiburg: Herder, 2016.

Di Cesare, Donatella. "Das Sein und der Jude: Heideggers metaphysischer Antisemitismus." In *Heidegger, die Juden, noch einmal,* ed. Peter Trawny and Andrew J. Mitchell, 55–74. Frankfurt: Vittorio Klostermann, 2015.

———. "Heidegger, das Sein und die Juden." *Information Philosophie,* February 2014, 8–21.

———. *Heidegger e gli ebrei: I "Quaderni neri."* Torino: Bollati Boringhieri, 2014.

———. "Heidegger—'Jews Self-destructed': New Black Notebooks Reveal Philosopher's Shocking Take on Shoah." February 9, 2015. Available at http://www.corriere.it/english/15_febbraio_09/heidegger-jews-self-destructed-47cd3930-b03b-11e4-8615-d0fd07eabd28.shtml.

———. "Heidegger's Metaphysical Anti-Semitism." In *Reading Heidegger's Black Notebooks 1931–1941,* ed. Ingo Farin and Jeff Malpas, 181–194. Cambridge: MIT Press, 2016.

———. "Heideggers metaphysischer Antisemitismus." In *Heidegger und der Antisemitismus: Positionen im Widerstreit, mit Briefen von Martin und Fritz Heidegger,* ed. Walter Homolka and Arnulf Heidegger, 212–219. Freiburg: Herder, 2016.

Dillard, Peter S. *Non-Metaphysical Theology After Heidegger.* New York: Palgrave Macmillan, 2016.

Dobie, Robert. "Meister Eckhart and Heidegger on *Gelassenheit.*" In *Martin Heidegger's Interpretations of Saint Augustine: Sein und Zeit und Ewigkeit,* ed. Frederick Van Fleteren, 351–382. Lewiston, NY: Edwin Mellen, 2005.

Donado, John Carlos. "Heidegger's Letter to Schmitt." Available at http://www.telospress.com/ heideggers-letter-to-schmitt/.

Duff, Alexander S. *Heidegger and Politics: The Ontology of Radical Discontent.* Cambridge: Cambridge University Press, 2015.
Düttmann, Alexander García. "Without Soil: A Figure in Adorno's Thought." In *Language Without Soil: Adorno and Late Philosophical Modernity*, ed. Gerhard Richter, 10–16. New York: Fordham University Press, 2010.
Eckhart, Meister. *The Complete Mystical Works of Meister Eckhart.* Ed. and trans. Maurice O'C. Walshe, revised with a foreword by Bernard McGinn. New York: Herder and Herder, 2009.
———. *Meister Eckhart: Die deutschen und lateinischen Werke*, vol. 1: *Meister Eckharts Predigten.* Ed. and trans. Josef Quint. Stuttgart: W. Kohlhammer, 1958.
Edel, Susanne. *Die individuelle Substanz bei Böhme und Leibniz: Die Kabbala als tertium comparationis für eine rezeptionsgeschichtliche Untersuchung.* Stuttgart: Franz Steiner, 1995.
———. "Kabbala in der Theosophie Jacob Böhmes und in der Metaphysik Leibnizens." In *Religion und Religiosität im Zeitalter des Barock*, ed. Dieter Breuer, 2:845–856. Wiesbaden: Harrassowitz, 1995.
———. "Métaphysique des idées et mystique des lettres: Leibniz, Böhme et la Kabbale prophétique." *Revue de l'Histoire des Religions* 213 (1996): 443–466.
Egginton, William. *The Philosopher's Desire: Psychoanalysis, Interpretation, and Truth.* Stanford: Stanford University Press, 2007.
Eliashiv, Solomon ben Ḥayyim. *Leshem Shevo we-Aḥlamah: Haqdamot u-Sheʻarim.* Jerusalem: Aaron Barzanai, 2006.
———. *Leshem Shevo we-Aḥlamah: Ḥeleq ha-Be'urim.* Jerusalem: Aaron Barzanai, 2011.
———. *Leshem Shevo we-Aḥlamah: Sefer ha-Deʻah.* Jerusalem: Aaron Barzanai, 2005.
———. *Leshem Shevo we-Aḥlamah: Sefer ha-Kelalim.* Jerusalem: Aaron Barzanai, 2010.
Epstein, Simon. "When the Demon Itself Complains of Being Demonized." In *Demonizing the Other: Antisemitism, Racism, and Xenophobia*, ed. Robert S. Wistrich, 236–243. London: Routledge, 1999.
Erlewine, Robert. *Judaism and the West: From Hermann Cohen to Joseph Soloveitchik.* Bloomington: Indiana University Press, 2016.
Escudero, Jesús Adrián. "Heidegger's *Black Notebooks* and the Question of Anti-Semitism." *Gatherings: The Heidegger Circle Annual* 5 (2015): 21–49.
Esposito, Roberto. *Communitas: The Origin and Destiny of Community.* Trans. Timothy Campbell. Stanford: Stanford University Press, 2010.
Ezrahi, Sidra DeKoven. *Booking Passage: Exile and Homecoming in the Modern Jewish Imagination.* Berkeley: University of California Press, 2000.
———. "Our Homeland, the Text . . . Our Text the Homeland: Exile and Homecoming in Modern Jewish Imagination." *Michigan Quarterly Review* 31 (1992): 463–497.
Fackenheim, Emil L. *Encounters Between Judaism and Modern Philosophy: A Preface to Future Jewish Thought.* New York: Schocken, 1980.
———. *To Mend the World: Foundations of Post-Holocaust Jewish Thought.* New York: Schocken, 1989.
Fagenblat, Michael. "'Heidegger' and the Jews." In *Reading Heidegger's Black Notebooks, 1931–1941*, ed. Ingo Farin and Jeff Malpas, 145–168. Cambridge: MIT Press, 2016.
———. "The Thing That Scares Me Most: Heidegger's Anti-Semitism and the Return to Zion." *Journal for Cultural and Religious Theory* 14 (2014): 8–24.

Farber, Marvin. "Heidegger on the Essence of Truth." *Philosophy and Phenomenological Research* 18 (1958): 523–532.

Farías, Victor. *Heidegger and Nazism*. Ed. Joseph Margolis and Tom Rockmore, trans. Paul Burrel and Dominic Di Bernardi. Philadelphia: Temple University Press, 1989.

Faye, Emmanuel. "Antisémitisme et extermination: Heidegger, l'Œuvre intégrale et les Cahiers noirs." *Cités: Philosophie, Politique, Histoire* 61 (2015): 107–122.

———. *Heidegger: The Introduction of Nazism Into Philosophy in Light of the Unpublished Seminars of 1933–1935*. Trans. Michael B. Smith, foreword by Tom Rockmore. New Haven: Yale University Press, 2011.

———. "Nazi Foundations in Heidegger's Work." *South Central Review* 23 (2006): 55–66.

Feinmann, José Pablo. *Heidegger's Shadow*. Trans. Joshua Price and María Constanza Guzmán. Lubbock: Texas Tech University Press, 2016.

Feldman, Matthew. "Between *Geist* and *Zeitgeist*: Martin Heidegger as Ideologue of 'Metapolitical Fascism.'" *Politics, Religion, and Ideology* 6 (2005): 175–198.

Ferber, Ilit. "Leibniz's Monad: A Study in Melancholy and Harmony." In *Philosophy's Moods: The Affective Grounds of Thinking*, ed. Hagi Kenaan and Ilit Ferber, 53–68. Dordrecht: Springer, 2011.

———. *Philosophy and Melancholy: Benjamin's Early Reflections on Theater and Language*. Stanford: Stanford University Press, 2013.

———. "*Stimmung*: Heidegger and Benjamin." In *Sparks Will Fly: Benjamin and Heidegger*, ed. Andrew Benjamin and Dimitris Vardoulakis, 67–93. Albany: State University of New York Press, 2015.

Fischer, Eugen, and Gerhard Kittel. "Das antike Weltjudentum." *Forschungen zur Judenfrage* 7 (1943): 1–236.

Fischer, Norbert. "Was ist Ewigkeit? Ein Denkanstoß Heideggers und eine Annäherung an die Antwort Augustins." In *Martin Heidegger's Interpretations of Saint Augustine: Sein und Zeit und Ewigkeit*, ed. Frederick Van Fleteren, 155–184. Lewiston, NY: Edwin Mellen, 2005.

Fleischacker, Samuel, ed. *Heidegger's Jewish Followers: Essays on Hannah Arendt, Leo Strauss, Hans Jonas, and Emmanuel Levinas*. Pittsburgh: Duquesne University Press, 2008.

Forster, Michael N. *German Philosophy of Language: From Schlegel to Hegel and Beyond*. Oxford: Oxford University Press, 2011.

Fort, Jeffrey. "Translator's Preface—Both/And: Heidegger's Equivocality." In Jean-Luc Nancy, *The Banality of Heidegger*, trans. Jeff Fort, vii–xvi. New York: Fordham University Press, 2017.

Fowl, Stephen. "A Very Particular Universalism: Badiou and Paul." In *Paul, Philosophy, and the Theopolitical Vision: Critical Engagements with Agamben, Badiou, Žižek, and Others*, ed. Douglas Harink, 119–134. Eugene: Cascade, 2010.

Franke, William. *A Philosophy of the Unsayable*. Notre Dame, IN: University of Notre Dame Press, 2014.

———. *Poetry and Apocalypse: Theological Disclosures of Poetic Language*. Stanford: Stanford University Press, 2009.

Franks, Paul. "Inner Anti-Semitism or Kabbalistic Legacy? German Idealism's Relationship to Judaism." *International Yearbook of German Idealism* 7 (2010): 254–279.

———. "Rabbinic Idealism and Kabbalistic Realism: Jewish Dimensions of Idealism and Idealist Dimensions of Judaism." In *The Impact of Idealism: The Legacy of*

Post-Kantian German Thought, vol. 4: *Religion*, ed. Nicholas Boyle, Liz Disley, and Nicholas Adams, 219–245. Cambridge: Cambridge University Press, 2013.

Freud, Sigmund. "Mourning and Melancholia." In *The Standard Edition of the Complete Psychological Works of Sigmund Freud*, trans. James Strachey, in collaboration with Anna Freud, assisted by Alix Strachey and Alan Tyson, 14:243–258. London: Hogarth, 1957.

Frey, Hans-Jost. *Interruptions*. Trans. with an introduction by Georgia Albert. Albany: State University of New York Press, 1996.

Fried, Gregory. *Heidegger's Polemos: From Being to Politics*. New Haven: Yale University Press, 2000.

——. "The King Is Dead: Heidegger's 'Black Notebooks': Gregory Fried on *Black Notebooks/Schwarze Hefte* Vols. 94–96." *Los Angeles Review of Books*, September 13, 2014. Available at http://lareviewofbooks.org/review/king-dead-heideggers-black-notebooks.

Friedman, Maurice. "Buber, Heschel, and Heidegger: Two Jewish Existentialists Confront a Great German Existentialist." *Journal of Humanistic Psychology* 51 (2011): 129–134.

Friedrich, Hans-Joachim. *Der Ungrund der Freiheit in Denken von Böhme, Schelling und Heidegger*. Stuttgart: Frommann-Holzboog, 2009.

Fritsche, Johannes. "Absence of Soil, Historicity, and Goethe in Heidegger's *Being and Time*: Sheehan on Faye." *Philosophy Today* 60 (2016): 429–445.

——. *Historical Destiny and National Socialism in Heidegger's* Being and Time. Berkeley: University of California Press, 1999.

——. "National Socialism, Anti-Semitism, and Philosophy in Heidegger and Scheler: On Peter Trawny's *Heidegger and the Myth of a Jewish World-Conspiracy*." *Philosophy Today* 60 (2016): 583–608.

Froment-Meurice, Marc. *Solitudes: From Rimbaud to Heidegger*. Trans. Peter Walsh, foreword trans. Douglas Brick. Albany: State University of New York Press, 1995.

Funkenstein, Amos. "An Escape from History: Rosenzweig on the Destiny of Judaism." *History and Memory* 2 (1990): 117–135.

——. *Perceptions of Jewish History*. Berkeley: University of California Press, 1993.

Galli, Barbara. *Franz Rosenzweig and Jehuda Halevi: Translating, Translations, and Translators*. Foreword by Paul Mendes-Flohr. Montreal: McGill-Queen's University Press, 1995.

Galli, Carlo. *Janus's Gaze: Essays on Carl Schmitt*. Ed. with an introduction by Adam Sitze, trans. Amanda Minervini. Durham: Duke University Press, 2015.

Gasché, Rodolphe. "Tuned to Accord: On Heidegger's Concept of Truth." In *Heidegger Toward the Turn: Essays on the Work of the 1930s*, ed. James Risser, 31–49. Albany: State University of New York Press, 1999.

Gignac, Alain. "Agamben's Paul: Thinker of the Messianic." In *Paul in the Grip of the Philosophers: The Apostle and Contemporary Continental Philosophy*, ed. Peter Frick, 165–192. Minneapolis: Fortress, 2013.

Gilman, Sander L. "Cosmopolitan Jews vs. Jewish Nomads: Sources of a Trope in Heidegger's *Black Notebooks*." In *Heidegger's Black Notebooks: Responses to Anti-Semitism*, ed. Andrew J. Mitchell and Peter Trawny, 18–35. New York: Columbia University Press, 2017.

Ginzberg, Louis. *The Legends of the Jews*, 7 vols. Philadelphia: Jewish Publication Society of America, 1968.

Givsan, Hassan. "Seyn und Macht. Seyn als Machenschaft, Seyn, die mythische Gewalt." In *Martin Heideggers "Schwarze Hefte": Eine philosophisch-politische Debatte*, ed. Marion Heinz and Sidonie Kellerer, with the collaboration of Tobias Bender, 78–99. Berlin: Suhrkamp, 2016.

Gonzalez, Francisco J. *Plato and Heidegger: A Question of Dialogue*. University Park: Pennsylvania State University Press, 2009.

Gordon, Haim. *The Heidegger-Buber Controversy: The Status of the I-Thou*. Westport, CT: Greenwood, 2001.

Gordon, Peter E. *Adorno and Existence*. Cambridge: Harvard University Press, 2016.

———. *Continental Divide: Heidegger, Cassirer, Davos*. Cambridge: Harvard University Press, 2010.

———. "Heidegger in Black." *New York Review of Books*, October 9, 2014. Available at http://www.nybooks.com/articles/archives/2014/oct/09/heidegger-in-black/.

———. "Heidegger in Purgatory." In Martin Heidegger, *Nature, History, State, 1933–1934*, ed. and trans. Gregory Fried and Richard Polt, 85–107. London: Bloomsbury, 2013.

———. *Rosenzweig and Heidegger: Between Judaism and German Philosophy*. Berkeley: University of California Press, 2003.

———. "Rosenzweig and Heidegger: Translation, Ontology, and the Anxiety of Affiliation." *New German Critique* 77 (1999): 113–148.

Gosetti-Ferencei, Jennifer Anna. *Heidegger, Hölderlin, and the Subject of Poetic Language: Towards a New Poetics of Dasein*. New York: Fordham University Press, 2004.

Greisch, Jean. *Ontologie et Temporalité: Esquisse d'une interprétation intégrale de Sein und Zeit*. Paris: Presses Universitaires de France, 1994.

Grugan, Arthur Anthony. "Thought and Poetry: Language as Man's Homecoming. A Study of Martin Heidegger's Question of Being and Its Ties to Friedrich Hölderlin's Experience of the Holy." Ph.D. dissertation, Duquesne University, 1972.

Grunenberg, Antonia. *Hannah Arendt and Martin Heidegger: History of a Love*. Trans. Peg Birmingham, Kristina Lebedeva, and Elizabeth von Witzke Birmingham. Bloomington: Indiana University Press, 2017.

———. *Hannah Arendt und Martin Heidegger: Geschichte einer Liebe*. Munich: Piper, 2006.

Habermas, Jürgen. "Dialectical Idealism in Transition to Materialism: Schelling's Idea of a Contraction of God and Its Consequences for the Philosophy of History." In *The New Schelling*, ed. Judith Norman and Alistair Welchman, 43–89. London: Continuum, 2004.

———. "The German Idealism of the Jewish Philosophers (1961)." In *Philosophical-Political Profiles*, trans. Frederick G. Lawrence, 21–43. Cambridge: MIT Press, 1983.

———. "Martin Heidegger: On the Publication of the Lectures of 1935." In *The Heidegger Controversy: A Critical Reader*, ed. Richard Wolin, 186–197. Cambridge: MIT Press, 1993.

———. *The Philosophical Discourse on Modernity: Twelve Lectures*. Trans. Frederick G. Lawrence. Cambridge: MIT Press, 1987.

Hallward, Peter. *Badiou: A Subject to Truth*. Foreword by Slavoj Žižek. Minneapolis: University of Minnesota Press, 2003.

BIBLIOGRAPHY

Hammer, Espen. "Being Bored: Heidegger on Patience and Melancholy." *British Journal for the History of Philosophy* 12 (2004): 277–295.

Hammermeister, Kai. "Heimat in Heidegger and Gadamer." *Philosophy and Literature* 24 (2000): 312–326.

Hansen, Ryan L. "Messianic or Apocalyptic? Engaging Agamben on Paul and Politics." In *Paul, Philosophy, and the Theopolitical Vision: Critical Engagements with Agamben, Badiou, Žižek, and Others*, ed. Douglas Harink, 198–223. Eugene: Cascade, 2010.

Haskell, Ellen D. *Mystical Resistance: Uncovering the Zohar's Conversations with Christianity*. New York: Oxford University Press, 2016.

Havas, Randall. "Nihilism and the Illusion of Nationalism." In *Martin Heidegger: Politics, Art, and Technology*, ed. Karsten Harries and Christoph Jamme, 197–209. New York: Holmes and Meier, 1994.

Hegel, Georg Wilhelm Friedrich. *Early Theological Writings*. Trans. Thomas Malcolm Knox, with an introduction and fragments translated by Richard Kroner. Philadelphia: University of Pennsylvania Press, 1971.

———. *Encyclopedia of the Philosophical Sciences in Basic Outline, part 1: Science of Logic*. Ed. and trans. Klaus Brinkmann and Daniel O. Dahlstrom. Cambridge: Cambridge University Press, 2010.

———. *Enzyklopädie der philosophischen Wissenschaften im Grundrisse (1830)*. Hauptwerke 6. Hamburg: Felix Meiner, 2015.

———. *Lectures on the History of Philosophy*, 3 vols. Trans. Elizabeth S. Haldane and Frances H. Simson. London: Routledge and Kegan Paul, 1968.

———. *Lectures on the Philosophy of Religion*, 3 vols. Ed. Peter C. Hodgson, trans. Robert F. Brown, Peter C. Hodgson, and J. McKellar Stewart, with the assistance of J. P. Fitzer and H. S. Harris. Berkeley: University of California Press, 1984–1987.

———. *Lectures on the Philosophy of Spirit, 1827–8*. Trans. with an introduction by Robert R. Williams. Oxford: Oxford University Press, 2007.

———. *The Science of Logic*. Ed. and trans. George di Giovanni. Cambridge: Cambridge University Press, 2010.

———. *System of Ethical Life (1802/3) and First Philosophy of Spirit (Part III of the System of Speculative Philosophy 1803/4)*. Ed. and trans. Henry S. Harris and Thomas M. Knox. Albany: State University of New York Press, 1979.

———. *Wissenschaft der Logik*. Hauptwerke 3. Hamburg: Felix Meiner, 2015.

Heidegger, Martin. *Anmerkungen I–V (Schwarze Hefte 1942–1948)* [GA 97]. Frankfurt: Vittorio Klostermann, 2015.

———. *Aus der Erfahrung des Denkens 1910–1976* [GA 13]. Frankfurt: Vittorio Klostermann, 2002.

———. *The Basic Problems of Phenomenology*. Trans. with an introduction and lexicon by Albert Hofstadter. Bloomington: Indiana University Press, 1982.

———. *Basic Questions of Philosophy: Selected "Problems" of "Logic."* Trans. Richard Rojcewicz and André Schuwer. Bloomington: Indiana University Press, 1994.

———. *Basic Writings*, rev. ed. Ed. David Farrell Krell, foreword by Taylor Carman. London: Harper Perennial, 2008.

———. *The Beginning of Western Philosophy: Interpretation of Anaximander and Parmenides*. Trans. Richard Rojcewicz. Bloomington: Indiana University Press, 2015.

———. *Being and Time.* Trans. Joan Stambaugh, revised with a foreword by Dennis J. Schmidt. Albany: State University of New York Press, 2010.
———. *Being and Truth.* Trans. Gregory Fried and Richard Polt. Bloomington: Indiana University Press, 2010.
———. *Beiträge zur Philosophie (Vom Ereignis)* [GA 65]. Frankfurt: Vittorio Klostermann, 1989.
———. *Besinnung* [GA 66]. Frankfurt: Vittorio Klostermann, 1997.
———. *Bremen and Freiburg Lectures: Insight Into That Which Is and Basic Principles of Thinking.* Trans. Andrew J. Mitchell. Bloomington: Indiana University Press, 2012.
———. *Bremer und Freiburger Vorträge* [GA 79]. Frankfurt: Vittorio Klostermann, 1994.
———. *The Concept of Time.* Trans. Ingo Farin with Alex Skinner. London: Continuum, 2011.
———. *The Concept of Time.* Trans. William McNeill. Oxford: Blackwell, 1992.
———. *Contributions to Philosophy (Of the Event).* Trans. Richard Rojcewicz and Daniela Vallega-Neu. Bloomington: Indiana University Press, 2012.
———. *Country Path Conversations.* Trans. Bret W. Davis. Bloomington: Indiana University Press, 2010.
———. "Critical Comments on Karl Jaspers's *Psychology of Worldviews.*" In *Becoming Heidegger: On the Trail of His Early Occasional Writings, 1910–1927*, ed. Theodore Kisiel and Thomas Sheehan, 110–149. Evanston: Northwestern University Press, 2007.
———. *Der Anfang der Abendländischen Philosophie: Auslegung des Anaximander und Parmenides* [GA 35]. Frankfurt: Vittorio Klostermann, 2012.
———. *Der Satz vom Grund* [GA 10]. Frankfurt: Vittorio Klostermann, 1997.
———. *Die Geschichte des Seyns* [GA 69]. Frankfurt: Vittorio Klostermann, 1998.
———. *Die Grundbegriffe der Metaphysik: Welt—Endlichkeit—Einsamkeit* [GA 29/30]. Frankfurt: Vittorio Klostermann, 1983.
———. *Die Grundprobleme der Phänomenologie* [GA 24]. Frankfurt: Vittorio Klostermann, 1997.
———. *Discourse on Thinking.* Trans. John M. Anderson and E. Hans Freund, with an introduction by John M. Anderson. New York: Harper and Row, 1966.
———. *Einführung in die Metaphysik* [GA 40]. Frankfurt: Vittorio Klostermann, 1983.
———. *Elucidations of Hölderlin's Poetry.* Trans. Keith Hoeller. Amherst: Humanity, 2000.
———. *The End of Philosophy.* Trans. with an introduction by Joan Stambaugh. New York: Harper and Row, 1973.
———. *Erläuterungen zu Hölderlins Dichtung* [GA 4]. Frankfurt: Vittorio Klostermann, 1996.
———. *The Essence of Human Freedom: An Introduction to Philosophy.* Trans. Ted Sadler. London: Continuum, 2002.
———. *The Essence of Truth: On Plato's Cave Allegory and Theaetetus.* Trans. Ted Sadler. New York: Continuum, 2002.
———. *Feldweg-Gespräche* [GA 77]. Frankfurt: Vittorio Klostermann, 1995.
———. *Four Seminars: Le Thor 1966, 1968, 1969, Zähringen 1973.* Trans. Andrew Mitchell and François Raffoul. Bloomington: Indiana University Press, 2003.

BIBLIOGRAPHY

——. *The Fundamental Concepts of Metaphysics: World, Finitude, Solitude.* Trans. William McNeill and Nicholas Walker. Bloomington: Indiana University Press, 1995.
——. *Gelassenheit.* Stuttgart: Neske, 1959.
——. *Grundfragen der Philosophie: Ausgewählte "Probleme" der "Logik"* [GA 45]. Frankfurt: Vittorio Klostermann, 1992.
——. "Hebel—Friend of the House." Trans. Bruce V. Foltz and Michael Heim. *Contemporary German Philosophy* 3 (1983): 89–101.
——. *The History of Beyng.* Trans. William McNeill and Jeffrey Powell. Bloomington: Indiana University Press, 2015.
——. *Hölderlin's Hymn "The Ister."* Trans. William McNeill and Julia Davis. Bloomington: Indiana University Press, 1996.
——. *Hölderlins Hymne "Der Ister"* [GA 53]. Frankfurt: Vittorio Klostermann, 1993.
——. *Hölderlins Hymnen "Germanien" und "Der Rhein"* [GA 39]. Frankfurt: Vittorio Klostermann, 1999.
——. *Hölderlin's Hymns "Germania" and "The Rhine."* Trans. William McNeill and Julia Ireland. Bloomington: Indiana University Press, 2014.
——. *Holzwege* [GA 5]. Frankfurt: Vittorio Klostermann, 1977.
——. "Homeland." Trans. Thomas F. O'Meara. *Listening* 6 (1971): 231–238.
——. *Identity and Difference.* Trans. and with an introduction by Joan Stambaugh. New York: Harper and Row, 1969.
——. *Interpretation of Nietzsche's Second Untimely Meditation.* Trans. Ulrich Haase and Mark Sinclair. Bloomington: Indiana University Press, 2016.
——. *Introduction to Metaphysics.* Trans. Gregory Fried and Richard Polt. New Haven: Yale University Press, 2000.
——. *Logic as the Question Concerning the Essence of Language.* Trans. Wanda Torres Gregory and Yvonne Unna. Albany: State University of New York Press, 2009.
——. *Logik als die Frage nach dem Wesen der Sprache* [GA 38]. Frankfurt: Vittorio Klostermann, 1998.
——. "Messkirch's Seventh Centennial." Trans. Thomas J. Sheehan. *Listening* 8 (1973): 40–57.
——. *Mindfulness.* Trans. Parvis Emad and Thomas Kalary. London: Continuum, 2006.
——. *Nature, History, State, 1933–1934.* Ed. and trans. Gregory Fried and Richard Polt. London: Bloomsbury, 2013.
——. *Nietzsche: Erster Band* [GA 6.1]. Frankfurt: Vittorio Klostermann, 1996.
——. *Nietzsche, Volume I: The Will to Power as Art.* Trans. with notes and analysis by David Farrell Krell. New York: Harper and Row, 1979.
——. *Off the Beaten Track.* Ed. and trans. Julian Young and Kenneth Haynes. Cambridge: Cambridge University Press, 2002.
——. *On the Essence of Language: The Metaphysics of Language and the Essencing of the Word, Concerning Herder's Treatise* On the Origin of Language. Trans. Wanda Torres Gregory and Yvonne Unna. Albany: State University of New York Press, 2004.
——. *On the Way to Language.* Trans. Peter D. Hertz. New York: Harper and Row, 1971.
——. *Parmenides* [GA 54]. Frankfurt: Vittorio Klostermann, 1992.
——. *Parmenides.* Trans. André Schuwer and Richard Rojcewicz. Bloomington: Indiana University Press, 1992.

——. *Pathmarks*. Ed. William McNeill. Cambridge: Cambridge University Press, 1998.
——. *Phänomenologie des religiösen Lebens* [GA 60]. Frankfurt: Vittorio Klostermann, 1995.
——. *The Phenomenology of Religious Life*. Trans. Matthias Fritsch and Jennifer Anna Gosetti-Ferencei. Bloomington: Indiana University Press, 2004.
——. *The Piety of Thinking: Essays by Martin Heidegger*. Trans. James G. Hart and John C. Maraldo. Bloomington: Indiana University Press, 1977.
——. *Poetry, Language, Thought*. Trans. and introduction by Albert Hofstadter. New York: Harper and Row, 1971.
——. *Ponderings II–VI: Black Notebooks 1931–1938*. Trans. Richard Rojcewicz. Bloomington: Indiana University Press, 2016.
——. *Ponderings VII–XI: Black Notebooks 1938–1939*. Trans. Richard Rojcewicz. Bloomington: Indiana University Press, 2017.
——. *Ponderings XII–XV: Black Notebooks 1939–1941*. Trans. Richard Rojcewicz. Bloomington: Indiana University Press, 2017.
——. *The Principle of Reason*. Trans. Reginald Lilly. Bloomington: Indiana University Press, 1991.
——. *Reden und Andere Zeugnisse eines Lebensweges 1910–1976* [GA 16]. Frankfurt: Vittorio Klostermann, 2000.
——. *Schelling: Vom Wesen der menschlichen Freiheit (1809)* [GA 42]. Frankfurt: Vittorio Klostermann, 1988.
——. *Schelling's Treatise on the Essence of Human Freedom*. Trans. Joan Stambaugh. Athens: Ohio University Press, 1985.
——. *Sein und Wahrheit* [GA 36/37]. Frankfurt: Vittorio Klostermann, 2001.
——. *Sein und Zeit*. Tübingen: Max Niemeyer, 1993.
——. *Sein und Zeit* [GA 2]. Frankfurt: Vittorio Klostermann, 1977.
——. *Die Selbstbehauptung der Deutschen Universität: Rede, gehalten bei der feierlichen Übernahme des Rektorats der Universität Freiburg i. Br. am 27.5.1933; Das Rektorat 1933/34: Tatsachen und Gedanken*. Frankfurt: Vittorio Klostermann, 1983.
——. *Seminare* [GA 15]. Frankfurt: Vittorio Klostermann, 2005.
——. "The Self-Assertion of the German University: Address, Delivered on the Solemn Assumption of the Rectorate of the University Freiburg; The Rectorate 1933/34: Facts and Thoughts." Trans. with an introduction by Karsten Harries. *Review of Metaphysics* 38 (1985): 467–502.
——. "Sprache und Heimat." In *Hebbel Jahrbuch*, ed. Ludwig Koopmann and Erich Trunz, 27–50. Heide: Westholsteinische Verlagsanstalt Boyens, 1960.
——. *Towards the Definition of Philosophy*. Trans. Ted Sadler. London: Athlone, 2000.
——. *Überlegungen II–VI (Schwarze Hefte 1931–1938)* [GA 94]. Frankfurt: Vittorio Klostermann, 2014.
——. *Überlegungen VII–XI (Schwarze Hefte 1938/39)* [GA 95]. Frankfurt: Vittorio Klostermann, 2014.
——. *Überlegungen XII–XV (Schwarze Hefte 1939–1941)* [GA 96]. Frankfurt: Vittorio Klostermann, 2014.
——. *Unterwegs zur Sprache* [GA 12]. Frankfurt: Vittorio Klostermann, 1985.
——. *Vom Wesen der menschlichen Freiheit: Einleitung in die Philosophie* [GA 31]. Frankfurt: Vittorio Klostermann, 1994.

BIBLIOGRAPHY

———. *Vom Wesen der Wahrheit: Zu Platons Höhlengleichnis und Theätet* [GA 34]. Frankfurt: Vittorio Klostermann, 1988.
———. *Vom Wesen des Sprache: Die Metaphysik der Sprache und Die Wesung des Wortes, Zu Herders Abhandlung "Über den Ursprung der Sprache"* [GA 85]. Frankfurt: Vittorio Klostermann, 1999.
———. *Vorträge und Aufsätze* [GA 7]. Frankfurt: Vittorio Klostermann, 2000.
———. *Was Heißt Denken?* [GA 8]. Frankfurt: Vittorio Klostermann, 2002.
———. *Wegmarken* [GA 9]. Frankfurt: Vittorio Klostermann, 1996.
———. *What Is Called Thinking?* Trans. Fred W. Wieck and J. Glenn Gray, with an introduction by J. Glenn Gray. New York: Harper and Row, 1968.
———. "Why Do I Stay in the Provinces?" (1934). In *Heidegger: The Man and the Thinker*, ed. Thomas Sheehan, 27–30. Chicago: Precedent, 1981.
———. *Zollikon Seminars: Protocols—Conversations—Letters*. Ed. Medard Boss, trans. with notes and afterwords by Franz Mayr and Richard Askay. Evanston: Northwestern University Press, 2001.
———. *Zum Ereignis-Denken* [GA 73.1]. Frankfurt: Vittorio Klostermann, 2013.
———. *Zum Ereignis-Denken* [GA 73.2]. Frankfurt: Vittorio Klostermann, 2013.
———. *Zum Wesen des Sprache und zur Frage nach der Kunst* [GA 74]. Frankfurt: Vittorio Klostermann, 2010.
———. *Zur Bestimmung der Philosophie* [GA 56/57]. Frankfurt: Vittorio Klostermann, 1987.
Heidegger, Martin, and Erhart Kästner. *Briefwechsel 1953–1974*. Ed. Heinrich W. Petzet. Frankfurt: Insel, 1986.
Heidegger, Martin, and Eugene Fink. *Heraclitus Seminar, 1966/67*. Trans. Charles H. Seibert. Tuscaloosa: University of Alabama Press, 1979.
The Heidegger-Jaspers Correspondence (1920–1963). Ed. Walter Biemel and Hans Saner, trans. Gary E. Aylesworth. Amherst: Humanity, 2003.
Heinz, Marion. "Seinsgeschichte und Metapolitik." In *Martin Heideggers "Schwarze Hefte": Eine philosophisch-politische Debatte*, ed. Marion Heinz and Sidonie Kellerer, with the collaboration of Tobias Bender, 122–143. Berlin: Suhrkamp, 2016.
Helbig, Daniela. "Denktagebücher? Zur textuellen Form der *Schwarzen Hefte*." In *Martin Heideggers "Schwarze Hefte": Eine philosophisch-politische Debatte*, ed. Marion Heinz and Sidonie Kellerer, with the collaboration of Tobias Bender, 310–325. Berlin: Suhrkamp, 2016.
Helting, Holger. *Heideggers Auslegung von Hölderlins Dichtung des Heiligen: Ein Beitrag zur Grundlagenforschung der Daseinanalyse*. Berlin: Duncker & Humblot, 1999.
Hemming, Paul. *Heidegger and Marx: A Productive Dialogue Over the Language of Humanism*. Evanston: Northwestern University Press, 2013.
Henry, Michel. *Marx: A Philosophy of Human Reality*. Trans. Kathleen McLaughlin. Bloomington: Indiana University Press, 1983.
Herf, Jeffrey. *The Jewish Enemy: Nazi Propaganda During World War II and the Holocaust*. Cambridge: Harvard University Press, 2006.
Hinchman, Lewis P., and Sandra K. Hinchman. "In Heidegger's Shadow: Hannah Arendt's Phenomenological Humanism." *Review of Politics* 46 (1984): 183–211.
Hitler, Adolf. *Mein Kampf: Zwei Bände in einem Band*. Munich: Franz Eher Nachf, 1943.

Hogan, Sinéad. "Hearing Heidegger: Proximities and Readings." In *Heidegger in the Twenty-First Century*, ed. Tziovanis Georgakis and Paul J. Ennis, 101–117. Dordrecht: Springer, 2015.

Hölderlin, Friedrich. *Poems and Fragments*. Trans. Michael Hamburger. Ann Arbor: University of Michigan Press, 1966.

Holub, Robert C. *Nietzsche's Jewish Problem: Between Anti-Semitism and Anti-Judaism*. Princeton: Princeton University Press, 2016.

Homolka, Walter, and Arnulf Heidegger, eds. *Heidegger und der Antisemitismus: Positionen im Widerstreit, mit Briefen von Martin und Fritz Heidegger*. Freiburg: Herder, 2016.

Horowitz, Elliott. *Reckless Rites: Purim and the Legacy of Jewish Violence*. Princeton: Princeton University Press, 2006.

Horwitz, Rivka. "Franz Rosenzweig and Gershom Scholem on Zionism and the Jewish People." *Jewish History* 6 (1992): 99–111.

Hsiao, Paul Shih-yi. "Heidegger and Our Translation of the *Tao Te Ching*." In *Heidegger and Asian Thought*, ed. Graham Parkes, 93–103. Honolulu: University of Hawaii Press, 1987.

Idel, Moshe. *Messianic Mystics*. New Haven: Yale University Press, 1998.

Imamichi, Tomonobu. "Philosophical Intuition of Religious Problems in Our Age." In *Philosophy of Religion*, vol. 10: *Contemporary Philosophy: A New Survey*, ed. Guttorm Fløistad, 17–34. Dordrecht: Springer, 2010.

Inkpin, Andrew. *Disclosing the World: On the Phenomenology of Language*. Cambridge: MIT Press, 2016.

IJsseling, Samuel. "Heidegger and Politics." In *Ethics and Danger: Essays on Heidegger and Continental Thought*, ed. Arleen B. Dallery and Charles E. Scott, with P. Holley Roberts, 3–10. Albany: State University of New York Press, 1992.

Irigaray, Luce. *An Ethics of Sexual Difference*. Trans. Carolyn Burke and Gillian C. Gill. Ithaca: Cornell University Press, 1993.

Janicaud, Dominique. *Heidegger in France*. Trans. François Raffoul and David Pettigrew. Bloomington: Indiana University Press, 2015.

——. *The Shadow of That Thought: Heidegger and the Question of Politics*. Evanston: Northwestern University Press, 1996.

Jaspers, Karl. *Notien zu Martin Heidegger*. Ed. Hans Saner. Munich: Piper, 1978.

——. *Philosophische Autobiographie*. Munich: Piper, 1977.

——. *Tragedy Is Not Enough*. Trans. Harald A. T. Reiche, Harry T. Moore, and Karl W. Deutsch. Boston: Beacon, 1952.

Jay, Martin. "Taking on the Stigma of Inauthenticity: Adorno's Critique of Genuineness." In *Language Without Soil: Adorno and Late Philosophical Modernity*, ed. Gerhard Richter, 17–29. New York: Fordham University Press, 2010.

Johnson, Ryan. "Thinking the Abyss of History: Heidegger's Critique of Hegelian Metaphysics." *Gatherings: The Heidegger Circle Annual* 6 (2016): 51–68.

Jonas, Hans. "Heidegger and Theology." *Review of Metaphysics* 18 (1964): 207–233.

——. *The Phenomenon of Life: Toward a Philosophical Biology*. With a foreword by Lawrence Vogel. Evanston: Northwestern University Press, 2001.

Jung, Carl G. *Civilization in Transition*, 2d ed [CW 10]. Trans. R. F. C. Hull. Princeton: Princeton University Press, 1970.

———. "Zur gegenwärtigen Lage der Psychotherapie." *Zentralblatt für Psychotherapie und ihre Grenzgebiete* 7 (1934): 1–16.
Jung Carl G., and Erich Neumann. *Analytical Psychology in Exile: The Correspondence of C. G. Jung and Erich Neumann.* Ed. Martin Liebscher, trans. Heather McCartney. Princeton: Princeton University Press, 2015.
Kahn, Charles H. *The Art and Thought of Heraclitus: An Edition of the Fragments with Translation and Commentary.* Cambridge: Cambridge University Press, 1979.
Kaufman, Eleanor. "The Saturday of Messianic Time: Agamben and Badiou on the Apostle Paul." In *Paul and the Philosophers*, ed. Ward Blanton and Hent de Vries, 297–309. New York: Fordham University Press, 2013.
Kavka, Martin. "Reading Messianically with Gershom Scholem." In *Rethinking the Messianic Idea in Judaism*, ed. Michael L. Morgan and Steven Weitzman, 404–418. Bloomington: Indiana University Press, 2015.
Kenny, Yoav. "The Geneses of the Animal and the Ends of Man: The Animalistic Origins of Derrida's Writings." *Epoché* 20 (2016): 497–516.
Kierkegaard, Søren. *The Lily of the Field and the Bird of the Air: Three Godly Discourses.* Trans. with an introduction by Bruce H. Kirmmse. Princeton: Princeton University Press, 2016.
Kisiel, Theodore. "Heidegger's Philosophical Geopolitics in the Third Reich." In *A Companion to Heidegger's Introduction to Metaphysics*, ed. Richard Polt and Gregory Fried, 226–249. New Haven: Yale University Press, 2001.
Klassen, Justin D. "Heidegger's Paul and Radical Orthodoxy on the Structure of Christian Hope." In *Paul, Philosophy, and the Theopolitical Vision: Critical Engagements with Agamben, Badiou, Žižek, and Others*, ed. Douglas Harink, 64–89. Eugene: Cascade, 2010.
Knepper, Timothy D. "Ineffability Investigations: What the Later Wittgenstein Has to Offer to the Study of Ineffability." *International Journal for Philosophy of Religion* 65 (2009): 65–76.
Kockelmans, Joseph J. *On Heidegger and Language.* Evanston: Northwestern University Press, 1972.
Koenker, Ernest B. "Grund and Ungrund in Jacob Boehme." *Philosophy Today* 15 (1971): 45–51.
Kotoh, Tetsuaki. "Language and Silence: Self-Inquiry in Heidegger and Zen." In *Heidegger and Asian Thought*, ed. Graham Parkes, 201–211. Honolulu: University of Hawaii Press, 1987.
Kovacs, George. *The Question of God in Heidegger's Phenomenology.* Evanston: Northwestern University Press, 1990.
Krell, David F. *Ecstasy, Catastrophe: Heidegger from Being and Time to the Black Notebooks.* Albany: State University of New York Press, 2015.
———. "Heidegger's *Black Notebooks*, 1931–1941." *Research in Phenomenology* 45 (2015): 127–160.
———. *Intimations of Mortality: Time, Truth, and Finitude in Heidegger's Thinking of Being.* University Park: Pennsylvania State University Press, 1986.
———. "Is There a Heidegger—or, for That Matter, a Lacan—Beyond All Gathering? διαφερόμενον in Heidegger's 'Logos: Heraclitus B 50' as a Possible Response to

Derrida's Disquiet." In *Heidegger and Language*, ed. Jeffrey Powell, 201–223. Bloomington: Indiana University Press, 2013.

———. "Spiriting Heidegger." In *Of Derrida, Heidegger, and Spirit*, ed. David Wood, 11–40. Evanston: Northwestern University Press, 1993.

———. *The Tragic Absolute: German Idealism and the Languishing of God*. Bloomington: Indiana University Press, 2005.

———. "Troubled Brows: Heidegger's *Black Notebooks*, 1942–1948." *Research in Phenomenology* 46 (2016): 309–335.

Kroeker, Travis. "Living 'As If Not': Messianic Becoming or the Practice of Nihilism?" In *Paul, Philosophy, and the Theopolitical Vision: Critical Engagements with Agamben, Badiou, Žižek, and Others*, ed. Douglas Harink, 37–63. Eugene: Cascade, 2010.

Kuenzli, Rudolf E. "The Nazi Appropriation of Nietzsche." *Nietzsche-Studien* 12 (1983): 428–435.

Lacan, Jacques. *Anxiety: The Seminar of Jacques Lacan, Book X*. Ed. Jacques-Alain Miller, trans. Adrian R. Price. Cambridge: Polity, 2014.

———. *Le Séminaire de Jacques Lacan, livre X: L'angoisse*. Ed. Jacques-Alain Miller. Paris: Seuil, 2004.

———. *The Seminar of Jacques Lacan, Book III: The Psychoses, 1955–1956*. Ed. Jacques-Alan Miller, trans. with notes by Russell Grigg. New York: Norton, 1993.

Lacoste, Jean-Yves. "The Phenomenality of Anticipation." In *Phenomenology and Eschatology: Not Yet in the Now*, ed. Neal DeRoo and John Panteleimon Manoussakis, 15–33. Surrey: Ashgate, 2008.

Lacoue-Labarthe, Philippe. *Heidegger and the Politics of Poetry*. Trans. with an introduction by Jeff Fort. Urbana: University of Illinois Press, 2007.

———. *Heidegger, Art, and Politics: The Fiction of the Political*. Trans. Chris Turner. Oxford: Basil Blackwell, 1990.

———. "Poetry's Courage." In *Walter Benjamin and Romanticism*, ed. Beatrice Hanssen and Andrew Benjamin, 163–179. London: Continuum, 2002.

———. *Typography: Mimesis, Philosophy, Politics*. Ed. Christopher Fynsk, with an introduction by Jacques Derrida. Stanford: Stanford University Press, 1998.

Lafont, Cristina. "World-Disclosure and Critique: Did Habermas Succeed in Thinking with Heidegger Against Heidegger?" *Telos* 145 (2008): 161–176.

Lang, Berel. *Heidegger's Silence*. Ithaca: Cornell University Press, 1996.

———. "Heidegger's Silence and the Jewish Question." In *Martin Heidegger and the Holocaust*, ed. Alan Rosenberg and Alan Milchman, 1–18. Atlantic Highlands, NJ: Humanities Press, 1994.

Lapidot, Elad. "Das Fremde im Denken." In *Heidegger und der Antisemitismus: Positionen im Widerstreit, mit Briefen von Martin und Fritz Heidegger*, ed. Walter Homolka and Arnulf Heidegger, 269–276. Freiburg: Herder, 2016.

Law, David R. "Negative Theology in Heidegger's *Beiträge zur Philosophie*." *International Journal for Philosophy of Religion* 48 (2000): 139–156.

Lettow, Susanne. "Heideggers Politik des Rassenbegriffs. Die *Schwarzen Hefte* im Kontext." In *Martin Heideggers "Schwarze Hefte": Eine philosophisch-politische Debatte*, ed. Marion Heinz and Sidonie Kellerer, with the collaboration of Tobias Bender, 234–250. Berlin: Suhrkamp, 2016.

Levinas, Emmanuel. *Beyond the Verse: Talmudic Readings and Lectures*. Trans. Gary D. Mole. London: Athlone, 1994.

———. *Collected Philosophical Papers*. Trans. Alphonso Lingis. Dordrecht: Martinus Nijhoff, 1987.
———. *Difficult Freedom: Essays on Judaism*. Trans. Seán Hand. Baltimore: Johns Hopkins University Press, 1990.
———. *God, Death, and Time*. Trans. Bettina Bergo. Stanford: Stanford University Press, 2000.
———. *Nine Talmudic Readings*. Trans. with an introduction by Annette Aronowicz. Bloomington: Indiana University Press, 1990.
———. *Of God Who Comes to Mind*. Trans. Bettina Bergo. Stanford: Stanford University Press, 1998.
———. *Proper Names*. Trans. Michael B. Smith. Stanford: Stanford University Press, 1996.
———. "Quelques réflexions sur le philosophie de l'Hitlérisme." *Espirit* 2 (1934): 199–208.
———. "Reflections on the Philosophy of Hitlerism." *Critical Inquiry* 17 (1990): 63–71.
———. *Totalité et infini: Essai sur l'extériorité*. The Hague: Martinus Nijhoff, 1980.
———. *Totality and Infinity: An Essay on Exteriority*. Trans. Alphonso Lingis. Dordrecht: Kluwer Academic, 1969.
———. "The Trace of the Other." In *Deconstruction in Context: Literature and Philosophy*, ed. Mark C. Taylor, 345–359. Chicago: University of Chicago Press, 1986.
Liebes, Yehuda. *On Sabbateanism and Its Kabbalah: Collected Essays*. Jerusalem: Bialik Institute, 1995 (Hebrew).
Lippi, Silvia. "Héraclite, Lacan: du logos au significant." *Recherches en Psychanalyse* 9 (2010): 55–62.
Löwith, Karl. "F. Rosenzweig and M. Heidegger on Temporality and Eternity." *Philosophy and Phenomenological Research* 3 (1942): 53–77.
———. "M. Heidegger und F. Rosenzweig. Ein Nachtrag zu 'Sein und Zeit.'" *Zeitschrift für philosophische Forschung* 12 (1958): 161–187.
———. *Martin Heidegger and European Nihilism*. Ed. Richard Wolin. New York: Columbia University Press, 1995.
———. *My Life in Germany Before and After 1933: A Report*. Trans. Elizabeth King. London: Athlone, 1994.
———. *Nature, History, and Existentialism*. Ed. Arnold Levison. Evanston: Northwestern University Press, 1966.
———. "The Political Implications of Heidegger's Existentialism." In *The Heidegger Controversy: A Critical Reader*, ed. Richard Wolin, 167–185. Cambridge: MIT Press, 1993.
Luz, Ehud. "Zionism and Messianism in the Thought of Franz Rosenzweig." *Jerusalem Studies in Jewish Thought* 2 (1983): 472–489 (Hebrew).
Lyotard, Jean-François. *Heidegger and "the jews."* Trans. Andreas Michel and Mark S. Roberts, foreword by David Carroll. Minneapolis: University of Minnesota Press, 1990.
Ma, Lin. *Heidegger on East-West Dialogue: Anticipating the Event*. New York: Routledge, 2008.
Macho, Thomas. "Zu Frage nach dem Preis des Messianismus. Der intellektuelle Bruch zwischen Gershom Scholem und Jacob Taubes als Erinnerung ungelöster Probleme des Messianismus." In *Gershom Scholem: Literatur und Rhetorik*, ed. Stéphane Mosès, 133–152. Cologne: Böhlau, 2000.

BIBLIOGRAPHY

Magid, Shaul. *From Metaphysics to Midrash: Myth, History, and the Interpretation of Scripture in Lurianic Kabbala.* Bloomington: Indiana University Press, 2008.
Malpas, Jeff. *Heidegger and the Thinking of Place: Explorations in the Topology of Being.* Cambridge: MIT Press, 2012.
———. *Heidegger's Topology: Being, Place, World.* Cambridge: MIT Press, 2006.
Marcuse, Herbert. *Heideggerian Marxism.* Ed. Richard Wolin and John Abromeit. Lincoln: University of Nebraska Press, 2005.
Marder, Michael. *Plant-Thinking: A Philosophy of Vegetal Life.* With a foreword by Gianni Vattimo and Santiago Zabala. New York: Columbia University Press, 2013.
Marrati, Paola. *Genesis and Trace: Derrida Reading Husserl and Heidegger.* Stanford: Stanford University Press, 2005.
Marten, Rainer. "Heideggers Geist." In *Die Heidegger Kontroverse*, ed. Jürg Altwegg, 226–229. Frankfurt: Athenaeum, 1988.
Masschelein, Anneleen. *The Unconcept: The Freudian Uncanny in Late-Twentieth-Century Theory.* Albany: State University of New York Press, 2011.
May, Reinhard. *Heidegger's Hidden Sources: East Asian Influences on His Work.* Trans. with a complementary essay by Graham Parkes. London: Routledge, 1996.
McCormick, Peter J. *Heidegger and the Language of the World: An Argumentative Reading of the Later Heidegger's Meditations on Language.* Ottawa: University of Ottawa Press, 1976.
———. "Saying and Showing in Heidegger and Wittgenstein." *Journal of the British Society of Phenomenology* 3 (1972): 27–35.
McCumber, John. "Essence and Subversion in Hegel and Heidegger." In *Writing the Politics of Difference*, ed. Hugh J. Silverman, 13–29. Albany: State University of New York Press, 1991.
McCutcheon, Felicity. *Religion Within the Limits of Language Alone: Wittgenstein on Philosophy and Religion.* Aldershot: Ashgate, 2001.
McNeill, William. *The Time of Life: Heidegger and Ēthos.* Albany: State University of New York Press, 2006.
Meillassoux, Quentin. *After Finitude: An Essay on the Necessity of Contingency.* Trans. Ray Brassier. London: Continuum, 2008.
Meir, Ephraim. "The Meaning of the Abrahamic Adventure in Levinas's Thought." In *Levinas Faces Biblical Figures*, ed. Yael Lin, 19–34. Lanham, MD: Lexington, 2014.
Mendes-Flohr, Paul. "Franz Rosenzweig and the Crisis of Historicism." In *The Philosophy of Franz Rosenzweig*, ed. Paul Mendes-Flohr, 138–161. Hanover, NH: University Press of New England, 1988.
———. "Martin Buber and Martin Heidegger in Dialogue." *Journal of Religion* 94 (2014): 2–25.
Mendieta, Eduardo. "Metaphysical Anti-Semitism and Worldlessness: On World Poorness, World Forming, and World Destroying." In *Heidegger's Black Notebooks: Responses to Anti-Semitism*, ed. Andrew J. Mitchell and Peter Trawny, 36–51. New York: Columbia University Press, 2017.
Merleau-Ponty, Maurice. *Phenomenology of Perception.* Trans. Donald A. Landes. London: Routledge, 2012.
Metcalf, Robert. "Rethinking 'Bodenständigkeit' in the Technological Age." *Research in Phenomenology* 42 (2012): 49–66.
Miller, James. "Heidegger's Guilt." *Salmagundi* 109/110 (1996): 178–243.

Mitchell, Andrew J. "Contamination, Essence, and Decomposition: Heidegger and Derrida." In *French Interpretations of Heidegger: An Exceptional Reception*, ed. David Pettigrew and François Raffoul, 131–150. Albany: State University of New York Press, 2008.

——. *The Fourfold: Reading the Late Heidegger*. Evanston: Northwestern University Press, 2015.

——. "Heidegger's Breakdown: Health and Healing Under the Care of Dr. V. E. von Gebsattel." *Research in Phenomenology* 46 (2016): 70–97.

——. "Heidegger's Later Thinking of Animality: The End of World Poverty." *Gatherings: The Heidegger Circle Annual* 1 (2011): 74–85.

Moran, Dermot. "Dasein as Transcendence in Heidegger and the Critique of Husserl." In *Heidegger in the Twenty-First Century*, ed. Tziovanis Georgakis and Paul J. Ennis, 23–45. Dordrecht: Springer, 2015.

Morgan, Michael L. *Discovering Levinas*. Cambridge: Cambridge University Press, 2007.

——. *Levinas's Ethical Politics*. Bloomington: Indiana University Press, 2016.

Mosès, Stéphane. *The Angel of History: Rosenzweig, Benjamin, Scholem*. Trans. Barbara Harshav. Stanford: Stanford University Press, 2009.

——. "Walter Benjamin and Franz Rosenzweig." *Philosophical Forum* 15 (1983–1984): 188–205.

Mugerauer, Robert. *Heidegger and Homecoming: The Leitmotif in the Later Writings*. Toronto: University of Toronto Press, 2008.

Müller-Doohm, Stefan. *Habermas: A Biography*. Trans. Daniel Steuer. Cambridge: Polity, 2016.

Myers, David N. *Resisting History: Historicism and Its Discontents in German-Jewish Thought*. Princeton: Princeton University Press, 2003.

Nagel, Mechthild. "Thrownness, Playing-in the-World, and the Question of Authenticity." In *Feminist Interpretations of Martin Heidegger*, ed. Nancy J. Holland and Patricia Huntington, 289–306. University Park: Pennsylvania State University Press, 2001.

Nancy, Jean-Luc. *The Banality of Heidegger*. Trans. Jeff Fort. New York: Fordham University Press, 2017.

Nancy, Jean-Luc, and Aurélien Barrau. *What's These Worlds Coming To?* Trans. Travis Holloway and Flor Méchain, foreword by David Pettigrew. New York: Fordham University Press, 2015.

Nietzsche, Friedrich. *The Pre-Platonic Philosophers*. Ed. and trans. with an introduction and commentary by Greg Whitlock. Urbana: University of Illinois Press, 2001.

——. *The Will to Power*. Ed. Walter Kaufmann, trans. Walter Kaufmann and R. J. Hollingdale. New York: Random House, 1967.

North, Paul. *The Yield: Kafka's Atheological Reformation*. Stanford: Stanford University Press, 2015.

Novak, David. "Buber's Critique of Heidegger." *Modern Judaism* 5 (1985): 125–140.

Novalis. *Novalis: Philosophical Writings*. Trans. Margaret Mahony Stoljar. Albany: State University of New York Press, 1997.

Oberst, Joachim L. *Heidegger on Language and Death: The Intrinsic Connection in Human Existence*. London: Continuum, 2009.

O'Brien, Mahon. *Heidegger, History and the Holocaust*. London: Bloomsbury Academic, 2015.

———. "Re-assessing the 'Affair': The Heidegger Controversy Revisited." *Social Science Journal* 47 (2010): 1–20.

O'Donoghue, Brendan. *A Poetics of Homecoming: Heidegger, Homelessness, and the Homecoming Venture*. Newcastle: Cambridge Scholars, 2011.

Olafson, Frederick A. "Being, Truth, and Presence in Heidegger's Thought." *Inquiry* 41 (1998): 45–64.

Oltermann, Philip. "Heidegger's 'Black Notebooks' Reveal Antisemitism at Core of His Philosophy." *Guardian*, March 12, 2014. Available at https://www.the guardian.com/books/2014/mar/13/martin-heidegger-black-notebooks-reveal-nazi-ideology-antisemitism.

O'Mahoney, Paul. "Opposing Political Philosophy and Literature: Strauss's Critique of Heidegger and the Fate of the 'Quarrel Between Philosophy and Poetry.'" *Theoria: A Journal of Social and Political Theory* 58 (2011): 73–96.

O'Regan, Cyril. *Gnostic Apocalypse: Jacob Boehme's Haunted Narrative*. Albany: State University of New York Press, 2002.

Ott, Hugo. "Heidegger's Catholic Origins: The Theological Philosopher." In *Martin Heidegger: Politics, Art, and Technology*, ed. Karsten Harries and Christoph Jamme, 18–33. New York: Holmes and Meier, 1994.

———. *Martin Heidegger: A Political Life*. Trans. Allan Blunden. New York: Basic Books, 1993.

Parkes, Graham. "Thoughts on the Way: *Being and Time* via Lao-Chuang." In *Heidegger and Asian Thought*, ed. Graham Parkes, 105–144. Honolulu: University of Hawaii Press, 1987.

Paslick, Robert H. "The Ontological Context of Gadamer's 'Fusion': Boehme, Heidegger, and Non-Duality." *Man and World* 18 (1985): 405–422.

Peckler, Mark A. "Imagination, Religious Practice, and World Transformations: Sophia, Heidegger, and Jacob Böhme's *The Way to Christ*." Ph.D. dissertation, University of Denver and Iliff School of Theology, 2009.

Penman, Leigh T. I. "Boehme's Intellectual Networks and the Heterodox Milieu of His Theosophy, 1600–1624." In *An Introduction to Jacob Boehme: Four Centuries of Thought and Reception*, ed. Ariel Hessayon and Sarah Apetrei, 57–76. New York: Routledge, 2014.

Pensky, Max. *Melancholy Dialectics: Walter Benjamin and the Play of Mourning*. Amherst: University of Massachusetts Press, 1993.

Petzet, Heinrich W. "Afterthoughts on the Spiegel Interview." In *Martin Heidegger and National Socialism: Questions and Answers*, ed. Günther Neske and Emil Kettering, trans. Lisa Harries, French portions trans. Joachim Neugroschel, introduction by Karsten Harries, 67–75. New York: Paragon House, 1990.

———. *Encounters and Dialogues with Martin Heidegger, 1929–1976*. Trans. Parvis Emad and Kenneth Maly. Chicago: University of Chicago Press, 1993.

Philipse, Herman. "Heidegger and Wittgenstein on External World Skepticism." In *Wittgenstein and Heidegger*, ed. David Egan, Stephen Reynolds, and Aaron James Wendland, 116–132. New York: Routledge, 2013.

Phillips, James. *Heidegger's Volk: Between National Socialism and Poetry*. Stanford: Stanford University Press, 2005.

Pöggeler, Otto. *Martin Heidegger's Path of Thinking*. Trans. Daniel Magurshak and Sigmund Barber. Atlantic Highlands, NJ: Humanities Press, 1987.
———. *The Paths of Heidegger's Life and Thought*. Trans. John Bailiff. Atlantic Highlands, NJ: Humanities Press, 1997.
Polt, Richard. "The Secret Homeland of Speech: Heidegger on Language, 1933-1934." In *Heidegger and Language*, ed. Jeffrey Powell, 63-85. Bloomington: Indiana University Press, 2013.
Rabinbach, Anson. "The Aftermath: Reflections on the Culture and Ideology of National Socialism." In *Weimar Thought: A Contested Legacy*, ed. Peter E. Gordon and John P. McCormick, 394-406. Princeton: Princeton University Press, 2013.
Radloff, Bernhard. *Heidegger and the Question of National Socialism: Disclosure and Gestalt*. Toronto: University of Toronto Press, 2007.
Raffoul, François. "The Ex-appropriation of Responsibility." In *Heidegger in the Twenty-First Century*, ed. Tziovanis Georgakis and Paul J. Ennis, 83-99. Dordrecht: Springer, 2015.
Richardson, S.J., William J. "Psychoanalysis and the Being-Question." In *Interpreting Lacan*, ed. Joseph H. Smith and William Kerrigan, 139-159. New Haven: Yale University Press, 1983.
———. *Through Phenomenology to Thought*, 3d ed. Preface by Martin Heidegger. The Hague: Martinus Nijhoff, 1974.
Richter, Gerhard. "The Debt of Inheritance Revisited: Heidegger's Mortgage, Derrida's Appraisal." *Oxford Literary Review* 37 (2015): 67-91.
Rickey, Christopher. *Revolutionary Saints: Heidegger, National Socialism, and Antinomian Politics*. University Park: Pennsylvania State University Press, 2002.
Riera, Gabriel. "Abyssal Grounds: Lacan and Heidegger on Truth." *Qui Parle* 9 (1996): 61-76.
Rockmore, Tom. *Heidegger and French Philosophy: Humanism, Antihumanism, and Being*. London: Routledge, 1995.
———. "Heidegger and Holocaust Revisionism." In *Martin Heidegger and the Holocaust*, ed. Alan Rosenberg and Alan Milchman, 113-126. Atlantic Highlands, NJ: Humanities Press, 1994.
———. *On Heidegger's Nazism and Philosophy*. Berkeley: University of California Press, 1997.
Rohkrämer, Thomas. "Heidegger, Kulturkritik und völkische Ideologie." In *Martin Heideggers "Schwarze Hefte": Eine philosophisch-politische Debatte*, ed. Marion Heinz and Sidonie Kellerer, with the collaboration of Tobias Bender, 258-274. Berlin: Suhrkamp, 2016.
Rojcewicz, Richard. *The Gods and Technology: A Reading of Heidegger*. Albany: State University of New York Press, 2006.
Romano, Claude. *At the Heart of Reason*. Trans. Michael B. Smith and Claude Romano. Evanston: Northwestern University Press, 2015.
Rorty, Richard. *Contingency, Irony, and Solidarity*. Cambridge: Cambridge University Press, 1989.
———. "Taking Philosophy Seriously." *New Republic* 11 (1988): 31-34.
Rosenzweig, Franz. *Die "Gritli"-Briefe: Briefe an Margrit Rosenstock-Huessy*. Ed. Inken Rühle and Reinhold Mayer, with a preface by Rafael Rosenzweig. Tübingen: Bilam, 2002.

———. *Der Mensch und sein Werk: Gesammelte Schriften II. Der Stern der Erlösung.* The Hague: Martinus Nijhoff, 1976.

———. "Scripture and Luther." In Martin Buber and Franz Rosenzweig, *Scripture and Translation*, trans. Lawrence Rosenwald with Everett Fox, 47–69. Bloomington: Indiana University Press, 1994.

———. *The Star of Redemption.* Trans. Barbara Galli. Madison: University of Wisconsin Press, 2000.

Roth, Michael. *The Poetics of Resistance: Heidegger's Line.* Evanston: Northwestern University Press, 1996.

Roudinesco, Elisabeth. *Freud: In His Time and Ours.* Trans. Catherine Porter. Cambridge: Harvard University Press, 2016.

———. *Jacques Lacan.* Trans. Barbara Bray. New York: Columbia University Press, 1997.

———. *Jacques Lacan & Co.: A History of Psychoanalysis in France, 1925–1985.* Trans. with a foreword by Jeffrey Mehlman. Chicago: University of Chicago Press, 1990.

Rubenstein, Mary-Jane. *Strange Wonder: The Closure of Metaphysics and the Opening of Awe.* New York: Columbia University Press, 2008.

Rusterholz, Sibylle. "Elemente der Kabbala bei Jacob Böhme." In *Mystik und Schriftkommentierung*, ed. Günther Bonheim and Petra Kattner, 15–45. Berlin: Weissensee, 2007.

Sacchi, Mario Enrique. *The Apocalypse of Being: The Esoteric Gnosis of Martin Heidegger.* Trans. Gabriel Xavier Martinez, foreword by Ralph McInerny. South Bend: St. Augustine's Press, 2002.

Sadler, Ted. *Heidegger and Aristotle: The Question of Being.* London: Athlone, 1996.

Sallis, John. "Interrupting Truth." In *Heidegger Toward the Turn: Essays on the Work of the 1930s*, ed. James Risser, 19–30. Albany: State University of New York Press, 1999.

Samuels, Andrew. *The Political Psyche.* London: Routledge, 1993.

Schaefer, Donovan O. *Religious Affects: Animality, Evolution, and Power.* Durham: Duke University Press, 2015.

Schalow, Frank. *Heidegger and the Quest for the Sacred: From Thought to the Sanctuary of Faith.* Dordrecht: Kluwer Academic, 2001.

Schelling, Friedrich Wilhelm Joseph. *The Ages of the World (Fragment) from the Handwritten Remains, Third Version (c. 1815).* Trans. with an introduction by Jason M. Wirth. Albany: State University of New York Press, 2000.

———. *Die Weltalter in den Urfassungen von 1811 und 1813 (Nachlaßband).* Ed. Manfred Schröter. Munich: Beck, 1946.

———. *Philosophical Investigations Into the Essence of Human Freedom.* Trans. and with an introduction by Jeff Love and Johannes Schmidt. Albany: State University of New York Press, 2006.

———. *Philosophie und Religion.* Ed. Alfred Denker and Holger Zaborowski. Munich: Karl Alber, 2008.

———. *Philosophy and Religion (1804).* Trans., annotated, and with an introduction by Klaus Ottmann. Putnam, CT: Spring, 2010.

———. *Sämmtliche Werke 1804*, vol. 6. Ed. Karl Friedrich August Schelling. Stuttgart: Cotta, 1860.

———. *Sämmtliche Werke*, vol. 7. Ed. Karl Friedrich August Schelling. Stuttgart: Cotta, 1860.

BIBLIOGRAPHY

———. *Sämmtliche Werke*, vol. 8. Ed. Karl Friedrich August Schelling. Stuttgart: Cotta, 1861.
Schmidt, Dennis J. *The Ubiquity of the Finite: Hegel, Heidegger, and the Entitlements of Philosophy*. Cambridge: MIT Press, 1988.
Schmidt-Biggemann, Wilhelm. "The Christian Kabbala: Joseph Gikatilla (1247–1305), Johannes Reuchlin (1455–1522), Paulus Ricius (d. 1541), and Jacob Böhme (1575–1624)." In *The Language of Adam, Die Sprache Adams*, ed. Allison Coudert, 81–121. Wiesbaden: Harrassowitz, 1999.
———. "Jakob Bohme und die Kabbala." In *Christliche Kabbala*, ed. Wilhelm Schmidt-Biggemann, 157–181. Ostfildem: Jan Thorbecke, 2003.
———. *Philosophia Perennis: Historical Outlines of Western Spirituality in Ancient, Medieval, and Early Modern Thought*. Dordrecht: Springer, 2004.
Schmitz-Berning, Cornelia. *Vokabular des Nationalsozialismus*. Berlin: Walter de Gruyter, 2007.
Scholem, Gershom. *The Fullness of Time: Poems*. Trans. Richard Sieburth, introduced and annotated by Steven M. Wasserstrom. Jerusalem: Ibis, 2003.
———. *The Messianic Idea and Other Essays on Jewish Spirituality*. New York: Schocken, 1971.
———. "The Name of God and the Linguistic Theory of the Kabbala." *Diogenes* 80 (1972): 164–194.
———. *On the Mystical Shape of the Godhead: Basic Concepts in the Kabbalah*. Ed. Jonathan Chipman, trans. Joachim Neugroschel. New York: Schocken, 1991.
Schrag, Calvin O. "Heidegger on Repetition and Historical Understanding." *Philosophy East and West* 20 (1970): 287–295.
Schulitz, John. *Jakob Böhme und die Kabbalah: Eine vergleichende Werkanalyse*. Frankfurt: Peter Lang, 1993.
Schulte, Christoph. "F. W. J. Schellings Ausleihe von Hand- und Druckschriften." *Zeitschrift für Religion und Geistesgeschichte* 45 (1993): 267–277.
———. "Zimzum bei Schelling." In *Kabbala und Romantik*, ed. Eveline Goodman-Thau, Gert Mattenklott, and Christoph Schulte, 97–118. Tubingen: Max Niemeyer, 1994.
———. *Zimzum: Gott und Weltursprung*. Berlin: Suhrkamp, 2014.
Schulze, Wilhelm August. "Jacob Boehme und die Kabbala." *Judaica* 11 (1955): 12–29.
Schürmann, Reiner. "A Brutal Awakening to the Tragic Condition of Being: On Heidegger's *Beiträge zur Philosophie*," in *Martin Heidegger: Politics, Art, and Technology*, ed. Karsten Harries and Christoph Jamme, 89–105. New York: Holmes and Meier, 1994.
———. *Broken Hegemonies*. Trans. Reginald Lilly. Bloomington: Indiana University Press, 2003.
———. *Meister Eckhart, Mystic and Philosopher: Translations with Commentary*. Bloomington: Indiana University Press, 1978.
Schwan, Alexander. "Heidegger's *Beiträge zur Philosophie* and Politics." In *Martin Heidegger: Politics, Art, and Technology*, ed. Karsten Harries and Christoph Jamme, 71–88. New York: Holmes and Meier, 1994.
Schwartz, Yossef. "Gustav Landauer and Gerhard Scholem: Anarchy and Utopia." In *Gustav Landauer: Anarchist and Jew*, ed. Paul Mendes-Flohr and Anya Mali, in collaboration with Hanna Delf von Wolzogen, 172–190. Berlin: Walter de Gruyter, 2015.

Schwarzschild, Steven. "An Introduction to the Thought of R. Isaac Hutner." *Modern Judaism* 5 (1985): 235–277.

———. *The Pursuit of the Ideal: Jewish Writings of Steven Schwarzschild*. Ed. Menachem Kellner. Albany: State University of New York Press, 1990.

Scult, Allen. *Being Jewish/Reading Heidegger: An Ontological Encounter*. New York: Fordham University Press, 2004.

———. "Forgiving 'La Dette Impensée': Being Jewish and Reading Heidegger." In *French Interpretations of Heidegger: An Exceptional Reception*, ed. David Pettigrew and François Raffoul, 231–244. Albany: State University of New York Press, 2008.

Sefer ha-Zohar. Ed. Reuven Margaliot. 3 vols. Jerusalem: Mosad ha-Rav Kook, 1978.

Segev, Alon. *Thinking and Killing: Philosophical Discourse in the Shadow of the Third Reich*. Berlin: Walter de Gruyter, 2013.

Seidman, Naomi. *Faithful Renderings: Jewish-Christian Difference and the Politics of Translation*. Chicago: University of Chicago Press, 2006.

Shapiro, Gary. "Subversion of System/Systems of Subversion." In *Writing the Politics of Difference*, ed. Hugh J. Silverman, 1–11. Albany: State University of New York Press, 1991.

Shapiro, Susan. "The Uncanny Jew: A Brief History of an Image." *Judaism* 46 (1997): 63–78.

Sheehan, Thomas. "Emmanuel Faye: The Introduction of Fraud Into Philosophy?" *Philosophy Today* 59 (2015): 367–400.

———. "Facticity and *Ereignis*." In *Interpreting Heidegger: Critical Essays*, ed. Daniel O. Dahlstrom, 42–68. Cambridge: Cambridge University Press, 2011.

———. "Heidegger and the Nazis." *New York Review of Books* 35, no. 10 (June 16, 1988): 38–47.

———. "Heidegger's 'Introduction to the Phenomenology of Religion,' 1920–21." In *A Companion to Heidegger's "Being and Time,"* ed. Joseph Kockelmans, 40–62. Washington, DC: University Press of America, 1986.

———. "Introduction: Heidegger, the Project and the Fulfillment." In *Heidegger: The Man and The Thinker*, ed. Thomas Sheehan, vii–xx. Chicago: Precedent, 1981.

———. *Making Sense of Heidegger: A Paradigm Shift*. London: Rowman and Littlefield, 2015.

———. "'Time and Being,' 1925–27." In *Martin Heidegger: Critical Assessments*, vol. 1: *Philosophy*, ed. Christopher Macann, 29–67. Routledge: London, 1992.

Sherratt, Yvonne. *Hitler's Philosophers*. New Haven: Yale University Press, 2013.

Sifre on Deuteronomy. Ed. Louis Finkelstein. New York: Jewish Theological Seminary of America, 1969.

Sikka, Sonia. *Forms of Transcendence: Heidegger and Medieval Mystical Theology*. Albany: State University of New York Press, 1997.

———. "Heidegger and Race." In *Race and Racism in Continental Philosophy*, ed. Robert Bernasconi, with Sybol Cook, 74–97. Bloomington: Indiana University Press, 2003.

Sluga, Hans. *Heidegger's Crisis: Philosophy and Politics in Nazi Germany*. Cambridge: Harvard University Press, 1993.

Smith, Steven B. "Destruktion or Recovery?: Leo Strauss's Critique of Heidegger." *Review of Metaphysics* 51 (1997): 345–377.

Soboczynski, Adam, and Alexander Cammann. "Heidegger and Anti-Semitism Yet Again: The Correspondence Between the Philosopher and His Brother Fritz Heidegger Exposed." *Los Angeles Review of Books*, December 25, 2016. Available at https://lareviewofbooks.org/article/heidegger-anti-semitism-yet-correspondence-philosopher-brother-fritz-heidegger-exposed/.

Sommer, Christian. "'Diktat des Seyns.' Zwölf Anmerkungen zu Heideggers politisch-theologischer Mythologie." In *Heidegger und der Antisemitismus: Positionen im Widerstreit, mit Briefen von Martin und Fritz Heidegger*, ed. Walter Homolka and Arnulf Heidegger, 353–362. Freiburg: Herder, 2016.

———. "Métapolitique de l'université. Le programme platonicien de Heidegger." *Les Études philosophiques* 93 (2010): 255–275.

Stambaugh, Joan. "Heidegger, Taoism, and the Question of Metaphysics." In *Heidegger and Asian Thought*, ed. Graham Parkes, 79–91. Honolulu: University of Hawaii Press, 1987.

———. *The Finitude of Being*. Albany: State University of New York Press, 1992.

Steiner, George. *After Babel: Aspects of Language and Translation*, 3d ed. Oxford: Oxford University Press, 1998.

———. *Grammars of Creation: Originating in the Gifford Lectures for 1990*. New Haven: Yale University Press, 2001.

———. *Lessons of the Masters*. Cambridge: Harvard University Press, 2003.

———. "Our Homeland, the Text." *Salmagundi* 66 (1985): 4–25.

———. *The Poetry of Thought: From Hellenism to Celan*. New York: New Directions, 2011.

Strauss, Leo. *The Rebirth of Classical Political Rationalism: An Introduction to the Thought of Leo Strauss*. Selected and introduced by Thomas L. Pangle. Chicago: University of Chicago Press, 1989.

Tanzer, Mark. "Heidegger on Animality and Anthropocentrism." *Journal of the British Society for Phenomenology* 47 (2016): 18–32.

Taubes, Jacob. *Occidental Eschatology*. Trans. with a preface by David Ratmoko. Stanford: Stanford University Press, 2009.

———. "The Price of Messianism." In *Essential Papers on Messianic Movements and Personalities in Jewish History*, ed. Marc Saperstein, 551–557. New York: New York University Press, 1992.

Taubes, Susan A. "The Gnostic Foundations of Heidegger's Nihilism." *Journal of Religion* 34 (1954): 155–172.

Tengelyi, László. "Transformations in Heidegger's Conception of Truth Between 1927 and 1930." In *Variations on Truth: Approaches in Contemporary Phenomenology*, ed. Pol Vandevelde and Kevon Hermberg, 94–108. London: Continuum, 2011.

Tezuka, Tomio. "Eine Stunde mit Heidegger." In *Japan und Heidegger: Gedenkschrift der Stadt Meßkirch zum hundertsten Geburtstag Martin Heideggers*, ed. Hartmut Buchner, 173–180. Sigmaringen: Thorbecke, 1989.

Thomä, Dieter. "Heidegger und der Nationalsozialismus. In der Dunkelkammer der Seinsgeschichte." In *Heidegger-Handbuch: Leben —Werk—Wirkung*, ed. Dieter Thomä, in collaboration with Florian Grosser, Katrin Meyer, and Hans Bernhard Schmid, rev. ed., 108–133. Stuttgart: J. B. Metzler, 2013.

———. "Wie antisemitisch ist Heidegger? Über die *Schwarzen Hefte* und die gegenwärtige Lage der Heidegger-Kritik." In *Martin Heideggers "Schwarze Hefte": Eine philosophisch-politische Debatte*, ed. Marion Heinz and Sidonie Kellerer, with the collaboration of Tobias Bender, 211–233. Berlin: Suhrkamp, 2016.

Thomson, Iain D. *Heidegger on Ontotheology: Technology and the Politics of Education*. Cambridge: Cambridge University Press, 2005.

Tishby, Isaiah. *The Wisdom of the Zohar: An Anthology of Texts*. Trans. David Goldstein. Oxford: Oxford University Press, 1989.
Trawny, Peter. *Freedom to Fail: Heidegger's Anarchy*. Trans. Ian Alexander Moore and Christopher Turner. Cambridge: Polity, 2015.
———. *Heidegger and the Myth of a Jewish World Conspiracy*. Trans. Andrew J. Mitchell. Chicago: University of Chicago Press, 2015.
———. "Heidegger, 'World Judaism,' and Modernity," *Gatherings: The Heidegger Circle Annual* 5 (2015): 1–20.
———. "The Universal and Annihilation: Heidegger's Being-Historical Anti-Semitism." In *Heidegger's Black Notebooks: Responses to Anti-Semitism*, ed. Andrew J. Mitchell and Peter Trawny, 1–17. New York: Columbia University Press, 2017.
Tropea, Gregory. *Religion, Ideology, and Heidegger's Concept of Falling*. Atlanta: Scholars Press, 1987.
Tugendhat, Ernst. "Heidegger's Idea of Truth." In *The Heidegger Controversy: A Critical Reader*, ed. Richard Wolin, 245–263. Cambridge: MIT Press, 1993.
———. *Der Wahrheitsbegriff bei Husserl und Heidegger*. Berlin: Walter de Gruyter, 1967.
Urbach, Ephraim E. *The World of the Sages: Collected Studies*. Jerusalem: Magnes, 1988 (Hebrew).
Vallega, Alejandro A. *Heidegger and the Issue of Space: Thinking on Exilic Grounds*. University Park: Pennsylvania State University Press, 2003.
Vallega-Neu, Daniela. "Heidegger's Reticence: From *Contributions* to *Das Ereignis* and toward *Gelassenheit*." *Research in Phenomenology* 45 (2015): 1–32.
Van Buren, John. *The Young Heidegger: Rumor of the Hidden King*. Bloomington: Indiana University Press, 1994.
Van der Heiden, Gert-Jan. "The Experience of Contingency and the Attitude to Life: Nietzsche and Heidegger on Paul." In *Rethinking Faith: Heidegger Between Nietzsche and Wittgenstein*, ed. Antonio Cimino and Gert-Jan van der Heiden, 161–177. New York: Bloomsbury, 2017.
Vandevelde, Pol. *Heidegger and the Romantics: The Literary Invention of Meaning*. New York: Routledge, 2012.
———. "Heidegger's Fluid Ontology in the 1930s: The Platonic Connection." In *Variations on Truth: Approaches in Contemporary Phenomenology*, ed. Pol Vandevelde and Kevon Hermberg, 109–126. London: Continuum, 2011.
———. "Translation as a Mode of Poetry: Heidegger's Reformulation of the Romantic Project." In *Phenomenology and Literature: Historical Perspectives and Systematic Accounts*, ed. Pol Vandevelde, 93–113. Würzburg: Königshausen & Neumann, 2010.
Vaughan, William. "Heidegger *silentio*." In *Martin Heidegger and the Holocaust*, ed. Alan Rosenberg and Alan Milchman, 70–101. Atlantic Highlands, NJ: Humanities Press, 1994.
Vattimo, Gianni. *Of Reality: The Purposes of Philosophy*. Trans. Robert T. Valgenti. New York: Columbia University Press, 2016.
Vedder, Ben. *Heidegger's Philosophy of Religion: From God to the Gods*. Pittsburgh: Duquesne University Press, 2007.
Vieillard-Baron, Jean-Louis. "Schelling et Jacob Böhme: Les Recherches de 1809 et la lecture de la *Lettre pastorale*." *Les Études philosophiques* 2 (1999): 223–242.
Vietta, Silvio. *Heideggers Kritik am Nationalsozialismus und an der Technik*. Berlin: Walter de Gruyter, 1989.

Villa, Dana R. "Arendt and Heidegger, Again." In *Heidegger's Jewish Followers: Essays on Hannah Arendt, Leo Strauss, Hans Jonas, and Emmanuel Levinas*, ed. Samuel Fleischacker, 43–82. Pittsburgh: Duquesne University Press, 2008.
——. *Arendt and Heidegger: The Fate of the Political*. Princeton: Princeton University Press, 1996.
Viṭal, Ḥayyim. *Eṣ Ḥayyim*. Jerusalem: Aharon Barzanai, 2004.
——. *Liqquṭei Torah*. Jerusalem: Yeshivat Qol Yehudah, 1995.
——. *Sha'ar ha-Pesuqim*. Jerusalem: Sitrei Ḥayyim, 2013.
Von Wolzogen, Christoph. "Heideggers Schweigen. Zur Rede 'Edmund Husserl zum siebenzigsten Geburtstag.'" In *Heidegger und der Nationalsozialismus, II: Interpretationen*, ed. Alfred Denker and Holger Zaborowski, 382–396. Freiburg: Karl Alber, 2009.
Waite, Geoff. "Heidegger, Schmitt, Strauss: The Hidden Monologue, or, Conserving Esotericism to Justify the High Hand of Violence." *Cultural Critique* 69 (2008): 113–144.
Ward, James F. *Heidegger's Political Thinking*. Amherst: University of Massachusetts Press, 1995.
Warminski, Andrzej. "Monstrous History: Heidegger Reading Hölderlin." In *The Solid Letter: Readings of Friedrich Hölderlin*, ed. Aris Fioretos, 201–214. Stanford: Stanford University Press, 1999.
Warnek, Peter. "Translating *Innigkeit*: The Belonging Together of the Strange." In *Heidegger and the Greeks: Interpretive Essays*, ed. Drew A. Hyland and John Panteleimon Manoussakis, 57–82. Bloomington: Indiana University Press, 2006.
Weeks, Andrew. *Boehme: An Intellectual Biography of the Seventeenth-Century Philosopher and Mystic*. Albany: State University of New York Press, 1991.
——. "Radical Reformation and the Anticipation of Modernism in Jacob Boehme." In *An Introduction to Jacob Boehme: Four Centuries of Thought and Reception*, ed. Ariel Hessayon and Sarah Apetrei, 38–56. New York: Routledge, 2014.
Weissblei, Gil. "The German Martin and the Jewish Mordechai: A Meeting Between Buber and Heidegger, 1957." Available at http://web.nli.org.il/sites/NLI/English/collections/personalsites/Israel-Germany/Division-of-Germany/Pages/Buber-Heidegger.aspx.
Wirth, Jason M. *Schelling's Practice of the Wild: Time, Art, Imagination*. Albany: State University of New York Press, 2015.
Withy, Katherine. *Heidegger on Being Uncanny*. Cambridge: Harvard University Press, 2015.
Wittgenstein, Ludwig. *Tractatus Logico-Philosophicus*. Trans. Charles K. Ogden, introduction by Bertrand Russell. London: Routledge, 1995.
Wolfe, Judith. *Heidegger and Theology*. London: Bloomsbury, 2014.
——. *Heidegger's Eschatology: Theological Horizons in Martin Heidegger's Early Work*. Oxford: Oxford University Press, 2013.
Wolfson, Elliot R. "Achronic Time, Messianic Expectation, and the Secret of the Leap in Habad." In *Habad Hasidism: History, Thought, Image*, ed. Jonatan Meir and Gadi Sagiv, 45–86 (English section). Jerusalem: Zalman Shazar, 2016.
——. *A Dream Interpreted Within a Dream: Oneiropoiesis and the Prism of Imagination*. New York: Zone, 2011.
——. *Alef, Mem, Tau: Kabbalistic Musings on Time, Truth, and Death*. Berkeley: University of California Press, 2006.

——. "Gazing Beneath the Veil: Apocalyptic Envisioning the End." In *Reinterpreting Revelation and Tradition: Jews and Christians in Conversation*, ed. with an introduction by John T. Pawlikowski, O.S.M. and Hayim Goren Perelmuter, 77–103. Franklin, WI: Sheed and Ward, 2000.

——. *Giving Beyond the Gift: Apophasis and Overcoming Theomania*. New York: Fordham University Press, 2014.

——. *Heidegger and Kabbalah: Hidden Gnosis and the Path of Poiēsis*. Bloomington: Indiana University Press, 2019.

——. *Language, Eros, Being: Kabbalistic Hermeneutics and Poetic Imagination*. New York: Fordham University Press, 2005.

——. "Left Contained in the Right: A Study in Zoharic Hermeneutics." *Association for Jewish Studies Review* 11 (1986): 27–52.

——. "Light Through Darkness: The Ideal of Human Perfection in the Zohar." *Harvard Theological Review* 81 (1988): 73–95.

——. *Luminal Darkness: Imaginal Gleanings from Zoharic Literature*. Oxford: Oneworld, 2007.

——. "Nihilating Nonground and the Temporal Sway of Becoming: Kabbalistically Envisioning Nothing Beyond Nothing." *Angelaki* 17 (2012): 31–45.

——. "Not Yet Now: Speaking of the End and the End of Speaking." In *Elliot R. Wolfson: Poetic Thinking*, ed. Hava Tirosh-Samuelson and Aaron W. Hughes, 127–193. Leiden: Brill, 2015.

——. "Skepticism and the Philosopher's Keeping Faith." In *Jewish Philosophy for the Twenty-First Century: Personal Reflections*, ed. Hava Tirosh-Samuelson and Aaron W. Hughes, 481–515. Leiden: Brill, 2014.

——. *Through a Speculum That Shines: Vision and Imagination in Medieval Jewish Mysticism*. Princeton: Princeton University Press, 1994.

——. *Venturing Beyond: Law and Morality in Kabbalistic Mysticism*. Oxford: Oxford University Press, 2006.

——. "Zeitliche Entzweiung und offenes System. Die Atonalität der Kabbala und Heideggers anfängliches Denken." In *Martin Heidegger: Die Falte der Sprache*, ed. Michael Friedman and Angelika Seppi, 121–167. Vienna: Turia and Kant, 2017.

Wolin, Richard. "An Exchange of Letters." In Richard Wolin, ed., *The Heidegger Controversy: A Critical Reader*. Cambridge: MIT Press, 1993.

——. *Heidegger's Children: Hannah Arendt, Karl Löwith, Hans Jonas, and Herbert Marcuse*. Princeton: Princeton University Press, 2001.

——. "Karl Löwith and Martin Heidegger—Contexts and Controversies: An Introduction," in Karl Löwith, *Martin Heidegger and European Nihilism*, ed. Richard Wolin, 1–25. New York: Columbia University Press, 1995.

——. "National Socialism, World Jewry, and the History of Being: Heidegger's *Black Notebooks*." *Jewish Review of Books* (Summer 2014). Available at http://jewishreviewofbooks.com/articles/993/national-socialism-world-jewry-and-the-history-of-being-heideggers-black-notebooks/.

——. *The Politics of Being: The Political Thought of Martin Heidegger*. New York: Columbia University Press, 2016.

——. *The Seduction of Unreason: The Intellectual Romance with Fascism from Nietzsche to Postmodernism*. Princeton: Princeton University Press, 2004.

Wolin, Richard, ed. *The Heidegger Controversy: A Critical Reader*. Cambridge: MIT Press, 1993.
Wrathall, Mark A. *Heidegger and Unconcealment: Truth, Language, and History*. Cambridge: Cambridge University Press, 2011.
———. "Heidegger on Plato, Truth, and Unconcealment: The 1931–32 Lecture on *The Essence of Truth*." *Inquiry* 47 (2004): 443–463.
———. "Heidegger, Truth, and Reference." *Inquiry* 45 (2002): 217–228.
Wurgaft, Benjamin Aldes. *Thinking in Public: Strauss, Levinas, Arendt*. Philadelphia: University of Pennsylvania Press, 2016.
Wyschogrod, Edith. *Spirit in Ashes: Hegel, Heidegger, and Man-Made Mass Death*. New Haven: Yale University Press, 1990.
Yisraeli, Oded. "Cain as the Scion of Satan: The Evolution of a Gnostic Myth in the *Zohar*." *Harvard Theological Review* 109 (2016): 56–74.
———. *Temple Portals: Studies in Aggadah and Midrash in the Zohar*. Trans. Liat Keren. Berlin: Walter de Gruyter, 2016.
Young, Iris Marion. "House and Home: Feminist Variations on a Theme." In *Feminist Interpretations of Martin Heidegger*, ed. Nancy J. Holland and Patricia Huntington, 252–288. University Park: Pennsylvania State University Press, 2001.
Young, Julian. *Heidegger, Philosophy, Nazism*. Cambridge: Cambridge University Press, 1997.
———. "Poets and Rivers: Heidegger on Hölderlin's "Der Ister."" In *Heidegger Reexamined*, vol. 3: *Art, Poetry, and Technology*, ed. with introductions by Hubert Dreyfus and Mark Wrathall, 79–104. New York: Routledge, 2002.
Young-Bruehl, Elisabeth. *Hannah Arendt: For Love of the World*. New Haven: Yale University Press, 1982.
Zabala, Santiago. *The Hermeneutic Nature of Analytic Philosophy: A Study of Ernst Tugendhat*. Foreword by Gianni Vattimo. New York: Columbia University Press, 2008.
Zaborowski, Holger. "Licht und Schatten: Zur Diskussion von Heideggers *Schwarzen Heften*." In *Heidegger und der Antisemitismus: Positionen im Widerstreit, mit Briefen von Martin und Fritz Heidegger*, ed. Walter Homolka and Arnulf Heidegger, 428–440. Freiburg: Herder, 2016.
———. "Metaphysics, Christianity, and the 'Death of God' in Heidegger's *Black Notebooks* (1931–1941)." In *Reading Heidegger's Black Notebooks, 1931–1941*, ed. Ingo Farin and Jeff Malpas, 195–204. Cambridge: MIT Press, 2016.
Zarader, Marlène. *The Unthought Debt: Heidegger and the Hebraic Heritage*. Trans. Bettina Bergo. Stanford: Stanford University Press, 2006.
Ziarek, Krzysztof. *Language After Heidegger*. Bloomington: Indiana University Press, 2013.
———. "On Heidegger's *Einmaligkeit* Again: The Single Turn of the Event." *Gatherings: The Heidegger Circle Annual* 6 (2016): 91–113.
Žižek, Slavoj. *Disparities*. London: Bloomsbury, 2016.
———. *Less Than Nothing: Hegel and the Shadow of Dialectical Materialism*. London: Verso, 2012.

INDEX

Abandonment, of being, 151–152. *See also* Seinsverlassenheit
Abgrund, xxii, 123, 142. *See also* Ungrund; Urgrund
Abraham, 73–74, 203*n*26, 222*n*236
Adorno, Theodor, 27, 47, 163–164, 195–196*n*161
Africans. *See* Black Africans
Agamben, Giorgio, 27, 47, 236*n*58
Agriculture, 146–147
Alchemy, 160; origin of German dialectic, 226*n*266
Alētheia, 58, 116, 134, 162–163, 253*n*27. *See also* Unconcealment
Alienation, 4, 66, 68; from being alienated, 68, 124; and the Jews, 37, 74, 83
Alterity, 129, 143, 155, 161, 172; of the foreign, 65; and the Jews, xxi, 85
Americanism, 63, 81, 227*n*274
"Andenken" (Hölderlin), 62
Animals, 39–41
Annihilation, xx, 34, 201*n*15
"Ansprache zum Heimatabend" (Heidegger), 66
Anthropocentrism: of language, 205*n*50; of metaphysics, 101
Antichrist, 36, 82–83

Antigone (Sophocles), 56–57
Anti-Semitism, xiii, 10; *The Black Notebooks* and, 31; metaphysics and, 29, 35–36, 81–86, 227*n*270. *See also* Heidegger, Martin, anti-Semitism of; Ontologischen Antisemitismus; Topologischer Antisemitismus
Apocalypse, 105–106, 234–235*n*56; hope and despair related to, 239–240*n*93
Apolitical, 50
Apophasis, 114, 116–117
Arendt, Hannah, xvii, 16–18, 47, 114–115, 188*n*96, 189*n*97, 189*n*101, 207–208*n*73
Aristotle, 237–238*n*69, 250*n*104
Aryan race, 33–34, 36, 44
Attunement, 40–41, 170; to being, 218*n*188; hermeneutic of, xix; melancholy and, 128; to the unthought, 114. *See also* Grundbefindlichkeit
Augustine, 49, 84, 94
Auschwitz, 113, 163–164
Aus der Erfahrung des Denkens (Heidegger), 139–140
Authentic temporality, 89
Autochthony, 68, 217*n*188, 226*n*268

INDEX

Babylonian Talmud, 21–22
Badiou, Alain, 18, 103, 189*n*101, 233*n*37
Balaam, 154–162, 166–168, 260*n*1, 261*n*5; Heidegger and, 161; represents Jesus, 157; the serpent and, 158, 263*n*19
Banality of Heidegger, The (Nancy), xv, 175*n*19, 183*n*41, 184*n*43, 200–201*n*12
Baudrillard, Jean, 7–8
Beginning, 102–104
Begriff der Zeit, Der (Heidegger), 96
Being, 2–3; abandonment of, 151–152; of animals, 40–41; belongingness in, 38, 53; clearing of, 171; of Dasein, 80, 90, 92; history of, 53; knowledge of, 126; language and, 38–39, 53; naming, 117; revealing, 83–84; singularity, uniqueness of, 101–102; struggle in, 34; tragedy of, 124–126; unconcealment of, 84, 132; in world, 39–40. *See also* Forgetttenness of being; Nonbeing
Being-away, 100
Being-in-the-world, 37, 69–71, 87, 150
Beings: being of, 136–137; comportment to, 40; consumption of, 152; in forgottenness of being, 100; ontology of, 81
Being-there, 38
Being-toward-death, 148–150
Beiträge zur Philosophie (Vom Ereignis) (Heidegger), 2, 19–20, 29, 234*n*50; on being-away, 100; on *Ereignis*, 148–149; on history, 91; on language, silence, 117; machination in, 165; on Marxism, 82–83; Nazism in, 190*n*109; nonbeing in, 143; on science, 36; on silence, 117–118
Belongingness in being, 38, 53
Belonging together, 6, 68. *See also* Zusammengehörigkeit
Benjamin, Walter, 129, 209*n*94, 251*n*106
Besinnung, 27, 80, 144
Besinnung (Heidegger), 13, 40
Beyng, 1–2; as appropriating event, 101; Dasein, in relation to, 100–101; death in, 148; eschatology of, 168; essence of, 148; in history, 91; mystery and, 117; negativity of, 143; poetry of, 48; silence of, 117–118; tragedy of, 123; truth of, 70, 77, 100–101, 118, 127
Bible. *See* Epistle to the Galatians; Genesis, Book of; Letter to the Thessalonians; Leviticus, Book of; Matthew, Gospel of; Numbers, Book of
Biemel, Walter, 15
Black Africans, 38–39
Black Notebooks, The (Heidegger), xxii, 8; anti-Semitism and, 31; on National Socialism, 13–14, 30–32; on people without space, 37. *See also* Ponderings II–VI; Ponderings VII–XI; Ponderings XII–XV
Blanchot, Maurice, 74, 184*n*47
Blickle, Peter, 47
Blindness, 46, 52, 184*n*42, 234*n*50, 265*n*66; Balaam and, 168; of the Germans, 247*n*78; of the Jews, 84
Blood and soil, 19, 33, 145–146, 199*n*3
Blood community, 71–72
Bodenständigkeit, 43, 68, 211*n*110. *See also* Groundlessness
Boehme, Jacob, 256*n*57
Böhme, Jacob, 142, 256–257*nn*57–58
Bolshevism, 81–82, 183*n*42
Bourdieu, Pierre, 4, 15–16, 211*n*109
Brassier, Ray, 258*n*65
Brencio, Francesca, 226–227*n*270
"Brief über den 'Humanismus'" (Heidegger), 52–53
Buber, Martin, 176–177*n*42, 205–206*n*50

Calculation, 36, 101, 152, 162, 201*n*16, 228*n*285; the Jews and, 36–37, 76, 83, 85, 101, 168, 227*n*270, 228*n*285. *See also* Rechnung
Calle-Gruber, Mireille, xvii, xxii–xxiii
Canetti, Elias, 47
Caputo, John, 38, 177*n*43, 226*n*268
Cassin, Barbara, 189*n*101, 208*n*73

INDEX

Cassirer, Ernst, 194–195n151; Heidegger's critique of, 228n285
Catholic philosophy, 78
Celan, Paul, 47, 54, 74
Chrétien, Jean-Louis, 246n59
Christ, 82, 87–88, 118, 157, 160–161
Christianity, 77–78; eschatology of, 96–98, 236n58; eschaton of, 88–89; facticity of, 88–89, 94; God in, 98; Heidegger on, 79–80, 88–89, 96; history and, 88–89; Judaism and, 82, 84, 97–98, 235n57; messianism in, 98–99, 236n58; metaphysics and, 78; Paul on, 87–88; space, time of, 82–83, 94; temporality of, 94–97; time in, 88; worldview of, 79–80
Circularity, 103–104; and the hermeneutical structure of human understanding, 5, 82, 104; and speaking about keeping silent, 116
Circular movement, 5
Clearing, the, xxi, 6, 22, 38–39, 52, 55, 58, 104, 106, 146, 171. *See also* Lichtung
Cohen, Hermann, 61, 215n161, 228–229n285
Collective unconscious, 207n65
Collins, Jeff, 194n147
Coming to be at home, 56
Comportment, to beings, 40
Comprehension, 79
Concealment, xxi, 6, 117; of being, 3; concealment of, 3, 133, 134, 146; disclosure as, 131, 140; errancy and, 55; language and, 64; overcoming, 132; in poetry, 58; truth as the unconcealing of, 135. *See also* Unconcealment
Conche, Marcel, 31–32
Confessions (Augustine), 49
Consumption, of beings, 152
Cooper, Andrew, 51–52
Counterturning, 55
Creation, 126, 128
Crucifixion, 88
Cultural criticism, 163

Dasein, 2, 22, 25; as being-in-the-world, 37, 87, 150; being of, 80, 90, 92; beyng and, 100–101; death in, 150; ek-sistence of, 55; freedom in, 146; as futural, 93; German, 27, 53; ground of, 29–31, 101, 137; historical, 47–49, 59; as historicity, 89, 92, 119; Jews and, 82; language and, 50–51, 118–119; relation of, to beyng, 100–101; science, in being of, 80; seeking in, 106; *Sein und Zeit* on, 43, 193n134; selfhood of, 106–107; silence of, 115, 118–119; as spatial, 43, 48; as temporal, 91–93; turning of, 55; *Volk* and, 29–30, 34
Davis, Bret W., 141
Death, 105, 138, 147–150, 256n57; of Christ, 200n6. *See also* Being-toward-death
De Beistegui, Miguel, xiii, 113, 199–200n6
Deception, 134
Deconcealment, 133, 137
Delusion, 132
Derrida, Jacques: on discourse, 80–81; on friendship, 244n34; on Heidegger, xii–xiv, xviii–xx, 10, 35, 41–42, 111, 169–170, 174n10; "Interpretations at War: Kant, the Jew, the German" by, 61; on Levinas, 223n238; on messianism, 105; on *Unheimliche*, 171
Destiny, 93, 99, 144
Dialectic, 67, 82–83, 103, 226n266
Differentiation, 133
Dillard, Peter S., 18–19
"Ding, Das" (Heidegger), 150
Disclosure: of beings as a concealing, 6; as a concealment, 131, 133, 140; of the disclosure, 138; as the grounding of the historicity of Dasein, 52; of the truth of being, 70
Discourse, 80–81, 115–116
Disparities (Žižek), 174n5, 185n61, 264n31
Displacement, 146
Double visage, 237n69
Duality, 143
Duff, Alexander, xv, 3–4

INDEX

Dwelling: earth as, 70; in homeland, 217n188; homelessness and, 58; poetry and, 49–50, 58, 76; speaking and, 59

Echontology, 38
Eckhart, Meister, 20, 141, 254–255n52
Einführung in die Metaphysik (Heidegger), 46, 50–51, 70, 80
Either-or, 143
Ek-sistence, of Dasein, 55
Eliashiv, Solomon ben Ḥayyim, 122
End, 103–105, 107–108
Enframing, 162–163, 165–166. *See also* Gestell
Entities, ontology of, 49
Epistle to the Galatians, 160–161
Ereignis, 19, 22, 38, 148–149
Errancy, 6, 55, 140–141, 146, 166, 180n23
Eschatology: of beyng, 168; of Christianity, 96–98, 236n58; Jewish, 97–98
Eschaton: of Christianity, 88–89; in Judaism, 105
Esotericism: and the gesture of unsaying, 140; Heidegger and, 181n35, 190n109, 211n109; kabbalah and, 51
Esposito, Roberto, 29
Essence: of beyng, 148; God and, 125; of technology, 162–163, 165; of temporality, 95–97; of truth, 5–7, 55, 112, 145. *See also* Nonessence; Unessence
Essential ground, 82
Estrangement, 66
Eternity, 94–97
Ethical universalism, 75
Ethnicity, 52
European society, 70–71
Evil, 122–124, 126, 156; Balaam and, 157–160; excess of, 121; insurrection of the ground's craving, 126; located in the ground of the nonground, 125; National Socialism and, 21; nonessence of being and, 35; obliteration of, 247n69
Exclusion, 84–85, 172

Exile, 73, 100, 219n206
Existence, 124
Existential ontology, 26
Existenz, 148
Expulsion, 76
Extermination, xx, 146, 190n105; of the Jews, 34, 111, 148, 201n12, 220n212

Fackenheim, Emil, 32, 198n192
Facticity, 38, 88–89, 94
Farías, Victor, xiii
Fatherland, 33–34, 48, 56
Feast, 78–79
Feinmann, Jose Pablo, 175n19, 182n37
Feldweg-Gespräche (Heidegger), 139
Ferber, Ilit, 250n105
Final solution, 34
Finitude, 58, 68; the temporalization of being and, 85
Flux, in temporality, 107–108
Foreign, the, 12, 56–57, 62–65, 75–76, 162, 171, 217n178
Forgiveness, 21–22
Forgottenness of being, 22, 100, 121, 255n52. *See also Seinsvergessenheit*
Fort, Jeff, 175n18
Frage der Technik, Die (Heidegger), 162
Franke, William, 5, 239–240n93
Freedom, 124–125, 135, 139, 141–142, 146, 163, 256n57; to give law to oneself, 19; melancholy and, 128; of the philosopher, xvii
Freud, Sigmund, 44–45, 55, 202n25, 237n65, 251n106
Frey, Hans-Jost, 104
Friendship, 244n34
Froment-Meurice, Marc, xx
From Metaphysics to Midrash (Magid), 261n5, 262n12
Führer, the, 18–19, 28, 151
Funkenstein, Amos, 24
Future, 90, 93, 99, 103, 108

Gadamer, Hans-Georg, xiv, xx, 23, 111
Genealogy, 29–30
Genesis, Book of, 73
Geography, 48

INDEX

German: Dasein, 27, 53; destiny, 99; the foreign, 65; Greek and, 61–64, 69, 80–81, 218n188; identity, 43, 47; intellectuals, 210n102; language, 38, 46–47, 52, 59–60, 64, 69, 215n163, 216n172; poetry, 48–49, 51, 53, 57; space, 43–44, 48; the unconscious of, 45; *Volk*, 19, 34, 45–48, 51, 78, 145
Germany: as fatherland, 33–34, 48, 56; rural, 69–70
Geschichtlichkeit, 40–41, 87, 167
Gestalt, 83; National Socialism and, 30; of truth, 116
Gestell, 163
God, 73, 79; in Christianity, 98; essence and, 125; as eternal, 95; existence of, 124; ground and, 126; kingdom of, 87–88; silence and, 245n47; transformation before, 94
Gods, 79–80, 102
Good and evil, 1–4, 141–142, 161–162, 170. *See also* Evil
Gordon, Peter, 72, 221n217
Gosetti-Ferencei, Jennifer Anna, 49
Greeks: Germans and, 61–64, 69, 80–81, 218n188; language of, 61–62, 64, 69; students and, 19; in translation, 56
Grimm, Hans, 37
Ground: of creation, 126; of Dasein, 29–31, 101, 137; essential, 82; God and, 126; tragedy and, 126–127; of truth, 135. *See also* Nonground
Groundlessness, 83–84, 100. *See also* Bodenständigkeit
Grundbefindlichkeit, 37
Grundbegriffe der Metaphysik, Die (Heidegger), 70, 95, 115

Habermas, Jürgen, xviii, 22, 109, 192n125
Hearth, 57–58
Hebrew, 73–74
Hegel, G. W. F., 60–61, 82–83, 103, 114, 126, 203n26, 226n266; on German language, 60, 215n158, 215n163
Heidegger, Martin: "Ansprache zum Heimatabend" by, 66; Arendt and, 16–18, 188n96; *Aus der Erfahrung des Denkens* by, 139–140; *Der Begriff der Zeit* by, 96; on being, 2–3; *Besinnung* by, 13, 40; *The Black Notebooks* by, xxii, 8; breakdown of, 198n186; "Brief über den 'Humanismus'" by, 52–53; on Christianity, 79–80, 88–89, 96; "Das Ding" by, 150; *Einführung in die Metaphysik* by, 46, 50–51, 70, 80; *Feldweg-Gespräche* by, 139; *Die Frage der Technik* by, 162; on German *Volk*, 45–47; *Die Grundbegriffe der Metaphysik* by, 70, 95, 115; on history, 4–5, 25–26; on Holocaust, 146–148; Husserl and, 224n248; on Judaism, 85, 97–100, 154, 177n43; on Judeo-Christian tradition, 38; kabbalah and, 154; legacy of, xvii–xviii; Levinas on, 20–22, 76; *Logik als die Frage nach dem Wesen der Sprache* by, 140–141; moral culpability of, 109–110; on Parmenides, 64; "Patmos" by, 162; phenomenology and, 88, 93–94, 232n34; on Plato, 131–136; "Platons Lehre von der Wahrheit" by, 115–116, 131–135, 137; *Ponderings II–VI* by, 211n110, 260n95; *Ponderings VII–XI* by, 183n42, 190n106, 205n42, 239n77, 247n75; racism of, 38–39; *Das Rektorat 1933/34: Tatsachen und Gedanken* by, 11–12, 186n72; rural life of, 69–70; on Schelling, 124–126, 231n13; *Schelling: Vom Wesen der Menschlichen Freiheit* by, 79, 95; *Schwarze Hefte* by, 33, 126–127, 181n35; on scripture, 87–88; on the Senegal Negro, 203n32; silence of, 109–114, 119, 129–130; Strauss on, 23–24; turn of, 49–50, 80; "Die Überwindung der Metaphysik" by, 38–39, 67, 150–151; "Der Ursprung des Kunstwerkes" by, 52; *Vom Wesen der Wahrheit* by, 34, 55, 116, 140; *Was Heißt Denken?* by, 147; *Was ist Metaphysik* by, 119; "Why Do I Stay in the Provinces?" by, 250n101; "Die Zeit des Weltbildes" by, 79, 138. *See also Beiträge zur Philosophie (Vom Ereignis)*; Black

INDEX

Heidegger, Martin (*cont.*)
  Notebooks, The; Derrida, Jacques;
  Hitler, Adolf; Hölderlin, Friedrich;
  Jaspers, Karl; *Sein und Zeit*
Heidegger, Martin, anti-Semitism of,
  170, 175*n*19, 242*n*17, 260*n*1; Levinas on,
  42; metaphysical, 81–86; *Seinsfrage*
  in, 77; topological, 37–38;
  worldlessness in, 70–71
Heidegger, Martin, on Jews, 38–43, 114,
  147–151; Balaam and, 167–168;
  being-in-the-world and, 69–71;
  calculation in, 101; caricature of, 30;
  dehumanization of, 35–36;
  groundlessness and, 83–84; Marx
  and, 82–83; metaphysics of, 85;
  time and, 87; in *Vom Wesen der
  Wahrheit*, 34–35; worldliness and,
  76–77
Heidegger, Martin, National Socialism
  and, 8–12, 91–92, 154; Antichrist trope
  in, 36; Arendt on, 17; *The Black
  Notebooks* on, 30–32; Derrida on, 111;
  IJsseling on, 113; in philosophy, 25–28;
  politicization of science and, 14–15
Heidegger, Martin, Nazism and, xi–xxi,
  1, 7–11, 26–33, 139, 170–172; Bourdieu
  on, 15–16; dehumanization of, 35–36;
  Führer and, 18–19; Habermas on,
  22–23; Hölderlin and, 53; Marcuse on,
  23; paganism in, 20–21; Sheehan on,
  24–25; silence on, 109–114; Strauss on,
  23–24
Heidegger and Theology (Wolfe), 209*n*96
Heidegger Controversy, The (Wolin),
  186*n*72, 188*n*94
Heidegger's Shadow (Feinmann), 175*n*19,
  182*n*37
Heimat, 13, 43, 49, 58–59, 66, 76, 210*n*109,
  217–218*n*188, 219*n*207, 226*n*268. *See
  also* Home
"Heimkunft/An die Verwandten"
  (Hölderlin), 52–53, 59–60, 121
Heimliche, 55
Heraclitus, 28, 125, 170, 199*n*5, 213*n*133
Hermeneutics: of circularity, 103–104;
  past in, 92–93; of truth, untruth, 140

Historical: destiny, 144; thinking as, 93
Historical in itself, 89–90
Historicism, 100
Historicity, 89, 92, 119
Historiographical explanation, 89–90
Historiography, 80, 231*n*13
Historiology, 91–92, 112, 205*n*42
History: of being, 53; beyng in, 91; black
  Africans and, 38–39; Christianity
  and, 88–89; comportment, to beings
  in, 40; Dasein in, 47–49, 59; as
  happening, 93; Heidegger on, 4–5,
  25–26; homeland and, 57; Jewish, 73;
  Jews and, 82, 99–100; language and,
  38–39, 46–47; prophecy and, 167; telos
  of, 105–106; unessence of, 140–141;
  world, 41. *See also* Future; Past;
  Temporality; Unhistorical
Hitler, Adolf, 5, 9, 11; final solution of, 34;
  Heidegger and, 14, 23, 25, 28, 32, 71,
  124, 151; ideology of, 152; on Jews, 71,
  196*n*168, 228*n*283; *Mein Kampf* by, 17,
  28, 187*n*90, 220*n*214
Hölderlin, Friedrich: "Andenken" by, 62;
  Heidegger on, 19–20, 47–49, 53–60,
  62, 66, 76, 97, 107, 127–128, 209*n*99,
  210*n*100; "Heimkunft/An die
  Verwandten" by, 52–53, 59–60, 121;
  "Der Ister" by, 53–56, 62;
  "Mnemosyne" by, 97; on river,
  of space and time, 107
Holiness, 155–156
Holocaust, 111–113, 121, 146–150
Holy Land, 73–75
Home: coming to be at, 56; Jews and,
  73–74, 76
Homecoming, 63, 65–66
Homeland, 52–53; dwelling as, 217*n*188;
  history and, 57; homesickness and,
  68; of Jews, 74; language and, 59; of
  poet, 58–59; technology and, 66,
  68–69; yearning for, 72–73. *See also*
  Fatherland
Homelessness, 53, 57, 66; dwelling and,
  58; plight and, 58–59
Homeliness, 54–57, 65–66
Homely. *See* Unhomeliness

INDEX

Homesickness, 66–69
Human being. *See* Being; Dasein
Human Condition, The (Arendt), 115
Husserl, Edmund, 23, 77, 88, 194*n*151, 224*nn*247–248, 241*n*16

Ideas, 136–137
IJsseling, Samuel, 113, 169
immigrant, 73
Ineffability, 115, 117, 243*n*25
Infinite Conversation, The (Blanchot), 184*n*47
Internment, 42
Interpretation, translation and, 63–64
"Interpretations at War: Kant, the Jew, the German" (Derrida), 61
Irigaray, Luce, xxii
Israel: election of, 223*n*238; holiness of, 75; knowledge of the holy, 157; land of, 73–75
"Ister, Der" (Hölderlin), 53–56, 62
Ivri, 73

Janicaud, Dominique, xxii, 25
Jaspers, Karl: on good and evil, 4; Heidegger and, 16–17, 31, 110–111, 186*n*77, 196*n*166, 198*n*187; *Psychologie der Weltanschauungen* by, 85; on shame, 31
Jesus Christ. *See* Christ
Jews: Dasein and, 82; ethical universalism of, 75; exclusion and, 84–85; in exile, 73, 100, 219*n*206; *Geschichtlichkeit* of, 40–41, 167; history and, 73, 82, 99–100; Hitler on, 71, 196*n*168, 228*n*283; home and, 73–74, 76; Israel and, 73–75; Jung on, 237*n*65; language of, 74; nomadism and, 37–38, 42–45; place and, 74–75; as rootless, 203*n*26; *Unheimlichkeit* of, 74; in world, 70–71, 76, 219*n*207. *See also* Anti-Semitism; Heidegger, Martin, on Jews
Jonas, Hans, 2–3
Journey, 107; circular nature of, 76; to the homeland, 57, 66; wandering and, 72

Judaism, 20–21, 74, 81; Christianity and, 82, 84, 97–98, 235*n*57; distinguished from Paganism, 75; eschatology of, 97–98; eschaton in, 105; future and, 99; Heidegger on, 85, 97–100, 154, 177*n*43; Marxism and, 227*n*271; messianism of, 98–99, 102, 105, 107–108; in modernity, 100. *See also* Anti-Semitism; Israel; Jews
Judenschaft, 82, 228*n*279
Judentum, 84
Judeo-Christian tradition, 38. *See also* Christianity
Jung, Carl G., 44–45, 207*n*65, 237*n*65

Kabbalah, 95, 101, 121–123, 125; Heidegger and, 154; on language, 47; Lurianic, 123, 158–161, 256*n*57; on metaphysical dichotomy, 162; transcendence in, 161
Kaffirs. *See* Black Africans
Kafka, Franz, 262–263*n*12
Kampf, 13–14, 100, 134, 145
Kataphasis, 116–117; the apophatic and, 104–105
Kehre, 66, 118, 192*n*124
Kierkegaard, Søren, 118
Knowledge, 11–12, 46, 126, 145–146; of Balaam, 156, 158–159, 263*n*20; of beyng, 123; of the demonic, 156, 158; of the essential occurrence of beyng, 78; of the futural ones, 4; of the holy, 157; of Moses, 156, 158–159; of the Most High, 158; scientific, 115; of self, 87, 118; of the State's leaders, 14; withholding of truths from, 119
Krell, David, 8, 22, 192*n*124, 228*n*279

Lacan, Jacques, 55, 213*n*133
Lacoue-Labarthe, Philippe, xviii–xix, 49, 111, 189*n*105, 212*n*132
Land. *See* Fatherland; Holy Land; Promised land; Soil
Language: anthropocentrism of, 205*n*50; being and, 38–39, 53; concealment and, 64; Dasein and, 50–51, 118–119; of the Greeks, 61–62, 64, 69; Hebrew as, 73–74; history and, 38–39, 46–47;

Language (*cont.*)
   homeland and, 59; of Jews, 74; kabbalah on, 47; limits of, 104–105; loss of, 42; poetry and, 48–51, 58; as saying, 120–121, 139–140; silence and, 117, 120–121; temporality of, 93; truth and, 166; unveils by veiling, 226n268. *See also* German
Last god, the, xx, 102, 112, 176n37, 183n42, 201n15
Leadership, 151–152
Leap, the, 102–103, 118
Letter to the Thessalonians, 87
Levinas, Emmanuel, 74–76, 99, 191n119, 205n50; on Abraham, 222n236; Derrida on, 223n238; on forgiveness, 21–22; on internment, anti-Semitism and, 42; on paganism, 20–21
Leviticus, Book of, 73
Liberation, 131, 135, 137
Lichtung, 6, 38–39
Life experience, 100
Locality, 107
Logik als die Frage nach dem Wesen der Sprache (Heidegger), 140–141
Löwith, Karl, 25–27
Lutheranism, 179n11
Lyotard, Jean-François, xxi, 109

Machenschaft, 13, 36, 68, 93. *See also* Machination
Machination, xvi, 36, 83, 165, 199n3. *See also Machenschaft*
Magid, Shaul, 261n5, 262n12
Marcuse, Herbert, 23, 28, 110, 220n212
Marxism, 82–83, 227n271
Mass production, 146–148
Mathematical. *See* Calculation
Matthew, Gospel of, 118
Mein Kampf (Hitler), 17, 28, 187n90, 220n214
Melancholy, 126, 128, 250n105, 251n106
Merleau-Ponty, Maurice, 129
Messiah, 75, 87, 98–99, 102, 105
Messianism: Christian, 98–99, 236n58; Derrida on, 105; Jewish, 98–99, 102, 105, 107–108

Metaphysical anti-Semitism, 81, 86, 226n269
Metaphysics: anthropocentrism of, 101; anti-Semitism and, 29, 35–36, 81–86, 227n270; Christianity and, 78; Jews in, 85; kabbalah and, 162; Nietzsche, on end of, 78–79; poetry overcoming, 127–128. *See also Einführung in die Metaphysik* (Heidegger); *From Metaphysics to Midrash* (Magid); *Grundbegriffe der Metaphysik, Die* (Heidegger); "Überwindung der Metaphysik, Die" (Heidegger); *Was ist Metaphysik?* (Heidegger)
Misinterpretation, of philosopher, 115
"Mnemosyne" (Hölderlin), 97
Modernity, 46, 79, 91–92, 100, 152–153
Moses, 155–160, 166, 261n5
Muttersprache, 47–48, 65
Mystery, 117, 164–165; veiling of, 116–117

Naming, 38, 117
Nancy, Jean-Luc, xiv–xvi, 81, 83–84, 175n19, 200n12
Nationalism, 9, 47, 51–52, 58, 208n73, 210n109
National Socialism, xvi, 1; in *Black Notebooks*, 13–14, 30–32; as collective unconscious, 207n65; Jung on, 45; leadership in, 152; Levinas on, 21; *Sein und Zeit* and, 25. *See also* Heidegger, Martin, National Socialism and
Nazi science, 78
Nazism: in *Beiträge*, 190n109; errancy of, 140–141; on homeliness, 65–66; nationalism of, 47, 51–52, 58; Nietzsche and, 10; paganism and, 20–21; on people without space, 37; on uniformity, 152–153. *See also* Heidegger, Martin, National Socialism and; Heidegger, Martin, Nazism and; Hitler, Adolf; National Socialism
Negation, 118
Negative Dialektik (Adorno), 163–164
Negativity, 143

INDEX

Neumann, Erich, 207n65
Nietzsche, Friedrich, 170, 228n281; aphorism of, 15; Arendt on, 18; on Christianity, 79; on end, of Western metaphysics, 78–79; Nazi use of, 10; on will to power, 30
Nihilism, 149
Nomadism: contrasted with parasitism, 71–72, 100, 220–221n214, 228n283; Heidegger's turn and the attitude toward, 66; Jews and, 28, 37–38, 42–45; turn and, 66
Nonbeing, 143
Nonessence, 35, 55, 125, 143
Nonground, xxii, 141–142; ground of the, 125; neither good nor evil, 125
Nonviolence, 50
Nothingness, 143
Not-knowing, 49, 209n90
Not-something, 143
Not talking, the negation of, 118
Novalis, 67
Numbers, Book of, 167

Objectivity: of the historical in itself, 89–90; subjectivity and, 92; of time, 94
Occurrence, of the nonoccurrence, 106–107
Ontologischen Antisemitismus, 226n269
Ontology: of beings, 81; of entities, 49; existential, 26; temporality and, 71–72
Ontotheology, 79, 225n260
Ordinary, the, 55; strife with the extraordinary, 103
Other, the, 55, 75–76, 161
Other Side, 122–123, 155–156
Overcoming: of concealing, 133; eternal joy of, 126; of the ground, 128; metaphysics, 35–36, 128, 204n37, 210n100; as undergoing, 4; violence, 50. See also *Überwindung*
Over-whelming, 214n148

Paganism, 20–21, 75–76
Parmenides, 64
Parousia, 93–94

Past, 89–91; future and, 103, 108; in hermeneutics, 92–93; narration of, 92
"Patmos" (Hölderlin), 162
Paul (apostle), 87–88, 94, 96–97, 233n37, 236n58
People. See Volk
People without space, 37
Petzet, Heinrich, 7, 69–70
Phenomenology, 88, 93–94, 150, 232n34
Philosopher: on death, 138; as liberator, 131; misinterpretation of, 115; as solitary, 132
Philosophie des Geistes (Hegel), 60
Philosophie und Religion (Schelling), 142
Philosophizing, xvii
Philosophy: Catholic, 78; Christian, 79; of Heidegger, National Socialism in, 25–28; melancholia, 128; politics of, 18; truth in, 118
Piety, 5, 166
Place, 74–75
Plato, 114–115, 131–136, 253n27
"Platons Lehre von der Wahrheit" (Heidegger), 115–116, 131–135, 137
Plight, homelessness and, 58–59
Poesy, 80
Poetry: of beyng, 48; concealment in, 58; dwelling and, 49–50, 58, 76; German, 48–49, 51, 53, 57; homeland and, 58–59; language and, 48–51, 58; metaphysics and, 127–128; politics of, 47, 51–52, 59, 76; silence and, 121; speaking and, 116; thinking and, 101. See also Hölderlin, Friedrich
Poiēsis, 51, 59, 76, 103, 114, 140, 163–165
Political: in historical destiny, 144; thought, 210n105
Politicization of science, 14–15
Politics: of philosophy, 18; of poetry, 47, 51–52, 59, 76
Polt, Richard, 50
Ponderings II–VI (Heidegger), 184n42, 201n15, 211n110, 250n101, 260n95, 265n66
Ponderings VII–XI (Heidegger), 183n42, 190n106, 205n42, 239n77, 247n75, 258n62

Ponderings XII–XV (Heidegger), 183–184n42, 210n100, 211n110, 227–228n274
Presence, 136, 139, 159
Problemata (Aristotle), 250n104
Promised land, 76
Prophecy, 167
Psychologie der Weltanschauungen (Jaspers), 85

Quietism, of Heidegger, 20

Race, 10, 34, 44, 77, 82–83, 182n37, 183n41, 199n1, 199n4, 211n110; blood and, 91; metaphysics of, 184n43; principle of, 83
Racism, 38–39, 42, 83, 110
Raffoul, François, 3
Ratmoko, David, 234n56
Rechnung, 36, 152. *See also* Calculation
Recollection, 69
Redemption, 99
Refinement, 258n62
Rektorat 1933/34, Das: Tatsachen und Gedanken (Heidegger), 11–12, 186n72
Releasement, 20
Religion, 93–94
Religiosity, 80, 89, 94
Republic (Plato), 131–132
Restlessness, 67
Restraint, 117
Reticence, 115, 123
Revealing, 83–84, 162, 165–166; concealing and, 135, 163; destiny of, 165; the domain of technology and, 163; mystery of, 166; poetic, 49, 163; self-concealing, 81, 208n73
Revolutionary Saints: Heidegger, National Socialism, and Antinomian Politics (Rickey), 179n11
Rickey, Christopher, 179n11, 187n81
River, of space and time, 107
Rootedness, 43–44, 68, 72–73, 171
Rootlessness, 76–77, 203n26
Rorty, Richard, 18
Rosenberg, Alfred, 9, 33, 182n37

Rosenzweig, Franz, 71–76, 94, 99, 128–129, 217n178, 221n217, 233n42

Saying, 120–121, 136, 139–140
Schelling, Friedrich Wilhelm Joseph, 123–126, 141–143, 231n13
Schelling: Vom Wesen der menschlichen Freiheit (Heiddeger), 79, 95
Schmitt, Carl, 28–29
Scholem, Gershom, 47, 98; on Husserl and Heidegger, 224n247; on the messianic idea, 235n57
Schürmann, Reiner, 3, 76, 124, 247n78
Schwarze Hefte (Heidegger), 33, 126–127, 181n35
Science: in being, of Dasein, 80; in the *Beiträge*, 36; Nazi, 78; politicization of, 14–15; reclaiming of, 46
Scripture, 87–88
Second World War, 15, 35, 121
Seeking, in Dasein, 106
Seinsfrage, 77
Seinsgeschichte, xxii, 29, 190n109
Seinsvergessenheit, 36, 255n52
Seinsverlassenheit, 20, 128, 144, 151, 201n15
Sein und Zeit (Heidegger), 23–26; on being, of animals, 40–41; being-toward-death in, 150; on Dasein, 43, 193n134; historiography in, 80; on silence, 115; temporality in, 89–91; on transcendence, 95–96; on uncanniness, 37
Self-annihilation, 36–37, 201n12, 201n15
Selfhood, of Dasein, 106
Senegal Negro, the, 203n32
Shadow, 132–133, 137–139; self-showing of, 133; substance of, 32; of technological hegemony, 70; transparency of, 6; of truth, 168; unmasking of, 5
Sheehan, Thomas, 24–25, 38, 88
Shibboleth, 54
Shyness, 146
Silence: of beyng, 117–118; of Dasein, 115, 118–119; discourse and, 115–116; God and, 245n47; of Heidegger, 109–114,

INDEX

119, 129–130; language and, 117, 120–121; as not talking, 118; poetry and, 121; *Sein und Zeit* on, 115; of solitude, 128; tragedy and, 128–129
Singularity, of being, 101–102
Slave revolt, 227*n*274
Socrates, 20–21
Soil, 43–44, 146
Solitude, 114–115, 127; of philosopher, 132; silence of, 128
Something, and the not-something, 143
Sophocles, 56–57
Space: Dasein in, 43–44, 48; time and, 49, 82–83, 89, 94, 107
Speaking: dwelling and, 59; poetry and, 116; saying and, 120
Speechlessness, 129
Spirit, 12, 70–71, 145–146
Stambaugh, Joan, 204*n*37
Strangers, 76
Strauss, Leo, 23–24, 193*n*131
Struggle, 34, 100, 145
Students, 19
Subject-object relation, 92

Taoism, 240*n*98
Taubes, Jacob, 234–235*nn*56–57
Technology: essence of, 162–163, 165; *Heimat* and, 66; homeland and, 66, 68–69; mystery and, 164–165; revealing, 163; in unconcealment, 162–163
Teleology, of *Volk*, 29–30
Telos, of history, 105–106
Temporality, 40–41; of Christianity, 94–97; of Dasein, 91–93; equiprimordiality of, 90; essence of, 95–97; flux in, 107–108; of language, 93; ontology and, 71–72; in *Sein und Zeit*, 89–91. *See also* Authentic temporality; Time
Text, as incomplete, 104–105
Theology, 79
Thinker, 115–116, 127
Thinking: as historical, 93; poetry and, 101; retrieval of, 69

Time: in Christianity, 88; circular linearity of, 104; Jewish, Heidegger on, 87; linear circularity of, 106; objectivity of, 94; reversal of, xix; space and, 49, 82–83, 89, 94, 107; true, 231*n*14
Timelessness, 94–95
Topography, 54, 71, 146
Topologischer Antisemitismus, 202*n*21
Topology, 37–38, 202*n*23. *See also* Fatherland
Tragedy, 4; of being, 124–126; of beyng, 123; ground and, 126–127; silence and, 128–129
Transcendence, 95–96, 161
Transformation, before God, 94
Translation: of Greek, 56; interpretation and, 63–64; truth and, 64–65; uncanniness and, 65
Trawny, Peter, 29, 36, 113–114, 211*n*114
True time, 231*n*14
Truth: of beyng, 70, 77, 100–101, 118, 127; essence of, 5–7, 55, 112, 145; ground of, 135; language and, 166; mystery and, 117; in philosophy, 118; struggle in, 145; translation and, 64–65; unconcealment of, 135; as unhiddenness, 135–136; untruth and, 131, 134, 140, 166; unveiling of what remains veiled, 140
Turn: of Dasein, 55; of Heidegger, 49–50, 80; nomadism and, 66

Überwindung, 4, 128, 133
"Überwindung der Metaphysik, Die" (Heidegger), 38–39, 67, 150–151
Uncanniness, 37, 54–58, 65, 80
Unconcealedness, 58
Unconcealment: of being, 59, 84; and the concealing of the unconcealed, 164; of the concealment, xxi, 162; of the end, 91; liberation as, 137; of light, 132; poetry as the saying of, 52; technology in, 162–163; of truth, 55, 116, 135, 165. *See also Alētheia*
Unconscious, the, 45, 207*n*65
Understanding, 40

Unessence, 140–141, 143–144
Ungrund, xxii, 125, 142
Unheimliche, 55, 171
Unheimlichkeit, 74
Unhiddenness, 134–137
Unhistorical, 143–144
Unhomeliness, 54–57, 76
Uniformity, 152–153
Uniqueness, of being, 101–102
Universalism, ethical, 75
Untruth, 131, 134, 140, 166
Unwesen, 6, 35, 55, 99, 119, 121, 140–141, 143, 145, 254–255*n*52, 258*n*62
Urgrund, xxii
Ursprung des deutschen Trauerspiels (Benjamin), 129
"Ursprung des Kunstwerkes, Der" (Heidegger), 52

Vattimo, Gianni, 27
Veil: appears as what veils, 163–164; of dejection, 126; unveiling of, 135, 139
Villa, Dana, 85
Viṭal, Ḥayyim, 158–160
Volk: Dasein and, 29–30, 34; German, 19, 34, 45–48, 51, 78, 145; teleology of, 29–30
Volksgeist, 71
Vollzugssinn, 88, 230*n*4
Vom Wesen der Wahrheit (Heidegger), 34–35, 55, 116, 140

War, 35
Warnek, Peter, 65
Was Heißt Denken? (Heidegger), 41, 120, 147
Was ist Metaphysik? (Heidegger), 119
Wholeness, of the world, 67–68

"Why Do I Stay in the Provinces?" (Heidegger), 250*n*101
Will, 19–20, 141–142
Will-to-not-will, 20
Will to power, 18, 30
Will to will, 150–151
Wissenschaft, 46
Wissenschaft der Logik (Hegel), 60–61
Wittgenstein, Ludwig, 114; Heidegger and, 243*n*25
Wolfe, Judith, 209*n*96
Wolin, Richard, 8, 186*n*72, 188*n*94
World: being in, 39–40; history, 41; Jews in, 70–71, 76, 219*n*207; spirit in, 70–71. *See also* Being-in-the-world
Worldhood, 71, 150; Jews alienated from, 37
Worldlessness, 70–71; of the Jews, 37, 291*n*207
Worldliness, 76–77, 219*n*207
World-picture, 164
Worldview: of Christianity, 79–80; of nihilism, 149
Wyschogrod, Edith, 8

Zarader, Marlène, 177*n*43
"Zeit des Weltbildes, Die" (Heidegger), 79, 138
Ziarek, Krzysztof, 102
Zionism, 71, 207*n*65, 223*n*241; as counter-nationalism, 235*n*57; Rosenzweig's rejection of, 217*n*178, 221*n*216, 223*n*243; Scholem's view of, 235*n*57
Žižek, Slavoj, 174*n*5, 185*n*61, 264*n*31
Zoharic literature, 155–159, 261*n*5, 263*nn*19–20
Zusammengehörigkeit, 6, 68–69, 133, 212*n*123

GPSR Authorized Representative: Easy Access System Europe, Mustamäe tee 50, 10621 Tallinn, Estonia, gpsr.requests@easproject.com

www.ingramcontent.com/pod-product-compliance
Lightning Source LLC
Chambersburg PA
CBHW021934290426
44108CB00012B/834